2014 Standards Supplement

American Correctional Association

In cooperation with the Commission on Accreditation for Corrections

March 2014

Mission of the American Correctional Association

The American Correctional Association provides a professional organization for all individuals and groups, both public and private that share a common goal of improving the justice system.

Information on accreditation may be obtained from:
American Correctional Association
Standards and Accreditation Department
206 N. Washington Street, Suite 200
Alexandria, VA 22314 (800) 222-5646

American Correctional Association Staff
Christopher Epps, President
James A. Gondles, Jr., CAE, Executive Director
Susan L. Clayton, MS, Director, Communications and Publications
Alice Heiserman, Manager of Publications and Research
Jeannelle Ferreira, Associate Editor
LeighAnn Brown, Graphics and Production Manager
Xavaire Bolton, Graphics and Production Associate
Cover Design by Xavaire Bolton

Printed in the United States of America by The P.A. Hutchinson Company, Mayfield, PA

Cover Photos:
We thank the Texas Department of Criminal Justice for the use of their photos.

ISBN 978-1-56991-283-6

This publication may be ordered from:
American Correctional Association
(800) 222-5646, ext. 0129
For information on publications and videos available from ACA, visit our website: www.aca.org/store.
For bulk copies of this publication, please call Bonnie Carpenter at (800) 222-5646, ext. 0197.

Introduction

ACA's standards uphold the ideal, recognize the reality, and expect a high level of operational effectiveness, efficiency, and proven outcomes. The standards address every area of correctional operations including health care. This *2014 Standards Supplement* updates ACA's entire collection of adult and juvenile standards manuals. It contains every addition, deletion, revision, and/or interpretation approved by the ACA Standards Committee through August 2013. These changes are a result of the Standards Committee's work in processing suggested revisions and changes received from the field. Convening twice a year to evaluate these suggestions, the committee is constantly striving to make sound judgments on correctional practices while balancing the goals of excellence with keeping expectations at a level that is achievable.

The Standards Committee continually reviews the standards based on evaluating documentation, expected practices, and outcomes. Additionally, with the increased research into the success rate of reentry and rehabilitation, correctional administrators' goals are evolving from not only accomplishing a safe and secure facility for staff and inmates but also to increasing programming for inmates to ensure success when they are released back into society. The committee strives to address the changing goals and needs within the field.

We welcome your comments on these revisions and additions. Together we can create a system that represents the ideals and best practices of our profession.

James A. Gondles, Jr., CAE
Executive Director
American Correctional Association

Standards Manuals Published by the American Correctional Association

2014 Standards Supplement
Core Jail Standards, 1st Edition
International Core Standards, 1st Edition
Standards for the Administration of Correctional Agencies, 2nd Edition
Performance-Based Standards for Adult Community Residential Services, 2nd Edition
Standards for Adult Correctional Boot Camp Programs, 1st Edition
Standards for Adult Correctional Institutions, 4th Edition
Standards for Adult Correctional Institutions (Spanish Version)
Performance-Based Standards for Adult Local Detention Facilities, 4th Edition
Standards for Adult Parole Authorities, 2nd Edition
Standards for Adult Probation and Parole Field Services, 3rd Edition
Performance-Based Standards for Correctional Health Care in Adult Correctional Institutions, 1st Edition
Performance-Based Standards for Correctional Industries, 2nd Edition
Performance-Based Standards for Therapeutic Communities, 1st Edition
Standards for Correctional Training Academies, 1st Edition
Standards for Electronic Monitoring Programs, 1st Edition
Standards for Juvenile Community Residential Facilities, 3rd Edition
Standards for Juvenile Correctional Boot Camp Programs, 1st Edition
Standards for Juvenile Day Treatment Programs, 1st Edition
Standards for Juvenile Detention Facilities, 3rd Edition
Standards for Juvenile Probation and Aftercare Services, 2nd Edition
Standards for Small Juvenile Detention Facilities, 1st Edition

Contents

COMMISSION ON ACCREDITATION FOR CORRECTIONS

Executive Committee of the Commission on Accreditation for Corrections

Luis Spencer, Massachusetts, Chair
Marge Webster, Puerto Rico, Vice Chair
Elias Diggins, Colorado
Clarence Williams Jr., Kentucky
Pamela Hearn, M.D., Louisiana

Commissioners

Lori Ammons, Kansas
Steve Andrashko, Virginia
Lynn Branham, Illinois
Patrick J. Curran, III, Tennessee
Hassan Davis, Kentucky
Kevin Downey, Texas
Mary S. Galey, Arizona
Angela Goehring, Florida
Bob P. Houston, Nebraska
James M. Le Blanc, Louisiana
Lester Lewis, M.D., Tennessee
Cherry Lindamood, Tennessee
Mark H. Luttrell, Tennessee
David R. McKune, Kansas
Jeaneene E. Miller, Colorado
Gloria Perry, Mississippi
Thomas J. Stickrath, Ohio
David L. Thomas, M.D., Florida

STANDARDS AND ACCREDITATION STAFF

Kathy Black-Dennis, Director
Ben Shelor, Deputy Director
Bridget Bayliss-Curren, Accreditation Specialist
Terry Carter, Accreditation Specialist
John Dowdy, Accreditation Specialist
Aquilah Munir, Standards Associate
Christina Randolph, Office Manager
Nadine Lee, Administrative Assistant

AMERICAN CORRECTIONAL ASSOCIATION 2014

Officers

Christopher Epps, Mississippi, President
Mary Livers, Louisiana, President-Elect
Daron Hall, Tennessee, Immediate Past President
Michael Wade, Virginia, Vice President
Lannette Linthicum, M.D., Texas, Treasurer
Burl Cain, Louisiana, Board of Governors Representative
Bill Peck, Tennessee, Board of Governors Representative
James A. Gondles, Jr., CAE, Executive Director

Board of Governors

Raul S. Banasco, Florida
Patricia Barnes-Goodwyn, Virginia
Kim B. Barnette, Louisiana
Michael Dempsey, Indiana
Kathleen Gebring, New York
John Gomez, Colorado
Gail M. Heller, Ohio
Reginald D. Hines, Oklahoma
Kenneth Lassiter, North Carolina
Jenny Nimer, Florida
Brian Patrick, Ohio
Allen L. Peaton, Alabama
Denise Robinson, Ohio
Robert Rosenbloom, Georgia
David Thomas, M.D., Florida
Tony Wilkes, Tennessee

Committee on Standards

Brad Livingston, Chair, Texas
James Le Blanc, Vice Chair, Louisiana
Michael Bradley, Florida
Elias Diggins, Colorado Justin Jones, Oklahoma
Harley G. Lappin, Tennessee
Cherry Lindamood, Tennessee
Gary C. Mohr, Ohio
Gloria Perry, M.D., Mississippi
Viola Riggin, Kansas
Michelle Robinette, Oklahoma
Denise Robinson, Ohio
Ramon C. Rustin, New Mexico
Charles Samuels, Washington, DC
Raman Singh, M.D., Louisiana
Luis Spencer, Massachusetts
Bonita Sweeney, Ohio
Marge Webster, Puerto Rico
John E. Wetzel, Pennsylvania
Clarence Williams, Kentucky

Executive Office

James A. Gondles, Jr., CAE, Executive Director
Jeffrey A. Washington, Deputy Executive Director
Debbi Seeger, Director, Executive Office
India Vargas, Senior Administrative Assistant

Introduction to Accreditation

The American Correctional Association (ACA) and the Commission on Accreditation for Corrections (CAC) are private, nonprofit organizations that administer the only national accreditation program for all components of adult and juvenile corrections. Their purpose is to promote improvement in the management of correctional agencies through the administration of a voluntary accreditation program and the ongoing development and revision of relevant, useful standards.

Accreditation, a process that began in 1978, involves a large number of detention facilities and approximately 80 percent of all state departments of correction and youth services as active participants. Also included are programs and facilities operated by the Federal Bureau of Prisons, the U.S. Parole Commission, and the District of Columbia. For all these agencies, the accreditation program offers the opportunity to evaluate their operations against national standards, remedy deficiencies, and upgrade the quality of correctional programs and services. The recognized benefits from such a process include improved management, a defense against lawsuits through documentation and the demonstration of a good-faith effort to improve conditions of confinement, increased accountability and enhanced public credibility for administrative and line staff, a safer and more humane environment for personnel and offenders, and the establishment of measurable criteria for upgrading programs, personnel, and the physical plant on a continuing basis.

The timelines, requirements, and outcomes of the accreditation process are the same for a state or federal prison, training school, local detention facility, private halfway house or group home, probation and parole field service agency, or paroling authority. All programs and facilities sign a contract, pay an accreditation fee, conduct a self-evaluation, and have a standards compliance audit by trained ACA auditors before an accreditation decision is made by the Commission on Accreditation for Corrections. Once accredited, all programs and facilities submit annual certification statements to ACA. Also, at ACA's expense and discretion, a monitoring visit may be conducted during the initial three-year accreditation period to ensure continued compliance with the appropriate standards.

Participation in the Accreditation Process

Invitations to participate in the accreditation process have been extended to all adult and juvenile agencies for which standards have been developed and published. Participating agencies include public and private, federal, state, and local agencies; and United States and international correctional agencies.

Accreditation activities are initiated voluntarily by correctional administrators. When an agency chooses to pursue accreditation, ACA staff will provide the agency with appropriate information and application materials. These include a contract, the applicable manual of standards, a policy and procedure manual, and an organization summary.

Eligibility Criteria

To be eligible for accreditation, an agency must be a part of a governmental or private entity or conform to the applicable federal, state, or local laws and regulations regarding corporate existence. The agency must: (1) hold under confinement pretrial or presentenced adults or juveniles who are being held pending a hearing for unlawful activity; or (2) hold under confinement sentenced adult offenders convicted of criminal activity or juveniles adjudicated to confinement; or (3) supervise in the community sentenced adult or adjudicated juvenile offenders, including juveniles placed in residential settings; and (4) have a single administrative officer responsible for agency operations. It is this administrative officer who makes formal application for admission for accreditation.

It is ACA's policy that nonadjudicated juveniles should be served outside the juvenile correctional system. Juvenile correctional facilities housing status offenders must remove them before the facility can be awarded accreditation. Detention facilities may house status offenders who have violated valid court orders by continued perpetration of status offenses. In such instances, the following conditions would apply: status offenders are separated by sight and sound from delinquent offenders; facility staff demonstrate attempts to mandate removal of all status offenders from detention centers; and special programs are developed for status offenders.

ACA does not prohibit community programs that house adjudicated juveniles with status offenders in nonsecure settings from participation in accreditation. However, ACA actively supports and requires exclusion of status offenders from the criminal and juvenile justice systems. Residential facilities and institutional programs that house adults and juveniles separated by sight and sound may become accredited. Individual cases may stipulate removal of juveniles before receiving an accreditation award.

Pre-Accreditation Assessment

Prior to signing an accreditation contract, an agency may request a pre-accreditation assessment. The assessment requires an ACA auditor to visit the agency. The auditor will assess strengths and areas for improvement, measure readiness to apply for accreditation, and identify steps required to achieve accreditation. The agency will receive a confidential, written report to assist in making the decision to apply for accreditation.

Accreditation Process

When the agency enters into the accreditation process, the administrator requests an information package from ACA. To confirm eligibility, determine appropriate fees, and schedule accreditation activities, the agency provides ACA with relevant narrative information through the organization summary. Applicant status begins when both the completed organization summary, which provides a written description of the facility/program, and the signed contract are returned to ACA. The association will notify the agency of its acceptance into the accreditation process within fifteen days of the receipt of the necessary application materials. ACA will then assign a standards specialist from the Standards and Accreditation Department as a permanent liaison to the agency. The agency will appoint an accreditation manager, who will be responsible for organizing and supervising agency resources and activities to achieve accreditation.

As defined in the contract, the fees for the accreditation period cover all services normally provided to an agency by ACA staff, auditors, and the commission. The fees are determined during the application period and are included in the contract signed by the agency and ACA.

Once the contract is signed, the agency conducts a self-assessment of its operations and completes a self-evaluation report, which specifies the agency's level of standards compliance. (Self-evaluation reports are optional for facilities signing a reaccreditation contract.)

At the agency's request and expense, an on-site accreditation orientation for staff and/or a field consultation may be scheduled. The object of the orientation is to prepare agency staff to complete the requirements of accreditation, including an understanding of self-evaluation activities, compilation of documentation, audit procedures, and standards interpretation. A field auditor provides information on accreditation policy and procedure, standards interpretations, and/or documentation requirements. Agency familiarity with standards and accreditation is the key factor in determining the need for these services.

The self-evaluation report includes the organization summary, a compliance tally, preliminary requests for waivers or plans of action, and a completed standards compliance checklist for each standard in the applicable manual.

The standards used for accreditation address services, programs, and operations essential to good correctional management, including administrative, staff, and fiscal controls, staff training and development, physical plant, safety and emergency procedures, sanitation, food service, rules and discipline, and a variety of subjects that comprise good correctional practice. These standards are under continual revision to reflect changing practice, current case law, new knowledge, and agency experience with their application. These changes are published by ACA in the *Standards Supplement.* ACA policy addresses the impact of the standards revisions on agencies involved in accreditation. Agencies signing contracts after the date that a *Standards Supplement* is published are held accountable for all standards changes in that supplement. Agencies are not held accountable for changes made after the contract is signed. The agencies may choose to apply new changes to the standards that have been issued following the program's entry into accreditation. Agencies must notify ACA of their decision before conducting the standards compliance audit.

For accreditation purposes, any new architectural design, building, and/or renovation of the institution must be in accordance with the current standards manual at the time of the design, building, and/or renovation. In such cases, different standards would be applied to separate parts of the institution, respective to these changes in the physical plant.

Standards Compliance Checklist

In completing a standards compliance checklist, the agency checks compliance, noncompliance, or not applicable for each standard. Checking compliance signifies complete compliance with the content of the standard at all times and that the agency has documentation (primarily written) available to support compliance. A finding of noncompliance indicates that all or part of the requirements stated in the standard have not been met. A not applicable response means that the standard/expected practice is clearly not relevant to the agency/facility being audited. A written statement supporting nonapplicability of the standard/expected practice is required.

At this time, the agency may request a waiver for one or more standards, provided that overall agency programming compensates for the lack of compliance. The waiver request must be accompanied by a clear explanation of the compensating conditions. The agency applies for a waiver only when the totality of conditions safeguards the life, health, and safety of offenders and staff. Waivers are not granted for standards/expected practices designated as mandatory and do not change the conclusion of noncompliance or the agency's compliance tally. When a waiver is requested during the self-evaluation phase, ACA staff renders a preliminary judgment. A final decision can be made only by the board of commissioners during the accreditation hearing. Most waivers granted are for physical plant standards.

The association requires that a self-evaluation report be completed by each applicant for accreditation. It is recommended that agencies entering into the accreditation process for the first time submit a written statement to ACA concerning their status at the completion of the evaluation. Information contained in this statement should include the percentage of compliance with mandatory and nonmandatory standards; a list of not applicable standards/expected practices; and a list of noncompliant standards and their deficiencies. Within sixty days of receipt of this statement, ACA staff will provide the agency administrator with a written response containing, where appropriate, comments on materials or information submitted to the association. The letter also provides notice to the agency of its acceptance to candidate status.

The compilation of written documentation requires the most time and effort during correspondent status. A separate documentation file, which documents compliance, is prepared for each standard. To request a standards compliance audit, an agency must comply with 100 percent of the standards/expected practices designated as mandatory and 90 percent of the nonmandatory standards/expected practices. Once an agency believes it has met or exceeded the compliance levels required for accreditation, an audit is scheduled. Final accreditation is not awarded until the Commission on Accreditation for Corrections awards accredited status. The accreditation award period is three years.

Standards Compliance Audit

The agency's request for an audit is made six-to-eight weeks before the desired audit dates. The purpose of the audit is to have the visiting committee measure the agency's operation against the standards based on the documentation provided by the agency. A visiting committee completes the audit and prepares a visiting committee report for submission to the commission. ACA designates a visiting committee chair to organize and supervise the committee's activities.

Prior to arrival at the audit site, each member of the visiting committee reviews the agency's descriptive narrative and any additional information that ACA may have provided, including pending litigation and court orders submitted by the agency, and any inmate correspondence. The visiting committee chair makes audit assignments to each auditor. For example, one auditor may audit the administrative, fiscal, and personnel standards/expected practices, while another audits standards/expected practices for the physical plant, sanitation, and security. Upon arrival, the visiting committee meets with the administrator, accreditation manager, and other appropriate staff to discuss the scope of the audit and the schedule of activities. This exchange of information provides for the development of an audit schedule that ensures the least amount of disruption to routine agency operation.

The exact amount of time required to complete the audit depends on the agency size, the number of applicable standards/expected practices, additional facilities to be audited, and accessibility and organization of the documentation. To hasten the audit, all documentation should be clearly referenced and located where the visiting committee is to work.

The accreditation manager's responsibilities include compiling and making accessible to all visiting committee members the standards-compliance documentation and release-of-information forms for personnel and offender records. Also, staff should be notified beforehand to ensure that they are available to discuss specific issues or conduct tours of the facility for the visiting committee.

During the audit, the members of the visiting committee tour the facility, review the documentation prepared for each standard/expected practice, and interview staff and offenders to make compliance decisions. The visiting committee reports its findings on the same standards-compliance checklist used by the agency in preparing its self-evaluation report. All members of the visiting committee review all mandatory standards/expected practices, all areas of noncompliance and nonapplicability, with decisions made collectively. (Final decisions on waivers can be approved only by the commission at the time of the agency's accreditation hearing.)

Interviewing staff and offenders is an integral part of the audit. In addition to speaking with those who request an interview with the team, the members of the visiting committee select other individuals to interview and with whom to discuss issues. Interviews are voluntary and occur randomly throughout the audit, and those interviewed are assured that their discussions are confidential.

In addition to auditing standards/expected practices documentation, auditors will evaluate the quality of life or conditions of confinement. An acceptable quality of life is necessary for an agency to be eligible for accreditation. Factors that the visiting committee consider include: the adequacy and quality of programs, activities, and services available to offenders and their involvement; occurrences of disturbances, serious incidents, assaults, or violence, including their frequency and methods of dealing with them to ensure the safety of staff and offenders or juveniles; and overall physical conditions, including conditions of confinement, program space, and institutional maintenance related to sanitation, health, and safety.

At the conclusion of the audit, the visiting committee again meets with the administrator, the accreditation manager, and any others selected by the administrator to discuss the results of the audit. During this exit interview, the visiting committee reports the compliance tally and all findings of noncompliance and nonapplicability, as well as preliminary decisions on waivers, stating the reasons for each decision.

The chair of the visiting committee then prepares and submits a copy of the visiting committee report to the ACA standards and accreditation specialist within ten days of the completion of the audit. ACA staff review the report for completeness, enter the data, and within fifteen days of the audit's completion, it is submitted to the agency administrator and other members of the visiting committee for concurrence. Upon receipt of the visiting committee report, the agency has seven days to submit its written response to the report to ACA staff and all members of the visiting committee.

The Accreditation Hearing

The Commission on Accreditation for Corrections is responsible for rendering accreditation decisions and is divided into accreditation panels authorized to render such decisions. Panels meet separately, or with a full board, and are composed of three-to-five commissioners.

The agency is invited to have representation at the accreditation hearing. Unless circumstances dictate otherwise, a member of the visiting committee is not present; however, an ACA staff member does participate. At the accreditation hearing, the agency representative provides information about the agency, speaks in support of its appeal and/or waiver requests, and addresses concerns the panel may have with regard to the accreditation application.

After completing its review, the accreditation panel votes to award or deny accreditation or continue the agency in candidacy status or place the agency on probation. When an agency receives a three- year accreditation award, a certificate with the effective date of the award is presented to the agency representative.

The board of commissioners may stipulate additional requirements for accreditation if, in its opinion, conditions exist in the facility or program that adversely affect the life, health, or safety of the staff or offenders. These requests are specific regarding activities required and timeliness for their completion. The panel advises the agency representative of all changes at the time the accreditation decision is made.

ACA and the commission may deny accreditation for insufficient standards/expected practices compliance, inadequate plans of action, or failure to meet other requirements as determined by the commission, including, but not limited to, the conditions of confinement in a given facility. In not awarding accreditation, the commission may extend an agency in candidate status for a specific period of time and for identified deficiencies, if in its judgment the agency is actively pursuing compliance. Those agencies denied accreditation, but not extended in candidate status, may reapply for accreditation after 180 days. The agency receives written notification of all decisions relative to its accreditation following the accreditation hearing.

Accredited Status

During the three-year accreditation period, ACA requires that accredited agencies submit annual certification statements confirming continued standards/expected practices compliance at levels necessary for accreditation. The report should include the agency's progress on completing plans of action and other significant events that may affect the accreditation award. In addition, ACA may require accredited agencies to submit written responses to public criticism, notoriety, or patterns of complaints about agency activity that suggest a failure to maintain standards/expected practices compliance. The association, at its own expense and with advance notice, may conduct on-site monitoring visits to verify continued standards/expected practices compliance or conditions of confinement.

Reconsideration Process

The goal of ACA's accreditation process is to ensure the equity, fairness, and reliability of its decisions, particularly those that constitute either denial or revocation of accredited status. Therefore, an agency may request reconsideration of any denial or revocation of accreditation. However, the reasonableness of ACA's standards, criteria, and/or procedures for accreditation may not serve as the basis for reconsideration.

A reconsideration request is based on the grounds that the adverse decision is (1) arbitrary, erratic, or otherwise in substantial disregard of the criteria and/or procedures for accreditation as stated by ACA, (2) based on incorrect facts or an incorrect interpretation of facts, or (3) unsupported by substantial evidence.

The agency submits a written request for reconsideration to ACA staff within thirty days of the adverse decision stating the basis for the request. The commission's Executive Committee reviews the request and decides whether there is sufficient evidence to warrant a reconsideration hearing before the board of commissioners. The agency is notified in writing of the Executive Committee's decision.

Revocation of Accreditation

An accredited agency that does not maintain the required levels of compliance throughout the three-year accreditation period, including continuous compliance with all mandatory standards/expected practices, may have its accreditation award revoked. The agency is notified of its deficiencies and given a specified amount of time to correct them. If the deficiencies continue, the Commission on Accreditation for Corrections may place the agency on probationary status for an additional stated period of time and require documentation of compliance. Should the agency fail to correct the deficiencies, the agency's accreditation may be revoked and the accreditation certificate returned to ACA. An accredited agency that has had its accreditation revoked for reasons of noncompliance also may use the reconsideration process.

Reaccreditation

To ensure continuous accredited status, accredited agencies should apply for reaccreditation approximately twelve months before the expiration of their current accreditation award.

The preceding information is provided as an overview of the accreditation process. Additional information on specific procedures and elements of the process is available from ACA's Standards and Accreditation Department.

Administration of Correctional Agencies (ACA), 2nd Edition

2-CO-1A-05

Revised January 2013. Policy, procedure, and practice govern the development and dissemination of agency policies.

COMMENT: Agency policies and related procedural rules and regulations are developed through a systematic and uniform process. All units of the agency should receive policies and revisions.

2-CO-1A-06

Revised January 2013. The qualifications, authority, and responsibilities of the director and other appointed personnel are specified in writing by statute or by the parent agency.

COMMENT: The administrator must balance the goals and objectives with available resources and assure that broad facility goals are translated into specific objectives.

2-CO-1A-06-1

Added August 2010. The facility/agency shall demonstrate it has examined, and where appropriate and feasible, implemented strategies that promote recycling, energy and water conservation, pollution reduction, and utilization of renewable energy alternatives.

COMMENT: Correctional facilities and programs have the responsibility to implement strategies that allow correctional facilities to be managed in ways that are most cost-effective and deliver superior performance, while improving environmental responsibility and sustainability. This includes recycling (including paper, metal, and plastic products), energy conservation (including building insulation, heating and ventilation, temperature controls, vehicle fuel efficiency, water economies, physical plant engineering, and energy measures), pollution reduction (including composting/sewer treatment, litter abatement, and carbon emissions), and utilization of renewable energy alternatives (bio-fuels, solar collection, turbine energy production, and methane collection).

2-CO-1A-08

Deleted January 2013.

2-CO-1A-11

Revised January 2000. The educational, operational, and administrative qualifications of the agency administrator are taken into consideration by the appointing authority in determining appointment to the position. These include, at a minimum: a baccalaureate degree, five years of related administrative experience or demonstrated administrative ability and leadership.

COMMENT: To ensure that only qualified persons are recruited and apply for the position of chief executive officer, the appointing authority should establish high qualifications and recruit and hire on the basis of these qualifications.

2-CO-1A-27-1

Added August 1993. Written policy, procedure, and practice establish the agency's commitment to informing the public and the media of events within the agency's areas of responsibility. The procedures address emergency and nonemergency responses to the media and, at a minimum, include the following:

- **the identification of areas in the facility that are accessible to media representatives**
- **the contact person for routine requests for information**
- **identification of data and information protected by federal or state privacy laws, or federal and state freedom of information laws**
- **special events coverage**
- **news-release policy**
- **the designation of individuals or positions within the agency authorized to speak with the media on behalf of the agency**

COMMENT: The complexity of the policy statement should be consistent with the size and complexity of the operation.

2-CO-1B-07

Revised January 2001. Written policy, procedure, and practice provide for an independent financial audit of the agency. This audit is conducted annually or as stipulated by statute or regulation, but at least every three years. If the agency is a part of a state system, an internal audits section or department of the agency's central administration and/or statutory agency shall be considered independent of the agency to be audited.

COMMENT: None.

2-CO-1C-09

Revised August 1995. Written policy specifies that equal employment opportunities exist for all positions. When deficiencies exist regarding the employment of minority groups and women, the institution can document the implementation of an affirmative action program that is approved by the appropriate government agency and can document annual reviews and the changes needed to keep the program current.

COMMENT: Equal employment opportunity is a public policy goal. All qualified persons should be able to compete equally for entry into and promotion within the institution, and the affirmative action program should actively encourage the participation of members of minority groups, individuals with disability, and women in the institution's staff development program. The affirmative action program also should include corrective actions, when needed, in policies regarding pay rate, demotion, transfer, layoff, termination, and upgrades.

2-CO-1C-09-1

Added August 1995. Written policy, procedure, and practice provide a mechanism to process requests for reasonable accommodation to the known physical and/or mental impairments of a qualified individual with a disability, either an applicant or an employee. The accommodation need not be granted if it would impose an undue hardship or direct threat.

COMMENT: *Reasonable accommodation* refers to modifications or adjustments, which enable qualified applicants with disabilities to access the job application process or which enable qualified employees with disabilities to perform the essential functions of the job and to enjoy the same terms, conditions, and privileges of employment that are available to persons without disabilities. Terms, conditions, and privileges of employment include, but are not limited to:

- recruitment, selection, and hiring
- salary and compensation
- benefits, holidays, leave, and work hours
- promotion and advancement
- staff development, including in-service training
- retirement, resignation, and termination

An *undue hardship* means significant difficulty or expense. *Direct threat* means a significant risk of substantial harm to the health or safety of any person, including the applicant or employee with a disability that cannot be eliminated or reduced by reasonable accommodation. A *qualified individual with a disability* means an individual with a disability who satisfies the requisite skill, experience, education, and other job-related requirements for the employment position such individual holds or desires, and who, with or without reasonable accommodation, can perform the essential functions of such position.

2-CO-1C-12 **Deleted August 1995.**

2-CO-1C-17 **Revised August 2009. Written agency policy, procedure, and practice require that employees of other public or private organizations providing a service to the agency are accountable to the administrative officer of the program in which they work.**

COMMENT: None.

2-CO-1C-20 **Revised January 2012. There is a written agency policy, procedure, and practice that specifies support for a drug-free workplace for all employees. This policy includes at a minimum the following:**

- **prohibition of the use of illegal drugs**
- **prohibition of possession of any illegal drug except in the performance of official duties**
- **the opportunities available for treatment and/or counseling for drug abuse**
- **the procedures to be used to ensure compliance**
- **the penalties for violation of the policy**

COMMENT: None.

2-CO-1C-23

Revised August 2010. The agency maintains a current, accurate, confidential personnel record on each employee except where state statutes require open public records and the personnel record cannot be maintained confidentially. Information obtained as part of a required medical examination (and/or inquiry) regarding the medical condition or history of applicants and employees is collected and maintained on separate forms and in separate medical files and treated as a confidential medical record.

COMMENT: The personnel record should contain the following: initial application; reference letters; results of employment investigation; verification of training and experience; wage and salary information; job performance evaluations; incident reports, if any; and commendations and disciplinary actions, if any.

2-CO-1D-02

Revised August 2007. Written policy, procedure, and practice specify training and staff development requirements for all employees. This training shall, at a minimum, include the following:

- **fire and emergency procedures**
- **safety procedures**
- **interpersonal relations**
- **communication skills**
- **sexual harassment**

The sophistication level and amount of training should be based on employees need to know and their job assignment.

COMMENT: Organizations are encouraged to train staff on agency operations.

2-CO-1D-07

Revised August 2000. Written policy, procedure, and practice provide that all administrative and managerial staff receive 40 hours of training in addition to orientation training during their first year of employment and 40 hours of training each year thereafter, in areas relevant to their position.

COMMENT: None.

2-CO-1E-01

Revised January 2012. Written agency policy, procedure, and practice governing case record management includes, but is not limited to, the establishment, use, content, privacy, security, preservation, and destruction of case records.

COMMENT: None.

2-CO-1F-01

Revised January 2012. Written agency policy provides for the uniform collecting, recording, organizing, and processing of data developed for management information purposes.

COMMENT: None.

2-CO-1F-13

Revised January 2011. Written policy and procedure governs voluntary participation in non-medical, non-pharmaceutical, and non-cosmetic testing.

COMMENT: Participation in nonmedical, nonpharmaceutical, and noncosmetic testing should be permitted only after a thorough review of the research.

2-CO-2B-04

Added August 1995. Reasonable accommodation is made to ensure that all parts of the institution that are accessible to the public are accessible and usable by staff and visitors with disabilities.

COMMENT: None.

2-CO-4G-02

Added January 1992. Written policy, procedure, and practice provide that consistent with the law of the jurisdiction, there is a system for providing notification to the registered victim(s) of a crime prior to any release from confinement of the convicted offender and/or escape from custody. Follow-up notification to victim(s) occurs when escapees are returned to custody.

COMMENT: An increasing number of jurisdictions are requiring notification of the victims of criminal act(s) prior to release of the person(s) convicted of the crime. When such legislation exists, the agency should provide the staff with a clear set of instructions to implement the legislation.

2-CO-5E-01

Revised August 2004. Written agency policy provides for religious programming for inmates/juveniles/residents, including:

- **program coordination and supervision**
- **opportunities to practice one's faith individually and corporately as authorized**
- **possession of authorized religious symbols and/or items essential for faith practice purchased through authorized vendors at the inmates'/juveniles'/residents' expense**
- **availability of religious program information to offenders**
- **access to approved publications related to religious beliefs and practices**
- **the observance of authorized religious diets, holy day ceremonies, work restrictions, and authorized communal sacramental rites (providing such rites do not conflict with existing procedures/policies or jeopardize the security and orderly running of the facility)**
- **distribution of resources among faith groups authorized to meet, commensurate with their representation within the population, to include the use of religious facilities and equipment**
- **accessibility by staff chaplains to all areas of the facility**
- **visitation of clergy/spiritual advisor to occur through established visiting procedures**
- **use of community resources to include the use of religious volunteers, consistent with the safety and security of the facility**

COMMENT: The size and complexity of the religious program will vary depending on the needs of the persons in the facilities. The central office policy should address the general goals of the religious program in sufficient detail to enable the managers of the facilities to develop more specific plans.

2-CO-5E-02 **Added August 2003. Written policy, procedure, and practice provide that a qualified senior staff member is responsible for coordinating the agency's religious program and that the staff member:**

- **specifies the lines of authority, responsibility, and accountability for the religious program**
- **enables juveniles/residents/inmates to identify religious preferences upon entering the system and provides a process where preferences may be changed (specifies if juveniles are required to obtain parental or legal guardian consent to change preference)**
- **ensures that juveniles/inmates/residents are not subjected to coercion, harassment, or ridicule due to religious affiliation**
- **describes the conditions and circumstances under which clergy's privileged communication exists. Circumstances under which privileged communication in the correctional setting does not apply should be clearly stated.**
- **ensures that staff who have direct contact with juveniles/residents/inmates are given training regarding religious practices**

COMMENT: The complexity of the provision of a religious services program requires the assignment of a person, preferably certified by a national professional chaplaincy organization, who will administer the program to help ensure that juveniles/residents/inmates are allowed equitable opportunities to practice the requirements of their faith and program development consistent with religious and spiritual needs of the populations being served, and professional development of the chaplaincy staff.

Appendix C. Revised January 2001. Refer to *Standards Supplement* Appendix D.

Performance-Based Standards for Adult Community Residential Services (ACRS), 4th Edition

4-ACRS-1A-07

Revised January 2008. Documentation is provided by a qualified source that lighting is at least 20 foot-candles at desk level and in personal grooming areas, and is checked at least once per accreditation cycle.

COMMENT: None.

PROTOCOLS: Written policy/procedure.

PROCESS INDICATORS: Documentation from qualified source.

4-ACRS-1A-08

Revised August 2002. Air circulation is at least 15 cubic feet of outside or recirculated filtered air per minute per person and is checked not less than once per accreditation cycle.

Interpretation August 2002. The words"accreditation cycle" are interpreted as within the past three years.

COMMENT: The facility should maintain strict adherence to local health codes requiring proper lighting and ventilation.

PROTOCOLS: Facility plans/specifications.

PROCESS INDICATORS: Documentation of air-circulation volume. Inspection reports from health agencies or other qualified independent sources. Measurement.

4-ACRS-1A-10

Deleted July 2012.

4-ACRS-1A-15

Revised January 2007. Offenders are permitted to decorate their living and sleeping quarters with personal possessions. Rules regarding the decoration of living/sleeping quarters are available to all offenders and staff. These rules are reviewed annually and revised, if necessary.

COMMENT: None.

PROTOCOLS: Written policy and procedure. Offender handbook and rules.

PROCESS INDICATORS: Documentation of annual review of rules. Observation. Interviews.

4-ACRS-1B-01

Revised August 2002 (Mandatory). An annual safety inspection of all vehicles is conducted by qualified individuals and in accordance with state statutes for any vehicle that is owned, leased, or used in the operation of the facility.

COMMENT: None.

PROTOCOLS: Written policy/procedure. Vehicle log format. Maintenance record format.

PROCESS INDICATORS: Inspection reports. Completed vehicle logs. Maintenance records and receipts. Reports of vehicle problems/requests for repair or maintenance. Credentials of inspector.

4-ACRS-1C-01-1

Added January 2003. Critical incidents are defined for the facility along with a debriefing to be conducted after each such incident. The debriefing process includes coordination and feedback about the incident with designated staff of the facility as soon as possible after the incident. A debriefing includes, but is not limited to:

- **a review of staff and offender actions during the incident**
- **a review of the incident's impact on staff and offenders**
- **a review of corrective actions taken and still needed**
- **plans for improvement to avoid another incident**

COMMENT: A critical incident is any event or situation that threatens staff or offenders in their community (criminal justice setting). While debriefings should occur as soon as possible, some information may not be available until later. All staff impacted by a critical incident should be included in the debriefings and referred to appropriate services to mitigate the stress associated with these events. All critical incidents should be reviewed by the administration, security, and health services. A two-week follow-up debriefing should occur to review the validity and appropriateness of all policies, plans, and information used during the critical incident and immediately after.

PROTOCOLS: Written policy/procedure. Definition of critical incidents.

PROCESS INDICATORS: Critical incident report. Minutes from debriefing. Interviews.

4-ACRS-1C-03

Deleted August 2007.

4-ACRS-1C-09

Revised August 2007 (Mandatory). There is a written evacuation plan to be used in the event of a fire. The plan is certified by an independent qualified agency or individual trained in the application of national fire safety codes. The plan is reviewed annually, updated, if necessary, and reissued to the local fire jurisdiction. The plan includes the following:

- **location of building/room floor plan**
- **use of exit signs and directional arrows that are easily seen and read**
- **location of publicly posted plan**
- **at least quarterly drills in all facility locations, and on every shift, including administrative areas**

COMMENT: The evacuation plan also should specify evacuation routes, subsequent disposition and temporary housing of offenders, and provision for medical care or hospital transportation for injured offenders and/or staff.

PROTOCOLS: Written policy/procedure. Facility plan/specifications. Written emergency plan.

PROCESS INDICATORS: Certification of emergency plan approval. Documentation of annual review by local fire jurisdiction. Documentation of credentials of person or agency that provided approval.

4-ACRS- 2B

Revised August 2000. Physical force is used only in instances of self-protection, protection of the offender or others, prevention of property damage, prevention of escape, or to maintain or regain control.

OUTCOME MEASURES FOR SECTION 2B

(1) Number of instances in which force was used in the past twelve months divided by the average daily offender population in the past twelve months.
(2) Number of times that staff's use of force was found to have been inappropriate in the past twelve months divided by the number of instances in which force was used in the past twelve months.
(3) Number of offender's grievances filed alleging inappropriate use of force in the past twelve months divided by the average daily offender population in the past twelve months.
(4) Number of grievances alleging inappropriate use of force decided in favor of offenders in the past twelve months divided by the number of grievances alleging inappropriate use of force filed in the past twelve months.
(5) Number of injuries requiring medical treatment resulting from staff use of force in the past twelve months divided by the average daily offender population in the past twelve months.

4-ACRS-2B-01

Revised August 2000. (Mandatory). A written report is prepared following all use of force and is submitted to the facility administrator. The report details all circumstances, lists those involved, including witnesses, and describes medical services provided.

COMMENT: It is important that records of all instances of use of force are maintained.

PROTOCOLS: Written policy/procedure. Incident report form.

PROCESS INDICATORS: Completed incident reports. Record of treatment provided. Offender records.

4-ACRS-2D-01 **Revised January 2001 (Mandatory). A control plan(s) for keys, tools, and utensils addresses access, use, and storage.**

COMMENT: Tools, keys, and utensils should be used in accordance with a prescribed system(s).

PROTOCOLS: Written policy/procedure. Key control plan. Tool control plan. Equipment control plan. Formats for control records/forms.

PROCESS INDICATORS: Facility logs. Key, tool, equipment control documentation (records, logs, forms).

4-ACRS-2D-02 **Revised January 2001 (Mandatory). Tools and utensils are used in accordance with the prescribed system.**

COMMENT: None.

PROTOCOLS: Written policy/procedure. Tool, utensil control plan.

PROCESS INDICATORS: Tool, utensil control records.

4-ACRS-2D-03 **Revised January 2001 (Mandatory). Keys are used in accordance with the prescribed system.**

COMMENT: None.

PROTOCOLS: Written policy/procedure. Key control plan

PROCESS INDICATORS: Key control records.

4-ACRS-3A-05 **Revised August 2013. Offenders receive written orientation materials and/or translations in their language, if they do not understand English. These materials may also be provided electronically, but inmates in segregation must be provided the information in a written format so that their access to the information is not impeded by their custody status. When a literacy problem exists, a staff member assists the offender in understanding the material.**

COMMENT: Orientation should include informal classes, distribution of written materials about the facility's programs (or how to access this information electronically, if available), rules and regulations, and discussions. Orientation also should be used to observe offender behavior and to identify special problems.

PROTOCOLS: Written policy/procedure.

PROCESS INDICATORS: Offender records. Facility logs.

4-ACRS-4A-01

Revised August 2010 (Mandatory). [Applicable only to facilities that prepare OR serve food to offenders]. If the facility prepares and/or serves food to offenders, dietary allowances are reviewed at least annually by a qualified nutritionist, dietitian, or physician to ensure that they meet the nationally recommended allowances for basic nutrition for the types of offenders housed in the facility.

COMMENT: None.

PROTOCOLS: Written policy/procedure. Format for food service records/forms.

PROCESS INDICATORS: Documentation of at least annual review by nutritionist or dietitian.

4-ACRS-4A-02

Revised August 2004. Therapeutic diets are provided as prescribed by appropriate clinicians. A therapeutic diet manual is available in health services and food services for reference and information. Prescriptions for therapeutic diets should be specific and complete, furnished in writing to the food service manager, and rewritten annually, or more often as clinically indicated.

COMMENT: Therapeutic diets are prepared and served to offenders according to the orders of the treating clinician or as directed by the responsible health authority. Therapeutic diets should be kept as simple as possible and should conform as closely as possible to the foods served to other offenders.

PROTOCOLS: Written policy/procedure. Format for food service records/forms. Format for offenders to request special diets. Offender handbook/rules.

PROCESS INDICATORS: Food service records. Offender medical records. Offender records.

4-ACRS-4A-04

Revised August 2010 (Mandatory). [Applicable only to facilities that prepare or serve food to offenders.] Food service staff complies with all sanitation and health codes enacted by state or local authorities.

COMMENT: All sanitation codes are to be strictly followed to ensure the health and welfare of the offenders. Local or state health regulations usually require some type of medical examination and certification for people preparing food.

PROTOCOLS: Written policy/procedure. Sanitation and health codes.

PROCESS INDICATORS: Documentation of compliance with sanitation and health codes. Documentation of medical examinations and certification, as applicable.

4-ACRS-4A-04-1

Added August 2011 [Applicable only to facilities that prepare or serve food to offenders]. All staff, contractors, and inmate workers who work in the food service department are trained in the use of food service equipment and in the safety procedures to be followed in the food service department.

COMMENT: All sanitation codes are to be strictly followed to ensure the health and welfare of the offenders. Local or state health regulations usually require some type of medical examination and certification for people preparing food.

PROTOCOLS: Written policy/procedure. Sanitation and health codes.

PROCESS INDICATORS: Documentation of compliance with sanitation and health codes. Documentation of medical examinations and certification, as applicable.

4-ACRS-4A-05

Revised August 2010. [Applicable only to facilities that prepare or serve food to offenders.] Adequate space is provided for food preparation and service and for an eating area and seating for all who dine at the same time.

COMMENT: None.

PROTOCOLS: Written policy/procedure. Facility plans/specifications.

PROCESS INDICATORS: Observation.

4-ACRS-4A-06

Revised August 2010. [Applicable only to facilities that prepare or serve food to offenders.] When the facility has a kitchen, dining or food storage areas, they are properly ventilated, properly furnished, and clean.

COMMENT: None.

PROTOCOLS: Written policy/procedure. Facility plans/specifications.

PROCESS INDICATORS: Documentation of adequate ventilation. Inspection records.

4-ACRS-4A-07

Revised August 2010. [Applicable only to facilities that prepare or serve food to offenders.] Food service practices provide for the following:

- **Weekly inspection of all food service areas, including dining and food preparation areas and equipment**
- **Sanitary, temperature-controlled storage facilities for all foods**
- **Daily checks of refrigerator and water temperatures**

COMMENT: Appropriate space and equipment should be available for the proper storage and refrigeration of food supplies. Dry food supplies are stored in a clean, dry, ventilated room not subject to wastewater backflow or other contamination. The American Dietary Association recommends storage temperatures for freezers to be -10 degrees to 0 degrees Fahrenheit, and refrigerated storage at 32 degrees to 36 degrees Fahrenheit.

PROTOCOLS: Written policy/procedure. Weekly inspection forms. Format for daily recording of refrigerator and water temperature.

PROCESS INDICATORS: Completed inspection forms and reports. Refrigerator and water temperature records. Documentation of actions taken in response to identified problems.

4-ACRS-4A-08

Revised August 2010. [Applicable only to facilities that prepare or serve food to offenders.] Toilet and washbasin facilities are available to food service personnel and offenders in close proximity to the food preparation area.

COMMENT: None.

PROTOCOLS: Written policy/procedure. Facility plans/specifications.

PROCESS INDICATORS: Observation. Inspect records (verify condition of fixtures).

4-ACRS-4B-04

Revised January 2001. Offenders are issued suitable, clean bedding and linen, including two sheets, a pillow and pillowcase, one mattress, not to exclude a mattress with integrated pillow, and sufficient blankets to provide comfort under existing temperature controls. There is provision for linen exchange, including towels, at least weekly.

COMMENT: None.

PROTOCOLS: Written policy and procedure. Format for recording linen exchanges.

PROCESS INDICATORS: Linen exchange records.

4-ACRS-4C-05

Revised August 2002. First aid kits are available in designated areas of the facility. Contents and locations are approved by the health authority. An automatic external defibrillator is available for use at the facility.

COMMENT: The availability and placement of first aid kits are determined by the designated health authority in conjunction with the facility administrator.

PROTOCOLS: Written policy/procedure. Facility plan with location of first aid kits are noted. List of required contents for first aid kits.

PROCESS INDICATORS: Documentation of approval by health authority. Inventories of first aid kits. Documentation of availability of equipment and supplies.

4-ACRS-4C-10

Revised January 2008. Policies direct actions to be taken by employees concerning offenders who have been diagnosed with HIV, including, at a minimum, the following:

- **appropriate safeguards for staff and offenders**
- **when and under what conditions offenders are to be separated**
- **staff and offender training procedures**
- **issues of confidentiality**
- **counseling and support services**

COMMENT: None.

PROTOCOLS: Written policy/procedure. Staff training curriculum. Offender training curriculum. Testing procedures. Offender handbook/rules.

PROCESS INDICATORS: Staff training records. Documentation of offender training. Documentation of testing. Health care provider records.

4-ACRS-4C-14-1

Added January 2003. Where nursing infants are allowed to remain with their mothers, provisions are made for a nursery, staffed by qualified persons, where the infants are placed when they are not in the care of their mothers.

COMMENT: *Qualified persons* may include offenders who have been trained in the competencies required for nursery care and who are working under appropriate supervision.
PROTOCOLS: Written policy/procedure.

PROCESS INDICATORS: Staff credentials. Facility layout to show location of nursery. Observations.

4-ACRS-5A-08

Revised January 2001. Provide for early identification and treatment of inmates with alcohol and drug abuse problems through a standardized battery assessment. This battery shall be documented and include, at a minimum, the following:

- **screening and sorting**
- **clinical assessment and reassessment**
- **medical assessment for drug and alcohol program assignment appropriate to the needs of the individual offenders**
- **referrals**

COMMENT: None.

PROTOCOLS: Assessment procedure and instruments.

PROCESS INDICATORS: Offender records. Documentation of referrals. Completed assessments.

4-ACRS-5A-18-1 **Added August 2003. An inmate is informed in a timely manner of the verifiable death or critical illness of an immediate family member. In case of the critical illness of an immediate family member, the inmate is allowed, whenever statutes and circumstances allow, to go to the bedside under escort or alone.**

COMMENT: Classification, status, geography, security level, and other specified criteria should determine eligibility. *Immediate family* is usually defined as parent, spouse, child, sibling, grandparent, or legal guardian.

PROTOCOLS: Written policy/procedure.

PROCESS INDICATORS: Notification to the facility of death or illness of immediate family member. Notification to the inmate of death or illness of immediate family member. Temporary release form. Interviews.

4-ACRS-5A-19 **Revised August 2002. There are telephone facilities on the premises, which provide for inmate access to public telephones. Inmates with hearing and/or speech disabilities, and inmates who wish to communicate with parties who have such disabilities, shall be afforded access to a Telecommunications Device for the Deaf (TDD), or comparable equipment. Public telephones with volume control also shall be made available to inmates with hearing impairments.**

COMMENT: Offenders should be permitted reasonable access to a telephone to make both personal and program-related calls. This may be a pay phone. Written policy specifies the hours of telephone availability and any limitations on telephone calls.

PROTOCOLS: Written policy/procedure. Facility plans/specifications. Offender handbook/rules. Format for transmitting messages to offenders.

PROCESS INDICATORS: Facility logs. Documentation of messages transmitted to offenders.

4-ACRS-5A-19-1 **Added August 2002. Offenders have access to reasonably priced telephone services. Correctional agencies ensure that:**

- **Contracts involving telephone services for offenders comply with all applicable state and federal regulations.**
- **Contracts are based on rates and surcharges that are commensurate with those charged to the general public for like services. Any deviation from ordinary consumer rates reflects actual costs associated with the provision of services in a correctional setting.**
- **Contracts for offender telephone services provide the broadest range of calling options determined by the agency administrator to be consistent with the requirements of sound correctional management.**

COMMENT: When procuring and renewing telephone services, correctional officials should inquire into the reasons for proposed deviations from standard charges and seek the best possible rates for the broadest possible range of calling options.

PROTOCOLS: Written policy/procedure. Applicable state and federal regulations.

PROCESS INDICATORS: Contract. Interstate Commerce Commission comparative rates.

4-ACRS-6A-01-1 **Added August 2002. Staff and offenders have access to an appropriately trained and qualified individual who is educated in the problems and challenges faced by offenders with physical and/or mental impairments, programs designed to educate and assist disabled offenders, and all legal requirements for the protection of offenders with disabilities.**

COMMENT: An *appropriately trained and qualified individual*, as used in this standard, is one who has been designated by the warden, superintendent, or other authority, to coordinate efforts to comply with and carry out responsibilities defined by the Americans with Disabilities Act. That individual should develop relationships with, and use the expertise of institutional staff, advocacy groups, nonprofit organizations, agencies of government, and others who have relevant knowledge and experience.

PROTOCOLS: Written policy/procedure.

PROCESS INDICATORS: Training records. Qualifications of individual(s). Interviews.

4-ACRS-6A-04-1 **Added January 2002. The assignment of appropriately trained individuals to assist disabled offenders who cannot otherwise perform basic life functions is provided.**

COMMENT: None.

PROTOCOLS: Written policy and procedure.

PROCESS INDICATORS: Training records. Interviews.

4-ACRS-6A-04-2 **Added August 2002. Education, equipment, and facilities, and the support necessary for inmates with disabilities to perform self-care and personal hygiene in a reasonably private environment are provided.**

COMMENT: A *reasonably private environment* will vary, depending on individual and institutional circumstances, but it is one which will maintain the dignity of the disabled individual in light of that person's disability.

PROTOCOLS: Written policy and procedure.

PROCESS INDICATORS: Education curriculum. Observations.

4-ACRS-6C-02 **Correction August 2001. Delete reference 3-ACRS-4D-07.**

4-ACRS-7B-01 **Revised August 2003. The qualifications for the position of facility administrator include, at a minimum, the following: a bachelor's degree in an appropriate discipline, five years of related administrative experience, and demonstrated administrative ability and leadership. The degree requirement may be satisfied by completion of a career development program that includes work-related experience, training, or college credits at a level of achievement equivalent to the bachelor's degree.**

COMMENT: Establishing high qualifications ensures that only experienced individuals are recruited and employed.

PROTOCOLS: Written policy/procedure. Job descriptions. Employee application and selection forms.

PROCESS INDICATORS: Personnel records. Employment applications.

4-ACRS-7B-02 **Revised January 2005 (Mandatory). All professional staff comply with applicable state and federal licensure, certification, or registration requirements. Verification of current credentials is on file in the facility.**

COMMENT: None.

PROTOCOL: Written policy and procedure. Copies of licensure requirements.

PROCESS INDICATORS: Personnel records. Documentation of licensure, certification or registration. Documentation of current credentials.

4-ACRS-7B-05 **Revised August 2007. A criminal record check is conducted on all new employees and volunteers in accordance with state and federal statutes. This record will include comprehensive identifier information to be collected and run against law enforcement indices. If suspect information on matters with potential terrorism connections is returned on a desirable applicant, it is forwarded to the local Joint Terrorism Task Force (JTTF) or another similar agency.**

COMMENT: The facility administrator should know of any criminal conviction that could directly affect an employee's job performance.

PROTOCOLS: Written policy/procedure.

PROCESS INDICATORS: Personnel records that include criminal record check.

4-ACRS-7B-15 **Revised August 2000. All administrative, managerial, and professional staff receive 40 hours of training in addition to orientation training during their first year of employment and 40 hours of training each year thereafter, in areas relevant to their position.**

COMMENT: Ongoing training in topics relevant to an employee's position enhances skill and job performance.

PROTOCOLS: Written policy and procedure. Training curriculum. Orientation training form.

PROCESS INDICATORS: Training records. Personnel records.

4-ACRS-7B-16 **Correction August 2001. Replace reference 3-ACRS-7B-16 with 3-ACRS-1D-12.**

4-ACRS-7B-17 **Revised August 2005. Written policy, procedure, and practice provide that all new offender care workers receive 120 hours of training during their first year of employment. At a minimum, this training covers the following areas:**

- **security and safety procedures**
- **emergency and fire procedures**
- **supervision of offenders**
- **suicide intervention/prevention**
- **use of force**
- **offender rights**
- **key control**
- **interpersonal relations**
- **communication skills**
- **standards of conduct**
- **cultural awareness**
- **sexual abuse/assault intervention**
- **code of ethics**

Additional topics may be added at the discretion of the agency or facility.

COMMENT: Since the duties of offender care workers frequently involve most institutional operations, their training should be comprehensive.

PROTOCOLS: Written policy/procedure. Training curriculum. Orientation training form.

PROCESS INDICATORS: Training records. Personnel records.

4-ACRS-7B-17-1 **Added August 2005. Written policy, procedure, and practice provide that all offender care workers receive at least 40 hours of annual training. This training shall include at a minimum the following areas:**

- **standards of conduct/ethics**
- **security/safety/fire/medical/emergency procedures**
- **supervision of offenders including training on sexual abuse and assault**
- **use of force**

Additional topics shall be included based upon a needs assessment of both staff and institution requirements.

COMMENT: This training will enable employees to sharpen skills, maintain certification, and keep abreast of changes in policies, procedures, and legislative, judicial, or executive actions.

PROTOCOLS: Written policy/procedure. Training curriculum. Orientation training form.

PROCESS INDICATORS: Training records. Personnel records.

4-ACRS-7D-01-1 **Added August 2010. The facility/agency shall demonstrate it has examined, and where appropriate and feasible, implemented strategies that promote recycling, energy and water conservation, pollution reduction, and utilization of renewable energy alternatives.**

COMMENT: Correctional facilities and programs have the responsibility to implement strategies that allow correctional facilities to be managed in ways that are most cost-effective and deliver superior performance, while improving environmental responsibility and sustainability. This includes recycling (including paper, metal, and plastic products), energy conservation (including building insulation, heating and ventilation, temperature controls, vehicle fuel efficiency, water economies, physical plant engineering, and energy measures), pollution reduction (including composting, sewer treatment, litter abatement, and carbon emissions), and utilization of renewable energy alternatives (bio-fuels, solar collection, turbine energy production, and methane collection).

PROTOCOLS: Written policy/procedure. Budget and planning documents.

PROCESS INDICATORS: Annual report. Board meeting minutes.

4-ACRS-7D-08

Revised January 2011. Procedures govern case record management, including, at a minimum, the following areas: the establishment, maintenance, use, and content of case records; right to privacy; secure placement and preservation of records; and schedule for retiring or destroying inactive records.

- **All entries in the case record are signed and dated.**
- **Appropriate safeguards exist to minimize the possibility of theft, loss, or destruction of records.**
- **Records are safeguarded from unauthorized and improper disclosure.**
- **When any part of the information system is computerized, security ensures confidentiality.**
- **The facility uses a "release of information consent form" that complies with applicable federal and state regulations and a copy of the form is maintained in the offender's case record.**
- **Employees, consultants, and contract personnel are informed in writing about the facility's policies on confidentiality of information and agree in writing to abide by them.**
- **The policies and procedures are reviewed annually.**

COMMENT: An orderly and timely system for recording, maintaining, and using data about offenders increases the efficiency and effectiveness of program and service delivery, and the transfer of information to the courts and release authorities. The policy should cover offenders' access to their files. An offender's constitutional right to privacy can be violated if records are improperly disseminated. The facility should establish procedures to limit access to records to persons and public agencies that have both a "need to know" and a "right to know" and can demonstrate that access to such information is necessary for criminal justice purposes. Written guidelines should regulate offender access to records. The written policies should specify what types of information are confidential between worker and offender, what types may be shared with other facility personnel, and what types can be communicated to persons outside the facility.

PROTOCOLS: Written policy/procedure. Case record management process. Confidentiality notice.

PROCESS INDICATORS: Case management records. Documentation of annual review. Documentation of staff agreement.

4-ACRS-7D-12

Revised January 2011. In facilities that engage in, or allow the conduct of research, the facility complies with state and federal guidelines for the use and dissemination of research findings, with accepted professional and scientific ethics, and issues of legal consent and release of information. Additionally, the facility also complies with the following:

- **The facility administrator reviews and approves all research projects prior to implementation.**
- **All research results are reviewed by the facility/agency administrator prior to publication or dissemination.**
- **Procedures govern the voluntary participation of offenders in non-medical, non-pharmaceutical, and non-cosmetic research programs.**

COMMENT: Researchers working in the facility should be informed of all policies relating to their research, especially those regarding confidentiality of information. Research should not be permitted to proceed until the research design and the requirements of the facility staff are understood and fully agreed upon.

PROTOCOLS: Written policy/procedure. Consent of Release of Information form. Copies of guidelines.

PROCESS INDICATORS: Offender records. Research reports. Completed offender consent forms.

4-ACRS-7D-24

Revised August 2001. There is an independent financial audit of the facility. This audit is conducted annually or as stipulated by statute or regulation, but at least every three years. If the facility is a part of a state system, an internal audits section or department of the agency's central administration and/or statutory agency shall be considered independent of the facility to be audited.

COMMENT: None.

PROTOCOLS: Written policy and procedure. Process for securing independent audit.

PROCESS INDICATORS: Audit reports.

4-ACRS-7D-33

Revised August 2007. Procedures specify to the offender how the amount of offender fees will be determined, and when and how they will be collected and recorded. If the program is provided by a contractor, the contractor will provide the contracting agency, at least monthly, with an accounting of fees received, including the amount paid and the payer.

COMMENT: None.

PROTOCOLS: Written policy/procedure.

PROCESS INDICATORS: Financial records. Offender records.

4-ACRS-7E-11

Revised August 2010. The institution maintains a current, accurate, confidential personnel record on each employee except where state statutes require open public records and the personnel record cannot be maintained confidentially. Information obtained as part of a required medical examination (and/or inquiry) regarding the medical condition or history of applicants and employees is collected and maintained on separate forms and in separate medical files and treated as a confidential medical record.

COMMENT: The personnel record should contain the following: initial application; reference letters; results of employment investigation; verification of training and experience; wage and salary information; job performance evaluations; incident reports, if any; and commendations and disciplinary actions, if any.

PROTOCOLS: Written policy/procedure.

PROCESS INDICATORS: Training records. Personnel records. Staff interviews.

Appendix C Revised January 2001. Refer to *Standards Supplement* Appendix D.

Adult Correctional Boot Camp Programs (ABC), 1st Edition

1-ABC-1A-07

Revised August 2003. To be considered qualified, a warden/superintendent at a minimum must possess the following: a bachelor's degree in an appropriate discipline, five years of related administrative experience, and demonstrated administrative ability and leadership. The degree requirement may be satisfied by completion of a career development program that includes work-related experience, training, or college credits at a level of achievement equivalent to the bachelor's degree.

COMMENT: Establishing high qualifications ensures that only qualified individuals are recruited and employed. It is the agency's responsibility to see that potential administrators receive the required education.

1-ABC-1A-16

Revised January 2003. Written policy, procedure, and practice provide for a system to monitor operations and programs through inspections and reviews. This monitoring is conducted by the administrator or designated staff at least annually, and by a qualified professional not affiliated with the facility or system at least once every three years.

COMMENT: Operations and programs should be implemented as outlined in policies and procedures. An audit system providing timely and periodic assessment of the various agency operations will reveal the degree of compliance. The internal administrative audit should exist apart from any external or continuing audit conducted by other agencies.

1-ABC-1A-18

Deleted August 2008.

1-ABC-1A-19

Deleted August 2008.

1-ABC-1A-20

Revised August 2008. Written policy, procedure, and practice establish the facility's commitment to informing the public and the media of events within the facility's areas of responsibility. The procedures address emergency and nonemergency responses to the media and, at a minimum, include the following:

- **identification of data and information protected by federal and state privacy laws or federal and state freedom of information laws**
- **facility tours**
- **special events coverage**
- **news release policy**
- **designation of individuals or positions within the facility authorized to speak with the media on behalf of the facility**
- **provide representatives of the media with access to the facility consistent with offenders' rights to confidentiality and privacy and the maintenance of order and security**

COMMENT: The complexity of the policy statement should be consistent with the size and complexity of the operation.

1-ABC-1B-11

Revised January 2001. Written policy, procedure, and practice provide for an independent financial audit of the facility. This audit is conducted annually or as stipulated by statute or regulation, but at least every three years. If the facility is a part of a state system, an internal audits section or department of the agency's central administration and/or statutory agency shall be considered independent of the facility to be audited.

COMMENT: None.

1-ABC-1C-04-1

Added August 1995. Written policy, procedure, and practice provide a mechanism to process requests for reasonable accommodation to the known physical and/or mental impairments of a qualified individual with a disability, either an applicant or an employee. The accommodation need not be granted if it would impose an undue hardship or direct threat.

COMMENT: *Reasonable accommodation* refers to modifications or adjustments, which enable qualified applicants with disabilities to access the job application process or which enable qualified employees with disabilities to perform the essential functions of the job and to enjoy the same terms, conditions, and privileges of employment that are available to persons without disabilities. *Terms, conditions, and privileges of employment* include, but are not limited to:

- recruitment, selection, and hiring
- salary and compensation
- benefits, holidays, leave, and work hours
- promotion and advancement
- staff development, including in-service training
- retirement, resignation, and termination

An *undue hardship* means significant difficulty or expense. *Direct threat* means a significant risk of substantial harm to the health or safety of any person, including the applicant or employee with a disability that cannot be eliminated or reduced by reasonable accommodation. A *qualified individual with a disability* means an individual with a disability who satisfies the requisite skill, experience, education, and other job-related requirements for the employment position such individual holds or desires, and who, with or without reasonable accommodation, can perform the essential functions of such position.

1-ABC-1C-06

Added January 2012. There is a written agency policy, procedure, and practice that specifies support for a drug-free workplace for all employees. This policy includes at a minimum the following:

- **prohibition of the use of illegal drugs**
- **prohibition of possession of any illegal drug except in the performance of official duties**
- **the opportunities available for treatment and/or counseling for drug abuse**
- **the procedures to be used to ensure compliance**
- **the penalties for violation of the policy**

COMMENT: None.

1-ABC-1C-12

Revised August 2007. Written policy, procedure, and practice provide that criminal record checks are conducted on all new employees and volunteers in accordance with state and federal statutes. This record will include comprehensive identifier information to be collected and run against law enforcement indices. If suspect information on matters with potential terrorism connections is returned on a desirable applicant, it is forwarded to the local Joint Terrorism Task Force (JTTF) or another similar agency.

COMMENT: The facility administrator should know of any criminal conviction that could directly affect an employee's job performance.

1-ABC-1C-13

Revised August 2008. Written policy, procedure, and practice provide that employees who have direct contact with inmates receive a physical examination prior to job assignment. All other employees receive a medical screening prior to the job assignment. Employees receive re-examinations according to a defined need or schedule.

COMMENT: Staff whose responsibilities include regular direct contact with offenders must have physical examinations to protect their health and ensure that they can carry out their assignments effectively. The basic health status of all employees should be evaluated against the specific requirements of their assignments. Physical examination and screening procedures may be established by the appropriate medical authority, if there are such applicable laws and regulations.

1-ABC-1C-15

Revised August 2010. The institution maintains a current, accurate, confidential personnel record on each employee except where state statutes require open public records and the personnel record cannot be maintained confidentially. Information obtained as part of a required medical examination (and/or inquiry) regarding the medical condition or history of applicants and employees is collected and maintained on separate forms and in separate medical files and treated as a confidential medical record.

COMMENT: The personnel record should contain the following: initial application; reference letters; results of employment investigation; verification of training and experience; wage and salary information; job performance evaluations; incident reports, if any; and commendations and disciplinary actions, if any.

1-ABC-1D-05

Revised August 2005. Written policy, procedure, and practice provide that all training programs are presented by persons who are qualified in the areas in which they conduct training. The training plan is reviewed annually.

COMMENT: None.

1-ABC-1D-09 **Revised August 2000. Written policy, procedure, and practice provide that all administrative and managerial staff receive 40 hours of training in addition to orientation training during their first year of employment and 40 hours of training each year thereafter, in areas relevant to their position.**

COMMENT: Ongoing training in topics relevant to an employee's position enhances skill and job performance.

Summary of Orientation and Minimum Training Hours

The following description of general job categories should be used in determining minimum training requirements as outlined in the standards. Contract or part-time employees should receive training similar to full-time employees in their particular category and pertinent to their role in working with adults. This chart replaces the chart on page 25 in *Standards for Adult Correctional Boot Camp Programs* published in January 1995.

CATEGORY	TYPICAL POSITION TITLES	BASIC ORIEN-TATION	TRAINING HOURS—FIRST YEAR ON THE JOB	TRAINING HOURS—EACH YEAR THERE-AFTER
CLERICAL/ SUPPORT (Minimum Contact)	Secretaries, clerks, typists, computer/ warehouse personnel, accountants, personnel staff	Yes	16	16
SUPPORT (Regular or Daily Contact)	Food service, industry work supervisors, maintenance work supervisors	Yes	40	40
PROFESSIONAL SPECIALIST	Case managers, counselors, social workers, teachers, psychologists, librarians, medical personnel, chaplains, recreation specialists	Yes	40	40
ALL OFFENDER SUPERVISION STAFF	All staff assigned to full-time supervision duties	Yes	120	40
ADMINIS-TRATIVE MANAGEMENT PERSONNEL	Superintendents, deputy or assistant superintendents, business managers, personnel directors, care supervisors, shift supervisors	Yes	40	40

Training: An organized, planned, and evaluated activity designed to achieve specific learning objectives. Training may occur on-site, at an academy or training center, at an institution of higher learning, through contract service, at professional meetings, or through closely supervised on-the-job training. Meetings of professional associations are considered training when there is clear evidence of specific learning objectives relative to the employee's career track. *See* Appendix F, "Revised Definitions of Learning and Training."

1-ABC-1D-10 **Revised August 2005. Written policy, procedure, and practice provide that all new correctional officers receive 120 hours of training during their first year of employment. At a minimum, this training covers the following areas:**

- **security and safety procedures**
- **emergency and fire procedures**
- **supervision of offenders**
- **suicide intervention/prevention**
- **use of force**
- **offender rights**
- **key control**
- **interpersonal relations**
- **communication skills**
- **standards of conduct**
- **cultural awareness**
- **sexual abuse/assault intervention**
- **code of ethics**

Additional topics may be added at the discretion of the agency or facility.

COMMENT: Since the duties of correctional officers frequently involve most boot camp operations, their training should be comprehensive.

1-ABC-1D-10-1 **Added August 2005. Written policy, procedure, and practice provide that all correctional officers receive at least 40 hours of annual training. This training shall include at a minimum the following areas:**

- **standards of conduct/ethics**
- **security/safety/fire/medical/emergency procedures**
- **supervision of offenders including training on sexual abuse and assault**
- **use of force**

Additional topics shall be included based upon a needs assessment of both staff and institution requirements.

COMMENT: This training will enable employees to sharpen skills, maintain certification, and keep abreast of changes in policies, procedures, and legislative, judicial, or executive actions.

1-ABC-1D-11 **Revised August 2007. Written policy, procedure and practice provide that correctional officers assigned to an emergency unit have at least one year of corrections and 40 hours of specialized training before undertaking their assignments. Other staff must have at least one year of experience in their specialty within a correctional setting. The specialized training may be part of their first-year training program. Officers and staff assigned to emergency units receive 40 hours of training annually, at least 16 hours of which is specifically related to the emergency unit assignment.**

COMMENT: None.

1-ABC-1D-12 **Revised August 2008. Written policy, procedure, and practice provide that all support employees who have regular or daily contact with offenders receive 40 hours of training in addition to orientation training during their first year of employment and 40 hours of training each year thereafter.**

COMMENT: Food service employees, industrial supervisors, and other support personnel whose work requires day-to-day contact with offenders should receive basic training in offender supervision and security, as well as specialized training in their field as it relates to the facility setting. These individuals should be familiar with policies and procedures of the facility, plus the basic rules of offender supervision and security. Ongoing training during subsequent years of employment enables employees to sharpen their skills and keep abreast of changes in operational procedures.

1-ABC-1E-01 **Revised January 2012. Procedures govern case record management, including, at a minimum, the following areas: the establishment, maintenance, use, and content of case records; right to privacy; secure placement and preservation of records; and schedule for retiring or destroying inactive records.**

- **All entries in the case record are signed and dated.**
- **Appropriate safeguards exist to minimize the possibility of theft, loss, or destruction of records.**
- **Records are safeguarded from unauthorized and improper disclosure.**
- **When any part of the information system is computerized, security ensures confidentiality.**
- **The facility uses a "release of information consent form" that complies with applicable federal and state regulations and a copy of the form is maintained in the offender's case record.**
- **Employees, consultants, and contract personnel are informed in writing about the facility's policies on confidentiality of information and agree in writing to abide by them.**

COMMENT: None.

1-ABC-1G-02 **Deleted August 2008.**

1-ABC-1G-03

Revised August 2008. Written policy and procedure specify who is responsible for operating a citizen involvement and volunteer service program, and his or her lines of authority, responsibility, and accountability.

COMMENT: Written policy should provide direction for the program, listing goals and objectives, types of services offered, population served, and so forth. Clear lines of accountability and authority should be established and communicated to staff and volunteers. Any volunteer activity that is shown to threaten order and security or the safety of a volunteer should be limited or discontinued until the problem is resolved.

1-ABC-2B-02

Deleted July 2012.

1-ABC-2C-01

Revised August 2002. Each sleeping area has, at a minimum, the following facilities and conditions:

- **25 square feet of unencumbered space per occupant**
- **access to toilets and a washbasin with hot and cold running water 24 hours a day**
- **a bed or bunk bed**
- **a mattress**
- **a pillow**
- **a writing surface**
- **a chair or stool**
- **hooks, closet space, or locker**
- **natural light**
- **temperatures that are appropriate to the summer and winter comfort zones**

COMMENT: The bed should be elevated from the floor and have a clean, covered mattress with blankets provided, as needed. Unencumbered space is usable space that is not encumbered by furnishings or fixtures. At least one dimension of the unencumbered space is not less than seven feet. In determining unencumbered space in the area, the total square footage is obtained and the square footage of fixtures and equipment is subtracted. All fixtures and equipment must be in an operational position. The facility must provide the following, at a minimum: one bed per offender or bunk beds for two offenders, plumbing fixtures (if inside the room), writing surface, locker, and chair or stool.

1-ABC-2C-03

Revised August 1998. Dayrooms provide sufficient seating and writing surfaces. Dayroom furnishings are consistent with the custody level of the offenders assigned.

COMMENT: The standard provides managers and designers with flexibility in designing and furnishing dayrooms and takes into consideration the range of activities that may occur (for example, dayroom activities usually include television viewing, reading, recreation, conversation, games, and sometimes include eating and work). In lower security settings, the use of normalized furnishings should be considered.

1-ABC-2C-06 **Revised August 1995. Inmates have access to operable showers with temperature-controlled hot and cold running water, at a minimum ratio of one shower for every eight inmates, unless national or state building or health codes specify a different ratio. Water for showers is thermostatically controlled to temperatures ranging from 100 degrees Fahrenheit to 120 degrees Fahrenheit to ensure the safety of inmates and to promote hygienic practice.**

COMMENT: Offenders can use scalding showers as a weapon against or punishment for other inmates. Also, accidental injury could occur when cold water is drawn in other areas, thereby unexpectedly elevating the hot water in showers to scalding temperatures. Water temperatures below 100 degrees Fahrenheit are uncomfortable and may deter an individual from pursuing good hygienic practices. The temperature controls should not preclude the use of water at higher temperatures, if needed, in other areas of the institution, such as kitchens.

1-ABC-2C-08 **Revised August 1995. Residents with disabilities are housed in a manner that provides for their safety and security. Housing used by residents with disabilities is designed for their use and provides for integration with other residents. Programs and services are accessible to residents with disabilities who reside in the facility.**

COMMENT: If the facility accepts individuals with a disability, it must provide for their housing and use of facility resources. Housing includes, but is not limited to, sleeping quarters/areas, furnishings, dayrooms, toilets, washbasins, showers/bathing facilities, and other common elements. Program and service areas include, but are not limited to, exercise and recreation areas, visiting rooms, laundry facilities, private counseling space, group meeting rooms, dining rooms, telephone facilities, admission and intake areas, and administrative areas, where appropriate.

1-ABC-2C-08-1 **Added January 2002. Written policy, procedure, and practice provide for the assignment of appropriately trained individuals to assist disabled offenders who cannot otherwise perform basic life functions.**

COMMENT: None.

1-ABC-2C-08-2 **Added August 2002. Written policy, procedure, and practice provide education, equipment, and facilities, and the support necessary for inmates with disabilities to perform self-care and personal hygiene in a reasonably private environment.**

COMMENT: A *reasonably private environment* will vary, depending on individual and institutional circumstances, but it is one which will maintain the dignity of the disabled individual in light of that person's disability.

1-ABC-2D-01 **Revised January 2008. Written policy, procedure, and practice provide that all sleeping quarters in the facility are well-lit and properly ventilated. Documentation shall be provided by a qualified source that lighting is at least 20 foot-candles at desk level and in personal grooming areas and air circulation is at least 15 cubic feet of outside or recirculated filtered air per minute per person. Air and light levels are checked at least once per accreditation cycle.**

COMMENT: The facility should maintain strict adherence to local health codes requiring proper lighting and ventilation.

1-ABC-2D-02 **Revised January 2012. Noise levels in inmate housing units do not exceed 70 dBA (A Scale). Measurements shall be conducted annually by a qualified source with at least one measurement taking place during night time and one measurement taking place during day time.**

COMMENT: None.

1-ABC-2D-02-1 **Deleted January 2013.**

1-ABC-2D-04 **Added August 2010. The facility/agency shall demonstrate it has examined, and where appropriate and feasible, implemented strategies that promote recycling, energy and water conservation, pollution reduction, and utilization of renewable energy alternatives.**

COMMENT: Correctional facilities and programs have the responsibility to implement strategies that allow correctional facilities to be managed in ways that are most cost-effective and deliver superior performance, while improving environmental responsibility and sustainability. This includes recycling (including paper, metal, and plastic products), energy conservation (including building insulation, heating and ventilation, temperature controls, vehicle fuel efficiency, water economies, physical plant engineering, and energy measures), pollution reduction (including composting sewer treatment, litter abatement, and carbon emissions), and utilization of renewable energy alternatives (bio-fuels, solar collection, turbine energy production, and methane collection).

1-ABC-2E-03 **Revised August 1995. Both outdoor and covered/enclosed exercise areas for general population inmates are provided in sufficient number to ensure that each inmate is offered at least one hour of access daily. Use of outdoor areas is preferred, but covered/enclosed areas must be available for use in inclement weather. Covered/enclosed areas can be designed for multiple uses as long as the design and furnishings do not interfere with scheduled exercise activities.**

The minimum space requirements for exercise areas are as follows:

- **Outdoor exercise areas in facilities where 100 or more inmates utilize one recreation area—15 square feet per inmate for the maximum number of inmates expected to use the space at one time, but not less than 1,500 square feet of unencumbered space.**
- **Outdoor exercise areas in facilities where less than 100 inmates have unlimited access to an individual recreation area—15 square feet per inmate for the maximum number of inmates expected to use the space at one time, but not less than 750 square feet of unencumbered space.**
- **Covered/enclosed exercise areas in facilities, where 100 or more inmates utilize one recreation area, should have 15 square feet per inmate for the maximum number of inmates expected to use the space at one time, with a minimum ceiling height of 18 feet, but not less than 1,000 square feet of unencumbered space.**
- **Covered/enclosed exercise areas in facilities where less than 100 inmates utilize one recreation area should have 15 square feet per inmate for the maximum number of inmates expected to use the space at one time, with a minimum ceiling height of 18 feet, but not less than 500 square feet of unencumbered space.**

COMMENT: Exercise/recreation spaces are not the same as dayrooms, although dayrooms can provide added opportunities for some exercise and recreation activities. The standard establishes performance requirements for exercise spaces, offering design and operational flexibility. It allows facilities in some climates to cover and/or enclose a yard, while others will have to provide indoor space; these spaces do not have to be indoors, but must be fully functional when the outdoor areas are not feasible for use.

1-ABC-2E-06 **Revised January 1999. Dining space should be large enough to allow for meals to be served, affording each offender the opportunity to have at least 20 minutes of dining time for each meal.**

COMMENT: None.

1-ABC-2G-01 **Deleted January 2007.**

1-ABC-3A-02 **Revised January 2007. Space is provided for a 24-hour control center for monitoring and coordinating the facility's security, safety, and communications systems. The control center provides access to a washbasin and toilet. There is a communication system between the control center and the offender living areas.**

COMMENT: A mechanical or audio communication system should be used to supplement direct staff supervision activities (for example, to advise staff of emergency needs), not as a substitute for staff supervision.

1-ABC-3A-12 **Revised August 2007. Written policy, procedure, and practice require that the chief security officer or qualified designee conduct at least weekly inspections of all security devices noting the items needing repair or maintenance. The inspections are reported in writing to the warden/superintendent and/or chief security officer.**

COMMENT: There should be a scheduled maintenance procedure to ensure that all locks, windows, doors, and other security devices are fully operational. Emergency keys should be checked at least quarterly to ensure that they are in working order. The results of all inspections should be submitted in writing to the facility administrator and/or the officer in charge of security.

1-ABC-3A-16-1 **Added August 2008. Written policy, procedure and practice, in general, prohibit the use of restraints on female offenders during active labor and the delivery of a child. Any deviation from the prohibition requires approval by and guidance on methodology from the medical authority and is based on documented serious security risks. The medical authority provides guidance on the use of restraints on pregnant offenders prior to active labor and delivery.**

COMMENT: Restraints on pregnant offenders during active labor and the delivery of a child should only be used in extreme instances and should not be applied for more time than is absolutely necessary. Restraints used on pregnant offenders prior to active labor and delivery should not put the pregnant offender nor the fetus at risk.

1-ABC-3A-20 **Revised August 2008 (Mandatory). Written policy, procedure, and practice govern the control, inventory, and use of tools, culinary and medical/dental instruments and supplies (syringes, needles and other sharps).**

COMMENT: None.

1-ABC-3A-21 **Deleted August 2008.**

1-ABC-3A-25 **Revised January 2008. Written policy, procedure, and practice govern the inventory, issuance, and accountability of routine and emergency distributions of security equipment.**

COMMENT: Written policy should delineate the process by which security equipment is distributed from the primary issue point to control points for both routine and emergency issuance. The policy should address how the facility tracks the issuance of security equipment (written log, chit system, and so forth) and the accountability of security equipment at end of the shift.

1-ABC-3A-30 **Revised January 200 (Mandatory). Written policy, procedure, and practice provide for the safe unloading and reloading of firearms.**

COMMENT: None.

1-ABC-3A-32 **Added January 1995.**

Preservation of Physical Evidence

Written policy, procedure, and practice, provide for the preservation, control, and disposition of all physical evidence obtained in connection with a violation of law and/or institutional regulation. At a minimum, the procedures shall address the following:

- **chain of custody**
- **evidence handling**
- **location and storage requirements**

COMMENT: Strict accountability of physical evidence collected in connection with a crime must be established to preserve the integrity of the disciplinary and/or legal process. Minor rule violations should be exempt from the procedural requirements of evidence control, preservation, and disposition.

1-ABC-3B-10 **Revised January 1998. Emergency equipment and systems are tested at least quarterly. Power generators are inspected weekly and load tested quarterly at a minimum or in accordance with manufacturer's recommendations and instruction manuals.**

COMMENT: Emergency equipment, such as standby lighting, batteries, power generators, firefighting apparatus, communications systems, and alarms should be checked frequently to ensure their reliability.

1-ABC-3B-12 **Revised January 2012 (Mandatory). All institution personnel are trained in the implementation of written emergency plans.**

COMMENT: Since the staff must be able to properly execute the plans, a review of the emergency plans should be an essential element of personnel orientation and in-service training. Dissemination of these plans to local authorities, such as law enforcement, state police, civil defense, and so forth, will keep them informed of their roles in the event of an emergency.

1-ABC-3B-14 **Revised January 2012. There is a written plan that provides for continuing operations in the event of a work stoppage or other job action. Copies of this plan are available only to appropriate supervisory or other personnel directly involved in the implementation of the plan.**

COMMENT: None.

1-ABC-3B-15 **Added January 2003. Written policy, procedure, and practice define critical incidents for the facility and provide for a debriefing to be conducted after each such incident. The debriefing process includes coordination and feedback about the incident with designated staff of the facility as soon as possible after the incident. A debriefing includes, but is not limited to:**

- **a review of staff and offender actions during the incident**
- **a review of the incident's impact on staff and offenders**
- **a review of corrective actions taken and still needed**
- **plans for improvement to avoid another incident**

COMMENT: A *critical incident* is any event or situation that threatens staff or offenders in their community (criminal justice setting). While debriefings should occur as soon as possible, some information may not be available until later. All staff impacted by a critical incident should be included in the debriefings and referred to appropriate services to mitigate the stress associated with these events. All critical incidents should be reviewed by the administration, security, and health services. A two-week follow-up debriefing should occur to review the validity and appropriateness of all policies, plans, and information used during the critical incident and immediately after.

1-ABC-3C-06 **Revised January 2008. Written policy, procedure, and practice provide that an offender charged with a major rule violation receives a written statement of the alleged violation(s), including a description of the incident and specific rules violated. The offender is given that statement at the same time the disciplinary report is filed with the disciplinary committee, but no less than 24 hours prior to the disciplinary hearing. The hearing may be held within 24 hours with the offender's written consent.**

COMMENT: None.

1-ABC-3D-04 **Revised August 1995. Written policy, procedure, and practice prohibit discrimination based on an inmate's race, religion, national origin, sex, disability, or political views in making administrative decisions and in providing access to programs.**

COMMENT: Inmates should be assured equal opportunities to participate in all institutional programs.

1-ABC-3D-06-1 **Added August 2002. Written policy, procedure, and practice ensure that information is provided to offenders about sexual abuse/assault including:**

- **prevention/intervention**
- **self-protection**
- **reporting sexual abuse/assault**
- **treatment and counseling**

The information is communicated orally and in writing, in a language clearly understood by the offender, upon arrival at the facility.

COMMENT: None.

1-ABC-3D-06-2 **Added January 2003. Inmates are screened within 24 hours of arrival at the facility for potential vulnerabilities or tendencies of acting out with sexually aggressive behavior. Housing assignments are made accordingly.**

COMMENT: None.

1-ABC-3D-06-3 **Added January 2003. Written policy, procedure, and practice require that an investigation is conducted and documented whenever a sexual assault or threat is reported.**

COMMENT: The agency should report occurrences/allegations of sexual assault or threat in accordance with the laws of the jurisdiction. The investigation may be limited by what is allowed by the laws of the jurisdiction.

1-ABC-3D-06-4 **Added January 2003. Written policy, procedure, and practice require that inmates identified as high risk with a history of sexually assaultive behavior are assessed by a mental health or other qualified professional. Inmates with a history of sexually assaultive behavior are identified, monitored, and counseled.**

COMMENT: None.

1-ABC-3D-06-5 **Added January 2003. Written policy, procedure, and practice provide that inmates identified as at risk for sexual victimization are assessed by a mental health or other qualified professional. Inmates at risk for sexual victimization are identified, monitored, and counseled.**

COMMENT: None.

1-ABC-3D-06-6 **Added January 2003. Written policy, procedure, and practice ensure that sexual conduct between staff and inmates, volunteers, or contract personnel and inmates, regardless of consensual status, is prohibited and subject to administrative and criminal disciplinary sanctions.**

COMMENT: None.

1-ABC-3D-06-7 **Added January 2003. Victims of sexual assault are referred under appropriate security provisions to a community facility for treatment and gathering of evidence. If these procedures are performed in-house, the following guidelines are used:**

- **A history is taken by a health care professional who conducts an examination to document the extent of physical injury and to determine if referral to another medical facility is indicated. With the victim's consent, the examination includes collection of evidence from the victim, using a kit approved by the appropriate authority.**
- **Provision is made for testing for sexually transmitted diseases (for example, HIV, gonorrhea, hepatitis, and other diseases) and counseling, as appropriate.**
- **Prophylactic treatment and follow-up for sexually transmitted diseases are offered to all victims, as appropriate.**
- **Following the physical examination, there is availability of an evaluation by a mental health professional to assess the need for crisis intervention counseling, and long-term follow-up.**
- **A report is made to the facility or program administrator or designee to assure separation of the victim from his or her assailant.**

COMMENT: None.

1-ABC-3D-06-8 **Added January 2003. Written policy, procedure, and practice provide that inmates who are victims of sexual abuse have the option to report the incident to a designated staff member other than an immediate point-of-contact line officer.**

COMMENT: None.

1-ABC-3D-06-9 **Added January 2003. Written policy, procedure, and practice provide that all case records associated with claims of sexual abuse, including incident reports, investigative reports, offender information, case disposition, medical and counseling evaluation findings, and recommendations for post-release treatment and/or counseling are retained in accordance with an established schedule.**

COMMENT: None.

1-ABC-4C-06 **Revised August 2004. Therapeutic diets are provided as prescribed by appropriate clinicians. A therapeutic diet manual is available in health services and food services for reference and information. Prescriptions for therapeutic diets should be specific and complete, furnished in writing to the food service manager, and rewritten annually, or more often as clinically indicated.**

COMMENT: Therapeutic diets are prepared and served to offenders according to the orders of the treating clinician or as directed by the responsible health authority. Therapeutic diets should be kept as simple as possible and should conform as closely as possible to the foods served to other offenders.

1-ABC-4C-09-1

Added August 2011. All staff, contractors, and inmate workers who work in the food service department are trained in the use of food service equipment and in the safety procedures to be followed in the food service department.

COMMENT: None.

1-ABC-4D-08

Revised August 2003. Written policy, procedure, and practice provide for the issue of suitable clothing to all inmates. Clothing is properly fitted, climatically suitable, durable, and presentable.

COMMENT: A standard wardrobe should be provided at the time of admission and should include, as appropriate, shirts, blouses, dresses, trousers, skirts, belts, undergarments, slips, socks, shoes, coats, jackets, and headwear. In addition to the standard issue of inmate clothing, civilian attire should be available in limited quantities for leisure, visiting, work release, and furloughs. Clothing provided should not be degrading or humiliating. Since the definition of these may be culturally determined, consideration should be given to the effect of clothing provided.

1-ABC-4D-12

Revised August 2007. Written policy, procedure, and practice provide for the issue of suitable, clean bedding and linen, including two sheets, pillow and pillowcase, one mattress, not to exclude a mattress with integrated pillow, and sufficient blankets to provide comfort under existing temperature controls. There is provision for linen exchange, including towels, at least weekly. Blanket exchange must be available at least quarterly.

COMMENT: None.

1-ABC-4D-14

Revised January 1998. Written policy, procedure, and practice require that articles necessary for maintaining proper personal hygiene are provided to all offenders.

COMMENT: As part of the admissions process, each offender should be given soap, a toothbrush, toothpaste or powder, a comb, and toilet paper. Shaving equipment should be made available upon request, and the special hygiene needs of females should be met. Proper personal hygiene improves offenders' health and medical conditions.

1-ABC-4E-04

Revised August 2003. Each policy, procedure, and program in the health care delivery system is reviewed at least annually by the appropriate health care authority and revised, if necessary.

COMMENT: None.

1-ABC-4E-15

Revised August 2008. Unless prohibited by state law, offenders (under staff supervision) may perform familial duties commensurate with their level of training. These duties may include the following:

- **peer support and education**
- **hospice activities**
- **assisting impaired offenders on a one-on-one basis with activities of daily living**
- **serving as a suicide companion or buddy, if qualified and trained through a formal program that is part of a suicide prevention plan**

Offenders are not to be used for the following duties:

- **performing direct patient care services**
- **scheduling health care appointments**
- **determining access of other offenders to health care services**
- **handling or having access to surgical instruments, syringes, needles, medications, or health records**
- **operating diagnostic or therapeutic equipment, except under direct supervision (by specially trained staff) in a vocational training program**

Correction August 1999. This standard is listed incorrectly as a mandatory standard in the *Standards for Adult Correctional Boot Camp* Programs, first edition. The standard is non-mandatory.

COMMENT: Offenders cannot operate medical equipment but should be able to perform maintenance and housekeeping services under close supervision of qualified staff. In addition, offenders participating in a certified vocational training program may perform direct services, such as dental chair side assistance. This also does not preclude familial-type duties including, but not limited to, assistance in feeding, lifting, assisting with ambulation, and helping to meet social/companionship needs (particularly in hospice situations). In summary, offenders should not be placed in a position of responsibility for the provision of medical care, but may function, with appropriate training and supervision, much like family members in the community would function in the home.

1-ABC-4E-23 **Revised January 2001. Written policy, procedure, and practice require that a comprehensive health appraisal for each inmate, excluding intrasystem transfers, is completed, as defined below after arrival at the facility. If there is documented evidence of a health appraisal within the previous 90 days, a new health appraisal is not required, except as determined by the designated health authority. Health appraisal includes the following:**

Within 14 days after arrival at the facility for all inmates as defined above:

- **review of the earlier receiving screening**
- **collection of additional data to complete the medical, dental, mental health, and immunization histories**
- **laboratory and/or diagnostic tests to detect communicable disease, including venereal disease and tuberculosis**
- **record of height, weight, pulse, blood pressure, and temperature**
- **other tests and examinations, as appropriate**

Within 14 days after arrival for inmates with identified significant health care problems:

- **medical examination, including review of mental and dental status (for those inmates with significant health problems discovered on earlier screening such as cardiac problems, diabetes, communicable diseases, and so forth)**
- **review of the results of the medical examination, tests, and identification of problems by a physician or other qualified health care personnel, if such is authorized in the medical practice act**
- **initiation of therapy, when appropriate**
- **development and implementation of treatment plan, including recommendations concerning housing, job assignment, and program participation**

Within 30 days after arrival at facility for inmates without significant health care problems:

- **medical examination, including a review of mental and dental status (for those inmates without significant health concerns identified during earlier screening; no identified acute or chronic disease, no identified communicable diseases, and so forth)**
- **review of the results of the medical examination, tests, and identification of problems by a physician or other qualified health care professional, if such is authorized in the medical practice act**
- **initiation of therapy, when appropriate**
- **development and implementation of treatment plan, including recommendations concerning housing, job assignment, and program participation**

COMMENT: When appropriate, additional investigation should be conducted into alcohol and drug abuse and other related problems. A routine appraisal by mental health staff should be completed within 30 days of admission of all new inmates. Test results, particularly for communicable diseases, should be received and evaluated before an inmate is assigned to housing in the general population. Information regarding the inmate's physical and mental status also may dictate housing and activity assignments. When appropriate, additional investigation should be conducted into alcohol and drug abuse and other related problems. A routine appraisal by mental health staff should be completed within 30 days of admission.

1-ABC- 4E-24

Revised August 2001. Written policy, procedure, and practice for the collection and recording of health appraisal data require the following:

- **The process is completed in a uniform manner as determined by the health authority**
- **Health history and vital signs are collected by health-trained or qualified health personnel**
- **Collection of all other health appraisal data is performed only by qualified health personnel**
- **Review of the results of the medical examination, tests, and identification of problems is performed by a physician or other health care personnel, if such is authorized in the medical practice act**

COMMENT: None.

1-ABC- 4E-25

Revised January 2001. Written policy and procedure require that dental care is provided to each inmate under the direction and supervision of a dentist, licensed in the state, as follows:

- **dental screening within 14 days of admission unless completed within the last six months, conducted on initial intake with instruction on dental hygiene**
- **dental examination by a dentist within 12 months, supported by x-rays, if necessary**
- **treatment, of dental pain; sedative fillings, extractions of nonrestorable teeth, gross debridement of symptomatic areas, and repair of partials and dentures for those inmates with less than 12-months' detention**
- **treatment plan with x-rays for those inmates who request care with more than 12-months' detention**

COMMENT: As part of the initial health screening, a dentist or health care personnel properly trained and designated by the dentist should perform a dental screening. The dental program also should provide inmates with instruction on the proper brushing of the teeth and other dental hygiene measures.

The dental examination should include taking or reviewing the patient's dental history and examination of hard and soft tissue of the oral cavity by means of an illuminator light, mouth mirror, and explorer. x-rays for diagnostic purposes should be available, if deemed necessary. The result of the dental examination and dental treatment plan are recorded on an appropriate uniform dental record using a numbered system such as the Federation Dental International System.

1-ABC- 4E-30

Revised August 2002. First aid kits are available in designated areas of the facility based on need and an automatic external defibrillator is available for use at the facility.

COMMENT: The availability and placement of first aid kits are determined by the designated health authority in conjunction with the facility administrator. The health authority approves the contents, number, location, and procedures for monthly inspection of the kits(s) and develops written procedures for the use of the kits by non-medical staff.

1-ABC- 4E-40-1

Added August 2008. Written policy, procedure and practice, in general, prohibit the use of restraints on female offenders during active labor and the delivery of a child. Any deviation from the prohibition requires approval by and guidance on methodology from the medical authority and is based on documented serious security risks. The medical authority provides guidance on the use of restraints on pregnant offenders prior to active labor and delivery.

COMMENT: Restraints on pregnant offenders during active labor and the delivery of a child should only be used in extreme instances and should not be applied for more time than is absolutely necessary. Restraints used on pregnant offenders prior to active labor and delivery should not put the pregnant offender nor the fetus at risk.

1-ABC- 4E-47

Revised January 1996. Written policy, procedure, and practice provide for the clinical management of chemically dependent inmates and include the following:

- **a standardized diagnostic needs assessment administered to determine the extent of use, abuse, dependency, and/or codependency**
- **a medical examination to determine medical needs and/or observational requirements**
- **an individualized treatment plan developed and implemented by a multidisciplinary team**
- **aftercare discharge plans shall include the inmate**

COMMENT: Primary goals with chemical dependency programs are assessment of needs and the development of a treatment plan. A key component to support the educational program, recovery process, and ongoing stability of the inmate includes relapse prevention. Relapse prevention is necessary to support long-term recovery and identify high-risk areas needing management. Referral resources for ongoing services should be updated and used in discharge planning for the inmate, as available.

1-ABC-4F-06 **Revised January 1996. The institution has a formal mechanism to determine appropriate levels of social services staffing. The mechanism used to determine such staffing levels includes at a minimum:**

- **type of inmate population served**
- **type of institution**
- **legal requirements**
- **goals to be accomplished**

The institution's use of a "team approach" and use of paraprofessionals, volunteers, and students also may influence the numbers of professional staff required.

COMMENT: Social services programs can assist offenders with family and personal problems through supportive guidance and professional assistance. A counseling program that is coordinated with the overall facility rehabilitation program can be effective in resolving personal and interpersonal problems.

1-ABC-4F-08 **Revised January 2001. Written policy, procedure, and practice provide for substance abuse programs, to include monitoring and drug testing, for inmates with drug and alcohol addiction problems.**

COMMENT: None.

1-ABC-4F-09 **Interpretation August 2003. The words "Where a drug program exists" are interpreted as a therapeutic community.**

1-ABC-4F-10 **Interpretation August 2003. The words "Where a drug program exists" are interpreted as a therapeutic community.**

1-ABC-4F-11 **Interpretation August 2003. The words "Where a drug program exists" are interpreted as a therapeutic community.**

1-ABC-4F-12 **Interpretation August 2003. The words "Where a drug program exists" are interpreted as a therapeutic community.**

1-ABC-4G-03 **Deleted August 2002.**

1-ABC-5A-01-1 **Revised August 2002. Written policy, procedure, and practice prohibit discrimination on the basis of disability in the provision of services, programs, and activities administered for program beneficiaries and participants.**

COMMENT: Services, programs, and activities include, but are not limited to, the following:

- academic and vocational education (including developmental and rehabilitative programs)
- work programs/work release programs (by providing reasonable accommodations or alternatives for offenders with disabilities so that the benefits of these programs, including sentence-reduction credits, are available to offenders with disabilities)
- recreation, exercise, and activities
- mail, telephone, visiting
- library
- religious programs
- reception and orientation
- transportation services (to provide for safety and security, and to avoid undue discomfort, in light of the offender's disabilities)
- classification
- food service
- sanitation and hygiene
- health care
- social services
- release
- discipline, grievance procedures, and due process proceedings
- safety and emergency procedures
- access to media, courts, counsel, and law library
- commissary/canteen
- volunteer programs
- psychological and psychiatric services

Program beneficiaries and participants include, but are not limited to: inmates, family members, clergy, attorneys, volunteers, and other authorized visitors.

The institution may be required to take remedial action, when necessary, to afford program beneficiaries and participants with disabilities an opportunity to participate in, and enjoy the benefit of services, programs, or activities. Remedial action may include, but is not limited to: 1) making reasonable modifications to policies, practices, or procedures, 2) providing auxiliary aids and services to the hearing and visually impaired, 3) constructing new or altering existing facilities, and 4) delivering of services and so on at alternate accessible sites.

1-ABC-5A-01-2 **Added August 2002. Written policy, procedure, and practice provide for staff and offender access to an appropriately trained and qualified individual who is educated in the problems and challenges faced by offenders with physical and/or mental impairments, programs designed to educate and assist disabled offenders, and all legal requirements for the protection of offenders with disabilities.**

COMMENT: An *appropriately trained and qualified individual*, as used in this standard, is one who has been designated by the warden, superintendent, or other authority, to coordinate efforts to comply with and carry out responsibilities defined by the Americans with Disabilities Act. That individual should develop relationships with, and use the expertise of institutional staff, advocacy groups, nonprofit organizations, agencies of government, and others that have relevant knowledge and experience.

1-ABC-5A-02 **Revised August 2008. Written policy, procedure, and practice require that all eligible offenders work unless assigned to an approved education or training program.**

COMMENT: All eligible inmates are expected to participate in work assignments, adult basic education programs, and programs ordered by the sentencing court or paroling authority or required by statute. Failure to participate in programs may result in administrative action.

1-ABC-5B-03 **Revised January 2012. Vocational training and/or vocational counseling programs are integrated with academic programs and are relevant to the vocational needs of the offender population and to employment opportunities in the community.**

COMMENT: Relevant vocational programs can occur through work assignments, apprenticeships, and on-the-job training. Employment opportunities can be assessed through contact with local businesses, industries, and trade groups.

1-ABC-5B-05 **Revised January 1994. [The standard was revised in January 1994, but was inadvertently omitted in *Adult Correctional Boot Camp Programs*, published in January 1995.] The institution uses business, industry, and community resources in developing academic and/or vocational education programs for selected inmates.**

COMMENT: None.

1-ABC-5C-03 **Deleted August 2003.**

1-ABC-5C-05 **Deleted August 2003.**

1-ABC-5D-06

Revised August 2002. Written policy, procedure, and practice specify that inmates are permitted to send sealed letters to a specified class of persons and organizations, including but not limited to the following: courts, counsel, officials of the confining authority, state and local chief executive officers, administrators of grievance systems, and members of the paroling authority. Staff, in the presence of the inmate, may be allowed to inspect outgoing privileged mail for contraband before it is sealed. Mail to inmates from this specified class of persons and organizations may be opened only to inspect for contraband and only in the presence of the inmate, unless waived in writing, or in circumstances, which may indicate contamination.

COMMENT: Suspicious mail may include packages and letters unusual in appearance or that appear different from mail normally received or sent by the individual; packages and letters of a size or shape not customarily received or sent by the individual; packages and letters with a city and/or state postmark that is different from the return address; or packages and letters leaking, stained, or emitting a strange or unusual odor, or that have a powdery residue.

1-ABC-5D-09

Revised August 2006. Written policy, procedure, and practice require that, excluding weekends and holidays, or emergency situations, incoming and outgoing letters are held for no more than 48 hours and packages (if allowed) are held no more than 72 hours.

Interpretation August 2002. The term *emergency situation* is interpreted as any significant disruption of normal facility or agency procedure, policy, or activity caused by riot, escape, fire, natural disaster, employee action, or other serious incident.

COMMENT: Inspection for contraband letters should take no longer than 48 hours to complete so that incoming letters should be distributed to inmates and outgoing letters sent to the post office within 48 hours of receipt. Similarly, inspection of packages normally should take no longer than 72 hours to complete. The standard does not prohibit the holding of mail for inmates who are temporarily absent from the facility (for example, in a hospital or court).

1-ABC-5D-11

Revised August 2002. Written policy, procedure, and practice provide for inmate access to public telephones. Inmates with hearing and/or speech disabilities, and inmates who wish to communicate with parties who have such disabilities, shall be afforded access to a Telecommunications Device for the Deaf (TDD), or comparable equipment. Public telephones with volume control also shall be made available to inmates with hearing impairments.

COMMENT: Offenders should have reasonable and equitable access to telephone facilities and be permitted a reasonable amount of privacy. Procedures should specify the hours during which the telephone is available, the maximum length of calls, and any limitation on calls. All long-distance calls should be made collect.

1-ABC-5D-11-1 **Added August 2002. Written policy, procedure, and practice ensure that offenders have access to reasonably priced telephone services. Correctional agencies ensure that:**

- **contracts involving telephone services for offenders comply with all applicable state and federal regulations**
- **contracts are based on rates and surcharges that are commensurate with those charged to the general public for like services. Any deviation from ordinary consumer rates reflects actual costs associated with the provision of services in a correctional setting**
- **contracts for offender telephone services provide the broadest range of calling options determined by the agency administrator to be consistent with the requirements of sound correctional management**

COMMENT: When procuring and renewing telephone services, correctional officials should inquire into the reasons for proposed deviations from standard charges and seek the best possible rates for the broadest possible range of calling options.

1-ABC-5D-14-1 **Added August 2003. Written policy, procedure, and practice require that an inmate is informed in a timely manner of the verifiable death or critical illness of an immediate family member. In case of the critical illness of an immediate family member, the inmate is allowed, whenever statutes and circumstances allow, to go to the bedside under escort or alone.**

COMMENT: Classification, status, geography, security level, and other specified criteria should determine eligibility. *Immediate family* is usually defined as parent, spouse, child, sibling, grandparent, or legal guardian.

1-ABC-5D-16 **Revised August 2007. Facility staff provide information to visitors regarding transportation to the facility and facilitate transportation between the facility and nearby public transit facilities.**

COMMENT: Facilities situated considerable distances from public transit terminals should try to provide transportation to visitors, particularly when transportation costs are significant.

1-ABC-5E-03 **Revised January 2003. Written policy, procedure, and practice provide that there is available to the facility a person with a master of library science, information resources, media services, or related degree who assists in coordinating and supervising library services and is responsible for training of all library staff.**

COMMENT: A qualified librarian should be available to assist the staff member who coordinates and supervises library services in the facility.

1-ABC-5F-03 **Revised August 2004. Written policy, procedure, and practice provide that assigned chaplain(s) (whether they be classified employees, contract employees, or volunteers), in consultation with and approval from facility administration, plans, directs, and supervises all aspects of the religious program, including approval and training of both lay and clergy volunteers from faiths represented in the inmate population.**

COMMENT: The religious program should be designed to fulfill the facility's responsibility of ensuring that all offenders voluntarily can exercise their constitutional right to religious freedom.

1-ABC-5F-05 **Revised August 2004. Written policy, procedure, and practice provide that the chaplain or designated staff develops and maintains close relationships with community religious resources.**

COMMENT: Community resources can help augment the delivery of appropriate religious services on special holidays or as needed to meet the requirements of the diversity of religious faith among offenders.

1-ABC-5F-07 **Deleted August 2004.**

1-ABC-5F-10 **Revised January 2012. The chaplain, in cooperation with the institutional administrator or designee, approves donations of equipment or materials for use in religious programs.**

COMMENT: Approval of donations helps ensure that equipment and materials are available for approved religious practices and helps avoid the accumulation of duplicate or inappropriate materials.

Appendix C Revised January 2001. Refer to *Standards Supplement* Appendix D.

Adult Correctional Institutions (ACI), 4th Edition

4-4003-1

Added August 2010. The facility/agency shall demonstrate it has examined, and where appropriate and feasible, implemented strategies that promote recycling, energy and water conservation, pollution reduction, and utilization of renewable energy alternatives.

COMMENT: Correctional facilities and programs have the responsibility to implement strategies that allow correctional facilities to be managed in ways that are most cost-effective and deliver superior performance, while improving environmental responsibility and sustainability. This includes recycling (including paper, metal, and plastic products), energy conservation (including building insulation, heating and ventilation, temperature controls, vehicle fuel efficiency, water economies, physical plant engineering, and energy measures), pollution reduction (including composting sewer treatment, litter abatement, and carbon emissions), and utilization of renewable energy alternatives (bio-fuels, solar collection, turbine energy production, and methane collection).

4-4006

Revised August 2008. Written policy, procedure, and practice provide that each institution is headed by a warden/superintendent, appointed by the administrator or governing board of the parent agency, who is in charge of all inmates, personnel, volunteers, programs, and activities connected with the institution.

COMMENT: The warden/superintendent's chain of command should extend directly to all staff. Similarly, all employees and units within the institution should ultimately be responsible to this individual.

4-4007

Deleted August 2008.

4-4009

Revised August 2003. To be considered qualified, a warden/superintendent at a minimum must possess the following: a bachelor's degree in an appropriate discipline, five years of related administrative experience, and demonstrated administrative ability and leadership. The degree requirement may be satisfied by completion of a career development program that includes work-related experience, training, or college credits at a level of achievement equivalent to the bachelor's degree.

COMMENT: Establishing high qualifications ensures that only qualified individuals are recruited and hired. It is the agency's responsibility to see that potential administrators receive the required education.

4-4011

Revised August 2009. The role and functions of employees of other public or private agencies providing a service to the institution are covered by written policy and procedure that specify their relation to the authority and the responsibility of the warden/superintendent.

COMMENT: The duties and responsibilities of personnel employed by other public or private agencies should be specific in a contract or other type of agreement.

4-4017 **Revised January 2003. Written policy, procedure, and practice provide for a system to monitor operations and programs through inspections and reviews. This monitoring is conducted by the warden/superintendent or designated staff at least annually and by qualified professionals not affiliated with the facility or system at least every three years.**

COMMENT: Timely and periodic assessment can reveal how well an institution's operation and programs are complying with policy and procedure. This internal administrative audit should be separate from any external or continuous inspection conducted by other agencies.

4-4020 **Deleted January 2010.**

4-4021 **Revised August 2008. Written policy, procedure, and practice establish the facility's commitment to informing the public and the media of events within the facility's areas of responsibility. The procedures address emergency and nonemergency responses to the media and, at a minimum, include the following:**

- **the identification of areas in the facility that are accessible to media representatives, consistent with preserving the inmate's right to privacy and maintaining order and security**
- **the contact person for routine requests for information**
- **identification of data and information protected by federal or state privacy laws, or federal and state freedom of information laws**
- **special events coverage**
- **news release policy**
- **the designation of individuals or positions within the facility authorized to speak with the media on behalf of the facility**

COMMENT: The complexity of the policy statement should be consistent with the size and complexity of the operation.

4-4022 **Deleted August 2008.**

4-4031 **Revised August 2009. Written policy, procedure, and practice demonstrate that the procedures for the collecting, safeguarding, and disbursing of monies comply with the accounting procedures established by the governing jurisdiction.**

COMMENT: The institution's fiscal policies and procedures should be patterned after those of the governing authority and should be compatible with the state's central accounting system. These include policies and procedures for fiscal recordkeeping, reports, reviews, audits, disbursements, position allocations, payroll, cash transactions, commissary/canteen operations, and inmate's personal funds, if any.

4-4057 **Revised January 2013. Written policy, procedure, and practice provide that all personnel are selected, retained, and promoted on the basis of merit and specified qualifications. New employees receive credit for their prior training.**

COMMENT: None.

4-4061 **Revised August 2007. A criminal record check is conducted on all new employees, contractors, and volunteers prior to assuming their duties to identify whether there are criminal convictions that have a specific relationship to job performance. This record will include comprehensive identifier information to be collected and run against law enforcement indices. If suspect information on matters with potential terrorism connections is returned on a desirable applicant, it is forwarded to the local Joint Terrorism Task Force (JTTF) or another similar agency.**

COMMENT: The institutions administrators should know of any criminal conviction that could directly affect an employee's job performance in an institutional setting. Comprehensive identifiers may include current name, birth name, date of birth, social security number, address, phone number, copy of driver's license, copy of passport (if any), and similar information. Such information is run against NCIC criminal histories, criminal indices, and wants and warrants.

4-4063 **Revised August 2009. There is a written policy and procedure that specifies support for a drug-free workplace for all employees. This policy includes at a minimum the following:**

- **prohibition of the use of illegal drugs**
- **prohibition of possession of any illegal drug except in the performance of official duties**
- **the procedures to be used to ensure compliance**
- **the opportunities available for treatment and/or counseling for drug abuse**
- **the penalties for violation of the policy**

COMMENT: None.

4-4067 **Revised August 2010. The institution maintains a current, accurate, confidential personnel record on each employee except where state statutes require open public records and the personnel record cannot be maintained confidentially. Information obtained as part of a required medical examination (and/or inquiry) regarding the medical condition or history of applicants and employees is collected and maintained on separate forms and in separate medical files and treated as confidential medical records.**

COMMENT: The personnel record should contain the following: initial application; reference letters; results of employment investigation; verification of training and experience; wage and salary information; job performance evaluations; incident reports, if any; and commendations and disciplinary actions, if any.

4-4069 **Revised January 2003. A written code of ethics shall require employees to conduct themselves and perform their duties in such a way as to set a good example for prisoners and thereby command their respect. The code of ethics shall prohibit employees from using their official position to secure privileges for themselves or others and from engaging in activities that constitute a conflict of interest. This code is available to all employees.**

COMMENT: To protect the integrity of the institution, its staff, and the parent agency, all personnel must be thoroughly familiar with the code of ethics, and the code must be strictly enforced.

4-4084 **Revised August 2005. Written policy, procedure, and practice provide that all new correctional officers receive 120 hours of training during their first year of employment. At a minimum, this training covers the following areas:**

- **security and safety procedures**
- **emergency and fire procedures**
- **supervision of offenders**
- **suicide intervention/prevention**
- **use of force**
- **offender rights**
- **key control**
- **interpersonal relations**
- **communication skills**
- **standards of conduct**
- **cultural awareness**
- **sexual abuse/assault intervention**
- **code of ethics**

Additional topics may be added at the discretion of the agency or facility.

COMMENT: Since the duties of correctional officers frequently involve most institutional operations, their training should be comprehensive.

4-4084-1 **Added August 2005. Written policy, procedure, and practice provide that all correctional officers receive at least 40 hours of annual training. This training shall include at a minimum the following areas:**

- **standards of conduct/ethics**
- **security/safety/fire/medical/emergency procedures**
- **supervision of offenders including training on sexual abuse and assault**
- **use of force**

Additional topics shall be included based upon a needs assessment of both staff and institution requirements.

COMMENT: This training will enable employees to sharpen skills, maintain certification, and keep abreast of changes in policies, procedures, and legislative, judicial, or executive actions.

4-4089 **Revised August 2007. Written policy, procedure and practice provide that correctional officers assigned to an emergency unit have at least one year of corrections and 40 hours of specialized training before undertaking their assignments. Other staff must have at least one year of experience in their specialty within a correctional setting. The specialized training may be part of their first year training program. Officers and staff assigned to emergency units receive 40 hours of training annually, at least 16 of which are specifically related to the emergency unit assignment.**

COMMENT: None.

4-4095 **Revised August 2009. Written policy and procedure govern case record management, including at a minimum the following areas: the establishment, use, and content of inmate records; right to privacy; secure placement and preservation of records; and schedule for retiring or destroying inactive records.**

COMMENT: An orderly and timely system for recording, maintaining, and using data about offenders increases the efficiency and effectiveness of the program and service delivery and the transfer of information to the courts and release authorities.

4-4105 **Revised August 2010. The institution's criteria for evaluating overall institutional performance are specific and defined in writing.**

COMMENT: Collecting, trending, and analyzing of data should be conducted on an ongoing basis to determine the internal order of the facility. Data collected should include, but not be limited to the following: escape rate; frequency and number of assaults of staff; group disturbances by inmates; assaults and homicides by inmates; weapons and/or illegal drugs found; major and minor disciplinary actions; and staff and inmate grievances. Management data on offenders permits categorization by age, sex, race, offense, and prior record.

4-4107 **Revised August 2010. Institutional programs are analyzed and evaluated at least every two years to determine their contribution to the institution's mission.**

COMMENT: Periodic program analyses and evaluations help the institution to identify which programs are productive and determine needed changes and/or the need for reordering priorities.

4-4112 **Revised January 2013. Written policy, procedure, and practice provide that the agency administrator or designee reviews and approves all research proposals and/or designs prior to their implementation.**

COMMENT: None.

4-4114 **Deleted August 2007.**

4-4115 **Revised August 2007. Written policy and procedure specify who is responsible for operating a citizen involvement and volunteer service program, and his or her lines of authority, responsibility, and accountability.**

COMMENT: Written policy should provide direction for the program, listing the goals and objectives, types of services offered, population served, and so forth. Clear lines of accountability and authority should be established and communicated to staff and volunteers. Any volunteer activity that is shown to threaten the institution's order and security or the safety of a volunteer should be limited or discontinued until the problem is resolved.

4-4123 **Revised July 2012. (Renovation, New Construction Only after January 1, 1990). The institution conforms to applicable federal, state, and/or local building codes.**

COMMENT: None.

4-4125 **Revised July 2012. (Renovation, New Construction Only after January 1, 1990). The physical plant design facilitates personal contact and interaction between staff and inmates.**

COMMENT: None.

4-4126 **Revised August 2003. The facility should encourage staff/inmate interaction. The facility has a management system that provides staff with the authority to make decisions, and the ability to make recommendations regarding security, classification, services, and programs for inmates.**

COMMENT: None.

4-4127 **Revised August 2003. The maximum size of a single management unit is variable and is based on the characteristics of its inmate population. The exact size of each management unit is determined by (1) the security classification of the inmate occupants (higher security levels require smaller unit size), and (2) the ability of staff to complete regular security checks, maintain visual and auditory contact, maintain personal contact and interaction with inmates, and be aware of unit conditions.**

COMMENT: The scale of the management unit should facilitate and encourage the involvement of all staff in decision making.

4-4128 **Revised July 2012 (New Construction Only after January 1, 1990). Single-cell living units shall not exceed 80 inmates.**

COMMENT: None.

4-4129 **Deleted July 2012.**

4-4130 **Deleted August 2004.**

4-4131 **Deleted August 2005.**

4-4132 **Revised January 2012. Cells/rooms used for housing inmates shall provide at a minimum, 25 square feet of unencumbered space per occupant. *Unencumbered space* is usable space that is not encumbered by furnishing or fixtures. At least one dimension of the unencumbered space is no less than seven feet. In determining unencumbered space in the cell or room, the total square footage is obtained and the square footage of fixtures and equipment is subtracted. All fixtures and equipment must be in operational position.**

COMMENT: None.

4-4133 **Revised January 2012. Written policy, procedure, and practice provide that single-occupancy cells/rooms shall be available, when indicated, for the following:**

- **inmates with severe medical disabilities**
- **inmates suffering from serious mental illness**
- **sexual predators**
- **inmates likely to be exploited or victimized by others**
- **inmates who have other special needs for single housing**

When confinement exceeds 10-hours a day, there is at least 80-square feet of total floor space, of which 35-square feet is unencumbered space.

COMMENT: The standard permits housing inmates of all security levels in multiple cells/rooms unless there is a need for single cells/rooms for an inmate in one of the groups listed. The caveat "when indicated" refers to determinations made by the classification system, medical diagnosis, or other professional conclusions.

4-4135 **Revised January 2012. Dayrooms with space for varied inmate activities are situated immediately adjacent to the inmate sleeping areas. Dayrooms provide sufficient seating and writing surfaces and all furnishings are consistent with the custody level of the inmates assigned. Dayrooms provide a minimum of 35-square feet of space per inmate (exclusive of lavatories, showers, and toilets) for the maximum number of inmates who use the dayroom at one time, and no dayroom encompasses less than 100 square feet of space (exclusive of lavatories, showers, and toilets).**

COMMENT: None.

4-4136 **Deleted January 2012.**

4-4137-1 **Added January 2012 (New Construction after June 2014). Inmates have access to toilets and hand-washing facilities 24-hours per day and are able to use toilet facilities without staff assistance when they are confined in their cells/sleeping areas. Toilets are provided at a minimum ratio of 1 for every 12 inmates in male facilities and 1 for every 8 inmates in female facilities. Urinals may be substituted for up to one-half of the toilets in male facilities. All housing units with 3 or more inmates have a minimum of 2 toilets. These ratios apply unless any applicable building or health codes require additional fixtures.**

COMMENT: None.

4-4138-1 **Added January 2012 (New Construction after June 2014). Inmates have access to operable washbasins with hot and cold running water in the housing units at a minimum ratio of 1 basin for every 12 occupants. These ratios apply unless any applicable building or health codes require additional fixtures.**

COMMENT: None.

4-4139-1 **Addition January 2012 (New Construction after June 2014). Inmates have access to operable showers with temperature-controlled hot and cold running water, at a minimum ratio of one shower for every twelve inmates, unless applicable codes require additional fixtures. Water for showers is thermostatically controlled to temperatures ranging from 100 degrees Fahrenheit to 120 degrees Fahrenheit to ensure the safety of inmates and promote hygienic practices.**

COMMENT: None.

4-4141 **Interpretation August 2004. The Standards Committee determined that segregation housing does not have to be single celled.**

4-4146 **Revised January 2008. Lighting in inmate rooms/cells is at least 20-foot-candles at desk level and in personal grooming areas, as documented by a qualified source, and is checked at least once per accreditation cycle.**

COMMENT: None.

4-4147 **Revised August 2006. (Existing only). All inmate rooms/cells provide access to natural light.**

COMMENT: None.

4-4147-1 **Revised July 2012. (Renovation, New Construction after June 1, 2008). All inmate rooms/cells provide inmates with access to natural light by means of at least three-square feet of transparent glazing, plus two additional square feet of transparent glazing per inmate in rooms/cells with three or more inmates.**

COMMENT: None.

4-4147-2 **Added January 2012. (New Construction or Renovation after June 1, 2014). Each dormitory provides inmates with access to natural light by means of at least 12 square feet, plus two additional square feet of transparent glazing per inmate in the dormitory.**

COMMENT: None.

4-4148 **Deleted January 2003.**

4-4149 **Revised July 2012. (New Construction Only after January 1, 1990). Each dayroom provides inmates with access to natural light by means of at least 12 square feet of transparent glazing in the dayroom, plus two additional square feet of transparent glazing per inmate whose room/cell is dependent on access to natural light through the dayroom.**

COMMENT: Many inmates spend most daylight hours outside of their cells, often in their dayroom, and the standard gives designers increased options for providing natural light.

4-4150 **Revised January 2012. Noise levels in inmate housing units do not exceed 70 dBA (A Scale). Measurements shall be conducted annually by a qualified source with at least one measurement taking place during night time and one measurement taking place during day time.**

COMMENT: None.

4-4150-1 **Deleted January 2013.**

4-4151 **Revised July 2012 (Renovation, New Construction Only after January 1, 1990). Circulation is at least 15 cubic feet of outside or recirculated filtered air per minute per occupant for cells/rooms, officer stations, and dining areas, as documented by a qualified technician and should be checked not less than once per accreditation cycle**

Interpretation August 2002. The words "accreditation cycle" are interpreted as within the past three years.

COMMENT: Mechanical ventilation may provide for recirculation of outside air except where prohibited by codes. The outside air requirements may be reduced to a minimum of 33 percent of the specified ventilated air quality if adequate temperature control is provided in addition to filtering equipment so that the maximum concentration of particles entering the space is reduced to acceptable limits. In no case should the outdoor air quantity be less than five cubic feet per minute per person.

4-4152 **Revised August 2007. (Existing). Circulation is at least 10-cubic feet of fresh or recirculated filtered air per minute per occupant for inmate rooms/cells, officer stations, and dining areas, as documented by a qualified technician and should be checked not less than once per accreditation cycle.**

Interpretation August 2002. The words "accreditation cycle" are interpreted as within the past three years.

COMMENT: None.

4-4153 **Revised August 2006. Temperatures in indoor living and work areas are appropriate to the summer and winter comfort zones.**

COMMENT: Temperature should be capable of being mechanically raised or lowered to an acceptable comfort level.

4-4155 **Revised August 2013. Segregation units have either outdoor uncovered or outdoor covered exercise areas. The minimum space requirements for outdoor exercise areas for segregation units are as follows:**

- **Group yard modules: 330-square feet of unencumbered space can accommodate two inmates. For each additional 150-square feet of unencumbered space, an additional inmate may use the exercise area simultaneously. (Formula: for each 150-square feet of unencumbered space exceeding the base requirement of 180-square feet for the first inmate, equals the maximum number of inmates who may use the recreation area space simultaneously). No more than five inmates are to use a group module at one time.**
- **Individual yard modules: 180-square feet of unencumbered space.**

In cases where cover is not provided to mitigate the inclement weather, appropriate weather-related equipment and attire should be available to the inmates who desire to take advantage of their authorized exercise time.

COMMENT: None.

4-4157 **Revised July 2012. (Renovation, New Construction Only after January 1, 1990). In institutions offering academic and vocational training programs, classrooms are designed in consultation with school authorities.**

COMMENT: None.

4-4158 **Revised January 2012. There is space for group dining except when security or safety considerations justify otherwise, and the space is large enough to allow for meals to be served, affording each inmate the opportunity to have at least 20 minutes of dining time for each meal.**

COMMENT: None.

4-4159 **Revised January 2012. There are sanitary, temperature-controlled facilities for the storage of all foods. The food preparation area includes a space for food preparation based on population size, type of food preparation, and methods of meal service.**

COMMENT: None.

4-4160 **Deleted January 2012.**

4-4170 **Deleted January 2007.**

4-4174 **Revised August 2009. There is a manual containing all procedures for institutional security and control, with detailed instructions for implementing these procedures. The manual is available to all staff.**

COMMENT: The manual should contain information on physical plant inspection, inmate counts, weapons and chemical agent control, contraband, key control, tool and equipment control, and emergency procedures.

4-4175 **Revised January 2007. Space is provided for a 24-hour continuously staffed secure control center for monitoring and coordinating the institution's security, life, safety, and communications systems. Staff assigned to a control center have access to a toilet and washbasin. There is a communication system between the control center and inmate living areas.**

COMMENT: None.

4-4176 **Deleted January 2007.**

4-4186 **Revised August 2007. Written policy, procedure, and practice require that the chief security officer or qualified designee conduct at least weekly inspections of all security devices, noting the items needing repair or maintenance. The inspections are reported in writing to the warden/superintendent and/or chief security officer.**

COMMENT: There should be a scheduled maintenance procedure to ensure that all bars, locks, windows, doors, and other security devices are fully operational. Emergency keys should be checked at least quarterly to ensure they are in working order. The results of all inspections should be submitted in writing to the warden/superintendent and/or the officer in charge of security.

4-4190-1 **Added August 2008. Written policy, procedure, and practice, in general, prohibit the use of restraints on female offenders during active labor and the delivery of a child. Any deviation from the prohibition requires approval by and guidance on methodology from the medical authority and is based on documented serious security risks. The medical authority provides guidance on the use of restraints on pregnant offenders prior to active labor and delivery.**

COMMENT: Restraints on pregnant offenders during active labor and the delivery of a child should only be used in extreme instances and should not be applied for more time than is absolutely necessary. Restraints used on pregnant offenders prior to active labor and delivery should not put the pregnant offender nor the fetus at risk.

4-4191 **Revised January 2011 (Mandatory). Four/five point restraints are used only in extreme instances and only when other types of restraints have proven ineffective or the safety of the inmate is in jeopardy. Advance approval is secured from the facility administrator/designee before an inmate is placed in a four/five point restraint. Subsequently, the health authority or designee must be notified to assess the inmate's medical and mental health condition, and to advise whether, on the basis of serious danger to self or others, the inmate should be in a medical/mental health unit for emergency involuntary treatment with sedation and/or other medical management, as appropriate. If the inmate is not transferred to medical/mental health unit and is restrained in a four/five point position, the following minimum procedures are followed:**

- **direct visual observation by staff is continuous prior to obtaining approval from the health authority or designee**
- **subsequent visual observation is made at least every 15 minutes**
- **restraint procedures are in accordance with guidelines approved by the designated health authority**
- **all decisions and actions are documented**

COMMENT: A four/five point restraint secures an inmate's arms and legs (four point) and head (five point). Restraint guidelines include consideration of an individual's physical conditions, such as body weight.

4-4192 **Revised August 2009. Written policy, procedure, and practice provide for searches of facilities and inmates to control contraband and provide for its disposition. These policies are made available to staff and inmates.**

COMMENT: The institution's search plans and procedures should include the following:

- unannounced and irregularly timed searches of cells, inmates, and inmate work areas
- inspection of all vehicular traffic and supplies coming into the institution
- use of metal detectors at compound gates and entrances into housing units
- complete search and inspection of each cell prior to occupancy by a new inmate
- avoidance of unnecessary force, embarrassment, or indignity to the inmate
- staff training in effective search techniques that protect both inmates and staff from bodily harm
- use of non-intensive sensors and other techniques instead of body searches, whenever feasible
- conduct of searches only as necessary to control contraband or to recover missing or stolen property
- respect of inmates' rights to authorized personal property
- use of only those mechanical devices absolutely necessary for security purposes

4-4196 **Revised January 2006 (Mandatory). Written policy, procedure, and practice govern the control, inventory, and use of tools, culinary and medical/dental instruments and supplies (syringes, needles and other sharps).**

COMMENT: None.

4-4200 **Revised January 2008. Written policy, procedure, and practice govern the inventory, issuance, and accountability of routine and emergency distributions of security equipment.**

COMMENT: Written policy should delineate the process by which security equipment is distributed from the primary issue point to control points for both routine and emergency issuance. The policy should address how the facility tracks the issuance of security equipment (written log, chit system, and so forth) and the accountability of security equipment at the end of the shift.

4-4212 **Revised August 2009 (Mandatory). Written policy, procedure, and practice provide for a comprehensive and thorough monthly inspection of the institution by a qualified fire and safety officer for compliance with safety and fire prevention standards. There is a weekly fire and safety inspection of the institution by a qualified departmental staff member.**

COMMENT: The qualified departmental staff member who conducts the weekly inspections may be an institutional staff member who has received training in and is familiar with the safety and sanitation requirements of the jurisdiction. At a minimum, it is expected that the safety/sanitation specialist will provide on-the-job training regarding applicable regulations and inspections, including the use of checklists and the methods of documentation.

4-4220 **Revised January 2012. All institution personnel are trained in the implementation of written emergency plans.**

COMMENT: Review of all emergency plans should be an essential element of personnel training and retraining programs. New employees should be familiar with all emergency plans prior to their permanent work assignments.

4-4223 **Revised January 2012. There is a written plan that provides for continuing operations in the event of a work stoppage or other job action. Copies of this plan are available only to appropriate supervisory or other personnel directly involved in the implementation of the plan.**

COMMENT: None.

4-4224 **Correction August 2010 (Mandatory). There are written plans that specify the procedures to be followed in situations that threaten institutional security. Such situations include but are not limited to riots, hunger strikes, disturbances, and taking of hostages. These plans are made available to all applicable personnel and are reviewed annually and updated, as needed.**

COMMENT: The plans should designate the personnel who are to implement the procedures, when and which authorities and media should be notified, how the problem should be contained, and the procedures to be followed after the incident is quelled. The plans presuppose regular inspection and maintenance of any specialized equipment necessary to implement the procedures. All personnel should be familiar with the plans. Hospital and medical personnel should be involved in the formulation of the plans, since they are responsible for the safety of their patients.

4-4225 **Revised August 2009. There are written procedures regarding escapes.**

COMMENT: Specific procedures that can be used quickly when an escape occurs should be made available to all personnel. Procedures should include the following: prompt reporting of the escape to the warden/superintendent; mobilizing of employees; implementing of a predetermined search plan; notifying law enforcement agencies, community groups, and relevant media; preparing escape circulars for distribution and mailing; and, after apprehension of the escapee, promptly notifying all who were previously alerted to the escape.

4-4225-1 **Added January 2003. Written policy, procedure, and practice define critical incidents for the facility and provide for a debriefing to be conducted after each such incident. The debriefing process includes coordination and feedback about the incident with designated staff of the facility as soon as possible after the incident. A debriefing includes, but is not limited to:**

- **a review of staff and offender actions during the incident**
- **a review of the incident's impact on staff and offenders**
- **a review of corrective actions taken and still needed**
- **plans for improvement to avoid another incident**

COMMENT: A critical incident is any event or situation that threatens staff or offenders in their community (criminal justice setting). While debriefings should occur as soon as possible, some information may not be available until later. All staff impacted by a critical incident should be included in the debriefings and referred to appropriate services to mitigate the stress associated with these events. All critical incidents should be reviewed by the administration, security, and health services. A two-week follow-up debriefing should occur to review the validity and appropriateness of all policies, plans, and information used during the critical incident and immediately after.

4-4226 **Revised August 2009. Written rules of inmate conduct specify acts prohibited within the institution and penalties that can be imposed for various degrees of violation.**

COMMENT: The rules should prohibit only observed behavior that can be shown clearly to have a direct, adverse effect on an inmate or on institutional order and security. The rules also should specify the range of penalties that can be imposed for violations. Penalties should be proportionate to the importance of the rule and the severity of the violation.

4-4227 **Revised August 2009. There is a written set of disciplinary procedures governing inmate rule violations.**

COMMENT: None.

4-4238 **Revised January 2008. Written policy, procedure, and practice provide that inmates charged with rule violations are scheduled for a hearing as soon as practicable but no later than seven days, excluding weekends and holidays, after being charged with a violation. Inmates are notified of the time and place of the hearing at least 24 hours in advance of the hearing.**

COMMENT: To ensure fairness and the integrity of the disciplinary process, inmates charged with rule violations should receive hearings as soon as possible unless the hearing is prevented by exceptional circumstances, unavoidable delays, or reasonable postponements. Reasons for all delays should be documented.

4-4255 **Revised August 2008. There is a sanctioning schedule for institutional rule violations. Continuous confinement for more than 30 days requires the review and approval of the warden/superintendent or designee. Inmates held in disciplinary detention for periods exceeding 60 days are provided the same program services and privileges as inmates in administrative segregation and protective custody.**

COMMENT: The time an inmate spends in disciplinary detention should be proportional to the offense committed, taking into consideration the inmate's prior conduct, specific program needs, and other relevant factors.

4-4257 **Revised August 2011. Written policy, procedure, and practice require that all special management inmates are personally observed by a correctional officer twice per hour, but no more than 40 minutes apart, on an irregular schedule. Inmates who are violent or mentally disordered or who demonstrate unusual or bizarre behavior receive more frequent observation; suicidal inmates are under continuing or continuous observation.**

COMMENT: None.

4-4264 **Revised January 2011. Alternative meal service may be provided to an inmate in segregation who uses food or food service equipment in a manner that is hazardous to self, staff, or other inmates. Alternative meal service is on an individual basis, is based on health or safety considerations only, meets basic nutritional requirements, and occurs with the written approval of the warden/superintendent, or designee and responsible health authority, or designee. The substitution period shall not exceed seven days.**

COMMENT: None.

4-4271 **Revised August 2005. Written policy, procedure, and practice provide that inmates in administrative segregation and protective custody are allowed telephone privileges.**

COMMENT: None.

4-4272 **Revised July 2012. Written policy, procedure and practice provide that an inmate in disciplinary detention is allowed limited telephone privileges unless phone restrictions have been invoked by the warden/superintendent or designee. Restrictions would not apply to calls related specifically to access to the attorney of record.**

COMMENT: None.

4-4281-1 **Added August 2002. Written policy, procedure, and practice ensure that information is provided to offenders about sexual abuse/assault including:**

- **prevention/intervention**
- **self-protection**
- **reporting sexual abuse/assault**
- **treatment and counseling**

The information is communicated orally and in writing, in a language clearly understood by the offender, upon arrival at the facility.

COMMENT: None.

4-4281-2 **Added January 2003. Inmates are screened within 24 hours of arrival at the facility for potential vulnerabilities or tendencies of acting out with sexually aggressive behavior. Housing assignments are made accordingly.**

COMMENT: None.

4-4281-3 **Added January 2003. Written policy, procedure, and practice require that an investigation is conducted and documented whenever a sexual assault or threat is reported.**

COMMENT: The agency should report occurrences/allegations of sexual assault or threat in accordance with the laws of the jurisdiction. The investigation may be limited by what is allowed by the laws of the jurisdiction.

4-4281-4 **Added January 2003. Written policy, procedure, and practice require that inmates identified as high risk with a history of sexually assaultive behavior are assessed by a mental health or other qualified professional. Inmates with a history of sexually assaultive behavior are identified, monitored, and counseled.**

COMMENT: None.

4-4281-5 **Added January 2003. Written policy, procedure, and practice provide that inmates identified as at risk for sexual victimization are assessed by a mental health or other qualified professional. Inmates at risk for sexual victimization are identified, monitored, and counseled.**

COMMENT: None.

4-4281-6 **Added January 2003. Written policy, procedure, and practice ensure that sexual conduct between staff and inmates, volunteers, or contract personnel and inmates, regardless of consensual status, is prohibited and subject to administrative and criminal disciplinary sanctions.**

COMMENT: None.

4-4281-7 **Added January 2003. Written policy, procedure, and practice provide that inmates who are victims of sexual abuse have the option to report the incident to a designated staff member other than an immediate point-of-contact line officer.**

COMMENT: None.

4-4281-8 **Added January 2003. Written policy, procedure, and practice provide that all case records associated with claims of sexual abuse, including incident reports, investigative reports, offender information, case disposition, medical and counseling evaluation findings, and recommendations for post-release treatment and/or counseling are retained in accordance with an established schedule.**

COMMENT: None.

4-4287 **Revised January 2006. Written policy, procedure, and practice provide for a reception program for new inmates upon admission to the correctional system. Except in unusual circumstances, initial reception and orientation of inmates is completed within 30 calendar days after admission.**

COMMENT: The daily program in the reception unit should include interviews, tests, and other admissions-related activities, including distribution of information on programs and services. New inmates should be provided reading materials, be permitted to attend religious services, receive exercise on the same schedule as the general population, and perform work assignments on the reception unit.

4288 **Revised August 2013. Written policy, procedure, and practice provide that new inmates receive written orientation materials and/or translations in their own language. These materials may also be provided electronically, but inmates in segregation must be provided the information in a written format so that their access to the information is not impeded by their custody status. When a literacy problem exists, a staff member assists the inmate in understanding the material. Completion of orientation is documented by a statement signed and dated by the inmate.**

COMMENT: Orientation should include formal classes, distribution of written materials about the institution's programs, rules, and regulations, and discussion. Orientation should also be used to observe inmate behavior and to identify special problems. The use of electronic kiosks is allowed as a means of providing the inmate handbook. Agencies using such kiosks should implement strategies to allow access to this information by general population inmates without interference by facility staff without a valid security-related reason. Inmates who are unable to read and write should be assisted through case management services provided by the facility.

4-4289 **Deleted January 2006.**

4-4290 **Revised January 2006. Written policy, procedure, and practice ensure that inmates transferred from other institutions within the correctional system receive an orientation to the new institution. Except in unusual circumstances, reception and orientation for inmates transferred from another institution within the system is completed within seven calendar days after admission.**

COMMENT: Every institution has procedures, rules, and regulations unique to its purposes, physical plant, and security status. Inmates transferred within the correctional system should be provided with the necessary information about the new institution.

4-4291 **Deleted January 2006.**

4-4292 **Revised January 2010. Written policy and procedure govern the control of personal property and funds belonging to inmates and are made available to inmates upon admission and when updated.**

COMMENT: None.

4-4295 **Revised August 2009. Written policy, procedure, and practice provide for a written inmate classification plan. The plan specifies the objectives of the classification system and methods for achieving them, and it provides a monitoring and evaluation mechanism to determine whether the objectives are being met.**

COMMENT: The classification system should consider an assessment of risk and the efficient management of the inmate population. No inmate should receive more surveillance or assistance than required or be kept in a more secure status than potential risk requires.

4-4312-1 **Added August 2005. Written policy, procedure, and practice provide for a system that identifies and monitors the movements and activities of inmates who pose a significant concern to the safety, security, and orderly management of correctional institutions. This system should ensure that appropriate staff are made aware of these inmates and that procedures exist to ensure information is current and communicated in a timely fashion.**

COMMENT: Inmates who pose a significant concern include but are not limited to disruptive gang members, domestic and international terrorists, and other inmates the facility determines are security threats.

4-4318 **Revised August 2004. Therapeutic diets are provided, as prescribed, by appropriate clinicians. A therapeutic diet manual is available in health services and food services for reference and information. Prescriptions for therapeutic diets should be specific and complete, furnished in writing to the food service manager, and rewritten annually, or more often, as clinically indicated.**

COMMENT: Therapeutic diets are prepared and served to offenders according to the orders of the treating clinician or as directed by the responsible health authority. Therapeutic diets should be kept as simple as possible and should conform as closely as possible to the foods served other offenders.

4-4321-1 **Added August 2011. All staff, contractors, and inmate workers who work in the food service department are trained in the use of food service equipment and in the safety procedures to be followed in the food service department.**

COMMENT: None.

4-4327 **Deleted January 2012.**

4-4336 **Revised August 2003. Written policy, procedure, and practice provide for the issue of suitable clothing to all inmates. Clothing is properly fitted, climatically suitable, durable, and presentable.**

COMMENT: A standard wardrobe should be provided at the time of admission and should include, as appropriate, shirts, blouses, dresses, trousers, skirts, belts, undergarments, slips, socks, shoes, coats, jackets, and headwear. In addition to the standard issue of inmate clothing, civilian attire should be available in limited quantities for leisure, visiting, work release, and furloughs. Clothing provided should not be degrading or humiliating. Since the definition of these may be culturally determined, consideration should be given to the effect of clothing provided.

4-4340 **Revised August 2007. Written policy, procedure, and practice provide for the issue of suitable, clean bedding and linen, including two sheets, pillow and pillowcase, one mattress, not to exclude a mattress with integrated pillow, and sufficient blankets to provide comfort under existing temperature controls. There is provision for linen exchange, including towels, at least weekly. Blanket exchange must be available at least quarterly.**

COMMENT: None.

4-4346 **Revised January 2006. There is a process for all offenders to initiate requests for health services on a daily basis. These requests are triaged daily by qualified health care professionals or health trained personnel. A priority system is used to schedule clinical services. Clinical services are available to offenders in a clinical setting at least five days a week and are performed by a health care practitioner or other qualified health care professional.**

COMMENT: A priority system addresses routine, urgent, and emergent complaints and conditions. Health care request forms must be readily available to all offenders. Clinical services include sick call, nursing assessments, and chronic care.

4-4347 **Revised January 2006. Continuity of care is required from admission to transfer or discharge from the facility, including referral to community-based providers, when indicated. Offender health care records should be reviewed by the facility's qualified health care professional upon arrival from outside health care entities including those from inside the correctional system.**

COMMENT: When health care is transferred to providers in the community, appropriate information should be shared with the new providers in accordance with consent requirements.

4-4348 **Revised January 2006. Offenders who need health care beyond the resources available in the facility, as determined by the responsible health care practitioner, are transferred under appropriate security provisions to a facility where such care is available. There is a written list of referral sources to include emergency and routine care. The list is reviewed and updated annually.**

COMMENT: Treatment of an offender's condition should not be limited by the resources and services available within a facility. Health care staff should collaborate with security personnel in determining conditions of transportation and necessary security precautions when an offender needs to be transported to another facility or provider.

4-4349 **Revised January 2006. A transportation system that assures timely access to services that are only available outside the correctional facility is required. Such a system needs to address the following issues:**

- **prioritization of medical need**
- **urgency (for example, ambulance versus standard transport)**
- **use of medical escort to accompany security staff, if indicated**
- **transfer of medical information**

The safe and timely transportation of offenders for medical, mental health, and dental clinic appointments, both inside and outside the correctional facility (for example, hospital, health care provider, or another correctional facility), is the joint responsibility of the facility or program administrator and the health services administrator.

COMMENT: It is essential that the medical and the custody staff work cooperatively in the design and implementation of the medical-transport system. Consideration should balance issues of security as well as medical or psychological concerns about the use of restraint devices that may affect the offender's health condition or access to care.

4-4350 **Revised January 2006. A written individual treatment plan is required for offenders requiring medical supervision, including chronic and convalescent care. This plan includes directions to health care and other personnel regarding their roles in the care and supervision of the patient, and is developed by the appropriate health care practitioner for each offender requiring a treatment plan.**

COMMENT: Offenders requiring treatment plans include the following: the chronically ill, offenders with serious communicable diseases, the physically disabled, pregnant offenders, the terminally ill, offenders with serious mental health needs, and the developmentally disabled.

4-4351 **Revised January 2006 (Mandatory). There is a written plan for access to 24-hour emergency medical, dental, and mental health services availability. The plan includes:**

- **on-site emergency first aid and crisis intervention**
- **emergency evacuation of the offender from the facility**
- **use of an emergency medical vehicle**
- **use of one or more designated hospital emergency rooms or other appropriate health facilities**
- **emergency on-call or available 24-hours per day, physician, dentist, and mental health professional services when the emergency health facility is not located in a nearby community**
- **security procedures providing for the immediate transfer of offenders, when appropriate**

COMMENT: In the event that primary health services are not available, and particularly in emergency situations, back-up facilities or providers should be predetermined. The plan may include the use of an alternative hospital emergency service or a physician on-call service.

4-4352 **Revised January 2006. Offenders are provided access to infirmary care either within the correctional setting or off site. If infirmary care is provided onsite, it includes, at a minimum, the following:**

- **definition of the scope of infirmary care services available**
- **a physician on call or available 24-hours per day**
- **health care personnel have access to a physician or a registered nurse and are on duty 24-hours per day when patients are present**
- **all offenders/patients are within sight or sound of a staff member**
- **an infirmary care manual that includes nursing care procedures**
- **compliance with applicable state statutes and local licensing requirements**

COMMENT: An *infirmary* is an area within the correctional setting or a specific area of a health care facility separate from other housing areas, where offenders are housed and provided health care. Admission and discharge from this area is controlled by medical orders or protocols.

4-4353 **Revised January 2003 (Mandatory). If female offenders are housed, access to pregnancy management is specific as it relates to the following:**

- **pregnancy testing**
- **routine prenatal care**
- **high-risk prenatal care**
- **management of the chemically addicted pregnant inmate**
- **postpartum follow-up**
- **unless mandated by state law, birth certificates/registry does not list a correctional facility as the place of birth**

COMMENT: Management should include family planning services prior to release.

4-4353-1

Added January 2003. Where nursing infants are allowed to remain with their mothers, provisions are made for a nursery, staffed by qualified persons, where the infants are placed when they are not in the care of their mothers.

COMMENT: Qualified persons may include offenders who have been trained in the competencies required for nursery care and who are working under appropriate supervision.

4-4354

Revised January 2006 (Mandatory). There is a written program to address the management of communicable and infectious diseases in offenders. The program plan shall include procedures for:

- **prevention to include immunizations, when applicable**
- **surveillance (identification and monitoring)**
- **offenders' education and staff training**
- **treatment to include medical isolation, when indicated**
- **follow-up care**
- **reporting requirements to applicable local, state, and federal agencies**
- **confidentiality/protected health information**
- **appropriate safeguards for offenders and staff**
- **post-exposure management protocols particularly for HIV and viral hepatitis infection**

Communicable disease and infection-control activities are discussed and reviewed at least quarterly by a multidisciplinary team that includes clinical, security, and administrative representatives.

COMMENT: Because of the serious nature, methods of transmission, and public sensitivity, communicable and infectious diseases require special attention. Agencies work with the responsible public health authority in establishing policy and procedures.

4-4354-1

Added August 2006. The management of offenders with Methicillin Resistant Staphylococcus Aureus (MRSA) infection includes requirements identified in the communicable disease and infection control program. In addition, the program for MRSA management shall include procedures for:

- **evaluating and treating infected inmates in accordance with an approved practice guideline**
- **medical isolation, when indicated**
- **follow-up care, including arrangements with appropriate health care authorities for continuity of care if offenders are relocated prior to the completion of therapy**

COMMENT: None.

4-4355 **Revised January 2006 (Mandatory). Management of tuberculosis (TB) in offenders includes procedures as identified in the communicable disease and infection control program. In addition, the program for TB management shall include procedures for:**

- **when and where offenders are to be screened/tested**
- **treatment, of latent tuberculosis infection and tuberculosis disease**
- **medical isolation, when indicated**
- **follow-up care, including arrangement with applicable departments of health for continuity of care if offender is released prior to completion of therapy**

COMMENT: Plans for the management of tuberculosis may be based on incidence and prevalence of the disease within the correctional agency's population and the surrounding community.

4-4356 **Revised January 2006 (Mandatory). Management of hepatitis A, B, and C in offenders includes procedures as identified in the communicable disease and infection control program. In addition, the program for hepatitis management shall include procedures for:**

- **when and where offenders are to be tested/screened**
- **hepatitis A and B immunization, when applicable**
- **treatment protocols**
- **when and under what conditions offenders are to be separated from the general population**

COMMENT: None.

4-4357 **Revised January 2006 (Mandatory). Management of HIV infection in offenders includes procedures as identified in the communicable disease and infection control program. In addition, the program for HIV management shall include:**

- **when and where offenders are to be HIV tested**
- **pre- and post-test counseling**
- **immunization and other prevention measures, when applicable**
- **treatment protocols**
- **confidentiality/protected health information**
- **when and under what conditions offenders are to be separated from the general population**

COMMENT: None.

4-4360 **Revised August 2013. Routine and emergency dental care is provided to each offender under the direction and supervision of a licensed dentist. There is a defined scope of available dental services, including emergency dental care, which includes the following:**

- **a dental screening (excluding intra-system transfers) upon admission by a qualified health care professional or health trained personnel**
- **a full dental examination (excluding intra-system transfers) by a dentist within 30 days**
- **oral hygiene, oral disease education, and self-care instruction are provided by a qualified health care provider within 30 days**
- **a defined charting system that identifies the oral health condition and specifies the priorities for treatment by category is completed**
- **consultation and referral to dental specialists, including oral surgery is provided, when necessary**

COMMENT: *Dental screening* is an assessment of dental pain, swelling, or functional impairment. As part of the initial health screening, a dentist or health care personnel properly trained and designated by the dentist should perform dental screenings. The dental program should also provide offenders with instruction on the proper brushing of teeth and other dental hygiene measures. The dental examination should include a periodontal examination (Periodontal Screening and Recording [PSR] or Community Periodontal Index of Treatment Needs [CPITN]) and taking or reviewing the patient's dental history. An examination of the hard and soft tissues of the oral cavity by means of an illuminator light, mouth mirror, and explorer should be performed. X-rays for diagnostic purposes should be available, if deemed necessary. The result of the dental examination and dental treatment plan are recorded on an appropriate uniform dental record using a numbered system such as the Federation Dental International System.

4-4362 **Revised January 2006 (Mandatory). Intake medical screening for offender transfers, excluding intra-system, commences upon the offender's arrival at the facility and is performed by health-trained or qualified health care personnel. All findings are recorded on a screening form approved by the health authority. The screening includes at least the following:**

Inquiry into:

- **any past history of serious infectious or communicable illness, and any treatment or symptoms (for example, a chronic cough, hemoptysis, lethargy, weakness, weight loss, loss of appetite, fever, night sweats that are suggestive of such illness), and medications**
- **current illness and health problems, including communicable diseases**
- **dental problems**
- **use of alcohol and other drugs, including type(s) of drugs used, mode of use, amounts used, frequency used, date or time of last use, and history of any problems that may have occurred after ceasing use (for example, convulsions)**
- **the possibility of pregnancy and history of problems (female only); and other health problems designated by the responsible physician**

Observation of the following:

- **behavior, including state of consciousness, mental status, appearance, conduct, tremor, and sweating**
- **body deformities, ease of movement, and so forth**
- **condition of the skin, including trauma markings, bruises, lesions, jaundice, rashes and infestations, recent tattoos and needle marks, or other indications of drug abuse**

Medical disposition of the offender:

- **general population**
- **general population with prompt referral to appropriate health care service**
- **referral to appropriate health care service for emergency treatment**

Offenders who are unconscious, semiconscious, bleeding, or otherwise obviously in need of immediate medical attention, are referred. When they are referred to an emergency department, their admission or return to the facility is predicated on written medical clearance. When screening is conducted by trained custody staff, procedures will require a subsequent review of positive findings by the licensed health care staff. Written procedures and screening protocols are established by the responsible physician in cooperation with the facility manager. Inmates confined within a correctional complex with consolidated medical services do not require health screening for intra-system transfers.

COMMENT: *Health screening* is a system of structured inquiry and observation to (1) prevent newly arrived offenders who pose a health or safety threat to themselves or others from being admitted to the general population; (2) identify offenders who require immediate medical attention.

Receiving screening can be performed at the time of admission by health care personnel or by a health-trained correctional officer. Facilities that have reception and diagnostic units or a holding room must conduct receiving screening on all offenders on their arrival at the facility as part of the admission procedures.

4-4363-1 **Correction 2003. The following standard was omitted from some versions of *Adult Correctional Institutions*, 4th edition.**

Written policy, procedure, and practice provide for early identification and treatment of offenders with alcohol and drug abuse problems through a standardized battery assessment. The battery shall be documented and include at a minimum the following:

- **screening and sorting**
- **clinical assessment and reassessment**
- **medical assessment for appropriate drug and alcohol program assignment to meet the needs of the individual inmates**
- **referral**

COMMENT: None.

4-4365 **Revised January 2006 (Mandatory). A comprehensive health appraisal for each offender, excluding intra-system transfers, is completed as defined below, after arrival at the facility. If there is documented evidence of a health appraisal within the previous 90 days, a new health appraisal is not required, except as determined by the designated health authority. Health appraisals include the following:**

Within 14 days after arrival at the facility:

- **review of the earlier receiving screen**
- **collection of additional data to complete the medical, dental, mental health, and immunization histories**
- **laboratory or diagnostic tests to detect communicable disease, including venereal disease and tuberculosis**
- **record of height, weight, pulse, blood pressure, and temperature**
- **other tests and examinations, as appropriate**

Within 14 days after arrival for inmates with identified significant health care problems:

- **medical examination, including review of mental and dental status (for those inmates with significant health problems discovered on earlier screening such as cardiac problems, diabetes, communicable diseases, and so forth)**
- **review of the results of the medical examination, tests, and identification of problems by a health care practitioner or other qualified health care professional, if such is authorized in the medical practice act**
- **initiation of therapy, when appropriate**
- **development and implementation of a treatment plan, including recommendations concerning housing, job assignment, and program participation**

Within 30 days after arrival for inmates without significant health care problems:

- **medical examination, including review of mental and dental status (for those inmates without significant health care concerns identified during earlier screening—no identified acute or chronic disease, no identified communicable disease, and so forth)**
- **review of the results of the medical examination, tests, and identification of problems by a health care practitioner or other qualified health care professional, if such is authorized in the medical practice act**
- **initiation of therapy, when appropriate**
- **development and implementation of a treatment plan, including recommendations concerning housing, job assignment, and program participation**

Interpretation January 2004. The criterion for testing for venereal diseases is at the discretion of the agency's/facility's health authority.

COMMENT: Test results, particularly for communicable diseases, should be received and evaluated before an offender is assigned to housing in the general population. Information regarding the offender's physical and mental status may also dictate housing and activity assignments. When appropriate, additional investigation should be conducted into alcohol and drug abuse and other related problems.

4-4366 **Revised January 2006. Health appraisal data collection and recording will include the following:**

- **a uniform process, as determined by the health authority**
- **health history and vital signs collected by health-trained or qualified health care personnel**
- **collection of all other health appraisal data performed only by qualified health professional(s)**
- **review of the results of the medical examination, tests, and identification of problems is performed by a physician or mid-level practitioner, as allowed by law**

COMMENT: None.

4-4367 **Revised January 2006. The conditions for periodic health examinations for offenders are determined by the health authority.**

COMMENT: All offenders should receive a thorough physical examination.

4-4368 **Revised January 2006 (Mandatory). The mental health program is approved by the appropriate mental health authority and includes at a minimum:**

- **screening on intake**
- **outpatient services for the detection, diagnosis, and treatment of mental illness**
- **crisis intervention and the management of acute psychiatric episodes**
- **stabilization of the mentally ill and the prevention of psychiatric deterioration in the correctional setting**
- **elective therapy services and preventive treatment, where resources permit**
- **provision for referral and admission to mental health facilities for offenders whose psychiatric needs exceed the treatment capability of the facility**
- **procedures for obtaining and documenting informed consent**

COMMENT: None.

4-4369 **Deleted January 2006.**

4-4370 **Revised January 2006 (Mandatory). All intersystem and intra-system transfer offenders will receive an initial mental health screening at the time of admission to the facility by a mental health trained or qualified mental health care professional. The mental health screening includes, but is not limited to:**

Inquiry into:

- **whether the offender has a present suicidal ideation**
- **whether the offender has a history of suicidal behavior**
- **whether the offender is presently prescribed psychotropic medication**
- **whether the offender has a current mental health complaint**
- **whether the offender is being treated for mental health problems**
- **whether the offender has a history of inpatient and outpatient psychiatric treatment**
- **whether the offender has a history of treatment for substance abuse**

Observation of:

- **general appearance and behavior**
- **evidence of abuse and/or trauma**
- **current symptoms of psychosis, depression, anxiety, and/or aggression**

Disposition of offender:

- **to the general population**
- **to the general population with appropriate referral to mental health care service**
- **referral to appropriate mental health care service for emergency treatment**

COMMENT: None.

4-4371 **Revised January 2006 (Mandatory). All intersystem offender transfers will undergo a mental health appraisal by a qualified mental health professional within 14 days of admission to a facility. If there is documented evidence of a mental health appraisal within the previous 90 days, a new mental health appraisal is not required, except as determined by the designated mental health authority. Mental health appraisals include, but are not limited to:**

- **review of available historical records of inpatient and outpatient psychiatric treatment**
- **review of history of treatment with psychotropic medication**
- **review of history of psychotherapy, psycho-educational groups, and classes or support groups**
- **review of history of drug and alcohol treatment**
- **review of educational history**
- **review of history of sexual abuse-victimization and predatory behavior**
- **assessment of current mental status and condition**
- **assessment of current suicidal potential and person-specific circumstances that increase suicide potential**

- **assessment of violence potential and person-specific circumstances that increase violence potential**
- **assessment of drug and alcohol abuse and/or addiction**
- **use of additional assessment tools, as indicated**
- **referral to treatment, as indicated**
- **development and implementation of a treatment plan, including recommendations concerning housing, job assignment, and program participation**

COMMENT: None.

4-4372 **Revised January 2006. Offenders referred for mental health treatment will receive a comprehensive evaluation by a qualified mental health practitioner. The evaluation is to be completed within 14 days of the referral request date and include at least the following:**

- **review of mental health screening and appraisal data**
- **direct observations of behavior**
- **collection and review of additional data from individual diagnostic interviews and tests assessing personality, intellect, and coping abilities**
- **compilation of the individuals' mental health history**
- **development of an overall treatment/management plan with appropriate referral to include transfer to mental health facility for offenders whose psychiatric needs exceed the treatment capability of the facility**

COMMENT: Comprehensive individual psychological evaluations should be performed when there is a reasonable expectation that such evaluation will serve a therapeutic or dispositional function useful to the overall interests of the offender. Written reports describing the results of the assessment should be prepared and all information should be appropriately filed.

4-4373 **Revised July 2012. There is a written suicide-prevention plan that is approved by the health authority and reviewed by the facility or program administrator. The plan includes staff and offender critical-incident debriefing that covers the management of suicidal incidents, suicide watch, and suicides. It ensures a review of suicidal incidents, suicide watch, and suicides by administration, security, and health services. All staff with responsibility for offender supervision are trained on an annual basis in the implementation of the program. Training should include but not be limited to:**

- **identifying the warning signs and symptoms of impending suicidal behavior**
- **understanding the demographic and cultural parameters of suicidal behavior, including incidence and variations in precipitating factors**
- **responding to suicidal and depressed offenders**
- **communication between correctional and health care personnel**
- **referral procedures**
- **housing observation and suicide watch level procedures**
- **follow-up monitoring of offenders who make a suicide attempt**

COMMENT: None.

4-4375

Revised January 2006. Medical or dental adaptive devices (eyeglasses, hearing aids, dentures, wheelchairs, or other prosthetic devices) are provided when medically necessary, as determined by the responsible health care practitioner.

COMMENT: Offenders may be required to provide copayments for these devices.

4-4376

Revised January 2006 (Mandatory). Detoxification is done only under medical supervision in accordance with local, state, and federal laws. Detoxification from alcohol, opiates, hypnotics, other stimulants, and sedative hypnotic drugs is conducted under medical supervision when performed at the facility or is conducted in a hospital or community detoxification center. Specific guidelines are followed for the treatment and observation of individuals manifesting mild or moderate symptoms of intoxication or withdrawal from alcohol and other drugs.

COMMENT: None.

4-4380

Revised January 2006 (Mandatory). The facility has a designated health authority with responsibility for ongoing health care services pursuant to a written agreement, contract, or job description. Such responsibilities include:

- **establish a mission statement, which defines the scope of health care services**
- **develop mechanisms, including written agreements, when necessary, to assure that the scope of services are provided and properly monitored**
- **develop a facility's operational health policies and procedures**
- **identify the type of health care staff needed to provide the determined scope of services**
- **establish systems for the coordination of care among multidisciplinary health care providers and**
- **develop a quality management program**

The health authority may be a physician, health services administrator, or health agency. When the health authority is other than a physician, final clinical judgments rest with a single, designated, responsible physician. The health authority is authorized and responsible for making decisions about the deployment of health resources and the day-to-day operations of the health services program.

COMMENT: The health authority and health services administrator may be the same person. The responsibility of the health authority includes arranging for all levels of health services, assuring the quality of all health services, and assuring that offenders have access to them. Health services provides for the physical and mental well-being of the offender population and should include providing medical and dental services, mental health services, nursing care, personal hygiene, dietary services, health education; and attending to environmental conditions. While overall responsibility may be assumed at the central office level, it is essential that each facility have an onsite health services administrator. The health authority and health services administrator may be the same person.

4-4381 **Revised January 2006 (Mandatory). Clinical decisions are the sole province of the responsible health care practitioner and are not countermanded by non-clinicians.**

COMMENT: The provision of health care is a joint effort of administrators and health care providers and can be achieved only through mutual trust and cooperation. The health authority arranges for the availability of health care services; the responsible clinician determines what services are needed; the official responsible for the facility provides the administrative support for making the services accessible to offenders.

4-4382 **Revised January 2006 (Mandatory). If the facility provides health care services, they are provided by qualified health care staff whose duties and responsibilities are governed by written job descriptions, contracts, or written agreements approved by the health authority. Verification of current credentials and job descriptions are on file in the facility.**

COMMENT: Job descriptions should include qualifications and specific duties and responsibilities. Verification consists of copies of credentials or a letter confirming credential status from the state licensing or certification body. Standing medical orders are for the definitive treatment of identified conditions and for the on-site emergency treatment of any person having such condition. Direct orders are those written specifically for the treatment of one person's particular condition.

4-4383 **Revised January 2006. When institutions do not have qualified health care staff, health-trained personnel coordinate the health delivery services in the institution under the joint supervision of the responsible health authority and warden or superintendent.**

COMMENT: The health-trained staff member (who is other than a nurse, mid-level practitioner, or emergency medical technician) may be full-time or part-time. Coordination duties may include reviewing receiving screening forms for needed follow-up, readying offenders and their records for sick call, and assisting in carrying out orders regarding such matters as diets, housing, and work assignments.

4-4384 **Deleted January 2006.**

4-4385 **Deleted January 2008.**

4-4386 **Revised January 2006. All direct care staff are screened for tuberculosis infection and disease prior to job assignment and periodically in accordance with recommendations from applicable local, state, and federal public health authorities.**

COMMENT: None.

4-4387 **Revised January 2006. All direct care staff are offered the hepatitis B vaccine series in accordance with the institution's exposure control plan.**

COMMENT: None.

4-4388 **Revised January 2006 (Mandatory). All health care staff in the facility are trained in the implementation of the facility's emergency plans. Health care staff are included in facility's emergency drills, as applicable.**

COMMENT: Emergency plans include those for fire, natural disaster, power outage, hostage situation, riot, and other disturbances.

4-4389 **Revised January 2006 (Mandatory). Designated correctional and all health care staff are trained to respond to health-related situations within a four-minute response time. The training program is conducted on an annual basis and is established by the responsible health authority in cooperation with the facility or program administrator and includes instruction on the following:**

- **recognition of signs and symptoms, and knowledge of action required in potential emergency situations**
- **administration of basic first aid**
- **certification in cardiopulmonary resuscitation (CPR) in accordance with the recommendations of the certifying health organization**
- **methods of obtaining assistance**
- **signs and symptoms of mental illness, violent behavior, and acute chemical intoxication and withdrawal**
- **procedures for patient transfers to appropriate medical facilities or health care providers**
- **suicide intervention**

COMMENT: The facility administrator or designee may designate those correctional officers and health care providers who have responsibility to respond to health care emergencies. Staff not physically able to perform CPR are exempt from the expected practice.

4-4390 **Revised July 2012. First aid kits are available in designated areas of the facility based on need and an automatic external defibrillator is available for use at the facility. The health authority approves the contents, number, location, and procedures for monthly inspection of the kits(s) and develops written procedures for the use of the kits by nonmedical staff.**

COMMENT: The availability and placement of first aid kits are determined by the designated health authority in conjunction with the facility administrator.

4-4393 **Revised August 2008. Unless prohibited by state law, offenders (under staff supervision) may perform familial duties commensurate with their level of training. These duties may include:**

- **providing peer support and education**
- **performing hospice activities**
- **assisting impaired offenders on a one-on-one basis with activities of daily living**
- **serving as a suicide companion or buddy if qualified and trained through a formal program that is part of suicide-prevention plan**
- **handling dental instruments for the purpose of sanitizing and cleaning, when directly supervised and in compliance with applicable tool-control policies, while in a dental assistant's training program certified by the state department of education or other comparable appropriate authority**

Offenders are not to be used for the following duties:

- **performing direct patient care services**
- **scheduling health care appointments**
- **determining access of other offenders to health care services**
- **handling or having access to surgical instruments, syringes, needles, medications, or health records**
- **operating diagnostic or therapeutic equipment except under direct supervision (by specially trained staff) in a vocational training program**

COMMENT: No offender, or group of offenders, is given control or authority over other offenders in the health care area.

4-4396 **Revised January 2006 (Mandatory). The principle of confidentiality applies to offender health records and information about offender health status.**

- **The active health record is maintained separately from the confinement case record.**
- **Access to the health record is in accordance with state and federal law.**
- **To protect and preserve the integrity of the facility, the health authority shares with the superintendent/warden information regarding an offender's medical management.**
- **The circumstances are specified when correctional staff should be advised of an offender's health status. Only that information necessary to preserve the health and safety of an offender, other offenders, volunteers/visitors, or the correctional staff is provided.**

- **Policy determines how information is provided to correctional/classification staff/volunteers/visitors to address the medical needs of the offender as it relates to housing, program placement, security, and transport.**
- **The release of health information complies with the Health Insurance Portability and Accountability Act (HIPAA), where applicable, in a correctional setting.**

COMMENT: The principle of confidentiality protects offender patients from disclosure of confidences entrusted to a health care provider during the course of treatment.

4-4399 **Revised January 2006. There is consultation between the facility and program administrator (or a designee) and the responsible health care practitioner (or designee) prior to taking action regarding chronically ill, physically disabled, geriatric, seriously mentally ill, or developmentally disabled offenders in the following areas:**

- **housing assignments**
- **program assignments**
- **disciplinary measures**
- **transfers to other facilities**

When immediate action is required, consultation to review the appropriateness of the action occurs as soon as possible, but no later than 72 hours.

COMMENT: Maximum cooperation between custody personnel and health care providers is essential so that both groups are aware of decisions and movements regarding mentally ill and developmentally disabled offenders.

4-4400 **Revised January 2006 (Mandatory). When an offender is transferred to segregation, health care staff will be informed immediately and will provide a screening and review, as indicated by the protocols established by the health authority. Unless medical attention is needed more frequently, each offender in segregation receives a daily visit from a qualified health care professional. The visit ensures that offenders have access to the health care system. The presence of a health care provider in segregation is announced and recorded. The frequency of physician visits to segregation units is determined by the health authority.**

COMMENT: Health care providers' visits are intended to be screening rounds and are not meant to be clinical encounters. Those offenders who request sick call are evaluated by a health care provider who determines the appropriate setting for further medical attention or examination. Health care providers may request that an offender be removed from a cell or housing area for medical attention or examination. All sick call encounters are documented in the offender's health record.

4-4402 **Revised January 2006 (Mandatory). The use of offenders for medical, pharmaceutical, or cosmetic experiments is prohibited. This does not preclude offender participation in clinical trials that are approved by an institutional review board based on his/her need for a specific medical intervention. Institutions electing to perform research will be in compliance with all state and federal guidelines.**

COMMENT: Experimental programs include aversive conditioning, psychosurgery, and the application of cosmetic substances being tested prior to sale to the general public. An individual's treatment with a new medical procedure by his or her physician should be undertaken only after the offender has received a full explanation of the positive and negative features of the treatment and only with informed consent.

4-4403-1 **Added January 2006. If Telehealth is used for patient encounters, the plan includes policies for:**

- **patient consent**
- **confidentiality/protected health information**
- **documentation**
- **integration of the report of the consultation into the primary health care record**

COMMENT: None.

4-4404 **Revised January 2005. A transfer that results in an offender's placement in a non-correctional facility or in a special unit within the facility or agency, specifically designated for the care and treatment of the severely mentally ill or developmentally disabled follows due process procedures as specified by federal, state, and local law prior to the move being effected. In emergency situations, a hearing is held as soon as possible after the transfer.**

COMMENT: The following are generally accepted as due process procedures: written notice to the offender of the proposed transfer; a hearing for the offender, with the right (unless limited for good cause) to call and cross-examine witnesses; a decision by an independent official not involved in treatment of the offender, with a statement of the reasons for transfer; and an independent adviser to assist the offender facing transfer.

4-4405 **Revised January 2006 (Mandatory). The use of restraints for medical and psychiatric purposes is defined, at a minimum by the following:**

- **conditions under which restraints may be applied**
- **types of restraints to be applied**
- **identification of a qualified medical or mental health care practitioner who may authorize the use of restraints after reaching the conclusion that less intrusive measures would not be successful**
- **monitoring procedures for offenders in restraints**

- **length of time restraints are to be applied**
- **documentation of efforts for less restrictive treatment alternatives as soon as possible**
- **an after-incident review**

COMMENT: Written policy should identify the authorization needed and when, where, and how restraints may be used and for how long.

4-4406 **Revised January 2013. (Mandatory). Victims of sexual assault are referred under appropriate security provisions to a community facility for treatment and gathering of evidence, or if these procedures are performed in-house, the following guidelines are used:**

- **A history is taken by health care professionals who conduct an examination to document the extent of physical injury and to determine if referral to another medical facility is indicated. With the victim's consent, the examination includes the collection of evidence from the victim, using a kit approved by the appropriate authority.**
- **Provision is made for testing of sexually transmitted diseases (for example, HIV, gonorrhea, hepatitis, other diseases) and counseling, as appropriate.**
- **Prophylactic treatment and follow-up for sexually transmitted diseases are offered to all victims, as appropriate.**
- **Following the physical examination, there is availability of an evaluation by a mental health professional to assess the need for crisis intervention counseling and long-term follow-up.**

A report is made to the facility or program administrator or designee to assure separation of the victim from his or her assailant.

COMMENT: None.

4-4409 **Deleted January 2006.**

4-4411 **Revised January 2006 (Mandatory). A documented peer review program for all health care practitioners and a documented external peer review program will be utilized for all physicians, psychologists, and dentists every two years.**

COMMENT: The credentialing and privileging process is an integral part of assuring the competence of the providers for the inmate patients they treat. This should be routine every two years with an ability to have an immediate review if problems of practice arise. Immediate reviews are serious and only should be permitted by a careful decision of the most senior physician responsible for the system or institution. A mechanism for patient care complaints, observations by other health services providers, security, or other nonmedical providers should be established so that the responsible physician can call a panel of independent physicians to review the practice and practice patterns of the physician on whom the complaint(s) has (have) been made. The investigation and its findings are confidential in most states by statute. The responsible physician should receive the report, take indicated action, and be prepared to demonstrate to the auditors, within the confines of confidentiality, the process, process indicators, and the actions available (for example, termination of the physician, required education in an area, prohibition against seeing a type of disease entity without another physician, and so forth). It is important that the auditors appreciate that the process is real and meaningful and that peer review is not simply a paper trail without substance.

4-4412 **Revised January 2006. The facility uses a health care staffing analysis to determine the essential positions needed to perform the health services mission and provide the defined scope of services. A staffing plan is developed and implemented from this analysis. There is an annual review of the staffing plan by the health authority to determine if the number and type of staff is adequate.**

COMMENT: Adequate staffing is based on variables such as facility size and configuration, location, and offender type. The staffing analysis is used to determine the types and numbers of staff needed to provide a defined scope of services (medical, dental, mental health, and infirmary).

4-4414 **Revised January 2006. Non-emergency offender transfers require the following:**

- **health record confidentiality to be maintained**
- **summaries, originals, or copies of the health record accompany the offender to the receiving facility. Health conditions, treatments, and allergies should be included in the record.**
- **determination of suitability for travel based on medical evaluation, with particular attention given to communicable disease clearance**
- **written instructions regarding medication or health interventions required en route should be provided to transporting officers separate from the medical record**
- **specific precautions (including standards) to be taken by transportation officers (for example, masks and gloves)**

A medical summary sheet is required for all inter- and intra-system transfers to maintain the provision of continuity of care. Information included does not require a release-of-information form.

Inmates confined within a correctional complex with consolidated medical services do not require health screening for intra-system transfers.

COMMENT: Transfers may be permanent or temporary (for consultative or diagnostic services).

4-4421 **Deleted January 2006.**

4-4424 **Revised August 2003. Each policy, procedure, and program in the health care delivery system is reviewed at least annually by the appropriate health care authority and revised, if necessary.**

COMMENT: None.

4-4426 **Revised January 2006. Adequate space is provided for administrative, direct care, professional, and clerical staff. This space includes conference areas, storage room for records, a public lobby, and toilet facilities.**

COMMENT: None.

4-4429 **Revised August 2002. Written policy, procedure, and practice prohibit discrimination on the basis of disability in the provision of services, programs, and activities administered for program beneficiaries and participants.**

COMMENT: Services, programs, and activities include, but are not limited to, the following:

- academic and vocational education (including developmental and rehabilitative programs)
- work programs/work release programs (by providing reasonable accommodations or alternatives for offenders with disabilities so that the benefits of these programs, including sentence-reduction credits, are available to offenders with disabilities)
- recreation, exercise, and activities
- mail, telephone, visiting
- library
- religious programs
- reception and orientation
- transportation services (to provide for safety and security, and to avoid undue discomfort, in light of the offenders' disabilities)
- classification
- food service
- sanitation and hygiene
- health care
- social services
- release
- discipline, grievance procedures, and due process proceedings
- safety and emergency procedures
- access to media, courts, counsel, and law library
- commissary/canteen
- volunteer programs
- psychological and psychiatric services

4-4429-1 **Added August 2002. Written policy, procedure, and practice provide for staff and offender access to an appropriately trained and qualified individual who is educated in the problems and challenges faced by offenders with physical and/or mental impairments, programs designed to educate and assist disabled offenders, and all legal requirements for the protection of offenders with disabilities.**

COMMENT: An *appropriately trained and qualified individual*, as used in this standard, is one who has been designated by the warden, superintendent, or other authority, to coordinate efforts to comply with and carry out responsibilities defined by the Americans with Disabilities Act. That individual should develop relationships with, and use the expertise of institutional staff, advocacy groups, nonprofit organizations, agencies of government, and others that have relevant knowledge and experience.

4-4438 **Revised August 2009. Where a drug treatment program exists, written policy, procedure, and practice provide that the alcohol and drug abuse treatment program has a written treatment philosophy within the context of the total corrections system, as well as goals and measurable objectives.**

COMMENT: None.

4-4438 – 4-4441 **The following interpretation applies to all standards from 4-4438 through 4-4441.**

Interpretation August 2003. The words "Where a drug program exists" are interpreted as a therapeutic community.

4-4443 **Revised July 2012. If a temporary release program is in place, it should include but not be limited to the following:**

- **written operational procedures**
- **careful screening and selection procedures**
- **written rules of conduct and sanctions**
- **a system of supervision to minimize inmate abuse of program privileges**
- **a complete recordkeeping system**
- **a system for evaluating program effectiveness**
- **efforts to obtain community cooperation and support**

COMMENT: None.

4-4447-1

Added January 2006. Written policy, procedure and practice provide that designated staff are responsible for coordination of victims' programs and that curriculum is established for providing training to staff involved with victims' issues. This curriculum includes the following topics:

- **specific services available to crime victims**
- **changes in laws impacting victims**
- **way(s) of gaining access to the services**
- **confidentiality of victim information**
- **way(s) for victims to communicate complaints and other concerns**
- **program-evaluation measures, which include victim input regarding the effectiveness of services and ways for them to make suggestions regarding agency policies and practices intended to assist crime victims**

COMMENT: None.

4-4448 – 4-4464

The following interpretation applies to all standards from 4-4448 through 4-4464.

Interpretation January 2002. This standard is applicable to all facilities. For reception and diagnostic centers, the standard only applies as follows:

1. **To reception and diagnostic centers with an average offender length of stay of 90 days or longer.**
2. **To reception and diagnostic centers with a cadre of offenders who are expected to serve more than 90 days of confinement within the facility, or for those sentenced offenders awaiting transfer to another facility whose stay exceeds 90 days.**

COMMENT: An inmate work program may include industrial, agricultural, maintenance, and service jobs. The plan should provide for employment for all eligible inmates although every inmate may not be actively involved in the plan all of the time.

4-4448

Revised July 2012. The institution maintains a written plan for full-time work and/or program assignments for all inmates in the general population. The plan also provides for employment for inmates with disabilities.

COMMENT: None.

4-4449

Revised August 2008. Written policy, procedure, and practice can require all eligible inmates to work unless assigned to an approved education or training program. Inmates have the option of refusing to participate in any rehabilitation or treatment program except adult basic education and programs required by statute or ordered by the sentencing court or paroling authority.

COMMENT: All eligible inmates are expected to participate in work assignments, adult basic education programs, and programs ordered by the sentencing court or paroling authority or required by statute. Failure to participate in programs may result in administrative action.

4-4450 **Deleted July 2012.**

4-4451

COMMENT: Whenever possible, inmates should gain work experience relevant to the current job market; assignments for female inmates should expand beyond the traditional tasks assigned to women.

4-4452

COMMENT: Inmates can do many necessary jobs related to maintenance and facility operations. Inmates may be assigned to construction work, conservation projects, or other work financed by public funds. These programs may be housed separately from the main facility. Staff supervising such inmates should be trained for such an assignment.

4-4453

COMMENT: The institution should actively pursue cooperation from labor and industry to help plan and evaluate its work programs and assist in work release, job training, and job placement. The establishment of advisory boards or joint councils should be considered.

4-4454

COMMENT: The number and duration of inmate work-day interruptions should be minimized as much as possible through rescheduling of staff assignments and inmate activities.

4-4455

COMMENT: The annual inspection can be conducted by a central office or regional safety inspector or by local qualified safety officials. Weekly inspections must be conducted by the institution's safety officer or by the industries/shops' administrative staff; the duty officer may not conduct these inspections unless qualified to do so.

4-4456

COMMENT: None.

4-4457

COMMENT: Appropriate industries' staff should evaluate and choose from the pool of potential employees made available by the classification committee. Responsibility for separation of inmates based on work performance resides with the industries' supervisor and is subject to review by the institution's industries manager and to applicable due process standards and procedures. Separation for reasons not related to job performance should be done by appropriate classification through the appropriate institutional committee. Inmates separated should be referred to the classification committee for reassignment.

4-4458

COMMENT: To ensure that realistic working conditions prevail, the industries' management should determine the number of workers necessary to handle the workload. Job descriptions outlining responsibilities and performance expectations should be available for each job.

4-4459

COMMENT: Quality control plans should include product specifications and tolerances or dimensions as well as production techniques, along with the use of appropriate measures for determining conformance to those standards. The plans should also stress periodic inspections throughout the entire production process, including inspection of the finished product, whether such inspections are of a random or statistical sampling or of all products made. Quality control records should be maintained and used for training purposes.

4-4460

COMMENT: The cost accounting system should be based on a chart of accounts and a general ledger that generate data for other fiscal reports. The system should include a means for recording and allocating the direct and indirect costs and the administrative overhead for each operating unit.

4-4461

COMMENT: Inmates should be compensated so that they can make purchases from the canteen and accumulate funds to assist them upon their release from incarceration.

4-4461-1 **Added January 2006. Written policy, procedure, and practice provide that, consistent with the laws and legal practices within the jurisdiction, restitution is collected and ultimately made available to the victims of crime and/or their survivors. Where supported by statute, and feasible, victim awareness classes are offered to help offenders understand the impact of their crimes on the victims, their communities, and their own families.**

COMMENT: Victim's programs should be overseen by someone in a management-level position who has easy access to the agency's top leadership and who is supported by staff trained to respond appropriately to crime victims who contact the agency.

4-4462

COMMENT: Reimbursement to the institution for room and board may be required

4-4463

COMMENT: Compensation, whether as part of a work-release program or an outside work assignment plan, should include all fringe benefits.

4-4464

COMMENT: A needs assessment of the institutional population is used to determine the type and number of programs needed to meet identified needs. A comprehensive education program may include other components in such areas as English as a second language, social and living skills, health education, pre-employment training, occupational training, and computer literacy.

4-4464 **Revised January 2012. Written policy, procedure, and practice provide for a comprehensive education program available to all inmates who are eligible that includes the following:**

- **educational philosophy and goals**
- **communication skills**
- **general education**
- **basic academic skills**
- **GED preparation**
- **special education**
- **vocational education**
- **postsecondary education**
- **other education programs that are consistent with the needs of the institutional and inmate population**

COMMENT: A needs assessment of the institutional population is used to determine the type and number of programs needed to meet identified needs. A comprehensive education program may include other components in such areas as English as a second language, social and living skills, health education, pre-employment training, occupational training, and computer literacy.

4-4465 **Deleted January 2012.**

4-4466

Interpretation January 2002. This standard is applicable to all facilities. For reception and diagnostic centers, the standard only applies as follows:

1. **To reception and diagnostic centers with an average offender length of stay of 90 days or longer**
2. **To reception and diagnostic centers with a cadre of offenders who are expected to serve more than 90 days of confinement within the facility or for those sentenced offenders awaiting transfer to another facility whose stay exceeds 90 days.**

COMMENT: None.

4-4467

Revised January 2012. Vocational training programs are integrated with academic programs and are relevant to the vocational needs of the inmate population and to employment opportunities in the community. For reception and diagnostic centers, the standard only applies as follows:

1. **To reception and diagnostic centers with an average offender length of stay of 90 days or longer**
2. **To reception and diagnostic centers with a cadre of offenders who are expected to serve more than 90 days of confinement within the facility or for those sentenced offenders awaiting transfer to another facility whose stay exceeds 90 days.**

COMMENT: None

4-4468

Deleted January 2012.

4-4469 - 4-4480

This interpretation applies to all standards from 4-4469 through 4-4480.

Interpretation January 2002. This standard is applicable to all facilities. For reception and diagnostic centers, the standard only applies as follows:

1. **To reception and diagnostic centers with an average offender length of stay of 90 days or longer**
2. **To reception and diagnostic centers with a cadre of offenders who are expected to serve more than 90 days of confinement within the facility or for those sentenced offenders awaiting transfer to another facility whose stay exceeds 90 days.**

COMMENT: None.

4-4470 **Revised August 2009. Written policy, procedure, and practice provide that the academic and vocational education programs are recognized, certified, or licensed by the state department of education or other recognized agency having jurisdiction. Programs up to the completion of high school and/or the GED are available at no cost to inmates.**

COMMENT: None.

4-4480 **Revised August 2009. Written policy, procedure, and practice provide incentives for educational and/or vocational participation and formal recognition of specific accomplishments.**

COMMENT: Recognition of academic and vocational achievements, such as certification or graduation, is helpful to inmates and provides general support for educational programs. Incentives may include pay, access to preferred jobs and/or educational programs, or other special privileges.

4-4482 **Revised August 2007. The education and experience of the recreation program supervisor are taken into consideration by the appointing authority in determining appointment to the position. These include education, correctional experience, training in recreation and/or leisure activities and the ability to supervise the program. In institutions with more than 100 inmates, the position is full-time.**

COMMENT: To ensure a high-quality leisure services program, it is important to have an administrator with training specific to recreation and/or leisure activities. This position may be filled by a volunteer or contract personnel.

4-4485 **Revised August 2013. Written policy, procedure, and practice provide for interaction with the community through various activities.**

COMMENT: None.

4-4487 **Revised August 2009. Written policy and procedure govern inmate correspondence.**

COMMENT: All regulations concerning inmate correspondence should be specified in writing and made available to staff members, inmates, and their correspondents.

4-4492 **Revised August 2002. Written policy, procedure, and practice specify that inmates are permitted to send sealed letters to a specified class of persons and organizations, including but not limited to the following: courts; counsel; officials of the confining authority; state and local chief executive officers; administrators of grievance systems; and members of the paroling authority. Staff, in the presence of the inmate, may be allowed to inspect outgoing privileged mail for contraband before it is sealed. Mail to inmates from this specified class of persons and organizations may be opened only to inspect for contraband and only in the presence of the inmate, unless waived in writing, or in circumstances, which may indicate contamination.**

COMMENT: Suspicious mail may include packages and letters unusual in appearance, or which appear different from mail normally received or sent by the individual; packages and letters of a size or shape not customarily received or sent by the individual; packages and letters with a city and/or state postmark that is different from the return address; or packages and letters leaking, stained, or emitting a strange or unusual odor, or which have a powdery residue.

4-4495 **Revised August 2006. Written policy, procedure, and practice require that, excluding weekends and holidays, or emergency situations, incoming and outgoing letters are held for no more than 48 hours and packages (if allowed) are held no more than 72 hours.**

Interpretation August 2002. The term *emergency situation* is interpreted as any significant disruption of normal facility or agency procedure, policy, or activity caused by riot, escape, fire, natural disaster, employee action, or other serious incident.

COMMENT: Inspection for contraband letters should take no longer than 48 hours to complete, so that incoming letters should be distributed to inmates and outgoing letters sent to the post office within 48 hours of receipt. Similarly, inspection of packages normally should take no longer than 72 hours to complete. The standard does not prohibit the holding of mail for inmates who are temporarily absent from the facility (for example, in a hospital or court).

4-4497-1 **Added August 2002. Written policy, procedure, and practice ensure that offenders have access to reasonably priced telephone services. Correctional agencies ensure that:**

- **contracts involving telephone services for offenders comply with all applicable state and federal regulations.**
- **contracts are based on rates and surcharges that are commensurate with those charged to the general public for like services. Any deviation from ordinary consumer rates reflects actual costs associated with the provision of services in a correctional setting**
- **contracts for offender telephone services provide the broadest range of calling options determined by the agency administrator to be consistent with the requirements of sound correctional management**

COMMENT: When procuring and renewing telephone services, correctional officials should inquire into the reasons for proposed deviations from standard charges and seek the best possible rates for the broadest possible range of calling options.

4-4500-1 **Added August 2003. Written policy, procedure, and practice require that an inmate is informed in a timely manner of the verifiable death or critical illness of an immediate family member. In case of the critical illness of an immediate family member, the inmate is allowed, whenever statutes and circumstances allow, to go to the bedside under escort or alone.**

COMMENT: Classification, status, geography, security level, and other specified criteria should determine eligibility. *Immediate family* is usually defined as parent, spouse, child, sibling, grandparent, or legal guardian.

4-4507 **Revised January 2003. There is available to the institution a person with a master's of library science, information resources, media services, or related degree who assists with coordinating and supervising library services and is responsible for training of all library staff.**

COMMENT: A qualified librarian should be available to assist the staff member who coordinates and supervises library services in the institution.

4-4510 **Revised August 2011. Library services are available daily, including evenings and weekends.**

COMMENT: There should be no restrictions on access to library services and facilities. Library services, which can include book carts, should be provided at prime program hours as well as at times that do not compete with work assignments, visitation, counseling, or other programs. Every inmate should have access to library services regardless of his or her work or visitation schedule. It is preferable that the facility's main library is available seven days per week; in lieu of this, library services are available seven days per week. All reasonable efforts should be made to ensure that inmates are provided access to varied reading materials.

4-4513 **Revised July 2012. In facilities with an average daily population of 500 or more inmates, there is a full-time chaplain (or chaplains). In facilities with less than 500 inmates, adequate religious staffing is available. The chaplain and/or religious staff has physical access to all areas of the institution to minister to inmates and staff.**

COMMENT: None.

4-4514 **Revised August 2004. Written policy, procedure, and practice provide that assigned chaplain(s) (whether they be classified employees, contract employees, or volunteers), in consultation with and approval from facility administration, plans, directs, and coordinates all aspects of the religious program, including approval and training of both lay and clergy volunteers from faiths represented by the inmate population.**

COMMENT: The religious program should be designed to fulfill the institution's responsibility of ensuring that all inmates can voluntarily exercise their constitutional right to religious freedom.

4-4515 **Deleted July 2012.**

4-4516 **Revised August 2004. The chaplain or designated staff develops and maintains close relationships with community religious resources.**

COMMENT: Community resources can help augment the delivery of appropriate religious services on special holidays or, as needed, to meet the requirements of the diversity of religious faiths among inmates.

4-4518 **Deleted August 2004.**

4-4519 **Revised August 2004. When a religious leader of an inmate's faith is not represented through the chaplaincy staff or volunteers, the chaplain or designated staff member assists the inmate in contacting a person who has the appropriate credentials from the faith judicatory. That person ministers to the inmate under the supervision of the chaplain.**

COMMENT: The religious leader can visit at designated regular times, with provision for emergency visits.

4-4521 **Revised January 2012. The chaplain, in cooperation with the institutional administrator or designee, approves donations of equipment or materials for use in religious programs.**

COMMENT: Approval of donations helps ensure that equipment and materials are available for approved religious practices and helps avoid the accumulation of duplicate or inappropriate materials.

4-4530 **Added January 2007.**

Added new section: Security Threat Groups

Written policy, procedure, and practice require that ongoing, but not less than semi-annually, consultation take place as determined by the agency or parent agency with the local Joint Terrorism Task Force (JTTF), or another similar agency, on all terrorism matters to include:

- **a list of known terrorist inmates in local custody**
- **intelligence regarding inmates with suspected terrorist ties**
- **information regarding specific incidents, events, or threats affecting the institution or detention facility that have a possible terrorism connection**

COMMENT: Examples of reportable intelligence might include attempts by such inmates to radicalize or recruit among fellow inmates, or efforts to continue contact with terrorist groups in the community. Documentation of the consultations should be determined by agency standards, and may include log books, e-mails exchanged with the JTTF or another like agency, or minutes of telephone calls.

Performance-Based Standards for Adult Local Detention Facilities (ALDF), 4th Edition

4-ALDF-1A-05 **Deleted July 2012.**

4-ALDF-1A-09 **Revised August 2008. Single cells in general population provide at least 35 square feet of unencumbered space. At least 70 square feet of total floor space is provided when the occupant is confined for more than 10 hours per day.**

COMMENT: *Unencumbered space* is usable space that is not encumbered by furnishings or fixtures. At least one dimension of the unencumbered space is no less than seven feet. In determining the unencumbered space, the total square footage is obtained and the square footage of the fixtures is subtracted. All fixtures must be in operational position for these calculations.

PROTOCOLS: Written policy and procedure. Facility plans/specifications.

PROCESS INDICATORS: Measurement. Observation.

4-ALDF-1A-14 **Revised January 2008. Light levels in inmate cells/rooms are at least 20 foot-candles in personal grooming areas and at the writing surface. Lighting throughout the facility is sufficient for the tasks performed. Measurements are documented by a qualified source and are checked at least once per accreditation cycle.**

COMMENT: None

PROTOCOLS: Written policy and procedure. Facility plans/specifications.

PROCESS: INDICATORS: Documentation from a qualified source. Measurement. Observation. Maintenance and repair records. Inmate and staff interviews.

4-ALDF-1A-15 **Revised August 2006. (Existing only) All inmate rooms/cells provide access to natural light.**

COMMENT: None.

PROTOCOLS: Written policy and procedure. Facility plans/specifications.

PROCESS INDICATORS: Observation.

4-ALDF-1A-16

Revised August 2006. (Renovation, Addition, New Construction only). All inmate rooms/cells provide the occupants with access to natural light by means of at least three-square feet of transparent glazing, plus two additional square feet of transparent glazing per inmate in rooms/cells with three or more inmates.

COMMENT: None.

PROTOCOLS: Written policy and procedure. Facility plans/specifications.

PROCESS INDICATORS: Measurement. Observation. Housing records and logs. Classification records.

4-ALDF-1A-18

Revised January 2012. Noise levels in inmate housing units do not exceed 70 dBA (A Scale). Measurements shall be conducted annually by a qualified source with at least one measurement taking place during night time and one measurement taking place during day time.

COMMENT: None.

PROTOCOLS: Written policy and procedure. Facility plans/specifications.

PROCESS INDICATORS: Observation. Measurement.

4-ALDF-1A-18-1

Deleted January 2013.

4-ALDF-1A-19

Revised August 2007. A ventilation system supplies at least 15-cubic feet per minute of circulated air per occupant with a minimum of five-cubic feet per minute of outside air. Toilet rooms, and cells with toilets, have no less than four air changes per hour unless state or local codes require a different number of air changes. Air quantities are documented by a qualified technician not less than once per accreditation cycle.

COMMENT: *Accreditation cycle* is defined as within the past three years.

PROTOCOLS: Written policy and procedure. Facility plans/specifications.

PROCESS INDICATORS: Measurement. Observation. Inmate and staff interviews. Maintenance and repair records. Report from independent source.

4-ALDF-1A-20 **Revised August 2006. Temperature is mechanically raised or lowered to acceptable comfort levels.**

COMMENT: None.

PROTOCOLS: Written policy and procedure. Facility plans/specifications.

PROCESS INDICATORS: Measurement. Inmate and staff interviews. Facility logs and records. Maintenance and repair records.

4-ALDF-1C-12 **Revised August 2005. Essential lighting and life-sustaining functions are maintained inside the facility and with the community in an emergency.**

COMMENT: None.

PROTOCOLS: Written policy and procedure. Facility plans/specifications.

PROCESS INDICATORS: Observation. Facility records and logs.

4-ALDF-2A-01 **Revised January 2007. Space is provided for a 24-hour continuously staffed secure control center for monitoring and coordinating the facility's security, life safety, and communications systems. Staff assigned to a control center have access to a toilet and washbasin. There are multiple communication systems between the control center and inmate occupied areas.**

COMMENT: None.

PROTOCOLS: Written policy and procedure. Facility plans/specifications. Staff plan and schedules.

PROCESS INDICATORS: Facility records and logs. Observation. Maintenance records. Staff deployment records. Staff interviews.

4-ALDF-2A-02 **Deleted January 2007.**

4-ALDF-2A-05 **Revised January 2013. Inmates classified as medium or maximum security risks are personally observed by an officer twice per hour, but no more than 40 minutes apart, on an irregular schedule. Inmates classified as minimum or low security risks are personally observed by an officer at least every 60 minutes on an irregular schedule.**

COMMENT: None.

PROTOCOLS: Written policy and procedure. Facility plans/specifications.

PROCESS INDICATORS: Observation. Staff and inmate interviews.

4-ALDF-2A-13 **Revised August 2007. Written policy, procedure, and practice require that the chief security officer or qualified designee conduct at least weekly inspections of all security devices noting the items needing repair or maintenance. The inspections are reported in writing to the warden/ superintendent and/or chief security officer.**

COMMENT: None.

PROTOCOLS: Written policy and procedure. Inspection forms and schedule.

PROCESS INDICATORS: Facility logs. Completed inspections forms and reports. Documentation of action taken to correct identified deficiencies. Maintenance records.

4-ALDF-2A-21 **Revised January 2007. Admission processes for a newly admitted inmate include, but are not limited to:**

- **recording basic personal data and information to be used for mail and visiting list**
- **criminal history check**
- **photographing and fingerprinting, including notation of identifying marks or other unusual physical characteristics**
- **assignment of registered number to the inmate**
- **medical, dental, and mental health screening**
- **screening to detect signs of drug/alcohol abuse**
- **suicide screening**
- **inventory of personal property**
- **secure storage of inmate property, including money and other valuables.**

The inmate is given a receipt for all property held until release.

COMMENT: None.

PROTOCOLS: Written policy and procedure. Intake and admission forms. Screening forms. Staff training curriculum. Inventory form. Receipt form.

PROCESS INDICATORS: Observation. Inmate records/files. Intake and admission records. Completed inventory forms. Intake records. Completed receipts.

4-ALDF-2A-23 **Deleted January 2007.**

4-ALDF-2A-27 **Revised August 2013. Prior to being placed in the general population, each inmate is provided with an orientation to the facility, which includes at a minimum:**

- **written information describing facility rules and sanctions**
- **explanation of mail and visiting procedures**
- **explanation of transportation options for visitors**
- **explanation of grievance procedures**

- **explanation of all fees, charges, or copayments that may apply**
- **description of services, programs, and eligibility requirements**
- **information on how to access medical care**
- **identification of available pretrial release options**

This information is provided to inmates in a written and/or electronic format. If the inmate handbook is provided electronically, inmates in segregation are provided the information in a written format so that their access to the information is not impeded by their custody status. The handbook is translated into those languages spoken by significant numbers of inmates.

COMMENT: The use of electronic kiosks is allowed as a means of providing the inmate handbook. Agencies using such kiosks should implement strategies to allow access to this information by general population inmates without interference by facility staff without a valid security-related reason. Inmates who are unable to read and write should be assisted through case management services provided by the facility.

PROTOCOLS: Written policy and procedure. Orientation information and process. Inmate handbook.

PROCESS INDICATORS: Observation. Intake records. Inmate interviews.

4-ALDF-2A-34 **Revised January 2007. Single occupancy cells/rooms are provided when indicated for the following:**

- **maximum and close custody**
- **inmates with severe medical disabilities**
- **inmates suffering from serious mental illness**
- **sexual predators**
- **inmates likely to be exploited or victimized by others**
- **inmates who have other special needs for single-occupancy housing**

No less than 10 percent of the rated capacity of the facility is available for single occupancy.

COMMENT: None.

PROTOCOLS: Written policy and procedure. Process for periodic review and appeal. Inmate handbook. Inmate orientation materials.

PROCESS INDICATORS: Classification records. Documentation of periodic review and appeal. Inmate interviews.

4-ALDF-2A-35 **Deleted January 2007.**

4-ALDF-2A-37 **Revised August 2008. Confinement of juveniles under the age of 18 is prohibited unless a court finds that it is in the best interest of justice and public safety that a juvenile awaiting trial or other legal process be treated as an adult for the purposes of prosecution, or unless convicted as an adult and required by statute to be confined in an adult facility.**

COMMENT: None.

PROTOCOLS: Written policy and procedure.

PROCESS INDICATORS: Observation. Interviews (staff, inmates). Admission and housing.

4-ALDF 2A-50 **Revised August 2008. There is a sanctioning schedule for rule violations. The maximum sanction for rule violations is no more than 60 days for all violations arising out of one incident. Continuous confinement for more than 30 days requires the review and approval of the facility administrator or designee.**

COMMENT: None.

PROTOCOLS: Written policy and procedure. Sanctioning schedule.

PROCESS INDICATORS: Documentation that sanctioning schedule has been communicated to inmates. Inmate interviews. Documentation of facility administrator review or designee approval.

4-ALDF 2A-51 **Interpretation August 2004. The Standards Committee determined that segregation housing does not have to be single celled.**

4-ALDF 2A-52 **Revised August 2011. Written policy, procedure, and practice require that all special management inmates are personally observed by a correctional officer twice per hour, but no more than 40 minutes apart, on an irregular schedule. Inmates who are violent or mentally disordered or who demonstrate unusual or bizarre behavior receive more frequent observation; suicidal inmates are under continuing or continuous observation.**

COMMENT: None.

PROTOCOLS: Written policy and procedure. Staffing plan. Log format.

PROCESS INDICATORS: Facility records and logs. Documentation of cell checks.

4-ALDF 2A-53 **Revised January 2005. Inmates in segregation receive daily visits from the facility administrator or designee, and members of the program staff, on request.**

COMMENT: None.

PROTOCOLS: Written policy and procedure. Log format.

PROCESS INDICATORS: Documentation of administrator/designee visits and health care visits. Inmate interviews. Completed logs.

4-ALDF 2A-54 **Revised August 2007. Staff assigned to work directly with inmates in special management units are selected based on criteria that includes:**

- **completion of probationary period**
- **experience**
- **suitability for this population**

Staff are closely supervised and their performance is documented at least annually. There are provisions for rotation to other duties.

COMMENT: None.

PROTOCOLS: Written policy and procedure. Staff schedule.

PROCESS INDICATORS: Documentation of supervision and rotation of staff. Inmate interviews. Staff interviews.

4-ALDF-2A-55 **Revised January 2007. Staff operating special management units maintain a permanent log that contains at a minimum the following information for each inmate admitted to segregation:**

- **name**
- **number**
- **housing location**
- **date admitted**
- **type of infraction or reason for admission**
- **tentative release date**
- **special medical or psychiatric problems or needs**

Officials who inspect the units, counsel the inmate on his or her behavior, and all releases also use the log to record all visits.

COMMENT: None.

PROTOCOLS: Written policy and procedure. Log format.

PROCESS INDICATORS: Completed log. Inmate records.

4-ALDF-2A-59 **(Revised January 2011): Alternative meal service may be provided to an inmate who uses food or food service equipment in a manner that is hazardous to self, staff, or other inmates. Alternative meal service is on an individual basis, is based on health or safety considerations only, meets basic nutritional requirements, and occurs with the written approval of the warden/superintendent, or designee and responsible health authority, or designee. The substitution period shall not exceed seven days.**

COMMENT: None.

PROTOCOLS: Written policy and procedure.

PROCESS INDICATORS: Documentation of approval. Segregation log. Inmate interviews.

4-ALDF-2B-02-1 **Added August 2008. Written policy, procedure and practice, in general, prohibit the use of restraints on female offenders during active labor and the delivery of a child. Any deviation from the prohibition requires approval by, and guidance on, methodology from the medical authority and is based on documented serious security risks. The medical authority provides guidance on the use of restraints on pregnant offenders prior to active labor and delivery.**

COMMENT: Restraints on pregnant offenders during active labor and the delivery of a child should only be used in extreme instances and should not be applied for more time than is absolutely necessary. Restraints used on pregnant offenders prior to active labor and delivery should not put the pregnant offender nor the fetus at risk.

PROTOCOLS: Written policy and procedure.

PROCESS INDICATORS: Escort logs. Inmate records. Medical records.

4-ALDF-2B-03 **Revised January 2011 (Mandatory). Four/five point restraints are used only in extreme instances and only when other types of restraints have proven ineffective or the safety of the inmate is in jeopardy. Advance approval is secured from the facility administrator/designee before an inmate is placed in a four/five point restraint. Subsequently, the health authority or designee must be notified to assess the inmate's medical and mental health condition, and to advise whether, on the basis of serious danger to self or others, the inmate should be in a medical/mental health unit for emergency involuntary treatment with sedation and/or other medical management, as appropriate. If the inmate is not transferred to a medical/mental health unit and is restrained in a four/five point position, the following minimum procedures are followed: direct visual observation by staff is continuous prior to obtaining approval from the health authority or designee; subsequent visual observation is made at least every 15 minutes; restraint procedures are in accordance with guidelines approved by the designated health authority; all decisions and actions are documented.**

COMMENT: A four/five point restraint secures an inmate's arms and legs (four point) and head (five point). Restraint guidelines include consideration of an individual's physical conditions, such as body weight.

PROTOCOLS: Written policy and procedure, forms.

PROCESS INDICATORS: Observation, facility records and logs, interviews with inmates and staff, documentation of approval(s) and observation.

4-ALDF-2B-06 **Revised January 2008. The facility maintains a record of routine and emergency distribution of security equipment. Firearms, chemical agents, and related security equipment are inventoried at least monthly to determine their condition and expiration dates.**

COMMENT: Written policy should delineate the process by which security equipment is distributed from the primary issue point to control points for both routine and emergency issuance. The policy should address how the facility tracks the issuance of security equipment (written log, chit system, and so forth) and the accountability of security equipment at the end of the shift.

PROTOCOLS: Written policy and procedure.

PROCESS INDICATORS: Completed distribution records. Completed inventory forms.

4-ALDF-2C-01 **Revised January 2007. Procedures guide searches of facilities and inmates to control contraband.**

COMMENT: None.

PROTOCOLS: Written policy and procedure. Search procedures.

PROCESS INDICATORS: Observation. Facility records and logs. Inmate and staff interviews.

4-ALDF 4A-09 **Revised August 2004. Therapeutic diets are provided as prescribed by appropriate clinicians. A therapeutic diet manual is available in health services and food services for reference and information. Prescriptions for therapeutic diets should be specific and complete, furnished in writing to the food service manager, and rewritten annually, or more often as clinically indicated.**

COMMENT: Therapeutic diets are prepared and served to offenders according to the orders of the treating clinician or as directed by the responsible health authority. Therapeutic diets should be kept as simple as possible and should conform as closely as possible to the foods served other offenders.

PROTOCOLS: Written policy and procedures. Diet manual. Diet request form.

PROCESS INDICATORS: Health records. Diet records or forms. Observation. Interviews.

4-ALDF 4A-12-1 **Deleted August 2013.**

4-ALDF 4A-16 **Revised August 2005. Stored shelf goods are maintained at 45 degrees to 80 degrees Fahrenheit, refrigerated foods at 35 degrees to 40 degrees Fahrenheit, and frozen foods at 0 degrees Fahrenheit or below, unless national or state health codes specify otherwise. Temperatures are checked and recorded daily.**

COMMENT: None.

PROTOCOLS: Written policy and procedure. Report and log formats.

PROCESS INDICATORS: Observation. Measurement. Documentation of daily temperature checks.

4-ALDF-4B-02 **Revised August 2007. Written policy, procedure, and practice provide for the issue of suitable, clean bedding and linen, including two sheets, pillow and pillowcase, one mattress, not to exclude a mattress with integrated pillow, and sufficient blankets to provide comfort under existing temperature controls. There is provision for linen exchange, including towels, at least weekly. Blanket exchange must be available at least quarterly.**

COMMENT: None.

PROTOCOLS: Written policy and procedure.

PROCESS INDICATORS: Documentation of issue and exchange.

4-ALDF 4C-24 **Interpretation January 2004 (Mandatory). The criterion for testing for venereal diseases is at the discretion of the agency's/facility's health authority.**

4-ALDF 4C-30 **Revised August 2005 (Mandatory). Inmates who are referred as a result of the mental health screening or by staff referral will receive a mental health appraisal by a qualified mental health person within 14 days of admission to the facility. If there is documented evidence of a mental health appraisal within the previous 90 days, a new mental health appraisal is not required, except as determined by the designated mental health authority. Mental health examinations include, but are not limited to:**

- **assessment of current mental status and condition**
- **assessment of current suicidal potential and person-specific circumstances that increase suicide potential**

- **assessment of violence potential and person-specific circumstances that increase violence potential**
- **review of available historical records of inpatient and outpatient psychiatric treatment**
- **review of history of treatment with psychotropic medication**
- **review of history of psychotherapy, psycho-educational groups, and classes or support groups**
- **review of history of drug and alcohol treatment**
- **review of educational history**
- **review of history of sexual abuse-victimization and predatory behavior**
- **assessment of drug and alcohol abuse and/or addiction**
- **use of additional assessment tools, as indicated**
- **referral to treatment, as indicated**
- **development and implementation of a treatment plan, including recommendations concerning housing, job assignment, and program participation**

COMMENT: None.

PROTOCOLS: Written policy and procedure. Mental health appraisal form.

PROCESS INDICATORS: Health records. Completed mental health appraisal forms. Transfer logs. Interviews.

4-ALDF 4D-05

Revised January 2005 (Mandatory). All professional staff comply with applicable state and federal licensure, certification, or registration requirements. Verification of current credentials is on file in the facility.

COMMENT: None.

PROTOCOLS: Written policy and procedure. Copies of licensure requirements.

PROCESS INDICATORS: Personnel record. Documentation of licensure, certification, or registration. Documentation of current credentials.

4-ALDF-4D-11

Revised August 2008. Unless prohibited by state law, offenders (under staff supervision) may perform familial duties commensurate with their level of training. These duties may include:

- **providing peer support and education**
- **engaging in hospice activities**
- **assisting impaired offenders on a one-on-one basis with activities of daily living**
- **serving as suicide companion or buddy, if qualified and trained through a formal program that is part of suicide-prevention plan**
- **handling dental instruments for the purpose of sanitizing and cleaning, when directly supervised and in compliance with applicable tool control policies, while in a dental assistant's training program certified by the state department of education or other comparable appropriate authority**

Offenders are not to be used for the following duties:

- **performing direct patient care services**
- **scheduling health care appointments**
- **determining access of other offenders to health care services**
- **handling or having access to surgical instruments, syringes, needles, medications, or health records**
- **operating diagnostic or therapeutic equipment except under direct supervision (by specially trained staff) in a vocational training program**

COMMENT: None.

PROTOCOLS: Written policy and procedure. Copies of licensure requirements.

PROCESS INDICATORS: Personnel records. Documentation of licensure, certification, or registration. Documentation of current credentials.

NOTE: This standard was incorrectly identified as 4-ALDF-6B-06 in the *2010 Standards Supplement.*

4-ALDF 4D-20

Revised January 2005. Due process is ensured prior to a transfer that results in an inmate's placement in a non-correctional facility or in a special unit within the facility or agency, specifically designated for the care and treatment of the severely mentally ill or developmentally disabled. Procedures for transfer comply with federal, state, and local law. In emergency situations, a hearing is held as soon as possible after the transfer.

COMMENT: The following are generally accepted as due process procedures: written notice to the inmate of the proposed transfer; a hearing for the inmate, with the right, unless limited for good cause, to call and cross-examine witnesses; a decision by an independent official not involved in treatment of the inmate, with a statement of the reasons for transfer; and an independent adviser to assist the inmate facing transfer.

PROTOCOLS: Written policy and procedure. State and local law.

PROCESS INDICATORS: Health records. Transfer logs. Interviews.

4-ALDF 4D-22

Deleted August 2005. This standard was deleted because it was a duplicate of 4-ALDF-2A-29. Standards 4-ALDF-4D-22-1 through 4-ALDF-4D-22-8 are still in effect, as originally published.

4-ALDF-5B-10

Revised August 2006. Excluding weekends and holidays, or emergency situations, incoming and outgoing letters are held for no more than 48 hours and packages (if allowed) are held no more than 72 hours.

COMMENT: An *emergency situation* is defined as any significant disruption of normal facility or agency procedure, policy, or activity caused by riot, escape, fire, natural disaster, employee action, or other serious incident.

PROTOCOLS: Written policy and procedure.

PROCESS INDICATORS: Mail records and logs.

4-ALDF-5B-18 **Revised January 2007. Procedures for releasing inmates from the facility at the end of their term include, but are not limited to, the following:**

- **identification of outstanding warrants, wants, or detainers**
- **verification of identity**
- **verification of release papers**
- **completion of release arrangements, including notification of the parole authorities in the jurisdiction of release, if required**
- **return of personal property**
- **verification that no facility property leaves the facility**
- **arrangements for completion of any pending action, such as grievances or claims for damages or lost possessions**
- **medical screening and arrangements for community follow-up, where needed, to include medication**
- **instructions for forwarding or return of mail**

COMMENT: None.

PROTOCOLS: Written policy and procedure. Release forms and procedures.

PROCESS INDICATORS: Completed release forms and documents. Facility records and logs. Inmate records. Observations.

4-ALDF-5C-04 **Revised August 2013. Segregation units have either outdoor uncovered or outdoor covered exercise areas. The minimum space requirements for outdoor exercise areas for segregation units are as follows:**

- **Group yard modules: 330-square feet of unencumbered space can accommodate two inmates. For each additional 150-square feet of unencumbered space, an additional inmate may use the exercise area simultaneously. (Formula: for each 150 square feet of unencumbered space exceeding the base requirement of 180 square feet for the first inmate, equals the maximum number of inmates who may use the recreation area space simultaneously). No more than five inmates are to use a group module at one time.**
- **Individual yard modules: 180 square feet of unencumbered space**

In cases where cover is not provided to mitigate the inclement weather, appropriate weather-related equipment and attire should be made available to the inmates who desire to take advantage of their authorized exercise time.

COMMENT: None.

PROTOCOLS: Written policy and procedure. Facility plans/specifications. Schedules.

PROCESS INDICATORS: Observation. Measurement. Facility logs and activity records.

4-ALDF-5C-20

Revised August 2004. Written policy, procedure, and practice provide that assigned chaplain(s)(whether they be classified employees, contract employees, or volunteers), in consultation with and approval from facility administration, plans, directs, and supervises all aspects of the religious program, including approval and training of both lay and clergy volunteers from faiths represented in the inmate population.

COMMENT: None.

PROTOCOLS: Written policy and procedure. Training curriculum. Plan.

PROCESS INDICATORS: Training records. Religious program records. Facility logs and records. Inmate interviews.

4-ALDF-5C-24

Revised January 2012. The chaplain, in cooperation with the institutional administrator or designee, approves donations of equipment or materials for use in religious programs.

COMMENT: Approval of donations helps ensure that equipment and materials are available for approved religious practices and helps avoid the accumulation of duplicate or inappropriate materials.

PROTOCOLS: Written policy and procedure.

PROCESS INDICATORS: Documentation of communications.

4-ALDF-6B-06

Revised August 2008. Appropriately trained individuals are assigned to assist disabled inmates who cannot otherwise perform basic life functions.

COMMENT: None.

PROTOCOLS: Written policy and procedure. Job descriptions. Staffing plan. Training curriculum.

PROCESS INDICATORS: Staff assignment records. Staff training records. Qualifications of persons assigned to assist disabled inmates.

4-ALDF 6C-09

Revised January 2008. Disciplinary hearings are convened as soon as practicable, but no later than seven days, excluding weekends and holidays, after being charged with a violation. Inmates are notified of the hearing at least 24 hours in advance of the hearing.

COMMENT: None.

PROTOCOLS: Written policy and procedure.

PROCESS INDICATORS: Disciplinary records.

4-ALDF 6C-18 **Revised August 2005. Inmates may appeal decisions of the disciplinary hearing officer(s) to the administrator or independent authority. The administrator or independent authority must affirm or reverse the decision of the disciplinary hearing officer(s) within 15 days of the appeal. For facilities that are part of an agency with a systemwide appeal process, the decision to affirm or deny the appeal is made within 30 days.**

COMMENT: None.

PROTOCOLS: Written policy and procedure.

PROCESS INDICATORS: Disciplinary records.

4-ALDF-7B-01 **Revised January 2013. Written policy, procedure, and practice provide that all personnel are selected, retained, and promoted on the basis of merit and specified qualifications. New employees receive credit for their prior training.**

COMMENT: None.

PROTOCOLS: Written policy and procedure. Job descriptions.

PROCESS INDICATORS: Verification of qualifications.

4-ALDF-7B-03 **Revised August 2007. A criminal record check is conducted on all new employees, contractors, and volunteers prior to their assuming duties to identify whether there are criminal convictions that have a specific relationship to job performance. This record will include comprehensive identifier information to be collected and run against law enforcement indices. If suspect information on matters with potential terrorism connections is returned on a desirable applicant, it is forwarded to the local Joint Terrorism Task Force (JTTF) or another similar agency.**

COMMENT: None.

PROTOCOLS: Written policy and procedure.

PROCESS INDICATORS: Personnel records.

4-ALDF 7B-08

Revised January 2005. All new professional and support employees, including contractors, who have regular or daily inmate contact receive training during their first year of employment. Forty hours are completed prior to being independently assigned to a particular job. An additional 40 hours of training is provided each subsequent year of employment. At a minimum, this training covers the following areas:

- **security procedures and regulations**
- **supervision of inmates**
- **signs of suicide risk**
- **suicide precautions**
- **use-of-force regulations and tactics**
- **report writing**
- **inmate rules and regulations**
- **key control**
- **rights and responsibilities of inmates**
- **safety procedures**
- **all emergency plan and procedures**
- **interpersonal relations**
- **social/cultural lifestyles of the inmate population**
- **cultural diversity**
- **communication skills**
- **CPR/first aid**
- **counseling techniques**
- **sexual harassment/sexual misconduct awareness**
- **code of ethics**

COMMENT: None.

PROTOCOLS: Written policy and procedure. Job descriptions. Training curriculum. Training record forms and formats.

PROCESS INDICATORS: Personnel records. Training records.

4-ALDF 7B-10

Revised August 2005. Written policy, procedure, and practice provide that all new correctional officers receive 120 hours of training during their first year of employment. At a minimum, this training covers the following areas:

- **security and safety procedures**
- **emergency and fire procedures**
- **supervision of offenders**
- **suicide intervention/prevention**
- **use of force**
- **offender rights**
- **key control**
- **interpersonal relations**
- **communication skills**
- **standards of conduct**
- **cultural awareness**
- **sexual abuse/assault intervention**
- **code of ethics**

Additional topics may be added at the discretion of the agency or facility.

COMMENT: Since the duties of correctional officers frequently involve most institutional operations, their training should be comprehensive.

PROTOCOLS: Written policy and procedure. Job descriptions. Training curriculum. Training record forms and formats.

PROCESS INDICATORS: Personnel records. Training records.

4-ALDF 7B-10-1

Added August 2005. Written policy, procedure, and practice provide that all correctional officers receive at least 40 hours of annual training. This training shall include at a minimum the following areas:

- **standards of conduct/ethics**
- **security/safety/fire/medical/emergency procedures**
- **supervision of offenders including training on sexual abuse and assault**
- **use of force**

Additional topics shall be included based upon a needs assessment of both staff and institution requirements.

COMMENT: This training will enable employees to sharpen skills, maintain certification and keep abreast of changes in policies, procedures, and legislative, judicial or executive actions.

PROTOCOLS: Written policy and procedure. Job descriptions. Training curriculum. Training record forms and formats.

PROCESS INDICATORS: Personnel records. Training records.

4-ALDF-7B-12

Revised August 2007. Written policy, procedure, and practice provide that correctional officers assigned to an emergency unit have at least one year of corrections and 40 hours of specialized training before undertaking their assignments. Other staff must have at least one year of experience in their specialty within a correctional setting. The specialized training may be part of their first-year training program. Officers and staff assigned to emergency units receive 40 hours of training annually, at least 16 of which are specifically related to emergency unit assignment.

COMMENT: None.

PROTOCOLS: Written policy and procedure. Job descriptions. Training curriculum. Training records and formats.

PROCESS INDICATORS: Personnel records. Training records.

4-ALDF-7C-01

Revised January 2012. The facility and administration affirm support for a drug-free workplace for all employees. The policy includes at a minimum:

- **prohibition of the use of illegal drugs**
- **prohibition of possession of any illegal drug except in the performance of official duties**
- **the procedures to be used to ensure compliance**
- **the opportunities available for treatment and/or counseling for drug abuse**
- **the penalties for violation of the policy**

COMMENT: None.

PROTOCOLS: Written policy and procedure. Drug-free workplace plan.

PROCESS INDICATORS: Staff interviews. Personnel records.

4-ALDF-7D-01-1

Added August 2010. The facility/agency shall demonstrate it has examined, and where appropriate and feasible, implemented strategies that promote recycling, energy and water conservation, pollution reduction, and utilization of renewable energy alternatives.

COMMENT: Correctional facilities and programs have the responsibility to implement strategies that allow correctional facilities to be managed in ways that are most cost-effective and deliver superior performance, while improving environmental responsibility and sustainability. This includes recycling (including paper, metal, and plastic products), energy conservation (including building insulation, heating and ventilation, temperature controls, vehicle fuel efficiency, water economies, physical plant engineering, and energy measures), pollution reduction (including composting sewer treatment, litter abatement, and carbon emissions), and utilization of renewable energy alternatives (bio-fuels, solar collection, turbine energy production, and methane collection).

PROTOCOLS: Written policy and procedure.

PROCESS INDICATORS: Observation. Log sheets. Documentation of services.

4-ALDF-7D-06

Revised January 2007. Written policies and procedures describe all facets of facility operation maintenance, and administration, and are reviewed annually. These are available to all employees unless security concerns justify limited access.

COMMENT: None.

PROTOCOLS: Written policy and procedure. Policy and procedure manual. Distribution lists.

PROCESS INDICATORS: Documentation of annual review.

4-ALDF 7D-12

Revised August 2005. The facility or parent agency fiscal process includes an independent financial audit of the facility annually, or as stipulated by statute or regulation, but at least every three years.

COMMENT: None.

PROTOCOLS: Written policy and procedure. Statutes and regulations.

PROCESS INDICATORS: Completed audits.

4-ALDF-7E-02

Revised August 2010. The institution maintains a current, accurate, confidential personnel record on each employee except where state statues require open public records and the personnel record cannot be maintained confidentially. Information obtained as part of a required medical examination (and/or inquiry) regarding the medical condition or history of applicants and employees is collected and maintained on separate forms and in separate medical files and treated as a confidential medical record.

COMMENT: None.

PROTOCOLS: Written policies and procedures. Statutes and regulations.

PROCESS INDICATORS: Personnel records.

4-ALDF-7G-01

Added January 2007.

Added new section: Security Threat Groups

Written policy, procedure, and practice require that ongoing, but not less than semi-annually, consultation takes place as determined by the agency or parent agency with the local Joint Terrorism Task Force (JTTF), or another similar agency, on all terrorism matters to include:

- **a list of known terrorist inmates in local custody**
- **intelligence regarding inmates with suspected terrorist ties**
- **information regarding specific incidents, events, or threats affecting the institution or detention facility that have a possible terrorism connection**

COMMENT: Examples of reportable intelligence might include attempts by such inmates to radicalize or recruit among fellow inmates, or efforts to continue contact with terrorist groups in the community. Documentation of the consultations should be determined by agency standards, and may include log books, e-mails exchanged with the JTTF or another like agency, or minutes of telephone calls.

PROTOCOLS: Written policy and procedure.

PROCESS INDICATORS: Inmate files/records. Completed logs. Staff interviews. Written correspondence with JTTF or like agency.

Adult Parole Authorities (APA), 2nd Edition

2-1012 **Revised August 1986. The parole authority has a written description and an organizational chart that accurately reflect the structure of authority, responsibility, and accountability within the agency. These documents are reviewed at least annually and are updated, if needed.**

COMMENT: A current organizational chart is necessary for providing a clear administrative picture. The chart should reflect the grouping of similar functions, the effective span of control, lines of authority, and an orderly channel of communication.

2-1020 **Deleted March 1983.**

Added August 2002. Written policy, procedure, and practice prohibit discrimination on the basis of disability in the provision of services, programs, and activities administered for program beneficiaries and participants.

COMMENT: None.

2-1021 **Deleted January 1988.**

2-1022 **Revised January 1988. The parole authority has a written set of long-range goals and objectives. They are reviewed, updated as needed, and evaluated for progress in meeting long-range goals.**

COMMENT: Long-range goals and objectives indicate that the parole authority is progressively preparing for the future.

2-1035 **Revised March 1983. At least two-thirds of the members of the parole authority have at least a baccalaureate degree or have completed a career development program that includes work-related experience, training, or college credits providing a level of achievement equivalent to the bachelor's degree.**

COMMENT: A parole authority must have a capacity for policy formulation and articulation, an awareness of contemporary research findings, correctional techniques, and skills in system planning and management.

2-1049 **Deleted January 1988.**

2-1050 **Revised January 1988. Written policy and procedure provide that the agency can document when deficiencies are noted in the implementation of its affirmative action program. The program is approved by the appropriate government agency, and is reviewed annually.**

COMMENT: An affirmative action program should contain necessary guidelines to accomplish the public policy goal of equal employment opportunity. All persons should be able to compete equally for entry into and promotion within the organization. The program also should be designed to seek out qualified minority groups and women.

2-1050-1 **Added January 1993. Written policy, procedure, and practice prohibit sexual harassment.**

COMMENT: Agency administrators should have as their objective the creation of a workplace that is free from all forms of discrimination, including sexual harassment. Agency policy clearly indicates that sexual harassment, either explicit or implicit, is strictly prohibited. Employees and agents of the agency, including volunteers, contractors, and vendors, must be advised that they are subject to disciplinary action, including dismissal and termination of contracts and/or services, if found guilty of sexual harassment charges brought by employees or inmates.

2-1051 **Deleted March 1983.**

2-1055 **Revised August 2005. Written policy, procedure, and practice provide that the authority's staff development training programs are planned, coordinated, and supervised by qualified employees. The training plan is reviewed annually.**

COMMENT: A qualified staff member, possibly in the parent agency, should have responsibility for planning and implementing the training program and coordinating it with other employee programs. While training may be conducted through institutes or other outside resources, the staff person coordinating the program should receive specialized training in the fundamentals of training and staff development.

2-1056-1 **Added August 1985. The training curriculum is developed, evaluated, and updated based on an annual needs assessment that identifies current job-related training needs.**

COMMENT: Training should be responsive to job requirements; professional development needs; new theories, techniques, and technologies; and current correctional issues. A needs assessment may entail observation and analysis of job tasks and components, surveys of staff to identify perceived training needs, reviews of agency/facility operations, reports and documents generated by staff, and use of previously developed resources in this area, with recommendations and specific objectives for training to be made based on findings from these efforts.

2-1059 **Revised April 1985. Parole authority members and all full-time employees, except clerical/support staff, receive a minimum of 40 hours of relevant training and education annually in addition to administrative staff meetings. Full-time clerical and support employees receive at least 16 hours of training annually.**

COMMENT: The authority's staff must have regular opportunities for training and continuing education related to their various functions as well as to broader issues involved in the authority's activities. Training may include: decision-making skills; new changes in law; court decisions; correctional policies and programs; communication skills; problem solving; reports on research; and specialized training for support staff. Such training may be in the form of relevant courses at colleges, universities, and professional institutes.

2-1074-1 **Added January 1988. Written policy and procedure provide that victims are given an opportunity to present information to the paroling authority. If requested, the parole authority notifies victims of the parole decision in writing.**

COMMENT: Victims should be given the opportunity to be involved in the parole process. They deserve to be informed of the outcome of the related case (if they choose to do so). They should have the opportunity to present their views of the offender to the paroling authority.

2-1076 **Deleted March 1983.**

2-1079 **Revised March 1983. The parole authority and the agency of which it may be a part have a written policy regarding the confidential nature of individual case information and have put into effect specific rules as to the source of the information, the persons who may have access to such information, and the staff who are responsible for the release of that information.**

COMMENT: Protection of the confidentiality of material available to the authority on individual cases is essential. The authority should have procedures that are clearly understood and that include the designation of the persons responsible for the release of case information as well as those to whom that information may be released. (*See* related standard 2-1064.)

2-1092-1 **Added January 1988. Written policy and procedure provide that inmates shall be allowed to have a representative present at all parole hearings.**

COMMENT: None.

2-1096-1 **Added January 1988. Written policy and procedure provide for a process that allows an inmate to appeal a decision to the paroling authority within 60 days of notification or a reasonable time constraint, as specified by the jurisdiction.**

COMMENT: None.

2-1099 **Revised January 1990. General conditions for release that apply to all parolees and mandatory releases under supervision include, at a minimum, requirements that a parolee observe the law, maintain appropriate contact with the parole system, have a visible means of support or a reasonable assurance of support, and notify the parole agency of changes of residence.**

COMMENT: None.

2-1102 **Revised August 1983. Written copies of the conditions of parole are furnished to the parolee and are explained to him or her. The parolee acknowledges in writing that he or she has received and understands the conditions, or there is certification to that effect.**

COMMENT: Conditions of parole should be reviewed with the parolee so that he or she fully understands them. A regular program should exist in the institution to assist parolees in understanding the conditions of their release and in dealing with any problems involved in their release plans.

2-1103 **Deleted August 1983.**

2-1117 **Interpretation March 1983. If the parolee is in jail pending a trial on new charges, must the revocation hearing be conducted within 60 days? No, the revocation hearing must be conducted within 60 days of return to prison on a finding of probable cause for a parole violation at a preliminary hearing that may be conducted after the trial on new charges. This conclusion is supported by the Supreme Court decision in *Moody v. Daggett,* 429 US 78 (1976).**

NOTE: In most cases, the issue of probation and parole violation is not addressed until new charges have been resolved.

2-1128-1 **Added January 1992. Written policy, procedure, and practice provide that consistent with the law of the jurisdiction, there is a system for providing notification to the registered victim(s) of a crime prior to any release from confinement of the convicted offender and/or escape from custody. Follow-up notification to victim(s) occurs when escapees are returned to custody.**

COMMENT: An increasing number of jurisdictions are requiring notification of the victims of criminal act(s) prior to release of the person(s) convicted of the crime. When such legislation exists, the agency should provide the staff with a clear set of instructions to implement the legislation.

2-1130 **Added August 1993. Written policy, procedure, and practice establish the agency's commitment to informing the public and the media of events within the agency's areas of responsibility. The procedures address emergency and nonemergency responses to the media and, at a minimum, include the following:**

- **the identification of areas in the facility that are accessible to media representatives**
- **the contact person for routine requests for information**
- **identification of data and information protected by federal or state privacy laws, or federal and state freedom of information laws**
- **special events coverage**
- **news release policy**
- **the designation of individuals or positions within the agency authorized to speak with the media on behalf of the agency**

COMMENT: The complexity of the policy statement should be consistent with the size and complexity of the operation.

Performance-Based Standards for Adult Probation and Parole Field Services (APPFS), 4th Edition

4-APPFS-3D-05-1

Added August 2010. The facility/agency shall demonstrate it has examined, and where appropriate and feasible, implemented strategies that promote recycling, energy and water conservation, pollution reduction and utilization of renewable energy alternatives.

COMMENT: Correctional facilities and programs have the responsibility to implement strategies that allow correctional facilities to be managed in ways that are most cost-effective and deliver superior performance, while improving environmental responsibility and sustainability. This includes recycling (including paper, metal, and plastic products), energy conservation (including building insulation, heating and ventilation, temperature controls, vehicle fuel efficiency, water economies, physical plant engineering, and energy measures), pollution reduction (including composting, sewer treatment, litter abatement, and carbon emissions), and utilization of renewable energy alternatives (bio-fuels, solar collection, turbine energy production, and methane collection).

PROTOCOLS: Written policy and procedure. Plan, objectives.

PROCESS INDICATORS: Agency records

4-APPFS-3D-28

Revised January 2012. Written agency policy, procedure and practice governing case record management includes, but is not limited to, the establishment, use, content, privacy, security, preservation, and destruction of case records.

COMMENT: None.

PROTOCOLS: Written policy and procedure.

PROCESS INDICATORS: Agency records. Observation.

4-APPFS-3E-12

Revised August 2010. The institution maintains a current, accurate, confidential personnel record on each employee except where state statues require open public records and the personnel record cannot be maintained confidentially. Information obtained as part of a required medical examination (and/or inquiry) regarding the medical condition or history of applicants and employees is collected and maintained on separate forms and in separate medical files and is treated as a confidential medical record.

COMMENT: The personnel record should contain the following: initial application; reference letters; results of employment investigation; verification of training and experience; wage and salary information; job performance evaluations; incident reports, if any; and commendations and disciplinary actions, if any.

PROTOCOLS: Written policy and procedure. Format for personnel records.

PROCESS INDICATORS: Staff records. Observation (provisions for confidentiality).

Core Jail Standards (CORE), 1st Edition

1-CORE-1A-10

Revised August 2013. A ventilation system supplies at least 15 cubic feet per minute of circulated air per occupant, with a minimum of five cubic feet per minute of outside air. Toilet rooms and cells with toilets have no less than four air changes per hour unless state or local codes require a different number of air changes. Air quantities are documented by a qualified technician and are checked not less than once per accreditation cycle. Temperatures are mechanically raised or lowered to acceptable comfort levels.

COMMENT: None.

1-CORE-2A-15

Revised August 2013. Prior to being placed in the general population, each inmate is provided with an orientation that includes facility rules and regulations, including access to medical care. Facility rules and regulations are available during their confinement. The written and/or electronic materials are translated into those languages spoken by a significant number of inmates.

COMMENT: The use of electronic kiosks is allowed as a means of providing the inmate handbook. Agencies using such kiosks should implement strategies to allow access to this information by general population inmates without interference by facility staff without a valid security-related reason. Inmates who are unable to read and write should be assisted through case management services provided by the facility.

1-CORE-2A-24

Revised January 2013. Inmates classified as medium or maximum security risks are personally observed by an officer twice per hour, but no more than 40 minutes apart, on an irregular schedule. Inmates classified as minimum or low security risks are personally observed by an officer at least every 60 minutes on an irregular schedule.

COMMENT: None.

1-CORE-2B-03-1

Added August 2008. Written policy, procedure and practice, in general, prohibit the use of restraints on female offenders during active labor and the delivery of a child. Any deviation from the prohibition requires approval by, and guidance on, methodology from the medical authority and is based on documented serious security risks. The medical authority provides guidance on the use of restraints on pregnant offenders prior to active labor and delivery.

COMMENT: None.

1-CORE-4A-03-1 **Revised August 2011. All staff, contractors, and inmate workers who work in the food service department are trained in the use of food service equipment and in the safety procedures to be followed in the food service department.**

COMMENT: None.

1-CORE-5C-03 **Revised August 2013. Segregation units have either outdoor uncovered or outdoor covered exercise areas. The minimum space requirements for outdoor exercise areas for segregation units are as follows:**

- **Group yard modules: 330 square feet of unencumbered space can accommodate two inmates. For each additional 150 square feet of unencumbered space, an additional inmate may use the exercise area simultaneously. (Formula: for each 150 square feet of unencumbered space exceeding the base requirement of 180 square feet for the first inmate, equals the maximum number of inmates who may use the recreation area space simultaneously). No more than five inmates are to use a group module at one time.**
- **Individual yard modules: 180 square feet of unencumbered space**

In cases where cover is not provided to mitigate the inclement weather, appropriate weather-related equipment and attire should be made available to the inmates who desire to take advantage of their authorized exercise time.

COMMENT: None.

1-CORE-7D-01-1 **Revised August 2010. The facility/agency shall demonstrate it has examined, and where appropriate and feasible, implemented strategies that promote recycling, energy and water conservation, pollution reduction and utilization of renewable energy alternatives.**

COMMENT: Correctional facilities and programs have the responsibility to implement strategies that allow correctional facilities to be managed in ways that are most cost-effective and deliver superior performance, while improving environmental responsibility and sustainability. This includes recycling (including paper, metal, and plastic products), energy conservation (including building insulation, heating and ventilation, temperature controls, vehicle fuel efficiency, water economies, physical plant engineering, and energy measures), pollution reduction (including composting, sewer treatment, litter abatement, and carbon emissions), and utilization of renewable energy alternatives (bio-fuels, solar collection, turbine energy production, and methane collection).

Performance-Based Standards for Correctional Health Care in Adult Correctional Institutions (HC), 1st Edition

In the original publication of the manual on page xxi, Summary of Mandatory Expected Practices, standard 1-HC-1A-37 was inadvertently omitted from the list.

1-HC-1A-03

Revised January 2006 (Ref. 4-4346). There is a process for all offenders to initiate requests for health services on a daily basis. These requests are triaged daily by qualified health care professionals or health-trained personnel. A priority system is used to schedule clinical services. Clinical services are available to offenders in a clinical setting at least five days a week and are performed by a health care practitioner or other qualified health care professional.

COMMENT: A priority system addresses routine, urgent, and emergent complaints and conditions. Health care request forms must be readily available to all offenders. Clinical services include sick call, nursing assessments, and chronic care.

PROTOCOLS: Written policy and procedure. Sick call request forms.

PROCESS INDICATORS: A health record. Sick call request forms. Clinical provider schedules. Observation. Interviews.

1-HC-1A-04

Revised January 2006 (Ref. 4-4347). Continuity of care is required from admission to transfer or discharge from the facility, including referral to community-based providers, when indicated. Offender health care records should be reviewed by the facility's qualified health care professional upon arrival from outside health care entities including those from inside the correctional system.

COMMENT: When health care is transferred to providers in the community, appropriate information should be shared with the new providers in accordance with consent requirements.

PROTOCOLS: Written policy and procedure. Referral transfer form.

PROCESS INDICATORS: Completed referral transfer forms. Health records. Facility logs. Interviews.

1-HC-1A-05

Revised January 2006 (Ref. 4-4348). Offenders who need health care beyond the resources available in the facility, as determined by the responsible health care practitioner, are transferred under appropriate security provisions to a facility where such care is available. There is a written list of referral sources to include emergency and routine care. The list is reviewed and updated annually.

COMMENT: Treatment of an offender's condition should not be limited by the resources and services available within a facility. Health care staff should collaborate with security personnel in determining conditions of transportation and necessary security precautions when an offender needs to be transported to another facility or provider.

PROTOCOLS: Written policy and procedure. Referral consult form.

PROCESS INDICATORS: Health records. Completed referral consult records. Documentation of annual list review. Transportation logs. Interviews.

1-HC-1A-06

Revised January 2006 (Ref. 4-4349). A transportation system that assures timely access to services that are only available outside the correctional facility is required. Such a system needs to address the following issues:

- **prioritization of medical need**
- **urgency (for example, ambulance versus standard transport)**
- **use of medical escort to accompany security staff, if indicated**
- **transfer of medical information**

The safe and timely transportation of offenders for medical, mental health, and dental clinic appointments, both inside and outside the correctional facility (for example, hospital, health care provider, or another correctional facility), is the joint responsibility of the facility or program administrator and the health services administrator.

COMMENT: It is essential that the medical and the custody staff work cooperatively in the design and implementation of the medical transport system. Consideration should balance issues of security as well as medical or psychological concerns about the use of restraint devices that may affect the offender's health condition or access to health care.

PROTOCOLS: Written policy and procedure. Transport form, log.

PROCESS INDICATORS: Health records. Completed transfer forms and log entries. Observations. Interviews.

1-HC-1A-07

Revised January 2006 (Ref. 4-4350). A written, individual treatment plan is required for offenders requiring medical supervision, including chronic and convalescent care. This plan includes directions to health care and other personnel regarding their roles in the care and supervision of the patient, and is developed by the appropriate health care practitioner for each offender requiring a treatment plan.

COMMENT: Offenders requiring treatment plans include the following: the chronically ill, offenders with serious communicable diseases, the physically disabled, pregnant offenders, the terminally ill, offenders with serious mental health needs, and the developmentally disabled.

PROTOCOLS: Written policy and procedure. Treatment plan format.

PROCESS INDICATORS: Health records. Interviews.

1-HC-1A-08

Revised January 2006 (Mandatory). There is a written plan for access to 24-hour emergency medical, dental, and mental health services availability. The plan includes:

- **on-site emergency first aid and crisis intervention**
- **emergency evacuation of the offender from the facility**
- **use of an emergency medical vehicle**
- **use of one or more designated hospital emergency rooms or other appropriate health facilities**
- **emergency on-call or available 24-hours per day, physician, dentist, and mental health professional services when the emergency health facility is not located in a nearby community**
- **security procedures providing for the immediate transfer of offenders, when appropriate**

COMMENT: In the event that primary health services are not available, and particularly in emergency situations, back-up facilities or providers should be predetermined. The plan may include the use of an alternative hospital emergency service or a physician on-call service.

PROTOCOLS: Written policy or procedure.

PROCESS INDICATORS: Designated facility. Provider lists. Transportation logs. Interviews.

1-HC-1A-09

Revised January 2006 (Ref. 4-4352). Offenders are provided access to infirmary care either within the correctional setting or offsite. If infirmary care is provided onsite, it includes, at a minimum, the following:

- **definition of the scope of infirmary care services available**
- **a physician on call or available 24 hours per day**
- **health care personnel have access to a physician or a registered nurse and are on duty 24 hours per day when patients are present**
- **all offenders/patients are within sight or sound of a staff member**
- **an infirmary care manual that includes nursing care procedures**
- **compliance with applicable state statutes and local licensing requirements**

COMMENT: An infirmary, within the correctional setting or a specific area of a health care facility separate from other housing areas, is where offenders are housed and provided health care. Admission and discharge from this area is controlled by medical orders or protocols.

PROTOCOLS: Written policy or procedures. Nursing manual. Licensing requirements and regulations.

PROCESS INDICATORS: Admission and inpatient records. Staffing schedules. Documentation of compliance with licensing requirements and regulations. Observation. Interviews.

1-HC-1A-11 **Revised January 2006 (Ref. 4-4354) (Mandatory). There is a written program to address the management of communicable and infectious diseases in offenders. The program plan shall include procedures for:**

- **prevention to include immunizations, when applicable**
- **surveillance (identification and monitoring)**
- **offender education and staff training**
- **treatment to include medical isolation, when indicated**
- **follow-up care**
- **reporting requirements to applicable local, state, and federal agencies**
- **confidentiality/protected health information**
- **appropriate safeguards for offenders and staff**
- **post-exposure management protocols particularly for HIV and viral hepatitis infection**

Communicable disease and infection control activities are discussed and reviewed at least quarterly by a multidisciplinary team that includes clinical, security, and administrative representatives.

COMMENT: Because of the serious nature, methods of transmission, and public sensitivity, communicable and infectious diseases require special attention. Agencies work with the responsible public health authority in establishing policy and procedures.

PROTOCOLS: Written policy; procedure; offender education and staff training curriculums; and treatment guidelines.

PROCESS INDICATORS: Health record entries; communicable and infectious diseases education and training records; minutes of committee meetings addressing communicable and infectious disease management; observations and interviews.

1-HC-1A-11-1 **Added August 2006. The management of offenders with Methicillin Resistant Staphylococcus Aureus (MRSA) infection includes requirements identified in the communicable disease and infection control program. In addition, the program for MRSA management shall include procedures for:**

- **evaluating and treating infected inmates in accordance with an approved practice guideline**
- **medical isolation, when indicated**
- **follow-up care, including arrangements with appropriate health care authorities for continuity of care if offenders are relocated prior to the completion of therapy**

COMMENT: None.

PROTOCOLS: Written policy and procedure. Treatment program.

PROCESS INDICATORS: Health records including laboratory reports, medical isolation logs, treatment plans, observations, and interviews.

1-HC-1A-12

Revised January 2006 (Ref. 4-4355) (Mandatory). Management of tuberculosis (TB) in offenders includes procedures as identified in the communicable disease and infection control program. In addition, the program for TB management shall include procedures for:

- **when and where offenders are to be screened/tested**
- **treatment, of latent tuberculosis infection and tuberculosis disease**
- **medical isolation, when indicated**
- **follow-up care, including arrangement with applicable departments of health for continuity of care if offender is released prior to completion of therapy**

COMMENT: Plans for the management of tuberculosis may be based on incidence and prevalence of the disease within the correctional agency's population and the surrounding community.

PROTOCOLS: Written policy; procedure and treatment guidelines.

PROCESS INDICATORS: Health records including tuberculosis testing, x-ray reports, laboratory reports, treatment plans, observations, and interviews.

1-HC-1A-13

Revised January 2006 (Ref. 4-4356) (Mandatory). Management of hepatitis A, B, and C in offenders includes procedures as identified in the communicable disease and infection control program. In addition, the program for hepatitis management shall include procedures for:

- **when and where offenders are to be tested/screened**
- **hepatitis A and B immunization, when applicable**
- **treatment protocols**
- **when and under what conditions offenders are to be separated from the general population**

COMMENT: None.

PROTOCOLS: Written policy/procedure and treatment guidelines.

PROCESS INDICATORS: Health records including laboratory reports, immunization administration records, and treatment plans; observations and interviews.

1-HC-1A-14

Revised January 2006 (Ref. 4-4357) (Mandatory). Management of HIV infection in offenders includes procedures as identified in the communicable disease and infection control program. In addition, the program for HIV management shall include:

- **when and where offenders are to be HIV tested**
- **pre- and post-test counseling**
- **immunization and other prevention measures, when applicable**
- **treatment protocols**
- **confidentiality/protected health information**
- **when and under what conditions offenders are to be separated from the general population**

COMMENT: None.

PROTOCOLS: Written policy, procedure, and treatment guidelines.

PROCESS INDICATORS: Health records including laboratory reports, pre- and post-test counseling documentation, treatment plans, observations, and interviews.

1-HC-1A-17

Revised January 2006 (Ref. 4-4360). Routine and emergency dental care is provided to each offender under the direction and supervision of a licensed dentist. There is a defined scope of available dental services, including emergency dental care, which includes the following:

- **a dental screening upon admission by a qualified health care professional or health-trained personnel**
- **a full dental examination by a dentist within 30 days**
- **oral hygiene, oral disease education, and self-care instruction are provided by a qualified health care provider within 30 days**
- **a defined charting system that identifies the oral health condition and specifies the priorities for treatment by category is completed**
- **consultation and referral to dental specialists, including oral surgery, is provided, when necessary**

COMMENT: Dental screening is an assessment of dental pain, swelling, or functional impairment. As part of the initial health screening, a dentist or health care personnel properly trained and designated by the dentist should perform dental screenings. The dental program should also provide offenders with instruction on the proper brushing of teeth and other dental hygiene measures.

The dental examination should include a periodontal examination (Periodontal Screening and Recording [PSR] or Community Periodontal Index of Treatment Needs [CPITN]) and taking or reviewing the patient's dental history. An examination of the hard and soft tissues of the oral cavity by means of an illuminator light, mouth mirror, and explorer should be performed. X-rays for diagnostic purposes should be available, if deemed necessary. The result of the dental examination and dental treatment plan are recorded on an appropriate uniform dental record using a numbered system such as the Federation Dental International System.

PROTOCOLS: Written policy and procedure. Dental screening forms. Dental request forms.

PROCESS INDICATORS: Dental records. Admission logs. Referral and consultation records. Dental request forms. Interviews.

1-HC-1A-19

Revised January 2006 (Ref. 4-4362) (Mandatory). Intake medical screening for offender transfers, excluding intra-system, commences upon the offender's arrival at the facility and is performed by health-trained or qualified health care personnel. All findings are recorded on a screening form approved by the health authority. The screening includes at least the following:

Inquiry into:

- **any past history of serious infectious or communicable illness, and any treatment or symptoms (for example, a chronic cough, hemoptysis, lethargy, weakness, weight loss, loss of appetite, fever, night sweats that are suggestive of such illness), and medications**
- **current illness and health problems, including communicable diseases**
- **dental problems**
- **use of alcohol and other drugs, including type(s) of drugs used, mode of use, amounts used, frequency used, date or time of last use, and history of any problems that may have occurred after ceasing use (for example, convulsions)**
- **the possibility of pregnancy and history of problems (female only); and other health problems designated by the responsible physician**

Observation of the following:

- **behavior, including state of consciousness, mental status, appearance, conduct, tremor, and sweating**
- **body deformities, ease of movement, and so forth**
- **condition of the skin, including trauma markings, bruises, lesions, jaundice, rashes and infestations, recent tattoos, and needle marks or other indications of drug abuse**

Medical disposition of the offender:

- **general population**
- **general population with prompt referral to appropriate health care service**
- **referral to appropriate health care service for emergency treatment**

Offenders, who are unconscious, semiconscious, bleeding, or otherwise obviously in need of immediate medical attention, are referred. When they are referred to an emergency department, their admission or return to the facility is predicated on written medical clearance. When screening is conducted by trained custody staff, procedures will require a subsequent review of positive findings by the licensed health care staff. Written procedures and screening protocols are established by the responsible physician in cooperation with the facility manager.

Inmates confined within a correctional complex with consolidated medical services do not require health screening for intra-system transfers.

COMMENT: Health screening is a system of structured inquiry and observation to (1) prevent newly arrived offenders who pose a health or safety threat to themselves or others from being admitted to the general population, and to (2) identify offenders who require immediate medical attention.

Receiving screening can be performed at the time of admission by health care personnel or by a health-trained correctional officer. Facilities that have reception and diagnostic units or a holding room must conduct receiving screening on all offenders on their arrival at the facility as part of the admission procedures.

PROTOCOLS: Written policy and procedure. Screening forms.

PROCESS INDICATORS: Health records. Completed screening forms. Transfer logs. Interviews.

1-HC-1A-22

Revised January 2006 (Ref. 4-4365) (Mandatory). A comprehensive health appraisal for each offender, excluding intra-system transfers, is completed as defined below, after arrival at the facility. If there is documented evidence of a health appraisal within the previous 90 days, a new health appraisal is not required, except as determined by the designated health authority. Health appraisals include the following:
Within 14 days after arrival at the facility:

- **review of the earlier receiving screen**
- **collection of additional data to complete the medical, dental, mental health, and immunization histories**
- **laboratory or diagnostic tests to detect communicable disease, including venereal disease and tuberculosis**
- **record of height, weight, pulse, blood pressure, and temperature**
- **other tests and examinations, as appropriate**

Within 14 days after arrival for inmates with identified significant health care problems:

- **medical examination, including review of mental and dental status (for those inmates with significant health problems discovered on earlier screening, such as cardiac problems, diabetes, communicable diseases, and so forth)**
- **review of the results of the medical examination, tests, and identification of problems by a health care practitioner or other qualified health care professional, if such is authorized in the medical practice act**
- **initiation of therapy, when appropriate**
- **development and implementation of a treatment plan, including recommendations concerning housing, job assignment, and program participation**

Within 30 days after arrival for inmates without significant health care problems:

- **medical examination, including review of mental and dental status (for those inmates without significant health care concerns identified during earlier screening—no identified acute or chronic disease, no identified communicable disease, and so forth)**
- **review of the results of the medical examination, tests, and identification of problems by a health care practitioner or other qualified health care professional, if such is authorized in the medical practice act**
- **initiation of therapy, when appropriate**
- **development and implementation of a treatment plan, including recommendations concerning housing, job assignment, and program participation**

COMMENT: Test results, particularly for communicable diseases, should be received and evaluated before an offender is assigned to housing in the general population. Information regarding the offender's physical and mental status may also dictate housing and activity assignments. When appropriate, additional investigation should be conducted into alcohol and drug abuse and other related problems.

PROTOCOLS: Written policy and procedure. Health appraisal form.

PROCESS INDICATORS: Health records. Completed health appraisal forms. Transfer logs. Interviews.

1-HC-1A-23 **Revised January 2006 (Ref. 4-4366). Health appraisal data collection and recording will include the following:**

- **a uniform process as determined by the health authority**
- **health history and vital signs collected by health-trained or qualified health care personnel**
- **collection of all other health appraisal data performed only by qualified health professional**
- **review of the results of the medical examination, tests**
- **identification of problems is performed by a physician or mid-level practitioner, as allowed by law**

COMMENT: None.

PROTOCOLS: Written policy and procedure.

PROCESS INDICATORS: Health records.

1-HC-1A-24 **Revised January 2006 (Ref. 4-4367). The conditions for periodic health examinations for offenders are determined by the health authority.**

COMMENT: All offenders should receive a thorough physical examination.

PROTOCOLS: Written policy and procedure.

PROCESS INDICATORS: Health records. Completed annual health appraisal forms. Interviews.

1-HC-1A-25 **Revised January 2006 (Ref. 4-4368) (Mandatory). The mental health program is approved by the appropriate mental health authority and includes at a minimum:**

- **screening on intake**
- **outpatient services for the detection, diagnosis, and treatment of mental illness**
- **crisis intervention and the management of acute psychiatric episodes**
- **stabilization of the mentally ill and the prevention of psychiatric deterioration in the correctional setting**

- **elective therapy services and preventive treatment where resources permit**
- **provision for referral and admission to mental health facilities for offenders whose psychiatric needs exceed the treatment capability of the facility**
- **procedures for obtaining and documenting informed consent**

COMMENT: An adequate number of qualified staff members should be available to deal directly with offenders who have severe mental health problems and to advise other correctional staff about their contacts with such individuals.

PROTOCOLS: Written policy and procedure. Screening form.

PROCESS INDICATORS: Health records. Completed screening forms. Provider qualifications and time and attendance records. Observations. Interviews.

1-HC-1A-26 **Deleted January 2006.**

1-HC-1A-27 **Revised January 2006 (Ref. 4-4370) (Mandatory). All intersystem and intra-system transfer offenders will receive an initial mental health screening at the time of admission to the facility by a mental health trained or qualified mental health care professional. The mental health screening includes, but is not limited to:**

Inquiry into:

- **whether the offender has a present suicidal ideation**
- **whether the offender has a history of suicidal behavior**
- **whether the offender is presently prescribed psychotropic medication**
- **whether the offender has a current mental health complaint**
- **whether the offender is being treated for mental health problems**
- **whether the offender has a history of inpatient and outpatient psychiatric treatment**
- **whether the offender has a history of treatment for substance abuse**

Observation of:

- **general appearance and behavior**
- **evidence of abuse and/or trauma**
- **current symptoms of psychosis, depression, anxiety, and/or aggression**

Disposition of offender:

- **to the general population**
- **to the general population with appropriate referral to mental health care service**
- **referral to appropriate mental health care service for emergency treatment**

COMMENT: None.

PROTOCOLS: Written policy and procedure. Mental health screening form.

PROCESS INDICATORS: Health records. Completed mental health screening forms. Transfer logs, interviews.

1-HC-1A-28

Revised January 2006 (Ref. 4-4371) (Mandatory). All intersystem offender transfers will undergo a mental health appraisal by a qualified mental health professional within 14 days of admission to a facility. If there is documented evidence of a mental health appraisal within the previous 90 days, a new mental health appraisal is not required, except as determined by the designated mental health authority. Mental health appraisals include, but are not limited to:

- **review of available historical records of inpatient and outpatient psychiatric treatment**
- **review of history of treatment with psychotropic medication**
- **review of history of psychotherapy, psycho-educational groups, and classes or support groups**
- **review of history of drug and alcohol treatment**
- **review of educational history**
- **review of history of sexual-abuse victimization and predatory behavior**
- **assessment of current mental status and condition**
- **assessment of current suicidal potential and person-specific circumstances that increase suicide potential**
- **assessment of violence potential and person-specific circumstances that increase violence potential**
- **assessment of drug and alcohol abuse and/or addiction**
- **use of additional assessment tools, as indicated**
- **referral to treatment, as indicated**
- **development and implementation of a treatment plan, including recommendations concerning housing, job assignment, and program participation**

COMMENT: None.

PROTOCOLS: Written policy and procedure. Mental health appraisal form.

PROCESS INDICATORS: Health records. Completed mental health appraisal forms. Transfer logs. Interviews.

1-HC-1A-29

Revised January 2006 (Ref. 4-4372). Offenders referred for mental health treatment will receive a comprehensive evaluation by a qualified mental health practitioner. The evaluation is to be completed within 14 days of the referral request date and include at least the following:

- **review of mental health screening and appraisal data**
- **direct observations of behavior**

- **collection and review of additional data from individual diagnostic interviews and tests assessing personality, intellect, and coping abilities**
- **compilation of the individuals mental health history**
- **development of an overall treatment/management plan with appropriate referral to include transfer to mental health facility for offenders whose psychiatric needs exceed the treatment capability of the facility**

COMMENT: Comprehensive individual psychological evaluations should be performed when there is a reasonable expectation that such evaluation will serve a therapeutic or dispositional function useful to the overall interests of the offender. Written reports describing the results of the assessment should be prepared and all information should be appropriately filed.

PROTOCOLS: Written policy and procedure. Mental health referral form.

PROCESS INDICATORS: Health records. Completed referral forms, interview with mental health provider(s). Clinic visit records.

1-HC-1A-32

Revised January 2006 (Ref. 4-4375). Medical or dental adaptive devices (eyeglasses, hearing aids, dentures, wheelchairs, or other prosthetic devices) are provided when medically necessary as determined by the responsible health care practitioner.

COMMENT: Offenders may be required to provide co-payments for these devices.

PROTOCOLS: Written policy and procedure.

PROCESS INDICATORS: Purchase records. Health records. Interviews.

1-HC-1A-33

Revised January 2006 (Ref. 4-4376) (Mandatory). Detoxification is done only under medical supervision in accordance with local, state, and federal laws. Detoxification from alcohol, opiates, hypnotics, other stimulants, and sedative hypnotic drugs is conducted under medical supervision when performed at the facility or is conducted in a hospital or community detoxification center. Specific guidelines are followed for the treatment and observation of individuals manifesting mild or moderate symptoms of intoxication or withdrawal from alcohol and other drugs.

COMMENT: None.

PROTOCOLS: Written policy and procedure. Community contract agreements.

PROCESS INDICATORS: Health records. Transfer records. Interviews.

1-HC-1A-38

Revised August 2004. Therapeutic diets are provided as prescribed by appropriate clinicians. A therapeutic diet manual is available in health services and food services for reference and information. Prescriptions for therapeutic diets should be specific and complete, furnished in writing to the food service manager, and rewritten annually, or more often as clinically indicated.

COMMENT: Therapeutic diets are prepared and served to offenders according to the orders of the treating clinician or as directed by the responsible health authority. Therapeutic diets should be kept as simple as possible and should conform as closely as possible to the foods served other offenders.

PROTOCOLS: Written policy and procedures. Diet manual. Diet request form.

PROCESS INDICATORS: Health records. Diet records or forms. Observation. Interviews.

1-HC-2A-01

Revised January 2006 (Ref. 4-4380) (Mandatory). The facility has a designated health authority with responsibility for ongoing health care services pursuant to a written agreement, contract, or job description. Such responsibilities include:

- **establish a mission statement, which defines the scope of health care services**
- **develop mechanisms, including written agreements, when necessary, to assure that the scope of services are provided and properly monitored**
- **develop a facility's operational health policies and procedures**
- **identify the type of health care staff needed to provide the determined scope of services**
- **establish systems for the coordination of care among multidisciplinary health care providers**
- **develop a quality management program**

The health authority may be a physician or health services administrator for a health agency. When the health authority is other than a physician, final clinical judgments rest with a single, designated, responsible physician. The health authority is authorized and responsible for making decisions about the deployment of health resources and the day-to-day operations of the health services program.

COMMENT: The health authority and health services administrator may be the same person. The responsibility of the health authority includes arranging for all levels of health services, assuring the quality of all health services, and assuring that offenders have access to them. Health services provides for the physical and mental well-being of the offender population and should include medical and dental services, mental health services, nursing care, personal hygiene, dietary services, health education, and attending to environmental conditions. While overall responsibility may be assumed at the central office level, it is essential that each facility have an on-site health services administrator. The health authority and health services administrator may be the same person.

PROTOCOLS: Written policy and procedure. Sample agreement or contract requirements. Job description.

PROCESS INDICATORS: Documentation of health authority designation. Contract. Billing records. Interviews. Documentation of mission statement, operational policies and procedures, scope of services and required personnel, coordination of care, and a quality management program.

1-HC-2A-02 **Revised January 2006 (Ref. 4-4381) (Mandatory). Clinical decisions are the sole province of the responsible health care practitioner and are not countermanded by non-clinicians.**

COMMENT: The provision of health care is a joint effort of administrators and health care providers and can be achieved only through mutual trust and cooperation. The health authority arranges for the availability of health care services; the responsible clinician determines what services are needed; the official responsible for the facility provides the administrative support for making the services accessible to offenders.

PROTOCOLS: Written policy and procedure.

PROCESS INDICATORS: Health record entries. Offender grievances. Interviews.

1-HC-2A-03 **Revised January 2006 (Ref. 4-4382) (Mandatory). If the facility provides health care services, they are provided by qualified health care staff whose duties and responsibilities are governed by written job descriptions, contracts or written agreements approved by the health authority. Verification of current credentials and job descriptions are on file in the facility.**

COMMENT: Job descriptions should include qualifications and specific duties and responsibilities. Verification consists of copies of credentials or a letter confirming credential status from a state licensing or certification body. Standing medical orders are for the definitive treatment of identified conditions and for the on-site emergency treatment of any person having such condition. Direct orders are those written specifically for the treatment of one person's particular condition.

PROTOCOLS: Written policy and procedure. Job descriptions. Standing orders.

PROCESS INDICATORS: Verification of credentials or licensure. Documentation of compliance with standing orders. Health record entries. Interviews.

1-HC-2A-04 **Revised January 2006 (Ref. 4-4383). When institutions do not have qualified health care staff, health-trained personnel coordinate the health delivery services in the institution under the joint supervision of the responsible health authority and the warden or superintendent.**

COMMENT: The health-trained staff member (who is other than a nurse, midlevel practitioner, or emergency medical technician) may be full-time or part-time. Coordination duties may include reviewing receiving screening forms for needed follow-up, readying offenders and their records for sick call, and assisting in carrying out orders regarding such matters as diets, housing, and work assignments.

PROTOCOLS: Written policy and procedure. Job description for health-trained personnel.

PROCESS INDICATORS: Health records. Observation. Interviews.

1-HC-2A-05 **Deleted January 2006.**

1-HC-2A-08 **Revised January 2006 (Ref. 4-4385). All full-time health care staff who have offender contact receive 40 hours of training in addition to orientation training during their first year of employment and 40 hours of training each year thereafter.**

COMMENT: None.

PROTOCOLS: Written policy and procedure.

PROCESS INDICATORS: Training records. Interviews.

1-HC- 2A-09 **Revised January 2006 (Ref. 4-4386). All direct care staff are screened for tuberculosis infection and disease prior to job assignment and periodically in accordance with recommendations from applicable local, state, and federal public health authorities.**

COMMENT: None.

PROTOCOLS: Written policy and procedure.

PROCESS INDICATORS: Employee records. Interviews.

1-HC-2A-10 **Revised January 2006 (Ref. 4-4387). All direct care staff are offered the hepatitis B vaccine series in accordance with the institution's exposure-control plan.**

COMMENT: None.

PROTOCOLS: Written policy and procedure.

PROCESS INDICATORS: Employment records. Interviews.

1-HC-2A-12

Revised January 2012. There is a written agency policy, procedure, and practice that specifies support for a drug-free workplace for all employees. This policy includes at a minimum the following:

- **prohibition of the use of illegal drugs**
- **prohibition of possession of any illegal drug except in the performance of official duties**
- **the opportunities available for treatment and/or counseling for drug abuse**
- **the procedures to be used to ensure compliance**
- **the penalties for violation of the policy**

COMMENT: None.

PROTOCOLS: Written policy and procedure. Drug-free workplace plan.

PROCESS INDICATORS: Documentation of annual review of the plan.

1-HC-2A-13

Revised January 2006 (Ref. 4-4220 and 4-4388) (Mandatory). All health care staff in the facility are trained in the implementation of the facility's emergency plans. Health care staff are included in facility's emergency drills, as applicable.

COMMENT: Emergency plans include those for fire, natural disaster, power outage, hostage situation, riot, and other disturbances.

PROTOCOLS: Written policy and procedure. Facility-plan specifications. A schedule for drills.

PROCESS INDICATORS: Documentation of drills. Facility logs. Interviews.

1-HC-2A-14

Revised January 2006 (Ref. 4-4389) (Mandatory). Designated correctional and all health care staff are trained to respond to health-related situations within a four-minute response time. The training program is conducted on an annual basis and is established by the responsible health authority in cooperation with the facility or program administrator and includes instruction on the following:

- **recognition of signs and symptoms, and knowledge of action required in potential emergency situations**
- **administration of basic first aid**
- **certification in cardiopulmonary resuscitation (CPR) in accordance with the recommendations of the certifying health organization**
- **methods of obtaining assistance**
- **signs and symptoms of mental illness, violent behavior, and acute chemical intoxication and withdrawal**
- **procedures for patient transfers to appropriate medical facilities or health care providers**
- **suicide intervention**

COMMENT: The facility administrator or designee may designate those correctional officers and health care providers who have responsibility to respond to health care emergencies. Staff not physically able to perform CPR are exempt from the expected practice.

PROTOCOLS: Written policy and procedure. Lesson plans and curriculum.

PROCESS INDICATORS: Verification of training. Records and certificates. Interviews.

1-HC-2A-15 **Revised August 2002. First aid kits are available in designated areas of the facility based on need and an automatic external defibrillator is available for use at the facility.**

COMMENT: The availability and placement of first aid kits are determined by the designated health authority in conjunction with the facility administrator. The health authority approves the contents, number, location, and procedures for monthly inspection of the kit(s) and develops written procedures for the use of the kits by nonmedical staff.

PROTOCOLS: Written policy and procedure.

PROCESS INDICATORS: List of first aid kit contents. Documentation of inspections.

1-HC-2A-18 **Revised August 2008. Unless prohibited by state law, offenders (under staff supervision) may perform familial duties commensurate with their level of training. These duties may include:**

- **providing peer support and education**
- **engaging in hospice activities**
- **assisting impaired offenders on a one-on-one basis with activities of daily living**
- **serving as a suicide companion or buddy if qualified and trained through a formal program that is part of a suicide-prevention plan**
- **handling dental instruments for the purpose of sanitizing and cleaning, when directly supervised and in compliance with applicable tool control policies, while in a dental assistant's training program certified by the state department of education or other comparable appropriate authority**

Offenders are not to be used for the following duties:

- **performing direct patient care services**
- **scheduling health care appointments**
- **determining access of other offenders to health care services**
- **handling or having access to surgical instruments, syringes, needles, medications, or health records**
- **operating diagnostic or therapeutic equipment except under direct supervision (by specially trained staff) in a vocational training program**

COMMENT: No offender, or group of offenders, is given control or authority over other offenders in the health care area.

PROTOCOLS: Written policy and procedure.

PROCESS INDICATORS: Observation. Interviews.

1-HC-3A-03

Revised January 2006 (Ref. 4-4396) (Mandatory). The principle of confidentiality applies to offender health records and information about offender health status.

- **The active health record is maintained separately from the confinement case record.**
- **Access to the health record is in accordance with state and federal law.**
- **To protect and preserve the integrity of the facility, the health authority shares with the superintendent/warden information regarding an offender's medical management.**
- **The circumstances are specified when correctional staff should be advised of an offender's health status. Only that information necessary to preserve the health and safety of an offender, other offenders, volunteers/visitors, or the correctional staff is provided.**
- **Policy determines how information is provided to correctional/ classification staff/volunteers/visitors to address the medical needs of the offender as it relates to housing, program placement, security, and transport.**
- **Complies with Health Insurance Portability and Accountability Act (HIPAA), where applicable in a correctional setting.**

COMMENT: The principle of confidentiality protects offender patients from disclosure of confidences entrusted to a health care provider during the course of treatment.

PROTOCOLS: Policy and procedure.

PROCESS INDICATORS: Observation. Interviews.

1-HC-3A-06

Revised January 2006 (Ref. 4-4399). There is consultation between the facility and program administrator (or a designee) and the responsible health care practitioner (or designee) prior to taking action regarding chronically ill, physically disabled, geriatric, seriously mentally ill, or developmentally disabled offenders in the following areas:

- **housing assignments**
- **program assignments**
- **disciplinary measures**
- **transfers to other facilities**

When immediate action is required, consultation to review the appropriateness of the action occurs as soon as possible, but no later than 72 hours.

COMMENT: Maximum cooperation between custody personnel and health care providers is essential so that both groups are aware of decisions and movements regarding mentally ill and developmentally disabled offenders.

PROTOCOLS: Written policy and procedure.

PROCESS INDICATORS: Documentation of consultation between facility or program administrator and clinician. Health records. Interviews.

1-HC-3A-06-1

Added January 2002. Written policy, procedure, and practice provide for the assignment of appropriately trained, individuals to assist disabled offenders who cannot otherwise perform basic life functions.

COMMENT: None.

PROTOCOLS: Written policy and procedure. Training curriculum.

PROCESS INDICATORS: Health records. Training logs. Observation. Interviews.

1-HC-3A-06-2

Added August 2002. Written policy, procedure, and practice provide education, equipment and facilities, and the support necessary for inmates with disabilities to perform self-care and personal hygiene in a reasonably private environment.

COMMENT: A *reasonably private environment* will vary, depending on individual and institutional circumstances, but is one which will maintain the dignity of the disabled individual in light of that person's disability.

PROTOCOLS: Written policy and procedure.

PROCESS INDICATORS: Building schematic. Medical record. Observation. Interviews.

1-HC-3A-06-3

Added August 2002. Written policy, procedure, and practice prohibit discrimination on the basis of disability in the provision of services, programs, and activities administered for program beneficiaries and participants.

COMMENT: Services, programs, and activities include, but are not limited to, the following:

- academic and vocational education (including developmental and rehabilitative programs)
- work programs/work release programs (by providing reasonable accommodations or alternatives for offenders with disabilities so that the benefits of these programs, including sentence-reduction credits, are available to offenders with disabilities)
- recreation, exercise, and activities

- mail, telephone, visiting
- library
- religious programs
- reception and orientation
- transportation services (to provide for safety and security, and to avoid undue discomfort, in light of the offender's disabilities)
- classification
- food service
- sanitation and hygiene
- health care
- social services
- release
- discipline, grievance procedures, and due process proceedings
- safety and emergency procedures
- access to media, courts, counsel, and law library
- commissary/canteen
- volunteer programs
- psychological and psychiatric services

Program beneficiaries and participants include, but are not limited to: inmates, family members, clergy, attorneys, volunteers, and other authorized visitors.

The institution may be required to take remedial action, when necessary, to afford program beneficiaries and participants with disabilities an opportunity to participate in, and enjoy the benefit of services, programs, or activities. may include, but is not limited to: 1) making reasonable modifications to policies, practices, or procedures, 2) providing auxiliary aids and services to the hearing and visually impaired, 3) constructing new or altering existing facilities, and 4) delivering of services, and so on at alternate accessible sites.

PROTOCOLS: Written policy and procedure.

PROCESS INDICATORS: Program, activities rosters. Photographs. Adaptive equipment purchase orders. Emergency/evacuation plan. Inmate files. Medical records. Visiting logs. Observation. Interviews.

1-HC-3A-06-4

Added August 2002. Written policy, procedure, and practice provide for staff and offender access to an appropriately trained and qualified individual who is educated in the problems and challenges faced by offenders with physical and/or mental impairments, programs designed to educate and assist disabled offenders, and all legal requirements for the protection of offenders with disabilities.

COMMENT: An appropriately trained and qualified individual, as used in this standard, is one who has been designated by the warden, superintendent, or other authority, to coordinate efforts to comply with and carry out responsibilities defined by the Americans with Disabilities Act. That individual should develop relationships with, and utilize the expertise of institutional staff, advocacy groups, nonprofit organizations, agencies of government, and others that have relevant knowledge and experience.

PROTOCOLS: Written policy and procedure. Job description.

PROCESS INDICATORS: Credential/license. Training curriculum. Training log. Observation. Interview.

1-HC-3A-07

Revised January 2006 (Ref. 4-4400) (Mandatory). When an offender is transferred to segregation, health care staff will be informed immediately and will provide a screening and review as indicated by the protocols established by the health authority. Unless medical attention is needed more frequently, each offender in segregation receives a daily visit from a qualified health care professional. The visit ensures that offenders have access to the health care system. The presence of a health care provider in segregation is announced and recorded. The frequency of physician visits to segregation units is determined by the health authority.

COMMENT: Health care provider's visits are intended to be screening rounds and are not meant to be clinical encounters. Those offenders who request sick call are evaluated by a health care provider who determines the appropriate setting for further medical attention or examination. Health care providers may request that an offender be removed from a cell or housing area for medical attention or examination.

PROTOCOLS: Written policy and procedure.

PROCESS INDICATORS: Health records. Segregation logs. Duty assignment roster for health care providers. Observation. Interviews.

1-HC-3A-09

Revised January 2006 (Ref. 4-4402) (Mandatory). The use of offenders for medical, pharmaceutical, or cosmetic experiments is prohibited. This does not preclude offender participation in clinical trials that are approved by an institutional review board based on his/her need for a specific medical intervention. Institutions electing to perform research will be in compliance with all state and federal guidelines.

COMMENT: None.

PROTOCOLS: Written policy and procedure. Laws and regulations.

PROCESS INDICATORS: Health records. Interviews.

1-HC-3A-10

Revised January 2006 (Ref. 4-4403). Health care encounters, including medical and mental health interviews, examinations and procedures should be conducted in a setting that respects the offender's privacy.

COMMENT: Offenders should be provided a same-sex escort except in emergency health care situations.

PROTOCOLS: Written policy and procedure. Facility diagram.

PROCESS INDICATORS: Observation. Interviews.

1-HC-3A-10-1

Added January 2006. If Telehealth is used for patient encounters, the plan includes policies for:

- **patient consent**
- **confidentiality/protected health information**
- **documentation**
- **integration of the report of the consultation into the primary health care record**

COMMENT: None.

PROTOCOLS: Written policy/ procedure; Telehealth appointment logs.

PROCESS INDICATORS: Patient consent form for Telehealth; health records; interviews.

1-HC-3A-12

Revised January 2006 (Ref. 4-4405) (Mandatory). The use of restraints for medical and psychiatric purposes is defined, at a minimum, by the following:

- **conditions under which restraints may be applied**
- **types of restraints to be applied**
- **identification of a qualified medical or mental health care practitioner who may authorize the use of restraints after reaching the conclusion that less intrusive measures would not be successful**
- **monitoring procedures for offenders in restraints**
- **length of time restraints are to be applied**
- **documentation of efforts for less-restrictive treatment alternatives as soon as possible**
- **an after-incident review**

COMMENT: Written policy should identify the authorization needed and when, where, and how restraints may be used and for how long.

PROTOCOLS: Written policy and procedure. Monitoring form.

PROCESS INDICATORS: Health records. Restraint logs. Completed monitoring forms. List of providers authorized to order restraints. Interviews.

1-HC-3A-12-1

Added August 2008. Written policy, procedure and practice, in general, prohibit the use of restraints on female offenders during active labor and the delivery of a child. Any deviation from the prohibition requires approval by, and guidance on, methodology from the medical authority and is based on documented serious security risks. The medical authority provides guidance on the use of restraints on pregnant offenders prior to active labor and delivery.

COMMENT: Restraints on pregnant offenders during active labor and the delivery of a child should only be used in extreme instances and should not be applied for more time than is absolutely necessary. Restraints used on pregnant offenders prior to active labor and delivery should not put the pregnant offender nor the fetus at risk.

PROTOCOLS: Written policy and procedure.

PROCESS INDICATORS: Escort logs. Inmate records. Medical records.

1-HC-3A-13-1 **Added August 2002. Written policy, procedure, and practice ensure that information is provided to offenders about sexual abuse/assault including:**

- **prevention/intervention**
- **self-protection**
- **reporting sexual abuse/assault**
- **treatment and counseling**

The information is communicated orally and in writing, in a language clearly understood by the offender, upon arrival at the facility.

COMMENT: None.

PROTOCOLS: Written policy and procedure.

PROCESS INDICATORS: Inmate records. Inmate handbook. Interviews.

1-HC-3A-13-2 **Added January 2003. Inmates are screened within 24 hours of arrival at the facility for potential vulnerabilities or tendencies of acting out with sexually aggressive behavior. Housing assignments are made accordingly.**

COMMENT: None.

PROTOCOLS: Written policy and procedure. Classification guidelines.

PROCESS INDICATORS: Inmates records. Housing roster. Observation. Interviews. Intake screening form.

1-HC-3A-13-3 **Added January 2003. Written policy, procedure, and practice require that an investigation is conducted and documented whenever a sexual assault or threat is reported.**

COMMENT: The agency should report occurrences/allegations of sexual assault or threat in accordance with the laws of the jurisdiction. The investigation may be limited by what is allowed by the laws of the jurisdiction.

PROTOCOLS: Written policy and procedure.

PROCESS INDICATORS: Written reports. Inmate records. Interviews.

1-HC-3A-13-4 **Added January 2003. Written policy, procedure, and practice require that inmates identified as high risk with a history of sexually assaultive behavior are assessed by a mental health or other qualified professional. Inmates with a history of sexually assaultive behavior are identified, monitored, and counseled.**

COMMENT: None.

PROTOCOLS: Written policy and procedure.

PROCESS INDICATORS: Classification records. Inmate records. Referral forms. Counseling records. Observation. Interviews.

1-HC-3A-13-5 **Added January 2003. Written policy, procedure, and practice provide that inmates identified as at risk for sexual victimization are assessed by a mental health or other qualified professional. Inmates at risk for sexual victimization are identified, monitored, and counseled.**

COMMENT: None.

PROTOCOLS: Written policy and procedure.

PROCESS INDICATORS: Intake assessment forms. Inmate records. Counseling logs. Observation. Interviews.

1-HC-3A-13-6 **Added January 2003. Written policy, procedure, and practice ensure that sexual conduct between staff and inmates, volunteers, or contract personnel and inmates, regardless of consensual status, is prohibited and subject to administrative and criminal disciplinary sanctions.**

COMMENT: None.

PROTOCOLS: Written policy and procedure.

PROCESS INDICATORS: Training curriculum. Training logs. Investigation reports. Observation. Interviews.

1-HC-3A-13-7 **Deleted August 2008.**

1-HC-3A-13-8 **Added January 2003. Written policy, procedure and practice provide that inmates who are victims of sexual abuse have the option to report the incident to a designated staff member other than an immediate point-of-contact line officer.**

COMMENT: None.

PROTOCOLS: Written policy and procedure.

PROCESS INDICATORS: Incident reports. Inmate records. Observation. Interviews.

1-HC-3A-13-9 **Added January 2003. Written policy, procedure, and practice provide that all case records associated with claims of sexual abuse, including incident reports, investigative reports, offender information, case disposition, medical and counseling evaluation findings, and recommendations for post-release treatment and/or counseling are retained in accordance with an established schedule.**

COMMENT: None.

PROTOCOLS: Written policy and procedure.

PROCESS INDICATORS: Observation. Interviews.

1-HC-4A-02 **(Ref. 4-4409) Deleted January 2006.**

1-HC-4A-04 **Revised January 2006 (Ref. 4-4411) (Mandatory). A documented peer review program for all health care practitioners and a documented external peer review program will be utilized for all physicians, psychologists, and dentists every two years.**

COMMENT: The credentialing and privileging process is an integral part of assuring the competence of the providers for the inmate patients they treat. This should be routine every two years with an ability to have an immediate review if problems of practice arise. Immediate reviews are serious and only should be permitted by a careful decision of the most senior physician responsible for the system or institution. A mechanism for patient care complaints, observations by other health services providers, security, or other nonmedical providers should be established so that the responsible physician can call a panel of independent physicians to review the practice and practice patterns of the physician of whom the complaints(s) has (have) been made. The investigation and its findings are confidential in most states by statute. The responsible physician should receive the report, take indicated action, and be prepared to demonstrate to the auditors, within the confines of confidentiality, the process, process indicators, and the actions available (in other words, terminations of the physician, required education in an area, prohibition against seeing a type of disease entity without another physician, and so forth). It is important that the auditors appreciate that the process is real and meaningful and that peer review is not simply a paper trail without substance.

PROTOCOLS: Written policy and procedure. Written agreement or contract.

PROCESS INDICATORS: Signed agreement or contract. Peer review reports.

1-HC-4A-05 **Revised January 2006 (Ref. 4-4051). The facility uses a health care staffing analysis to determine the essential positions needed to perform the health services mission and provide the defined scope of services. A staffing plan is developed and implemented from this analysis. There is an annual review of the staffing plan by the health authority to determine if the number and type of staff is adequate.**

COMMENT: Adequate staffing is based on variables such as, facility size and configuration, location, and offender type. The staffing analysis is used to determine the types and numbers of staff needed to provide a defined scope of services (medical, dental, mental health, and infirmary).

PROTOCOLS: Written policy and procedure.

PROCESS INDICATORS: Documentation of annual staffing plan review. Staffing analysis plan. Interviews.

1-HC-4A-07

Revised January 2006 (Ref. 4-4414). Non-emergency offender transfers require the following:

- **health record confidentiality to be maintained**
- **summaries, originals, or copies of the health record accompany the offender to the receiving facility. Health conditions, treatments, and allergies should be included in the record.**
- **determination of suitability for travel based on medical evaluation, with particular attention given to communicable disease clearance**
- **written instructions regarding medication or health interventions required en route should be provided to transporting officers separate from the medical record**
- **specific precautions (including standard) to be taken by transportation officers (for example, masks or gloves)**

A medical summary sheet is required for all inter and intra-facility transfers in order to maintain the provision of continuity of care. Information included does not require a release-of-information form.

Inmates confined within a correctional complex with consolidated medical services do not require health screening for intra-system transfers.

COMMENT: Transfers may be permanent or temporary (for consultative or diagnostic services).

PROTOCOLS: Written policy and procedure. Transfer and transportation form(s).

PROCESS INDICATORS: Health records. Completed forms. Observations. Interviews.

1-HC-6A-13

Revised January 2003 (Mandatory). Revision for the *Performance-Based Standards for Correctional Health Care in Adult Correctional Institutions*, 1st Edition, manual only. This change was made in the *Adult Correctional Institutions* manual but was not changed in the health care manual.

Written policy, procedure, and practice provide for adequate health protection for all inmates and staff in the institution, and inmates and other persons working in the food service, including the following:

- **where required by the laws and/or regulations applicable to food service employees in the community where the facility is located, all persons involved in the preparation of food receive a pre-assignment medical examination and periodic reexaminations to ensure freedom from diarrhea, skin infections, and other illnesses transmissible by food or utensils; all examinations are conducted in accordance with local requirements**
- **when the institutions' food services are provided by an outside agency or individual, the institution has written verification that the outside provider complies with the state and local regulations regarding food service**
- **all food handlers are instructed to wash their hands upon reporting to duty and after using toilet facilities**
- **inmates and other persons working in food service are monitored each day for health and cleanliness by the director of food services (or designee)**

COMMENT: All employee health and sanitation codes are to be strictly followed to ensure the health and welfare of offenders and staff.

PROTOCOLS: Written policy and procedure. State or local sanitation and health codes or regulations.

PROCESS INDICATORS: Documentation of health exams and daily monitoring of food service workers. Observation. Interviews.

1-HC-7A-05 **Revised January 2006 (Ref. 4-4425). Authorities having jurisdiction are promptly notified of an offender's death. Procedures specify and govern the actions to be taken in the event of the death of an offender.**

COMMENT: A postmortem examination should be performed in accordance with statute.

PROTOCOLS: Written policy and procedure.

PROCESS INDICATORS: Documentation of actions taken.

1-HC-7A-08 **Revised January 2006 (Ref. 4-4426). Adequate space is provided for administrative, direct care, professional, and clerical staff. This space includes conference areas, storage room for records, a public lobby, and toilet facilities.**

COMMENT: None.

PROTOCOLS: Written policy and procedure. Program plans and specifications.

PROCESS INDICATORS: Observation.

1-HC-7B-05 **Revised August 2010. The institution maintains a current, accurate, confidential personnel record on each employee except where state statutes require open public records and the personnel record cannot be maintained confidentially. Information obtained as part of a required medical examination (and/or inquiry) regarding the medical condition or history of applicants and employees is collected and maintained on separate forms and in separate medical files and treated as a confidential medical record.**

COMMENT: The personnel record should contain the following: initial application; reference letters; results of employment investigation; verification of training and experience; wage and salary information; job performance evaluations; incident reports, if any; and commendations and disciplinary actions, if any.

PROTOCOLS: Written policy and procedure. Applicable statutes. Personnel forms.

PROCESS INDICATORS: Personnel records.

Performance-Based Standards for Correctional Industries (CI), 2nd Edition

2-CI-1B-1-1

Added August 2003 (Mandatory). All flammable materials are controlled, safely handled, and securely stored. Where smoking is permitted, noncombustible receptacles for smoking materials and separate containers for other combustible refuse are provided at approved locations. Special containers for flammable liquids and for rags used with flammable liquids are provided. All receptacles and containers are emptied and cleaned daily.

COMMENT: None.

PROTOCOLS: Written policy/procedure. Inventory forms. Facility plans/ specifications. Staff, contractor, inmate and volunteer training curriculum. Offender handbook/ rules. Internal inspection forms.

PROCESS INDICATORS: Staff, contractor, inmate, and volunteer training records. Documentation of inventory. Internal inspection results. Documentation of incidents that involve flammable materials.

2-CI-1B-4

Added August 2003 (Mandatory). All toxic and caustic materials are controlled and secure.

COMMENT: None.

PROTOCOLS: Written policy/procedure. Inventory forms. Internal inspection forms.

PROCESS INDICATORS: Documentation of perpetual inventory. Observation. Interviews. Results of internal inspections. Inspection reports from external authorities.

2-CI-6A-5

Revised August 2003. The actual performance of each new cost accounting center is analyzed at the end of the first year of operation and annually thereafter.

COMMENT: None.

PROTOCOLS: Written policy/procedure. Specifications, drawings, and bills for materials.

PROCESS INDICATORS: Completed year-end financial statements and performance reports. Documentation of analysis. Variance reports.

Correctional Training Academies (CTA), 1st Edition

1-CTA-1A-06 **Revised January 2013. The qualifications, authority, and responsibilities of the director and other appointed personnel are specified in writing by statute or by the parent agency.**

COMMENT: None.

1-CTA-1A-07 **Revised August 2003. To be considered qualified, a director, at a minimum, must possess the following: a bachelor's degree in an appropriate discipline, five years of related administrative experience, and demonstrated administrative ability and leadership. The degree requirement may be satisfied by completion of a career development program that includes work-related experience, training, or college credits at a level of achievement equivalent to a bachelor's degree.**

COMMENT: Establishing high qualifications ensures that only qualified individuals are recruited and hired. It is the agency's responsibility to see that potential administrators receive the required education.

1-CTA-1A-08 **Deleted January 2002.**

1-CTA-1B-06 **Revised January 2003. The accounting system is designed to show the current status of appropriations and expenditures.**

COMMENT: Current information is needed to meet objectives, prevent budget discrepancies, respond to emerging needs, and ensure that the flow of funds is proceeding as planned.

1-CTA-1B-07 **Revised January 2001. Written policy, procedure, and practice provide for an independent financial audit of the facility. This audit is conducted annually or as stipulated by statute or regulation, but at least every three years. If the facility is a part of a state system, an internal audits section or department of the agency's central administration and/or statutory agency shall be considered independent of the facility to be audited.**

COMMENT: None.

1-CTA-1C-03 **Revised August 1995. Written policy specifies that equal employment opportunities exist for all positions. When deficiencies exist regarding the employment of minority groups and women, the institution can document the implementation of an affirmative action program that is approved by the appropriate government agency and can document annual reviews and the changes needed to keep the program current.**

COMMENT: Equal employment opportunity is a public policy goal. All qualified persons should be able to compete equally for entry into and promotion within the institution, and the affirmative action program should actively encourage the participation of members of minority groups, individuals with disability, and women in the institution's staff development program. The affirmative action program also should include corrective actions, when needed, in policies regarding pay rate, demotion, transfer, layoff, termination, and upgrades.

1-CTA-1C-03-1

Added August 1995. Written policy, procedure, and practice provide a mechanism to process requests for reasonable accommodation to the known physical and/or mental impairments of a qualified individual with a disability, either an applicant or an employee. The accommodation need not be granted if it would impose an undue hardship or direct threat.

COMMENT: *Reasonable accommodation* refers to modifications or adjustments, which enable qualified applicants with disabilities to access the job application process or which enable qualified employees with disabilities to perform the essential functions of the job and to enjoy the same terms, conditions, and privileges of employment that are available to persons without disabilities. Terms, conditions, and privileges of employment include, but are not limited to:

- recruitment, selection, and hiring
- salary and compensation
- benefits, holidays, leave, and work hours
- promotion and advancement
- staff development, including in-service training
- retirement, resignation, and termination

An *undue hardship* means significant difficulty or expense. *Direct threat* means a significant risk of substantial harm to the health or safety of any person, including the applicant or employee with a disability that cannot be eliminated or reduced by reasonable accommodation. A *qualified individual with a disability* means an individual with a disability who satisfies the requisite skill, experience, education, and other job-related requirements for the employment position such individual holds or desires, and who, with or without reasonable accommodation, can perform the essential functions of such position.

1-CTA-1C-06

Revised August 2007. A criminal record check is conducted on all new employees in accordance with the laws of the authority having jurisdiction over the academy. The purpose of the check is to detect any criminal convictions that relate specifically to job performance. This record will include comprehensive identifier information to be collected and run against law enforcement indices. If suspect information on matters with potential terrorism connections is returned on a desirable applicant, it is forwarded to the local Joint Terrorism Task Force (JTTF) or another similar agency.

COMMENT: The academy's administrators should know of any criminal conviction that could directly affect an employee's job performance in an institutional or correctional training setting.

1-CTA-1C-07

Revised January 2012. There is a written agency policy, procedure, and practice that specifies support for a drug-free workplace for all employees. This policy includes at a minimum the following:

- **prohibition of the use of illegal drugs**
- **prohibition of possession of any illegal drug except in the performance of official duties**
- **the opportunities available for treatment and/or counseling for drug abuse**
- **the procedures to be used to ensure compliance**
- **the penalties for violation of the policy**

COMMENT: None.

1-CTA-1C-11

Revised August 2010. The institution maintains a current, accurate, confidential personnel record on each employee except where state statutes require open public records and the personnel record cannot be maintained confidentially. Information obtained as part of a required medical examination (and/or inquiry) regarding the medical condition or history of applicants and employees is collected and maintained on separate forms and in separate medical files and is treated as a confidential medical record.

COMMENT: The personnel record should contain the following: initial application; reference letters; results of employment investigation; verification of training and experience; wage and salary information; job performance evaluations; incident reports, if any; and commendations and disciplinary actions, if any.

1-CTA-2D-03

Revised August 1995. Reasonable accommodation is made to ensure that all parts of the facility that are accessible to the public are accessible and usable by staff and visitors with disabilities.

COMMENT: None.

1-CTA-3A-01

Revised August 2005. Written policy, procedure, and practice provide that the academy's/authority's staff development and student training programs are planned, coordinated, and supervised by qualified employees. The training plan is reviewed annually.

COMMENT: None.

1-CTA-3A-03 **Revised August 2005. Training plans are developed, evaluated, and updated based on a valid annual assessment that identifies current job-related training needs.**

COMMENT: Training should be responsive to position requirements, professional development needs, current correctional issues, and new theories, techniques, and technologies.

1-CTA-3A-22 **Revised August 2008. Written policy, procedure, and practice provide that correctional officers assigned to an emergency unit have at least one year of corrections and 40 hours of specialized training before undertaking their assignments. Other staff must have at least one year of experience in their specialty within a correctional setting. The specialized training may be part of their first-year-training program. Officers and staff assigned to emergency units receive 40 hours of training annually, at least 16 of which are specifically related to emergency unit assignment.**

COMMENT: None.

1-CTA-3B-02 **Revised January 2001 (Mandatory). Written policy and procedure govern the control and use of tools, training equipment, and keys.**

COMMENT: None.

1-CTA-3B-09 **Revised January 2001 (Mandatory). Written policy, procedure, and practice provide for the safe unloading and reloading of firearms.**

COMMENT: None.

1-CTA-3D-02-1 **Added August 2011. All staff, contractors, and inmate workers who work in the food service department are trained in the use of food service equipment and in the safety procedures to be followed in the food service department.**

COMMENT: None.

1-CTA-3F-03 **Revised August 2002. First aid kits are available in designated areas of the facility based on need, and an automatic external defibrillator is available for use at the facility.**

COMMENT: The availability and placement of first aid kits and an automatic external defibrillator are determined by the designated health authority in conjunction with the facility administrator. The health authority approves the contents, number, location, and procedures for monthly inspection of the kits(s), and develops written procedures for the use of the kits by nonmedical staff.

Appendix C Revised January 2001. Refer to *Standards Supplement* Appendix D.

Electronic Monitoring (EM), 1st Edition

1-EM-1A-04-1

Added August 2010. The facility/agency shall demonstrate it has examined, and where appropriate and feasible, implemented strategies that promote recycling, energy and water conservation, pollution reduction, and utilization of renewable energy alternatives.

COMMENT: Correctional facilities and programs have the responsibility to implement strategies that allow correctional facilities to be managed in ways that are most cost-effective and deliver superior performance, while improving environmental responsibility and sustainability. This includes recycling (including paper, metal, and plastic products), energy conservation (including building insulation, heating and ventilation, temperature controls, vehicle fuel efficiency, water economies, physical plant engineering, and energy measures), pollution reduction (including composting, sewer treatment, litter abatement, and carbon emissions), and utilization of renewable energy alternatives (bio-fuels, solar collection, turbine energy production, and methane collection).

1-EM-1B-09

Revised January 2001. Written policy, procedure, and practice provide for an independent financial audit of the agency. This audit is conducted annually or as stipulated by statute or regulation, but at least every three years. If the agency is a part of a state system, an internal audits section or department of the agency's central administration and/or statutory agency shall be considered independent of the agency to be audited.

COMMENT: None.

1-EM-1C-04-1

Added August 1995. Written policy, procedure, and practice provide a mechanism to process requests for reasonable accommodation to the known physical and/or mental impairments of a qualified individual with a disability, either an applicant or an employee. The accommodation need not be granted if it would impose an undue hardship or direct threat.

COMMENT: *Reasonable accommodation* refers to modifications or adjustments, which enable qualified applicants with disabilities to access the job application process or which enable qualified employees with disabilities to perform the essential functions of the job and to enjoy the same terms, conditions, and privileges of employment that are available to persons without disabilities. *Terms, conditions, and privileges of employment* include, but are not limited to:

- recruitment, selection, and hiring
- salary and compensation
- benefits, holidays, leave, and work hours
- promotion and advancement
- staff development, including in-service training
- retirement, resignation, and termination

An *undue hardship means* significant difficulty or expense. *Direct threat* means a significant risk of substantial harm to the health or safety of any person, including the applicant or employee with a disability that cannot be eliminated or reduced by reasonable accommodation. A *qualified individual with a disability* means an individual with a disability who satisfies the requisite skill, experience, education, and other job-related requirements for the employment position such individual holds or desires, and who, with or without reasonable accommodation, can perform the essential functions of such position.

1-EM-1C-06

Revised January 2012. There is a written agency policy, procedure, and practice that specifies support for a drug-free workplace for all employees. This policy includes at a minimum the following:

- **prohibition of the use of illegal drugs**
- **prohibition of possession of any illegal drug except in the performance of official duties**
- **the opportunities available for treatment and/or counseling for drug abuse**
- **the procedures to be used to ensure compliance**
- **the penalties for violation of the policy**

COMMENT: None.

1-EM-1C-09

Revised August 2007. Written policy, procedure, and practice provide that criminal record checks are conducted on all new employees and volunteers in accordance with state and federal statutes. This record will include comprehensive identifier information to be collected and run against law enforcement indices. If suspect information on matters with potential terrorism connections is returned on a desirable applicant, it is forwarded to the local Joint Terrorism Task Force (JTTF) or another similar agency.

COMMENT: The program administrator should know of any criminal conviction that could directly affect an employee's job performance.

1-EM-1C-11

Revised August 2010. The institution maintains a current, accurate, confidential personnel record on each employee except where state statutes require open public records and the personnel record cannot be maintained confidentially. Information obtained as part of a required medical examination (and/or inquiry) regarding the medical condition or history of applicants and employees is collected and maintained on separate forms and in separate medical files and treated as a confidential medical record.

COMMENT: The personnel record should contain the following: initial application; reference letters; results of employment investigation; verification of training and experience; wage and salary information; job performance evaluations; incident reports, if any; and commendations and disciplinary actions, if any.

1-EM-1D-02

Revised August 2005. Written policy, procedure, and practice provide that a training plan is developed, evaluated, and updated based on a valid annual assessment that identifies current job-related training needs.

COMMENT: Training should be responsive to position requirements, professional development needs, current issues, and new theories, techniques, and technologies. The needs assessment may require information from many sources; observation and analysis of job components; staff surveys regarding training needs; reviews of program operations; staff reports; and evaluations and findings from sources within and outside the jurisdiction.

\

1-EM-1D-09

Revised August 2000. Written policy, procedure, and practice provide that all administrative and managerial staff receive 40 hours of training in addition to orientation training during their first year of employment and 40 hours of training each year thereafter, in areas relevant to their position.

COMMENT: Ongoing training in topics relevant to an employee's position enhances skill and job performance.

1-EM-1E-01

Revised January 2012. Written agency policy, procedure and practice governing case record management includes, but is not limited to, the establishment, use, content, privacy, security, preservation, and destruction of case records.

COMMENT: None.

Appendix C Revised January 2001. Refer to *Standards Supplement* Appendix D.

Juvenile Community Residential Facilities (JCRF), 3rd Edition

3-JCRF-1A-05-1 **Added August 2010. The facility/agency shall demonstrate it has examined, and where appropriate and feasible, implemented strategies that promote recycling, energy and water conservation, pollution reduction, and utilization of renewable energy alternatives.**

COMMENT: Correctional facilities and programs have the responsibility to implement strategies that allow correctional facilities to be managed in ways that are most cost-effective and deliver superior performance, while improving environmental responsibility and sustainability. This includes recycling (including paper, metal, and plastic products), energy conservation (including building insulation, heating and ventilation, temperature controls, vehicle fuel efficiency, water economies, physical plant engineering, and energy measures), pollution reduction (including composting, sewer treatment, litter abatement, and carbon emissions), and utilization of renewable energy alternatives (bio-fuels, solar collection, turbine energy production, and methane collection).

3-JCRF-1A-07 **Revised August 2003. The qualifications for the position of facility administrator include, at a minimum, the following: a bachelor's degree in an appropriate discipline; five years of related administrative experience; and demonstrated administrative ability and leadership. The degree requirement may be satisfied by completion of a career development program that includes work-related experience, training, or college credits at a level of achievement equivalent to the bachelor's degree.**

COMMENT: Establishing high qualifications ensures that only qualified individuals are recruited and employed. It is the agency's responsibility to see that potential administrators receive the required education.

3-JCRF-1B-10 **Revised January 2001. Written policy, procedure, and practice provide for an independent financial audit of the facility. This audit is conducted annually or as stipulated by statute or regulation, but at least every three years. If the facility is a part of a state system, an internal audits section or department of the agency's central administration and/or statutory agency shall be considered independent of the facility to be audited.**

COMMENT: None.

3-JCRF-1B-12 **Deleted January 2005.**

3-JCRF-1C-03 **Revised August 1995. Written policy specifies that equal employment opportunities exist for all positions. When deficiencies exist regarding the employment of minority groups and women, the facility can document the implementation of an affirmative action program that is approved by the appropriate government agency and can document annual reviews and the changes needed to keep the program current.**

COMMENT: Equal employment opportunity is a public policy goal. All qualified persons should be able to compete equally for entry into and promotion within the facility, and the affirmative action program should actively encourage the participation of members of minority groups, individuals with disability, and women in the facility's staff development program. The affirmative action program also should include corrective actions, when needed, in policies regarding pay rate, demotion, transfer, layoff, termination, and upgrades.

Summary of Orientation and Minimum Training Hours

The following description of general job categories should be used in determining minimum training requirements as outlined in the standards. Contract or part-time employees should receive training similar to full-time employees in their particular category and pertinent to their role in working with juveniles. This chart replaces the chart on page 18 in Juvenile Community *Residential Facilities*, Third Edition, published in January 1994.

CATEGORY	TYPICAL POSITION TITLES	BASIC ORIEN-TATION	TRAINING HOURS—FIRST YEAR ON THE JOB	TRAINING HOURS—EACH YEAR THERE-AFTER
CLERICAL/ SUPPORT (Minimum Contact)	Secretaries, clerks, typists, computer/ warehouse personnel, accountants, personnel staff	Yes	16	16
SUPPORT (Regular or Daily Contact)	Food service, industry work supervisors, maintenance work supervisors	Yes	40	40
PROFESSIONAL SPECIALIST	Case managers, counselors, social workers, teachers, psychologists, librarians, medical personnel, chaplains, recreation specialists	Yes	40	40
ALL OFFENDER SUPERVISION STAFF	All staff assigned to full-time supervision duties	Yes	120	40
ADMINIS-TRATIVE MANAGEMENT PERSONNEL	Superintendents, deputy or assistant superintendents, business managers, personnel directors, care supervisors, shift supervisors	Yes	40	40

Training: An organized, planned, and evaluated activity designed to achieve specific learning objectives. Training may occur onsite, at an academy or training center, at an institution of higher learning, through contract service, at professional meetings, or through closely supervised on-the-job training. Meetings of professional associations are considered training when there is clear evidence of specific learning objectives relative to the employee's career track. *See* Appendix F, "Revised Definitions of Learning and Training."

3-JCRF-1C-03-1 **Added August 1995. Written policy, procedure, and practice provide a mechanism to process requests for reasonable accommodation to the known physical and/or mental impairments of a qualified individual with a disability, either an applicant or an employee. The accommodation need not be granted if it would impose an undue hardship or direct threat.**

COMMENT: *Reasonable accommodation* refers to modifications or adjustments, which enable qualified applicants with disabilities to access the job application process or which enable qualified employees with disabilities to perform the essential functions of the job and to enjoy the same terms, conditions, and privileges of employment that are available to persons without disabilities. *Terms, conditions, and privileges of employment* include, but are not limited to:

- recruitment, selection, and hiring
- salary and compensation
- benefits, holidays, leave, and work hours
- promotion and advancement
- staff development, including in-service training
- retirement, resignation, and termination

An *undue hardship* means significant difficulty or expense. *Direct threat* means a significant risk of substantial harm to the health or safety of any person, including an applicant or employee with a disability that cannot be eliminated or reduced by reasonable accommodation. A *qualified individual with a disability* means an individual with a disability who satisfies the requisite skill, experience, education, and other job-related requirements for the employment position such individual holds or desires, and who, with or without reasonable accommodation, can perform the essential functions of the position.

3-JCRF-1C-05 **Revised January 2012. There is a written agency policy, procedure, and practice that specifies support for a drug-free workplace for all employees. This policy includes at a minimum the following:**

- **prohibition of the use of illegal drugs**
- **prohibition of possession of any illegal drug except in the performance of official duties**
- **the opportunities available for treatment and/or counseling for drug abuse**
- **the procedures to be used to ensure compliance**
- **the penalties for violation of the policy**

COMMENT: None.

3-JCRF-1C-10

Revised August 2007. A criminal record check is conducted on all new employees in accordance with state and federal statutes. This record will include comprehensive identifier information to be collected and run against law enforcement indices. If suspect information on matters with potential terrorism connections is returned on a desirable applicant, it is forwarded to the local Joint Terrorism Task Force (JTTF) or another similar agency.

COMMENT: The facility administrator should know of any criminal conviction that could directly affect an employee's job performance.

3-JCRF-1C-14

Revised August 2010. The institution maintains a current, accurate, confidential personnel record on each employee except where state statutes require open public records and the personnel record cannot be maintained confidentially. Information obtained as part of a required medical examination (and/or inquiry) regarding the medical condition or history of applicants and employees is collected and maintained on separate forms and in separate medical files and treated as a confidential medical record.

COMMENT: The personnel record should contain the following: initial application; reference letters; results of employment investigation; verification of training and experience; wage and salary information; job performance evaluations; incident reports, if any; and commendations and disciplinary actions, if any.

3-JCRF-1D-09

Revised August 2000. Written policy, procedure, and practice provide that all administrative, managerial, and professional staff receive 40 hours of training in addition to orientation training during their first year of employment and 40 hours of training each year thereafter, in areas relevant to their position.

COMMENT: Ongoing training in topics relevant to an employee's position enhances skill and job performance.

3-JCRF-1D-10

Revised August 2005. Written policy, procedure, and practice provide that all new juvenile care workers receive 120 hours of training during their first year of employment. At a minimum, this training covers the following areas:

- **security and safety procedures**
- **emergency and fire procedures**
- **supervision of offenders**
- **suicide intervention/prevention**
- **use of force**
- **offender rights**
- **key control**
- **interpersonal relations**
- **communication skills**
- **standards of conduct**

- **cultural awareness**
- **sexual abuse/assault intervention**
- **code of ethics**

Additional topics may be added at the discretion of the agency or facility.

COMMENT: Since the duties of juvenile care workers frequently involve most institutional operations, their training should be comprehensive.

3-JCRF-1D-10-1 **Added August 2005. Written policy, procedure, and practice provide that all juvenile care workers receive at least 40 hours of annual training. This training shall include at a minimum the following areas:**

- **standards of conduct/ethics**
- **security/safety/fire/medical/emergency procedures**
- **supervision of offenders including training on sexual abuse and assault**
- **use of force**

Additional topics shall be included based upon a needs assessment of both staff and institution requirements.

COMMENT: This training will enable employees to sharpen skills, maintain certification, and keep abreast of changes in policies, procedures, and legislative, judicial, or executive actions.

3-JCRF-1G-01 **Deleted August 2007.**

3-JCRF-1G-02 **Revised August 2007. Written policy and procedure specify who is responsible for operating a citizen involvement and volunteer service program, and his or her lines of authority, responsibility, and accountability.**

COMMENT: A citizen involvement and volunteer service program can generate a wide variety of services for juveniles during confinement and after release; for example, information on referrals to release programs and recreational and cultural activities in the community. The staff member responsible for the program may be full-time or part-time, and the position may be filled by volunteer or contract personnel. The responsible person should have or receive appropriate training. Written policy should provide direction for the program, listing the goals and objectives, types of services offered, and so forth. Clear lines of accountability and authority should be established and communicated to staff and volunteers. Any volunteer activity that is shown to threaten order and security or the safety of a volunteer should be limited or discontinued until the problem is resolved.

3-JCRF-2A-01

Correction August 1998. This standard is listed incorrectly as a mandatory standard in the *Standards for Juvenile Community Residential Facilities*, Third Edition. The standard is non-mandatory.

3-JCRF-2B-02

Revised August 2006. (Existing only). Written policy, procedure, and practice provide that no more than 25 juveniles are housed in each living unit in the facility.

COMMENT: A small living and treatment unit is more conducive to enhancing student and staff interaction. The living unit's maximum size should be no more than 25; however, smaller units of 10, 15, or 20 permit services on a more manageable scale.

3-JCRF-2B-02-1

Added August 2006. (Renovations, Additions, New Construction). Written policy, procedure, and practice provide that no more than 16 juveniles are housed in each living unit in the facility.

COMMENT: A small living and treatment unit is more conducive to enhancing student and staff interaction.

3-JCRF-2B-03

Deleted July 2012.

3-JCRF-2C-05

Revised August 1995. Juveniles have access to operable showers with temperature-controlled hot and cold running water, at a minimum ratio of one shower for every eight juveniles, unless national or state building or health codes specify a different ratio. Water for showers is thermostatically controlled to temperatures ranging from 100 degrees Fahrenheit to 120 degrees Fahrenheit to ensure the safety of juveniles and to promote hygienic practices.

COMMENT: Juveniles can use scalding showers as a weapon against, or punishment for, other juveniles. Also, accidental injury could occur when cold water is drawn in other areas, thereby unexpectedly elevating the hot water in showers to scalding temperatures. Water temperatures below 100 degrees Fahrenheit are uncomfortable and may deter an individual from pursuing good hygienic practices. The temperature controls should not preclude the use of water at higher temperatures, if needed, in other areas of the facility, such as kitchens.

3-JCRF-2C-08

Revised August 1995. Juveniles with disabilities are housed in a manner that provides for their safety and security. Housing used by juveniles with disabilities is designed for their use and provides integration with other juveniles. Programs and services are accessible to juveniles with disabilities who reside in the facility.

COMMENT: If the facility accepts individuals with disabilities, it must provide for their housing and use of facility resources. Housing includes, but is not limited to, sleeping quarters/areas, furnishings, dayrooms, toilets, washbasins, showers/bathing facilities, and other common elements. Program and service areas include, but are not limited to, exercise and recreation areas, visiting rooms, laundry facilities, private counseling space, group meeting rooms, dining rooms, telephone facilities, admission and intake areas, and administrative areas, where appropriate.

3-JCRF-2C-09 **Added January 2002. Written policy, procedure, and practice provide for the assignment of appropriately trained individuals to assist disabled juveniles who cannot otherwise perform basic life functions.**

COMMENT: None.

3-JCRF-2C-10 **Added August 2002. Written policy, procedure, and practice provide education, equipment, and facilities, and the support necessary for juveniles with disabilities to perform self-care and personal hygiene in a reasonably private environment.**

COMMENT: A *reasonably private environment* will vary, depending on individual and institutional circumstances, but is one which will maintain the dignity of the disabled individual in light of that person's disability.

3-JCRF-2D-01 **Revised January 2008. Written policy, procedure, and practice provide that all sleeping quarters are well-lighted and properly ventilated. Natural lighting should be provided, wherever possible. Documentation shall be provided by a qualified source that lighting is at least 20 foot-candles at desk level and air circulation is at least 15 cubic feet of outside or re-circulated filtered air per minute per occupant for rooms, housing areas, staff stations, and dining areas. Air and light levels should be checked at least once per accreditation cycle.**

Interpretation August 2002. The words "accreditation cycle" is interpreted as within the past three years.

COMMENT: The facility should maintain strict adherence to local health codes requiring proper lighting and ventilation.

3-JCRF-2D-02 **Revised August 2006. Temperatures in indoor living and work areas are appropriate to the summer and winter comfort zones.**

COMMENT: Temperature should be capable of being mechanically raised or lowered to an acceptable comfort level.

3-JCRF-2E-03

Revised January 2005. Written policy, procedure, and practice, provide for adequate and appropriate areas for visiting.

COMMENT: An important part of the residential program is providing for relatives and friends to visit the juveniles at the facility.

3-JCRF-2F-02

Revised August 1995. Reasonable accommodation is made to ensure that all parts of the facility that are accessible to the public are accessible and usable by staff and visitors with disabilities.

COMMENT: None.

3-JCRF-3A-02

Revised August 2000 (Mandatory). Written policy, procedure, and practice restrict the use of physical force to instances of justifiable self-defense, protection of the juveniles or others, protection of property, prevention of escapes, and to maintain or regain control, and then only as a last resort and in accordance with appropriate statutory authority. In no event is physical force justifiable as punishment. A written report is prepared following all uses of force and is submitted to administrative staff for review.

COMMENT: Correctional personnel should be prepared to justify their use of physical force. The phrase "as a last resort" may be defined through appropriate statutory authority.

3-JCRF-3A-07

Revised August 1997. Written policy, procedure, and practice provide that staff conduct a daily inspection, including holidays and weekends, of all areas occupied by juveniles and submit a daily written report to the facility administrator or designee.* Unoccupied areas are to be inspected weekly.

COMMENT: Matters requiring further attention (for example, concerns of staff, juveniles, and unsafe or unsanitary conditions) should be reported in writing for review and further action.

*The intent of the Standards Committee was to lower the reporting requirements below that of the facility administrator.

3-JCRF-3A-13

Revised January 2001 (Mandatory). Written policy, procedure, and practice govern the control and use of tools, equipment, and keys.

COMMENT: Tools and utensils should be used in accordance with a prescribed system.

3-JCRF-3A-14

Added new subtitle January 1995.

Preservation of Physical Evidence

Written policy, procedure, and practice provide for the preservation, control, and disposition of all physical evidence obtained in connection with a violation of law and/or facility regulation. At a minimum, the procedures shall address the following:

- **chain of custody**
- **evidence handling**
- **location and storage requirements**

COMMENT: Strict accountability of physical evidence collected in connection with a crime must be established to preserve the integrity of the disciplinary and/or legal process. Minor rule violations should be exempt from the procedural requirements of evidence control, preservation, and disposition.

3-JCRF-3B-13

Added January 2003. Written policy, procedure, and practice define critical incidents for the facility and provide for a debriefing to be conducted after each such incident. The debriefing process includes coordination and feedback about the incident with designated staff of the facility as soon as possible after the incident. A debriefing includes, but is not limited to:

- **a review of staff and juvenile actions during the incident**
- **a review of the incident's impact on staff and juveniles**
- **a review of corrective actions taken and still needed**
- **plans for improvement to avoid another incident**

COMMENT: A *critical incident* is any event or situation that threatens staff or juveniles in their community (criminal justice setting). While debriefings should occur as soon as possible, some information may not be available until later. All staff impacted by a critical incident should be included in the debriefings and referred to appropriate services to mitigate the stress associated with these events. All critical incidents should be reviewed by the administration, security, and health services. A two-week follow-up debriefing should occur to review the validity and appropriateness of all policies, plans, and information used during the critical incident and immediately after.

3-JCRF-3C-06

Revised January 2008. Written policy, procedure, and practice provide that juveniles are scheduled for a hearing as soon as practicable but no later than seven days, excluding weekends and holidays, after being charged with a violation. Juveniles are notified of the time and place of the hearing at least 24 hours in advance of the hearing.

COMMENT: To ensure fairness and the integrity of the disciplinary process, juveniles charged with major rule violations should receive hearings as soon as possible, unless the hearing is prevented by exceptional circumstances, unavoidable delays, or reasonable postponements. Reasons for all delays should be documented. If the process could result in the transfer of a juvenile to a more restrictive setting, staff or volunteers may assist the juvenile.

3-JCRF-3D-03 **Revised August 1995. Written policy, procedure, and practice prohibit discrimination based on a juvenile's race, religion, national origin, sex, disability, or political views in making administrative decisions and in providing access to programs.**

COMMENT: Juveniles should be assured equal opportunities to participate in all facility programs.

3-JCRF-3D-04-1 **Deleted January 2013.**

3-JCRF-3D-04-2 **Added August 2008. Written policy, procedure, and practice ensure that information is provided to juveniles about sexual abuse/assault including:**

- **prevention/intervention**
- **self-protection**
- **reporting sexual abuse/assault**
- **treatment and counseling**

The information is communicated orally and in writing, in a language clearly understood by the juvenile, upon arrival at the facility.

COMMENT: None.

3-JCRF-3D-04-3 **Added August 2008. Juveniles are screened within 24 hours of arrival at the facility for potential vulnerabilities or tendencies of acting out with sexually aggressive behavior. Housing assignments are made accordingly.**

COMMENT: None.

3-JCRF-3D-04-4 **Added August 2008. Written policy, procedure, and practice require that an investigation is conducted and documented whenever a sexual assault is alleged, threatened, or occurs.**

COMMENT: None.

3-JCRF-3D-04-5 **Added August 2008. Written policy, procedure, and practice require that juveniles identified as high risk with a history of assaultive behavior are assessed by a mental health or other qualified professional. Such juveniles are identified, monitored, counseled, and provided appropriate treatment.**

COMMENT: None.

3-JCRF-3D-04-6 **Added August 2008. Written policy, procedure, and practice require that juveniles identified as at risk for sexual victimization are assessed by a mental health or other qualified professional. Such juveniles are identified, monitored, and counseled.**

COMMENT: None.

3-JCRF-3D-04-7 **Added August 2008. Written policy, procedure, and practice ensure that sexual conduct between staff and juveniles, volunteers, or contract personnel and juveniles, regardless of consensual status, is prohibited and subject to administrative and criminal disciplinary sanctions.**

COMMENT: None.

3-JCRF-3D-04-8 **Added August 2008. Victims of sexual assault are referred under appropriate security provisions to a community facility for treatment and gathering of evidence. If these procedures are performed in house, the following guidelines are used:**

- **Health care professionals take a history and conduct an examination to document the extent of physical injury and to determine if referral to another medical facility is indicated. With the victim's consent, the examination includes collection of evidence from the victim, using a kit approved by the appropriate authority.**
- **Provision is made for testing for sexually transmitted diseases (for example, HIV, gonorrhea, hepatitis, and other diseases) and counseling, as appropriate.**
- **Prophylactic treatment and follow-up for sexually transmitted diseases are offered to all victims, as appropriate.**
- **Following the physical examination, there is availability of an evaluation by a mental health professional to assess the need for crisis intervention counseling and long-term follow-up.**
- **A report is made to the facility or program administrator or designee to assure separation of the victim from his or her assailant.**

COMMENT: None.

3-JCRF-3D-04-9 **Added August 2008. Written policy, procedure, and practice provide that juveniles who are victims of sexual abuse have the option to report the incident to a designated staff member other than an immediate point-of-contact line staff member.**

COMMENT: None.

3-JCRF-3D-04-10 **Added August 2008. Written policy, procedure, and practice provide that all case records associated with claims of sexual abuse and/or assault, including incident reports, investigative reports, juvenile information, case disposition, medical and counseling evaluation findings, and recommendations for post-release treatment and/or counseling are retained in accordance with an established schedule.**

COMMENT: None.

3-JCRF-4A-05 **Revised August 2004. Therapeutic diets are provided as prescribed by appropriate clinicians. A therapeutic diet manual is available in health services and food services for reference and information. Prescriptions for therapeutic diets should be specific and complete, furnished in writing to the food service manager, and rewritten annually, or more often as clinically indicated.**

COMMENT: Therapeutic diets are prepared and served to offenders according to the orders of the treating clinician or as directed by the responsible health authority. Therapeutic diets should be kept as simple as possible and should conform as closely as possible to the foods served other offenders.

3-JCRF- 4A-07-1 **Added August 2011. All staff, contractors, and inmate workers who work in the food service department are trained in the use of food service equipment and in the safety procedures to be followed in the food service department.**

COMMENT: None.

3-JCRF-4B-08 **Revised August 2007. Written policy, procedure, and practice provide for the issue of suitable, clean bedding and linen, including two sheets, pillow and pillowcase, one mattress, not to exclude a mattress with integrated pillow, and sufficient blankets to provide comfort under existing temperature controls. There is provision for linen exchange, including towels, at least weekly. Blanket exchange must be available at least quarterly.**

COMMENT: Collection, storage, and exchange methods for bedding and linens should be done hygienically; that is, blankets, pillows, and mattresses should be cleaned before reissue.

3-JCRF-4B-09 **Revised January 1998. Written policy, procedure, and practice require that articles necessary for maintaining proper personal hygiene are provided to all juveniles.**

COMMENT: As part of the admissions process, each juvenile should be given soap, a toothbrush, toothpaste or powder, a comb, and toilet paper. Shaving equipment should be made available upon request, and the special hygiene needs of females should be met. Proper personal hygiene improves juveniles' health and medical conditions.

3-JCRF-4C-03 **Revised January 2005. Appropriate state and federal licensure, certification, or registration requirements, and restrictions apply to personnel who provide health care services to juveniles. The duties and responsibilities of such personnel are governed by written job descriptions approved by the health authority. Verification of current credentials is on file in the facility.**

COMMENT: Only qualified health care personnel should determine and supervise health care procedures. Written job descriptions should include the required professional qualifications and the individual's specific role in the health care delivery system. Verification of qualifications may consist of copies of current credentials or a letter from the state licensing or certifying body regarding current credential status. Nursing services are performed in accordance with professionally recognized standards of nursing practice and the jurisdiction's Nurse Practice Act.

3-JCRF-4C-06

Revised August 1994 (Mandatory). There is a written suicide prevention and intervention program that is reviewed and approved by a qualified medical or mental health professional. All staff with responsibility for juvenile supervision are trained in the implementation of the program.

COMMENT: The program should include specific procedures for intake screening, identifying, and supervising of suicide-prone juveniles.

3-JCRF-4C-09-1

Added August 1994. Written policy, procedure, and practice provide for early identification and treatment of juveniles with alcohol and drug abuse problems through a standardized battery assessment. This battery shall be documented and include, at a minimum, the following:

- **screening and sorting**
- **clinical assessment and reassessment**
- **medical assessment for drug and alcohol program assignment appropriate to the needs of the individual juveniles**
- **referrals**
- **monitoring and drug testing**

COMMENT: None.

3-JCRF-4C-15

Correction December 1999 (Mandatory). Written policy, procedure, and practice provide that care worker staff and other personnel are trained to respond to health-related situations within a four-minute response time. A training program is established by the responsible health authority in cooperation with the facility administrator that includes the following:

- **recognition of signs and symptoms and knowledge of action required in potential emergency situations**
- **administration of first aid and cardiopulmonary resuscitation (CPR)**
- **knowledge of methods of obtaining assistance**
- **recognizing signs and symptoms of mental illness, retardation, and chemical dependency**
- **knowing procedures for patient transfers to appropriate medical facilities or health care providers**

COMMENT: With even the most adequate staff of qualified health care personnel, emergencies can occur in distant parts of the facility; too much time can be lost in getting staff promptly on the scene to handle emergency matters. All juvenile care staff should have standard first aid training. Minimally, one juvenile care worker per shift should be trained in cardiopulmonary resuscitation (CPR) and in recognition of symptoms of illnesses most common to juveniles.

3-JCRF-4C-16

Revised August 2002. The facility has available at all times, first aid kit equipment approved by a recognized health authority. An automatic external defibrillator is available for use at the facility.

COMMENT: The health authority develops written procedures outlining the use of first aid kits and an automatic external defibrillator by nonmedical staff.

3-JCRF-4C-23-1

Added August 1994. Where a drug treatment program exists, written policy, procedure, and practice provide that the alcohol and drug abuse treatment program has a written treatment philosophy within the context of the total correctional system, as well as goals and measurable objectives. These documents are reviewed at least annually and updated, as needed.

Interpretation August 2003. The words "Where a drug program exists" are interpreted as a therapeutic community.

COMMENT: None.

3-JCRF-4C-23-2

Added August 1994. Where a drug treatment program exists, written policy, procedure, and practice provide for an appropriate range of primary treatment services for alcohol and other drug-abusing juveniles that include, at a minimum, the following:

- **juvenile diagnosis**
- **identified problem areas**
- **individual treatment objectives**
- **treatment goals**
- **counseling needs**
- **drug education plan**
- **relapse prevention and management**
- **culturally sensitive treatment objectives, as appropriate**
- **the provision of self-help groups as an adjunct to treatment**
- **prerelease and transitional service needs**
- **coordination efforts with community supervision and treatment staff during the prerelease phase to ensure a continuum of supervision and treatment**

Interpretation August 2003. The words "Where a drug program exists" are interpreted as a therapeutic community.

COMMENT: None.

3-JCRF-4C-23-3

Added August 1994. Where a drug treatment program exists, written policy, procedure, and practice provide that the facility uses a coordinated staff approach to deliver treatment services. This approach to service delivery shall be documented in treatment planning conferences and in individual treatment files.

Interpretation August 2003. The words "Where a drug program exists" are interpreted as a therapeutic community.

COMMENT: None.

3-JCRF-4C-23-4

Added August 1994. Where a drug treatment program exists, written policy, procedure, and practice provide incentives for targeted treatment programs to increase and maintain the juvenile's motivation for treatment.

Interpretation August 2003. The words "Where a drug program exists" are interpreted as a therapeutic community.

COMMENT: These incentives may include a variety of options such as preferences in housing, clothing, award certificates, or other items consistent with the goals of the facility.

3-JCRF-5A-01-1

Added August 1995. Written intake criteria prohibit discrimination in accepting referrals on the basis of sex, disability, race, creed, or national origin.

COMMENT: None.

3-JCRF-5B-01-1

Revised August 2002. Written policy, procedure, and practice prohibit discrimination on the basis of disability in the provision of services, programs, and activities administered for program beneficiaries and participants.

COMMENT: Services, programs, and activities include, but are not limited to, the following:

- academic and vocational education (including developmental and rehabilitative programs)
- work programs/work release programs (by providing reasonable accommodations or alternatives for juveniles with disabilities so that the benefits of these programs, including sentence-reduction credits, are available to juveniles with disabilities)
- recreation, exercise, and activities
- mail, telephone, and visiting
- library
- religious programs
- reception and orientation
- transportation services (to provide for safety and security, and to avoid undue discomfort, in light of the juvenile's disabilities)

- classification
- food service
- sanitation and hygiene
- health care
- social services
- release
- discipline, grievance procedures, and due process proceedings
- safety and emergency procedures
- access to media, courts, counsel, and law library
- commissary/canteen
- volunteer programs
- psychological and psychiatric services

Program beneficiaries and participants include, but are not limited to: juveniles, family members, clergy, attorneys, volunteers, and other authorized visitors.

The institution may be required to take remedial action, when necessary, to afford program beneficiaries and participants with disabilities an opportunity to participate in, and enjoy the benefit of services, programs, or activities. Remedial action may include, but is not limited to: 1) making reasonable modifications to policies, practices, or procedures, 2) providing auxiliary aids and services to the hearing and visually impaired, 3) constructing new or altering existing facilities, and 4) delivering services and so on at alternative accessible sites.

3-JCRF-5B-01-2 **Added August 2002. Written policy, procedure, and practice provide for staff and juvenile access to an appropriately trained and qualified individual who is educated in the problems and challenges faced by juveniles with physical and/or mental impairments, programs designed to educate and assist disabled juveniles, and all legal requirements for the protection of juveniles with disabilities.**

COMMENT: An appropriately trained and qualified individual, as used in this standard, is one who has been designated by the warden, superintendent, or other authority, to coordinate efforts to comply with and carry out responsibilities defined by the Americans with Disabilities Act. That individual should develop relationships with, and use the expertise of institutional staff, advocacy groups, nonprofit organizations, agencies of government, and others that have relevant knowledge and experience.

3-JCRF-5E-01 **Revised January 2005. Written policy, procedure, and practice provide for adequate and appropriate areas for indoor and outdoor recreational and leisure time needs of juveniles. Juveniles should be encouraged to be physically active, dependent upon their capabilities, and receive at least two hours of planned recreation per day.**

COMMENT: Provision should be made for periodic group activities outside the facility. Also, there should be space for indoor leisure time activities, such as television, games, reading, and studying.

3-JCRF-5G-05 **Revised August 2002. Written policy, procedure, and practice provide for juvenile access to public telephones. Juveniles with hearing and/or speech disabilities, and juveniles who wish to communicate with parties who have such disabilities, shall be afforded access to a Telecommunications Device for the Deaf (TDD), or comparable equipment. Public telephones with volume control also shall be made available to juveniles with hearing impairments.**

COMMENT: Sufficient telephone facilities should permit reasonable and equitable access to all juveniles and permit a reasonable amount of privacy. Procedures should specify the hours during which the telephone is available, the maximum length of calls, and any limitation on calls. All long distance calls should be made collect.

3-JCRF-5G-05-1 **Added August 2002. Written policy, procedure, and practice ensure that offenders have access to reasonably priced telephone services. Correctional agencies ensure that:**

- **Contracts involving telephone services for offenders comply with all applicable state and federal regulations.**
- **Contracts are based on rates and surcharges that are commensurate with those charged to the general public for like services. Any deviation from ordinary consumer rates reflects actual costs associated with the provision of services in a correctional setting.**
- **Contracts for offender telephone services provide the broadest range of calling options determined by the agency administrator to be consistent with the requirements of sound correctional management.**

COMMENT: When procuring and renewing telephone services, correctional officials should determine the reasons for proposed deviations from standard charges and seek the best possible rates for the broadest possible range of calling options.

3-JCRF-5G-08 **Added August 2003. Written policy, procedure, and practice require that a juvenile is informed in a timely manner of the verifiable death or critical illness of an immediate family member. In case of the critical illness of an immediate family member, the juvenile is allowed, whenever statutes and circumstances allow, to go to the bedside under escort or alone.**

COMMENT: Classification, status, geography, security level, and other specified criteria should determine eligibility. Immediate family is usually defined as parent, spouse, child, sibling, grandparent, or legal guardian.

Appendix B Revised January 2001. Refer to *Standards Supplement* Appendix D.

Juvenile Correctional Boot Camp Programs (JBC), 1st Edition

1-JBC-1A-05-1 **Added August 2010. The facility/agency shall demonstrate it has examined, and where appropriate and feasible, implemented strategies that promote recycling, energy and water conservation, pollution reduction, and utilization of renewable energy alternatives.**

COMMENT: Correctional facilities and programs have the responsibility to implement strategies that allow correctional facilities to be managed in ways that are most cost-effective and deliver superior performance, while improving environmental responsibility and sustainability. This includes recycling (including paper, metal, and plastic products), energy conservation (including building insulation, heating and ventilation, temperature controls, vehicle fuel efficiency, water economies, physical plant engineering, and energy measures), pollution reduction (including composting, sewer treatment, litter abatement, and carbon emissions), and utilization of renewable energy alternatives (bio-fuels, solar collection, turbine energy production, and methane collection).

1-JBC-1A-07 **Revised January 2013. The qualifications, authority, and responsibilities of the boot camp program administrator and other appointed personnel are specified in writing by statute or by the parent agency.**

COMMENT: None.

1-JBC-1A-08 **Revised August 2003. To be considered qualified, a boot camp program administrator must possess at a minimum, the following: a bachelor's degree in an appropriate discipline, two years of related administrative experience, and demonstrated administrative ability and leadership. The degree requirement may be satisfied by completion of a career development program that includes work-related experience, training, or college credits at a level of achievement equivalent to the bachelor's degree.**

COMMENT: Establishing high qualifications for the position of boot camp program administrator ensures that only qualified individuals are recruited and hired. It is the agency's responsibility to see that potential administrators receive the required education.

1-JBC-1A-09 **Deleted August 2002.**

1-JBC-1B-11 **Revised January 2001. Written policy, procedure, and practice provide for an independent financial audit of the facility. This audit is conducted annually or as stipulated by state regulation, but at least every three years. If the facility is a part of a state system, an internal audits section or department of the agency's central administration and/or statutory agency shall be considered independent of the facility to be audited.**

COMMENT: None.

1-JBC-1C-06 **Revised August 1995. Written policy specifies that equal employment opportunities exist for all positions. When deficiencies exist regarding the employment of minority groups and women, the institution can document the implementation of an affirmative action program that is approved by the appropriate government agency and can document annual reviews and the changes needed to keep the program current.**

COMMENT: Equal employment opportunity is a public policy goal. All qualified persons should be able to compete equally for entry into and promotion within the institution, and the affirmative action program should actively encourage the participation of members of minority groups, individuals with disability, and women in the institution's staff development program. The affirmative action program also should include corrective actions, when needed, in policies regarding pay rate, demotion, transfer, layoff, termination, and upgrades.

1-JBC-1C-06-1 **Added August 1995. Written policy, procedure, and practice provide a mechanism to process requests for reasonable accommodation to the known physical and/or mental impairments of a qualified individual with a disability, either an applicant or an employee. The accommodation need not be granted if it would impose an undue hardship or direct threat.**

COMMENT: *Reasonable accommodation* refers to modifications or adjustments, which enable qualified applicants with disabilities to access the job application process or which enable qualified employees with disabilities to perform the essential functions of the job and to enjoy the same terms, conditions, and privileges of employment that are available to persons without disabilities. *Terms, conditions, and privileges of employment* include, but are not limited to:

- recruitment, selection, and hiring
- salary and compensation
- benefits, holidays, leave, and work hours
- promotion and advancement
- staff development, including in-service training
- retirement, resignation, and termination

An *undue hardship* means significant difficulty or expense. *Direct threat* means a significant risk of substantial harm to the health or safety of any person, including the applicant or employee with a disability that cannot be eliminated or reduced by reasonable accommodation. A *qualified individual with a disability* means an individual with a disability who satisfies the requisite skill, experience, education, and other job-related requirements for the employment position such individual holds or desires, and who, with or without reasonable accommodation, can perform the essential functions of such position.

1-JBC-1C-12

Revised August 2007. A criminal record check is conducted on all new employees and volunteers in accordance with state and federal statutes. This record will include comprehensive identifier information to be collected and run against law enforcement indices. If suspect information on matters with potential terrorism connections is returned on a desirable applicant, it is forwarded to the local Joint Terrorism Task Force (JTTF) or another similar agency.

COMMENT: The program administrator should know of any criminal conviction that could directly affect an employee's job performance in a boot camp setting.

1-JBC-1C-14

Revised January 2012. There is a written agency policy, procedure, and practice that specifies support for a drug-free workplace for all employees. This policy includes at a minimum the following:

- **prohibition of the use of illegal drugs**
- **prohibition of possession of any illegal drug except in the performance of official duties**
- **the opportunities available for treatment and/or counseling for drug abuse**
- **the procedures to be used to ensure compliance**
- **the penalties for violation of the policy**

COMMENT: None.

1-JBC-1C-17

Revised August 2010. The institution maintains a current, accurate, confidential personnel record on each employee except where state statutes require open public records and the personnel record cannot be maintained confidentially. Information obtained as part of a required medical examination (and/or inquiry) regarding the medical condition or history of applicants and employees is collected and maintained on separate forms and in separate medical files and treated as a confidential medical record.

COMMENT: The personnel record should contain the following: initial application; reference letters; results of employment investigation; verification of training and experience; wage and salary information; job performance evaluations; incident reports, if any; and commendations and disciplinary actions, if any.

1-JBC-1D-08

Revised August 2000. Written policy, procedure, and practice provide that all administrative and managerial staff receive 40 hours of training in addition to orientation training during their first year of employment and 40 hours of training each year thereafter, in areas relevant to their position.

COMMENT: Ongoing training in topics relevant to an employee's position enhances skill and job performance.

1-JBC-1D-09 **Revised August 2005. Written policy, procedure, and practice provide that all newly hired professional specialists and juvenile care workers receive 120 hours of training during their first year of employment. At a minimum, this training covers the following areas:**

- **security procedures**
- **supervision of juveniles**
- **suicide intervention/prevention**
- **use of discipline in boot camps**
- **use of force**
- **juvenile rules and regulations**
- **program rules and regulations**
- **safety procedures**
- **firearms training**
- **key control**
- **interpersonal relations**
- **cultural diversity training**
- **communication skills**
- **cultural awareness**
- **crisis intervention**
- **sexual harassment**
- **legal issues**
- **specialized training, such as physical fitness, drill and ceremonies, various program components, aftercare issues, and so forth**
- **sexual abuse/assault**
- **code of ethics**

Additional topics may be added at the discretion of the agency or facility.

COMMENT: Since the duties of juvenile care workers frequently involve most institutional operations, their training should be comprehensive.

1-JBC-1D-09-1 **Added August 2005. Written policy, procedure, and practice provide that all juvenile care workers receive at least 40 hours of annual training. This training shall include at a minimum the following areas:**

- **standards of conduct/ethics**
- **security/safety/fire/medical/emergency procedures**
- **supervision of offenders including training on sexual abuse and assault**
- **use of force**

Additional topics shall be included based upon a needs assessment of both staff and institution requirements.

COMMENT: This training will enable employees to sharpen skills, maintain certification, and keep abreast of changes in policies, procedures, and legislative, judicial, or executive actions.

1-JBC-1D-10 **Revised August 2002. Written policy, procedure, and practice provide that all support employees who have regular or daily contact with juveniles receive 40 hours of training in addition to orientation training during their first year of employment and 40 hours of training each year thereafter. At a minimum, this training covers the following areas:**

- **security procedures**
- **supervision of juveniles**
- **signs of suicide risks and suicide precautions**
- **use of discipline**
- **use-of-force regulations and restraint techniques**
- **report writing**
- **juvenile rules and regulations**
- **boot camp program rules and regulations**
- **rights and responsibilities of juveniles**
- **fire and emergency procedures**
- **safety procedures**
- **firearms training**
- **key control**
- **interpersonal relations**
- **social/cultural lifestyles of the juvenile population**
- **cultural diversity training**
- **communication skills**
- **first aid/cardiopulmonary resuscitation (CPR)**
- **counseling techniques**
- **crisis intervention**
- **sexual harassment**
- **legal issues**
- **specialized training, such as physical fitness, drill and ceremonies, various program components, aftercare issues, and so forth**
- **sexual abuse/assault prevention**

COMMENT: Food service employees, industrial supervisors, and other support personnel whose work requires day-to-day contact with juveniles should receive basic training in juvenile supervision and security as well as specialized training in their field as it relates to the boot camp program setting. These individuals should be familiar with policies and procedures of the boot camp program, plus the basic rules of juvenile supervision and security. Ongoing training during subsequent years of employment enables employees to sharpen skills and keep abreast of changes in operational procedures.

1-JBC-1E-01 **Revised January 2012. Written agency policy, procedure and practice governing case record management includes, but is not limited to, the establishment, use, content, privacy, security, preservation, and destruction of case records.**

COMMENT: None.

1-JBC-2B-07 **Deleted July 2012.**

1-JBC-2C-01

Revised August 2002. Each sleeping area has, at a minimum, the following facilities and conditions:

- **25 square feet of unencumbered space per occupant**
- **access to toilets and a washbasin with hot and cold running water 24 hours a day without staff assistance**
- **a bed or bunk bed, mattress, pillow, writing surface, chair or stool, and hooks or closet space, or locker**
- **natural light**
- **temperatures that are appropriate to the summer and winter comfort zones**

COMMENT: Beds should be elevated from the floor and have clean, covered mattresses with blankets provided, as needed. *Unencumbered space* is usable space that is not encumbered by furnishings or fixtures. At least one dimension of the unencumbered space is no less than seven feet. In determining unencumbered space in the area, the total square footage is obtained and the square footage of fixtures and equipment is subtracted. All fixtures and equipment must be in operational position. The facility must provide the following, at a minimum: one bed per juvenile or bunk beds for two juveniles, plumbing fixtures (if inside the room), writing surface, locker, and chair or stool.

1-JBC-2C-03

Revised August 1998. Dayrooms provide sufficient seating and writing surfaces. Dayroom furnishings are consistent with the custody level of the juveniles assigned.

COMMENT: The standard provides managers and designers with flexibility in designing and furnishing dayrooms and takes into consideration the range of activities that may occur (for example, dayroom activities usually include television viewing, reading, recreation, conversation, and games, and sometimes include eating and work). In lower security settings, the use of "normalized" furnishings should be considered.

1-JBC-2C-06

Revised August 1995. Juveniles have access to operable showers with temperature-controlled hot and cold running water, at a minimum ratio of one shower for every eight juveniles, unless national or state building or health codes specify a different ratio. Water for showers is thermostatically controlled to temperatures ranging from 100 degrees Fahrenheit to 120 degrees Fahrenheit to ensure the safety of juveniles and to promote hygienic practices.

COMMENT: Juveniles can use scalding showers as a weapon against, or punishment for, other juveniles. Also, accidental injury could occur when cold water is drawn in other areas, thereby unexpectedly elevating the hot water in showers to scalding temperatures. Water temperatures below 100 degrees Fahrenheit are uncomfortable and may deter an individual from pursuing good hygienic practices. The temperature controls should not preclude the use of water at higher temperatures, if needed, in other areas of the institution, such as kitchens.

1-JBC-2C-07 **Revised August 1995. Juveniles with disabilities are housed in a manner that provides for their safety and security. Housing used by juveniles with disabilities is designed for their use and provides for integration with other juveniles. Programs and services are accessible to juveniles with disabilities who reside in the facility.**

COMMENT: If the facility accepts individuals with disabilities, it must provide for their housing and use of facility resources. Housing includes, but is not limited to, sleeping quarters/areas, furnishings, dayrooms, toilets, washbasins, showers/bathing facilities, and other common elements. Program and service areas include, but are not limited to, exercise and recreation areas, visiting rooms, laundry facilities, private counseling space, group meeting rooms, dining rooms, telephone facilities, admission and intake areas, and administrative areas, where appropriate.

1-JBC-2C-07-1 **Added January 2002. Written policy, procedure, and practice provide for the assignment of appropriately trained, individuals to assist disabled juveniles who cannot otherwise perform basic life functions.**

COMMENT: None.

1-JBC-2C-07-2 **Added August 2002. Written policy, procedure, and practice provide education, equipment, and facilities, and the support necessary for juveniles with disabilities to perform self-care and personal hygiene in a reasonably private environment.**

COMMENT: A *reasonably private environment* will vary, depending on individual and institutional circumstances, but is one which will maintain the dignity of the disabled individual in light of that person's disability.

1-JBC-2D-01 **Revised January 2008. Written policy, procedure, and practice require that all housing areas provide, at a minimum, the following:**

- **lighting of at least 20 foot-candles at desk level and in the personal grooming area, as documented by a qualified source, at least once per accreditation cycle**
- **natural light**
- **other lighting requirements for boot camps program determined by tasks to be performed**
- **access to a drinking fountain**
- **heating, ventilation, and acoustical systems to ensure healthful and adequate living and working conditions for juveniles and staff**

COMMENT: None.

1-JBC-2D-02

Revised January 2012. Noise levels in inmate housing units do not exceed 70 dBA (A Scale). Measurements shall be conducted annually by a qualified source with at least one measurement taking place during night time and one measurement taking place during day time.

COMMENT: None.

1-JBC-2D-02-1

Deleted January 2013.

1-JBC-2D-03

Revised August 2007. Circulation is at least 15 cubic feet of outside or re-circulated filtered air per minute per occupant for rooms, housing areas, staff stations, and dining areas, as documented by a qualified technician and should be checked not less than once per accreditation cycle.

Interpretation August 2002. The words "accreditation cycle" are interpreted as within the past three years.

COMMENT: Mechanical ventilation may provide for recirculation of outside air except where prohibited by codes. The outside air requirements may be reduced to a minimum of 33 percent of the specified ventilated air quality if adequate temperature control is provided in addition to filtering equipment so that the maximum concentration of particles entering the space is reduced to acceptable limits. In no case should the outdoor air quantity be less than five cubic feet per minute per person.

1-JBC-2D-04

Revised August 2006. Temperatures in indoor living and work areas are appropriate to the summer and winter comfort zones.

COMMENT: Temperature should be capable of being mechanically raised or lowered to an acceptable comfort level

1-JBC-2E-02

Revised August 1995. Both outdoor and covered/enclosed exercise areas for general population juveniles arc provided in sufficient number to ensure that each juvenile is offered at least one hour of access daily. Use of outdoor areas is preferred, but covered/enclosed areas must be available for use in inclement weather. Covered/enclosed areas can be designed for multiple uses as long as the design and furnishings do not interfere with scheduled exercise activities.

The minimum space requirements for exercise areas are as follows:

- **Outdoor exercise areas in facilities where 100 or more juveniles utilize one recreation area—15 square feet per juvenile for the maximum number of juveniles expected to use the space at one time, but not less than 1,500 square feet of unencumbered space.**

- **Outdoor exercise areas in facilities where less than 100 juveniles have unlimited access to an individual recreation area—15 square feet per juvenile for the maximum number of juveniles expected to use the space at one time, but not less than 750 square feet of unencumbered space.**
- **Covered/enclosed exercise areas in facilities where 100 or more juveniles utilize one recreation area should have 15 square feet per juvenile for the maximum number of juveniles expected to use the space at one time, with a minimum ceiling height of 18 feet, but not less than 1,000-square feet of unencumbered space.**
- **Covered/enclosed exercise areas in facilities where less than 100 juveniles utilize one recreation area should have 15 square feet per juvenile for the maximum number of juveniles expected to use the space at one time, with a minimum ceiling height of 18 feet, but not less than 500 square feet of unencumbered space.**

COMMENT: Exercise/recreation spaces are not the same as dayrooms, although dayrooms can provide added opportunities for some exercise and recreation activities. The standard establishes performance requirements for exercise spaces, offering design and operational flexibility. It allows facilities in some climates to cover and/or enclose a yard, while others will have to provide indoor space; these spaces do not have to be "indoors" but must be fully functional when the outdoor areas are not feasible for use.

1-JBC-2F-02 **Revised August 1995. Reasonable accommodation is made to ensure that all parts of the facility that are accessible to the public are accessible and usable by staff and visitors with disabilities.**

COMMENT: None.

1-JBC-2G-01 **Deleted January 2007.**

1-JBC-3A-02 **Revised January 2007. Space is provided for a 24 hour control center for monitoring and coordinating the facility's security, safety, and communications systems. The control center provides access to a washbasin and toilet. There is a communication system between the control center and juvenile living areas.**

COMMENT: The control center should contain sufficient space for monitoring and coordinating all internal and external security systems, safety alarms, detection systems, and other mechanical and electrical systems. A mechanical or audio communication system should be used to supplement direct staff supervision activities (for example, to advise staff of emergency needs), not as a substitute for staff supervision.

1-JBC-3A-16 **Revised August 2000 (Mandatory). Written policy, procedure, and practice restrict the use of physical force to instances of justifiable self-defense, protection of others, protection of property, prevention of escapes, and to maintain or regain control, and then only as a last resort and in accordance with appropriate statutory authority. In no event is physical force justifiable as punishment. A written report is prepared following all uses of force and is submitted to administrative staff for review.**

COMMENT: Correctional personnel should be prepared to justify their use of physical force. The phrase "as a last resort" may be defined through appropriate statutory authority.

1-JBC-3A-24 **Revised January 1994. [The standard was revised in January 1994, but the revision was inadvertently omitted from *Standards for Juvenile Correctional Boot Camp Programs*, published in January 1995.] Written policy, procedure, and practice provide that, except in emergency situations, visual inspections of juvenile body cavities are conducted by officers of the same sex and in private and based on reasonable belief that the juvenile is carrying contraband or other prohibited material. Reasonable belief is not required when juveniles return from contact with the general public or from outside the institution. In all cases, this inspection is conducted by trained personnel.**

COMMENT: None.

1-JBC-3A-25 **Revised August 2000 (Mandatory). Written policy, procedure, and practice govern the control and use of keys.**

COMMENT: None.

1-JBC-3A-26 **Revised August 2000 (Mandatory). Written policy, procedure, and practice govern the control and use of tools, and culinary and medical equipment.**

COMMENT: Nonc.

1-JBC-3A-32 **Added new subtitle January 1995.**

Preservation of Physical Evidence

Written policy, procedure, and practice provide for the preservation, control, and disposition of all physical evidence obtained in connection with a violation of law and/or institutional regulation. At a minimum, the procedures shall address the following:

- **chain of custody**
- **evidence handling**
- **location and storage requirements**

COMMENT: Strict accountability of physical evidence collected in connection with a crime must be established to preserve the integrity of the disciplinary and/or legal process. Minor rule violations should be exempt from the procedural requirements of evidence control, preservation, and disposition.

1-JBC-3B-08

Revised January 1998. Emergency equipment and systems are tested at least quarterly. Power generators are inspected weekly and load tested quarterly at a minimum or in accordance with manufacturer's recommendations and instruction manuals.

COMMENT: Emergency equipment, such as standby lighting, batteries, power generators, fire-fighting apparatus, communications systems, and alarms should be checked frequently to ensure their reliability.

1-JBC-3B-12

Revised August 2007 (Mandatory). All institution personnel are trained in the implementation of written emergency plans. Work stoppage plans are communicated only to appropriate supervisory or other personnel directly involved in the implementation of those plans.

COMMENT: A contingency plan for maintaining essential services is crucial. This plan might involve agreements with other law enforcement agencies, such as local or state police. Additionally, the administrator should attempt to ensure the safety and well-being of employees who do not participate in the job action.

1-JBC-3B-16

Added January 2003. Written policy, procedure, and practice define critical incidents for the facility and provide for a debriefing to be conducted after each such incident. The debriefing process includes coordination and feedback about the incident with designated staff of the facility as soon as possible after the incident. A debriefing includes, but is not limited to:

- **a review of staff and juvenile actions during the incident**
- **a review of the incident's impact on staff and juveniles**
- **a review of corrective actions taken and still needed**
- **plans for improvement to avoid another incident**

COMMENT: A *critical incident* is any event or situation that threatens staff or juveniles in their community (criminal justice setting). While debriefings should occur as soon as possible, some information may not be available until later. All staff impacted by a critical incident should be included in the debriefings and referred to appropriate services to mitigate the stress associated with these events. All critical incidents should be reviewed by the administration, security, and health services. A two-week follow-up debriefing should occur to review the validity and appropriateness of all policies, plans, and information used during the critical incident and immediately after.

1-JBC-3C-14

Revised January 2008. Written policy, procedure, and practice provide that juveniles are scheduled for a hearing as soon as practicable but no later than seven days, excluding weekends and holidays, after being charged with a violation. Juveniles are notified of the time and place of the hearing at least 24-hours in advance of the hearing.

COMMENT: To ensure fairness and the integrity of the disciplinary process, juveniles charged with rule violations should receive hearings as soon as possible unless the hearing is prevented by exceptional circumstances, unavoidable delays, or reasonable postponements. Reasons for all delays should be documented.

1-JBC-3D-04

Revised August 1995. Written policy, procedure, and practice prohibit discrimination based on a juvenile's race, religion, national origin, sex, disability, or political views in making administrative decisions and in providing access to programs.

COMMENT: Juveniles should be assured equal opportunities to participate in all institutional programs.

1-JBC-3D-06-1

Added August 2002. Written policy, procedure, and practice ensure that information is provided to juveniles about sexual abuse/assault including:

- **prevention/intervention**
- **self-protection**
- **reporting sexual abuse/assault**
- **treatment and counseling**

The information is communicated orally and in writing, in a language clearly understood by the juvenile, upon arrival at the facility.

COMMENT: None.

1-JBC-3D-06-2

Added January 2003. Juveniles are screened within 24 hours of arrival at the facility for potential vulnerabilities or tendencies of acting out with sexually aggressive behavior. Housing assignments are made accordingly.

COMMENT: None.

1-JBC-3D-06-3

Added January 2003. Written policy, procedure, and practice require that an investigation is conducted and documented whenever a sexual assault is alleged, threatened, or occurs.

COMMENT: The agency should report occurrences/allegations of sexual assault or threat in accordance with the laws of the jurisdiction. The investigation may be limited by what is allowed by the laws of the jurisdiction.

1-JBC-3D-06-4 **Added January 2003. Written policy, procedure, and practice require that juveniles identified as high risk with a history of assaultive behavior are assessed by a mental health or other qualified professional. Such juveniles are identified, monitored, counseled, and provided appropriate treatment.**

COMMENT: None.

1-JBC-3D-06-5 **Added January 2003. Written policy, procedure, and practice require that juveniles identified as at risk for sexual victimization are assessed by a mental health or other qualified professional. Such juveniles are identified, monitored, and counseled.**

COMMENT: None.

1-JBC-3D-06-6 **Added January 2003. Written policy, procedure, and practice ensure that sexual conduct between staff and juveniles, volunteers, or contract personnel and juveniles, regardless of consensual status, is prohibited and subject to administrative and criminal disciplinary sanctions.**

COMMENT: None.

1-JBC-3D-06-7 **Added January 2003. Victims of sexual assault are referred under appropriate security provisions to a community facility for treatment and gathering of evidence. If these procedures are performed in-house, the following guidelines are used:**

- **A history is taken by health care professionals who conduct an examination to document the extent of physical injury and to determine if referral to another medical facility is indicated. With the victim's consent, the examination includes collection of evidence from the victim, using a kit approved by the appropriate authority.**
- **Provision is made for testing for sexually transmitted diseases (for example, HIV, gonorrhea, hepatitis, and other diseases) and counseling, as appropriate.**
- **Prophylactic treatment and follow-up for sexually transmitted diseases are offered to all victims, as appropriate.**
- **Following the physical examination, there is availability of an evaluation by a mental health professional to assess the need for crisis-intervention counseling and long-term follow-up.**
- **A report is made to the facility or program administrator or designee to assure separation of the victim from his or her assailant.**

COMMENT: None.

1-JBC-3D-06-8 **Added January 2003. Written policy, procedure, and practice provide that juveniles who are victims of sexual abuse have the option to report the incident to a designated staff member other than an immediate point-of-contact line staff member.**

COMMENT: None.

1-JBC-3D-06-9 **Added January 2003. Written policy, procedure, and practice provide that all case records associated with claims of sexual abuse, including incident reports, investigative reports, juvenile information, case disposition, medical and counseling evaluation findings, and recommendations for post-release treatment and/or counseling are retained in accordance with an established schedule.**

COMMENT: None.

1-JBC-4A-05 **Revised August 2004. Therapeutic diets are provided as prescribed by appropriate clinicians. A therapeutic diet manual is available in health services and food services for reference and information. Prescriptions for therapeutic diets should be specific and complete, furnished in writing to the food service manager, and rewritten annually, or more often as clinically indicated.**

COMMENT: Therapeutic diets are prepared and served to offenders according to the orders of the treating clinician or as directed by the responsible health authority. Therapeutic diets should be kept as simple as possible and should conform as closely as possible to the menus served to other offenders.

1-JBC-4A-08-1 **Added August 2011. All staff, contractors, and inmate workers who work in the food service department are trained in the use of food service equipment and in the safety procedures to be followed in the food service department.**

COMMENT: None.

1-JBC-4A-10 **Revised August 1999. Written policy, procedure, and practice provide that stored shelf goods are maintained at 45 degrees-to-80 degrees Fahrenheit, refrigerated foods at 35 degrees-to-40 degrees Fahrenheit, and frozen foods at 0 degrees Fahrenheit or below, unless national or state health codes specify otherwise.**

COMMENT: None.

1-JBC-4B-10 **Revised August 2007. Written policy, procedure, and practice provide for the issue of suitable, clean bedding and linen, including two sheets, pillow and pillowcase, one mattress, not to exclude a mattress with integrated pillow, and sufficient blankets to provide comfort under existing temperature controls. There is provision for linen exchange, including towels, at least weekly. Blanket exchange must be available at least quarterly.**

COMMENT: Collection, storage, and exchange methods for bedding and linens should be done hygienically; that is, blankets, pillows, mattresses covers, and mattresses should be clean before reissue, and linen and towels must be laundered before reissue.

1-JBC-4B-12

Revised January 1998. Written policy, procedure, and practice require that articles necessary for maintaining proper personal hygiene are provided to all juveniles.

COMMENT: As part of the admissions process, each juvenile should be given soap, a toothbrush, toothpaste or powder, a comb, and toilet paper. Shaving equipment should be made available upon request, and the special hygiene needs of females should be met. Proper personal hygiene improves juveniles' health and medical conditions.

1-JBC-4C-22-1

Revised January 2001. Written policy, procedure, and practice provide for early identification and treatment of juveniles with alcohol and drug abuse problems through a standardized battery assessment. This battery shall be documented and include, at a minimum, the following:

- **screening and sorting**
- **clinical assessment and reassessment**
- **medical assessment for appropriate drug and alcohol program assignment based on the needs of the individual juveniles**
- **referrals**
- **monitoring and drug testing**

COMMENT: None.

1-JBC-4C-25

Revised August 2001. Written policy, procedure, and practice for the collection and recording of health appraisal data require the following:

- **The process is completed in a uniform manner as determined by the health authority.**
- **Health history and vital signs are collected by health-trained or qualified health personnel.**
- **Review of the results of the medical examination, tests, and identification of problems is performed by a physician or other health care personnel, if such is authorized in the medical practice act.**
- **Collection of all other health appraisal data is performed only by qualified health personnel.**

COMMENT: None.

1-JBC-4C-30

Revised August 2002. Written policy, procedure, and practice require that first aid kit(s) are available. The responsible physician approves the contents, number, location, and procedure for periodic inspection of the kit(s). An automatic external defibrillator is available for use at the facility.

COMMENT: The medical staff develops written procedures outlining the use of first aid kits by nonmedical staff.

1-JBC-5A-05 **Revised August 2013. Written policy, procedure, and practice provide that new juveniles receive written orientation materials and/or translations in their own language if they do not understand English. These materials may also be provided electronically, but inmates in segregation must be provided the information in a written format so that their access to the information is not impeded by their custody status. When a literacy problem exists, a staff member helps the juvenile in understanding the material. Completion of orientation is documented by a statement signed and dated by the juvenile.**

COMMENT: Orientation should include informal classes, distribution of written materials about the facility's programs (or how to access this information electronically, if available), rules and regulations, and discussions. Orientation also should be used to observe offender behavior and to identify special problems. The use of electronic kiosks is allowed as a means of providing the inmate handbook. Agencies using such kiosks should implement strategies to allow access to this information by general population inmates without interference by facility staff without a valid security-related reason. Inmates who are unable to read and write should be assisted through case management services provided by the facility.

1-JBC-5B-02-1 **Revised August 2002. Written policy, procedure, and practice prohibit discrimination on the basis of disability in the provision of services, programs, and activities administered for program beneficiaries and participants.**

COMMENT: Services, programs, and activities include, but are not limited to, the following:

- academic and vocational education (including developmental and rehabilitative programs)
- work programs/work release programs (by providing reasonable accommodations or alternatives for juveniles with disabilities so that the benefits of these programs, including sentence-reduction credits, are available to juveniles with disabilities)
- recreation, exercise, and activities
- mail, telephone, and visiting
- library
- religious programs
- reception and orientation
- transportation services (to provide for safety and security, and to avoid undue discomfort, in light of the juvenile's disabilities)
- classification
- food service
- sanitation and hygiene
- health care
- social services
- release
- discipline, grievance procedures, and due process proceedings
- safety and emergency procedures
- access to media, courts, counsel, and law library

- commissary/canteen
- volunteer programs
- psychological and psychiatric services

Program beneficiaries and participants include, but are not limited to: juveniles, family members, clergy, attorneys, volunteers, and other authorized visitors.

The institution may be required to take remedial action, when necessary, to afford program beneficiaries and participants with disabilities an opportunity to participate in, and enjoy the benefit of services, programs, or activities. Remedial action may include, but is not limited to: 1) making reasonable modifications to policies, practices, or procedures, 2) providing auxiliary aids and services to the hearing and visually impaired, 3) constructing new or altering existing facilities, and 4) delivering services and so on at alternate accessible sites.

1-JBC-5B-02-2

Added August 2002. Written policy, procedure, and practice provide for staff and juvenile access to an appropriately trained and qualified individual who is educated in the problems and challenges faced by juveniles with physical and/or mental impairments, programs designed to educate and assist disabled juveniles, and all legal requirements for the protection of juveniles with disabilities.

COMMENT: An *appropriately trained and qualified individual,* as used in this standard, is one who has been designated by the warden, superintendent, or other authority, to coordinate efforts to comply with and carry out responsibilities defined by the Americans with Disabilities Act. That individual should develop relationships with, and use the expertise of institutional staff, advocacy groups, nonprofit organizations, agencies of government, and others that have relevant knowledge and experience.

1-JBC-5B-05

Revised August 2000. A personalized program is designed with multidisciplinary input from the facility for and with each juvenile, and whenever appropriate and feasible, with participation from parents, which includes measurable criteria of expected behavior and accomplishments and a time schedule for achievement. The program is documented by staff and juvenile signatures.

COMMENT: None.

1-JBC-5C-05

Revised January 1996. The institution has a formal mechanism to determine appropriate levels of social services staffing. The mechanism used to determine such staffing levels includes at a minimum:

- **type of juvenile population served**
- **type of institution**
- **legal requirements**
- **goals to be accomplished**

The institution's use of a "team" approach and use of paraprofessionals, volunteers, and students also may influence the numbers of professional staff required.

COMMENT: Social services programs can assist juveniles with family and personal problems through supportive guidance and professional assistance. A counseling program that is coordinated with the overall facility rehabilitation program can be effective in resolving personal and interpersonal problems.

1-JBC-5C-10 **Revised January 2001. Written policy, procedure, and practice provide for early identification and treatment of juveniles with alcohol and drug abuse problems through a standardized battery assessment. This battery shall be documented and include, at a minimum, the following:**

- **screening and sorting**
- **clinical assessment and reassessment**
- **medical assessment for drug and alcohol program assignment appropriate to the needs of the individual juveniles**
- **referrals**

COMMENT: None.

1-JBC-5C-13 **This interpretation (listed as 1-JBC-5C-16) applies to all standards from 1-JBC-5C-13 through 1-JBC-5C-16.**

1-JBC-5C-16 **Interpretation August 2003. The words "Where a drug program exists" are interpreted as a therapeutic community.**

1-JBC-5D-07 **Revised January 2012. Vocational training and/or vocational counseling programs are integrated with academic programs and are relevant to the vocational needs of the juvenile population and to employment opportunities in the community.**

COMMENT: Relevant vocational programs can occur through work assignments, apprenticeships, and on-the-job training. Employment opportunities can be assessed through contact with local businesses, industries, and trade groups.

1-JBC-5D-15 **Added August 1995. The juvenile work plan provides for employment for juveniles with disabilities.**

COMMENT: None.

1-JBC-5G-08 **Revised August 2004. The chaplain or staff person develops and maintains close relationships with religious sources in the community.**

COMMENT: Community resources can help administer religious services on special holidays or as needed to meet the requirements of the diversity of religious faiths among juveniles.

1-JBC-5H-04 **Revised August 2002. Written policy, procedure, and practice specify that juveniles are permitted to send sealed letters to a specified class of persons and organizations, including but not limited to the following: courts, counsel, officials of the confining authority, administrators of grievance systems, and members of the releasing authority. Staff, in the presence of the juvenile, may be allowed to inspect outgoing privileged mail for contraband before it is sealed. Mail to juveniles from this specified class of persons and organizations may be opened only to inspect for contraband and only in the presence of the juveniles, unless waived in writing, or in circumstances which may indicate contamination.**

COMMENT: Suspicious mail may include packages and letters unusual in appearance or which appear different from mail normally received or sent by the individual; packages and letters of a size or shape not customarily received or sent by the individual; packages and letters with a city and/or state postmark that is different from the return address; or packages and letters leaking, stained, or emitting a strange or unusual odor, or which have a powdery residue.

1-JBC-5H-08 **Revised August 1994. [The standard was revised in January 1994, but the revision was inadvertently omitted in *Standards for Juvenile Correctional Boot Camp Programs*, published in January 1995.] Written policy, procedure, and practice require that all funds received through the mail are held for the juvenile in accordance with procedures approved by the parent agency. The facility may refuse acceptance of cash or personal checks by returning the items to the sender.**

COMMENT: The administration should have discretion to control the flow of cash to juveniles. However, when cash is intercepted and withheld by the facility, it must be in accordance with written procedures that specify who is responsible for the cash, where it is to be deposited, and the method of return or transferal on the juvenile's release or placement.

1-JBC-5H-09 **Revised August 2006. Written policy, procedure, and practice require that, excluding weekends and holidays, or emergency situations, incoming and outgoing letters are held for no more than 48 hours and packages (if allowed) are held no more than 72 hours.**

Interpretation August 2002. The term *emergency situation* is interpreted as any significant disruption of normal facility or agency procedure, policy, or activity caused by riot, escape, fire, natural disaster, employee action, or other serious incident.

COMMENT: Inspection for contraband letters should take no longer than 48 hours to complete so that incoming letters should be distributed to inmates and outgoing letters sent to the post office within 48 hours of receipt. Similarly, inspection of packages normally should take no longer than 72 hours to complete. The standard does not prohibit the holding of mail for inmates who are temporarily absent from the facility (for example, in a hospital or court).

1-JBC-5H-11

Revised August 2002. Written policy, procedure, and practice provide for juvenile access to public telephones. Juveniles with hearing and/or speech disabilities, and juveniles who wish to communicate with parties who have such disabilities, shall be afforded access to a Telecommunications Device for the Deaf (TDD), or comparable equipment. Public telephones with volume control also shall be made available to juveniles with hearing impairments.

COMMENT: Sufficient telephone facilities should permit reasonable and equitable access to all inmates and permit a reasonable amount of privacy. Procedures should specify the hours during which the telephone is available, the maximum length of calls, and any limitation on calls. All long distance calls should be made collect.

1-JBC-5H-11-1

Added August 2002. Written policy, procedure, and practice ensure that juveniles have access to reasonably priced telephone services. Correctional agencies ensure that:

- **Contracts involving telephone services for juveniles comply with all applicable state and federal regulations.**
- **Contracts are based on rates and surcharges that are commensurate with those charged to the general public for like services. Any deviation from ordinary consumer rates reflects actual costs associated with the provision of services in a correctional setting.**
- **Contracts for juvenile telephone services provide the broadest range of calling options determined by the agency administrator to be consistent with the requirements of sound correctional management.**

COMMENT: When procuring and renewing telephone services, correctional officials should inquire into the reasons for proposed deviations from standard charges and seek the best possible rates for the broadest possible range of calling options.

1-JBC-5H-14-1

Added August 2003. Written policy, procedure, and practice require that a juvenile is informed in a timely manner of the verifiable death or critical illness of an immediate family member. In case of the critical illness of an immediate family member, the juvenile is allowed, whenever statutes and circumstances allow, to go to the bedside under escort or alone.

COMMENT: Classification, status, geography, security level, and other specified criteria should determine eligibility. Immediate family is usually defined as parent, spouse, child, sibling, grandparent, or legal guardian.

Appendix B Revised (January 2001). Refer to *Standards Supplement* Appendix D.

Juvenile Correctional Facilities (JCF), 4th Edition

4-JCF-1C-01

Revised January 2013. Living units that are designed primarily for single occupancy provide:

- **Some degree of privacy with at least 35 unencumbered square feet per occupant**
- **When confinement exceeds 10 hours per day, there are at least 80 square-feet per occupant**
- **A bed for each juvenile**
- **Adequate storage space for clothing and personal belongings for each juvenile**
- **A desk and a chair or stool for each juvenile**
- **Access to toilets and a washbasin with hot and cold running water 24 hours per day without staff assistance**

COMMENT: None.

4-JCF-2A-18

Revised January 2011 (Mandatory). Four/five point restraints are used only in extreme instances and only when other types of restraints have proven ineffective or the safety of the juvenile is in jeopardy. Advance approval is secured from the facility administrator/designee before a juvenile is placed in a four/five point restraint. Subsequently, the health authority or designee must be notified to assess the juvenile's medical and mental health condition, and to advise whether, on the basis of serious danger to self or others, the juvenile should be in a medical/mental health unit for emergency involuntary treatment with sedation and/or other medical management, as appropriate. If the juvenile is not transferred to a medical/mental health unit and is restrained in a four/five point position, the following minimum procedures are followed:

- **Direct visual observation by staff is continuous prior to obtaining approval from the health authority or designee;**
- **Subsequent visual observation is made at least 15 minutes;**
- **Restraint procedures are in accordance with guidelines approved by the designated health authority;**
- **All decisions and actions are documented.**

COMMENT: None.

4-JCF-2A-18-1

Added August 2008. Written policy, procedure and practice, in general, prohibit the use of restraints on female juveniles during active labor and the delivery of a child. Any deviation from the prohibition requires approval by, and guidance on, methodology from the medical authority and is based on documented serious security risks. The medical authority provides guidance on the use of restraints on pregnant offenders prior to active labor and delivery.

COMMENT: None.

1-JCF-3B-01

Revised August 2013. Within 24 hours of admission, facility staff provide a rulebook and discuss with the juvenile:

- **rules governing conduct**
- **chargeable offenses**
- **the range of penalties**
- **disciplinary procedures**
- **incentives for good behavior**

This information is provided to juveniles in a written and/or electronic format. If the juvenile handbook is provided electronically, juveniles in segregation are provided the information in a written format so that their access to the information is not impeded by their custody status. The handbook is translated into those languages spoken by significant numbers of juveniles.

COMMENT: The use of electronic kiosks is allowed as a means of providing the juvenile handbook. Agencies using such kiosks should implement strategies to allow access to this information by general population juveniles without interference by facility staff without a valid security-related reason. Juveniles who are unable to read and write should be assisted through case management services provided by the facility.

4-JCF-3C-03

Revised January 2012. The following procedure is followed for any juvenile placed in room confinement:

- **Checked visually by staff at least every 15 minutes**
- **Visited at least once each day by personnel from administrative, clinical, social work, religious, and/or medical units. As safety and security permit, actual entry into the room of confinement with the juvenile or removal of the juvenile from the room for the purpose of discussion or counseling constitutes a visit.**
- **A log is kept recording:**
  a. the name and title of the individual who authorized the confinement
  b. name and title of persons visiting the juvenile
  c. record of time checks
  d. the person authorizing release from confinement
  e. the time of release
- **Suicidal juveniles are under continuous one-to one observations until evaluated by a mental health professional.**

COMMENT: None.

4-JCF-4A-10-1

Added August 2011. All staff, contractors, and juveniles that work in the food service department are trained in the use of food service equipment and in the safety procedures to be followed in the food service department.

COMMENT: None.

4-JCF-5D-06

Revised January 2012. Vocational training programs are integrated with academic programs, are age appropriate, and are relevant to the vocational needs of the juvenile population and employment opportunities.

COMMENT: None.

4-JCF-6A-07

Revised January 2013. The qualifications, authority, and responsibilities of the facility administrator and other appointed personnel are specified in writing by statute or in position descriptions of the parent agency.

COMMENT: None.

4-JCF-6A-09-1

Added August 2010. The facility/agency shall demonstrate it has examined, and, where appropriate and feasible, implemented strategies that promote recycling, energy and water conservation, pollution reduction, and utilization of renewable energy alternatives.

COMMENT: Correctional facilities and programs have the responsibility to implement strategies that allow correctional facilities to be managed in ways that are most cost-effective and deliver superior performance, while improving environmental responsibility and sustainability. This includes recycling (including paper, metal, and plastic products), energy conservation (including building insulation, heating and ventilation, temperature controls, vehicle fuel efficiency, water economies, physical plant engineering, and energy measures), pollution reduction (including composting, sewer treatment, litter abatement, and carbon emissions), and utilization of renewable energy alternatives (bio-fuels, solar collection, turbine energy production, and methane collection).

4-JCF-6D-03

Revised January 2012. There is a written agency policy, procedure, and practice that specifies support for a drug-free workplace for all employees. This policy includes at a minimum the following:

- **prohibition of the use of illegal drugs**
- **prohibition of possession of any illegal drug except in the performance of official duties**
- **the opportunities available for treatment and/or counseling for drug abuse**
- **the procedures to be used to ensure compliance**
- **the penalties for violation of the policy**

COMMENT: None.

4-JCF-6D-11 **Revised August 2010. The institution maintains a current, accurate, confidential personnel record on each employee except where state statutes require open public records and the personnel record cannot be maintained confidentially. Information obtained as part of a required medical examination (and/or inquiry) regarding the medical condition or history of applicants and employees is collected and maintained on separate forms and in separate medical files and treated as a confidential medical record.**

COMMENT: None.

Juvenile Day Treatment Programs (JDTP), 1st Edition

1-JDTP-1A-01-1

Added August 2010. The facility/agency shall demonstrate it has examined, and where appropriate and feasible, implemented strategies that promote recycling, energy and water conservation, pollution reduction and utilization of renewable energy alternatives.

COMMENT: Correctional facilities and programs have the responsibility to implement strategies that allow correctional facilities to be managed in ways that are most cost-effective and deliver superior performance, while improving environmental responsibility and sustainability. This includes recycling (including paper, metal, and plastic products), energy conservation (including building insulation, heating and ventilation, temperature controls, vehicle fuel efficiency, water economies, physical plant engineering, and energy measures), pollution reduction (including composting, sewer treatment, litter abatement, and carbon emissions), and utilization of renewable energy alternatives (bio-fuels, solar collection, turbine energy production, and methane collection).

1-JDTP-1A-11

Revised January 2013. The qualifications, authority, and responsibilities of the program administrator and other appointed personnel are specified in writing by statute or by the parent agency.

COMMENT: None.

1-JDTP-1A-12

Revised August 2003. To be considered qualified, a program administrator, at a minimum, must possess the following: a bachelor's degree in an appropriate discipline, two years of related administrative experience, and demonstrated administrative ability and leadership. The degree requirement may be satisfied by the completion of a career development program that includes work-related experience, training, or college credits at a level of achievement equivalent to a bachelor's degree.

COMMENT: Establishing high qualifications ensures that only qualified individuals are recruited and hired. It is the agency's responsibility to see that potential administrators receive the required education.

1-JDTP-1A-13

Deleted August 2002.

1-JDTP-1B-08

Revised January 2003. The accounting system is designed to show the status of income and expenditures.

COMMENT: Current information is needed to meet objectives, prevent budget discrepancies, respond to emerging needs, and ensure that the flow of funds is proceeding as planned.

1-JDTP-1B-12

Revised January 2001. Written policy, procedure, and practice provide for an independent financial audit of the facility. This audit is conducted annually or as stipulated by statute or regulation, but at least every three years. If the facility is a part of a state system, an internal audits section or department of the agency's central administration and/or statutory agency shall be considered independent of the facility to be audited.

COMMENT: None.

1-JDTP-1C-07

Revised August 1995. Written policy specifies that equal employment opportunities exist for all positions. When deficiencies exist regarding the employment of minority groups and women, the institution can document the implementation of an affirmative action program that is approved by the appropriate government agency and can document annual reviews and the changes needed to keep the program current.

COMMENT: Equal employment opportunity is a public policy goal. All qualified persons should be able to compete equally for entry into and promotion within the institution, and the affirmative action program should actively encourage the participation of members of minority groups, individuals with disability, and women in the institution's staff development program. The affirmative action program also should include corrective actions, when needed, in policies regarding pay rate, demotion, transfer, layoff, termination, and upgrades.

1-JDTP-1C-07-1

Added August 1995. Written policy, procedure, and practice provide a mechanism to process requests for reasonable accommodation to the known physical and/or mental impairments of a qualified individual with a disability, either an applicant or an employee. The accommodation need not be granted if it would impose an undue hardship or direct threat.

COMMENT: *Reasonable accommodation* refers to modifications or adjustments, which enable qualified applicants with disabilities to access the job application process or which enable qualified employees with disabilities to perform the essential functions of the job and to enjoy the same terms, conditions, and privileges of employment that are available to persons without disabilities. *Terms, conditions, and privileges of employment* include, but are not limited to:

- recruitment, selection, and hiring
- salary and compensation
- benefits, holidays, leave, and work hours
- promotion and advancement
- staff development, including in-service training
- retirement, resignation, and termination

An *undue hardship* means significant difficulty or expense. *Direct threat* means a significant risk of substantial harm to the health or safety of any person, including the applicant or employee with a disability that cannot be eliminated or reduced by reasonable accommodation. A *qualified individual with a disability* means an individual with a disability who satisfies the requisite skill, experience, education, and other job-related requirements for the employment position such individual holds or desires, and who, with or without reasonable accommodation, can perform the essential functions of such position.

1-JDTP-1C-16

Revised August 2007. A criminal record check is conducted on all new employees in accordance with state and federal statutes. This record will include comprehensive identifier information to be collected and run against law enforcement indices. If suspect information on matters with potential terrorism connections is returned on a desirable applicant, it is forwarded to the local Joint Terrorism Task Force (JTTF) or another similar agency.

COMMENT: The administrator should know of any criminal conviction that could directly affect an employee's job performance in a program setting.

1-JDTP-1C-18

Revised January 2012. There is a written agency policy, procedure, and practice that specifies support for a drug-free workplace for all employees. This policy includes at a minimum the following:

- **prohibition of the use of illegal drugs**
- **prohibition of possession of any illegal drug except in the performance of official duties**
- **the opportunities available for treatment and/or counseling for drug abuse**
- **the procedures to be used to ensure compliance**
- **the penalties for violation of the policy**

COMMENT: None.

1-JDTP-1C-22

Revised August 2010. The institution maintains a current, accurate, confidential personnel record on each employee except where state statutes require open public records and the personnel record cannot be maintained confidentially. Information obtained as part of a required medical examination (and/or inquiry) regarding the medical condition or history of applicants and employees is collected and maintained on separate forms and in separate medical files and treated as a confidential medical record.

COMMENT: The personnel record should contain the following: initial application; reference letters; results of employment investigation; verification of training and experience; wage and salary information; job performance evaluations; incident reports, if any; and commendations and disciplinary actions, if any.

1-JDTP-1D-01

Revised August 2005. Written policy, procedure, and practice provide that the staff development and training program is planned, coordinated, and supervised by a qualified employee who has completed training-for-trainers' training or its equivalent. The training plan is reviewed annually.

COMMENT: The training plan should include all pre-service, in-service, and specialized training curriculums, with specific timelines for completing each training unit. The plan should consider the program's mission, physical characteristics, and specific juvenile populations.

1-JDTP-1D-07

Revised August 2000. Written policy, procedure, and practice provide that all administrative and managerial staff receive 40 hours of training in addition to orientation training during their first year of employment and 40 hours of training each year thereafter, in areas relevant to their position.

COMMENT: Ongoing training in topics relevant to an employee's position enhances skills and job performance.

1-JDTP-1D-08

Revised August 2005. Written policy, procedure, and practice provide that all new juvenile care workers receive 120 hours of training during their first year of employment. At a minimum, this training covers the following areas:

- **security and safety procedures**
- **emergency and fire procedures**
- **supervision of offenders**
- **suicide intervention/prevention**
- **use of force**
- **offender rights**
- **key control**
- **interpersonal relations**
- **communication skills**
- **standards of conduct**
- **cultural awareness**
- **sexual abuse/assault intervention**
- **code of ethics**

Additional topics may be added at the discretion of the agency or facility.

COMMENT: Since the duties of juvenile care workers frequently involve most institutional operations, their training should be comprehensive.

1-JDTP-1D-08-1

Added August 2005. Written policy, procedure, and practice provide that all juvenile care workers receive at least 40 hours of annual training. This training shall include at a minimum the following areas:

- **standards of conduct/ethics**
- **security/safety/fire/medical/emergency procedures**
- **supervision of offenders including training on sexual abuse and assault prevention**
- **use of force**

Additional topics shall be included based upon a needs assessment of both staff and institution requirements.

COMMENT: This training will enable employees to sharpen skills, maintain certification, and keep abreast of changes in policies, procedures, and legislative, judicial, or executive actions.

1-JDTP-1E-01

Revised January 2012. Written agency policy, procedure and practice governing case record management includes, but is not limited to, the establishment, use, content, privacy, security, preservation, and destruction of case records.

COMMENT: None.

1-JDTP-1G-01

Deleted August 2007.

1-JDTP-1G -02

Revised August 2007. Written policy and procedure specify who is responsible for operating a citizen involvement and volunteer service program, and his or her lines of authority, responsibility, and accountability.

COMMENT: A citizen involvement and volunteer service program can generate a wide variety of services for juveniles during program participation and after release; for example, information on referrals to work and study release programs and recreational and cultural activities in the community. The staff member responsible for the program may be full-time or part-time, and the position may be filled by volunteer or contract personnel. The responsible person should have or receive appropriate training. Some jurisdictions mandate a citizen advisory board for each program. Written policy should provide direction for the program, listing the goals and objectives, types of services offered, population served, and so forth. Clear lines of accountability and authority should be established and communicated to staff and volunteers.

1-JDTP-2A-04 **Revised August 2002. Natural lighting should be provided, wherever possible. Documentation shall be provided by an independent, qualified source that lighting is at least 20 foot-candles at desk level and air circulation is at least 15 cubic feet of outside or recirculated filtered air per minute per person and should be checked not less than once per accreditation cycle.**

Interpretation August 2002. The words "accreditation cycle" are interpreted as within the past three years.

COMMENT: None.

Summary of Orientation and Minimum Training Hours

CATEGORY	TYPICAL POSITION TITLES	BASIC ORIEN-TATION	TRAINING HOURS—FIRST YEAR ON THE JOB	TRAINING HOURS—EACH YEAR THERE-AFTER
CLERICAL/ SUPPORT (Minimum Contact)	Secretaries, clerks, typists, computer/ warehouse personnel, accountants, personnel staff	Yes	16	16
SUPPORT (Regular or Daily Contact)	Food service, industry work supervisors, maintenance work supervisors	Yes	40	40
PROFESSIONAL SPECIALIST	Case managers, counselors, social workers, teachers, psychologists, librarians, medical personnel, chaplains, recreation specialists	Yes	40	40
ALL OFFENDER SUPERVISION STAFF	All staff assigned to full-time supervision duties	Yes	120	40
ADMINIS-TRATIVE MANAGEMENT PERSONNEL	Superintendents, deputy or assistant superintendents, business managers, personnel directors, care supervisors, shift supervisors	Yes	40	40

The following description of general job categories should be used in determining minimum training requirements as outlined in the standards. Contract or part-time employees should receive training similar to full-time employees in their particular category and pertinent to their role in working with juveniles. This chart replaces the chart on page 84 in *Standards for Juvenile Day Treatment Programs*, published in July 1993.

Training: An organized, planned, and evaluated activity designed to achieve specific learning objectives. Training may occur on-site, at an academy or training center, at an institution of higher learning, through contract service, at professional meetings, or through closely supervised on-the-job training. Meetings of professional associations are considered training when there is clear evidence of specific learning objectives relative to the employee's career track. *See* Appendix F, "Revised Definitions of Learning and Training."

1-JDTP-2A-09 **Revised August 1995. Reasonable accommodation is made to ensure that all parts of the facility that are accessible to the public are accessible and usable by staff and visitors with disabilities.**

COMMENT: None.

1-JDTP-2C-01-1 **Added August 2005 (Mandatory). Written policy, procedure, and practice govern the control and use of all flammable, toxic, and caustic materials.**

COMMENT: The following definitions apply to this standard: *flammable materials*—liquids with a flash point below 100 degrees F; *toxic materials*—substances that through chemical reaction or mixture can produce possible injury or harm to the body by entering through the skin, digestive tract, or respiratory tract (for example, zinc chromate paint, ammonia, chlorine, antifreeze, herbicides, pesticides); *caustic materials*—substances that can destroy or eat away by chemical reaction (for example, lye, caustic soda, sulfuric acid). If a substance possesses more than one of the above properties, the safety requirements for all applicable properties should be considered.

All flammable, toxic, and caustic materials should be stored in secure areas that are inaccessible to juveniles, and a prescribed system should be used to account for their distribution. Juveniles should never possess such items unless they are under the close supervision of qualified staff.

Substances that do not contain one or more of the above properties but that are labeled "Keep Out of the Reach of Children" or "May Be Harmful If Swallowed" are not prohibited; their use and control, however, should be addressed in agency policy.

1-JDTP-3A-02-1 **Added August 2011. All staff, contractors, and juveniles who work in the food service department are trained in the use of food service equipment and in the safety procedures to be followed in the food service department.**

COMMENT: None.

1-JDTP-3A-05 **Revised August 2004. Therapeutic diets are provided as prescribed by appropriate clinicians. A therapeutic diet manual is available in health services and food services for reference and information. Prescriptions for therapeutic diets should be specific and complete, furnished in writing to the food service manager, and rewritten annually, or more often as clinically indicated.**

COMMENT: Therapeutic diets are prepared and served to offenders according to the orders of the treating clinician or as directed by the responsible health authority. Therapeutic diets should be kept as simple as possible and should conform as closely as possible to the foods served other offenders.

1-JDTP-3A-07 **Revised August 2002. All foods brought into the facility are properly stored at all times.**

COMMENT: None.

1-JDTP-3B-07 **Revised August 2002. The day treatment program has available at all times first-aid equipment approved by a recognized health authority, and an automatic external defibrillator is available for use at the facility.**

COMMENT: The health authority may be a physician, health administrator, or organization that has the expertise to determine the potential first-aid needs of the program and to evaluate the condition of the first-aid supplies and equipment.

1-JDTP-3D-01-1 **Revised August 2002. Written policy, procedure, and practice prohibit discrimination on the basis of disability in the provision of services, programs, and activities administered for program beneficiaries and participants.**

COMMENT: Services, programs, and activities include, but are not limited to, the following:

- academic and vocational education (including developmental and rehabilitative programs)
- work programs/work release programs (by providing reasonable accommodations or alternatives for juveniles with disabilities so that the benefits of these programs, including sentence-reduction credits, are available to juveniles with disabilities)
- recreation, exercise, and activities
- mail, telephone, and visiting
- library
- religious programs
- reception and orientation
- transportation services (to provide for safety and security, and to avoid undue discomfort, in light of the juvenile's disabilities)
- classification
- food service
- sanitation and hygiene
- health care
- social services
- release
- discipline, grievance procedures, and due process proceedings
- safety and emergency procedures
- access to media, courts, counsel, and law library
- commissary/canteen
- volunteer programs
- psychological and psychiatric services

Program beneficiaries and participants include, but are not limited to: juveniles, family members, clergy, attorneys, volunteers, and other authorized visitors.

The institution may be required to take remedial action, when necessary, to afford program beneficiaries and participants with disabilities an opportunity to participate in, and enjoy the benefit of services, programs, or activities. Remedial action may include, but is not limited to: 1) making reasonable modifications to policies, practices, or procedures, 2) providing auxiliary aids and services to the hearing and visually impaired, 3) constructing new or altering existing facilities, and 4) delivering services, and so on, at alternative accessible sites.

1-JDTP-3D-14-1 **Added August 1995. Written policy, procedure, and practice prohibit discrimination based on a juvenile's race, religion, national origin, sex, disability, or political views in making administrative decisions and in providing access to programs.**

COMMENT: Juveniles should be assured equal opportunities to participate in all institutional programs.

1-JDTP-3D-20 **Revised January 2005. In its use of community resources, the facility maintains and annually updates an inventory and evaluation of community agencies with which the facility interacts.**

COMMENT: The evaluation should be a simple assessment of the quality of services provided to the juveniles by each community agency with which the facility interacts.

1-JDTP-3E-12 **Revised January 2001 (Mandatory). Written policy, procedure, and practice provide for a key inventory system that considers the safety of staff and juveniles and assists in protecting and preserving personal and facility property.**

COMMENT: All keys should be issued from a central office. A log should be used to record the movement of all keys, including the key numbers, location of locks, number of keys to each lock, and names of employees possessing keys. Control of keys requires a suitable storage unit mounted in a manner to show the presence or absence of keys. All juveniles should have a key to their locker.

Appendix B Revised January 2001. Refer to *Standards Supplement* Appendix D.

Juvenile Detention Facilities (JDF), 3rd Edition

3-JDF-1A-04-1

Added January 1990. Written policy, procedure, and practice provide that the facility is used solely for pretrial holding and not as a post-trial treatment center. Juveniles may be held post-trial awaiting placement.

COMMENT: None.

3-JDF-1A-04-2

Added August 2010. The facility/agency shall demonstrate it has examined, and where appropriate and feasible, implemented strategies that promote recycling, energy and water conservation, pollution reduction, and utilization of renewable energy alternatives.

COMMENT: Correctional facilities and programs have the responsibility to implement strategies that allow correctional facilities to be managed in ways that are most cost-effective and deliver superior performance, while improving environmental responsibility and sustainability. This includes recycling (including paper, metal, and plastic products), energy conservation (including building insulation, heating and ventilation, temperature controls, vehicle fuel efficiency, water economies, physical plant engineering, and energy measures), pollution reduction (including composting sewer treatment, litter abatement, and carbon emissions), and utilization of renewable energy alternatives (bio-fuels, solar collection, turbine energy production, and methane collection).

3-JDF-1A-15

Revised January 2013. The qualifications, authority, and responsibilities of the facility administrator and other appointed personnel are specified in writing by statute or by the parent agency.

COMMENT: None.

3-JDF-1A-16

Revised August 2003. To be considered qualified, a warden/superintendent, at a minimum, must possess the following: a bachelor's degree in an appropriate discipline; five years of related administrative experience; and demonstrated administrative ability and leadership. The degree requirement may be satisfied by completion of a career development program that includes work-related experience, training, or college credits at a level of achievement equivalent to the bachelor's degree.

COMMENT: Establishing high qualifications ensures that only qualified individuals are recruited and employed. It is the agency's responsibility to see that potential administrators receive the required education.

3-JDF-1A-17

Deleted August 2002.

3-JDF-1A-31-1

Added August 1993. Written policy, procedure, and practice establish the facility's commitment to informing the public and the media of events within the facility's areas of responsibility. The procedures address emergency and nonemergency responses to the media and, at a minimum, include the following:

- **the identification of areas in the facility that are accessible to media representatives**
- **the contact person for routine requests for information**
- **identification of data and information protected by federal or state privacy laws, or federal and state freedom of information laws**
- **special events coverage**
- **news release policy**
- **the designation of individuals or positions within the facility authorized to speak with the media on behalf of the facility**

COMMENT: The complexity of the policy statement should be consistent with the size and complexity of the operation.

3-JDF-1B-09

Revised January 2003. The accounting system is designed to show the current status of income and expenditures.

COMMENT: Current information is needed to meet objectives, prevent budget discrepancies, respond to emerging needs, and ensure that the flow of funds is proceeding as planned.

3-JDF-1B-13

Revised January 2001. Written policy, procedure, and practice provide for an independent financial audit of the facility. This audit is conducted annually or as stipulated by statute or regulation, but at least every three years. If the facility is a part of a state system, an internal audits section or department of the agency's central administration and/or statutory agency shall be considered independent of the facility to be audited.

COMMENT: None.

3-JDF-1B-20

Deleted August 1993.

3-JDF-1C-05

Revised August 1995. Written policy specifies that equal employment opportunities exist for all positions. When deficiencies exist regarding the employment of minority groups and women, the facility can document the implementation of an affirmative action program that is approved by the appropriate government agency and can document annual reviews and the changes needed to keep the program current.

COMMENT: Equal employment opportunity is a public policy goal. All qualified persons should be able to compete equally for entry into and promotion within the facility, and the affirmative action program should actively encourage the participation of members of minority groups, individuals with a disability, and women in the facility's staff development program. The affirmative action program also should include corrective actions, when needed, in policies regarding pay rate, demotion, transfer, layoff, termination, and upgrades.

3-JDF-1C-05-1 **Added January 1993. Written policy, procedure, and practice prohibit sexual harassment.**

COMMENT: Facility administrators should have as their objective the creation of a workplace that is free from all forms of discrimination, including sexual harassment. Facility policy clearly indicates that sexual harassment, either explicit or implicit, is strictly prohibited. Employees and agents of the facility, including volunteers, contractors, and vendors, must be advised that they are subject to disciplinary action, including dismissal and termination of contracts and/or services, if found guilty of sexual harassment charges brought by employees or juveniles.

Summary of Orientation and Minimum Training Hours

The following description of general job categories should be used in determining minimum training requirements as outlined in the standards. Contract or part-time employees should receive training similar to full-time employees in their particular category and pertinent to their role in working with juveniles. This chart replaces the chart on page 23 in *Standards for Juvenile Detention Facilities*, Third Edition, published in May 1991.

CATEGORY	TYPICAL POSITION TITLES	BASIC ORIEN-TATION	TRAINING HOURS—FIRST YEAR ON THE JOB	TRAINING HOURS—EACH YEAR THERE-AFTER
CLERICAL/ SUPPORT (Minimum Contact)	Secretaries, clerks, typists, computer/ warehouse personnel, accountants, personnel staff	Yes	16	16
SUPPORT (Regular or Daily Contact)	Food service, industry work supervisors, maintenance work supervisors	Yes	40	40
PROFESSIONAL SPECIALIST	Case managers, counselors, social workers, teachers, psychologists, librarians, medical personnel, chaplains, recreation specialists	Yes	40	40
ALL OFFENDER SUPERVISION STAFF	All staff assigned to full-time supervision duties	Yes	120	40
ADMINIS-TRATIVE MANAGEMENT PERSONNEL	Superintendents, deputy or assistant superintendents, business managers, personnel directors, care supervisors, shift supervisors	Yes	40	40

Training: An organized, planned, and evaluated activity designed to achieve specific learning objectives. Training may occur on-site, at an academy or training center, at an institution of higher learning, through contract service, at professional meetings, or through closely supervised on-the-job training. Meetings of professional associations are considered training when there is clear evidence of specific learning objectives relative to the employee's career track. *See* Appendix F, "Revised Definitions of Learning and Training."

3-JDF-1C-05-2 **Added August 1995. Written policy, procedure, and practice provide a mechanism to process requests for reasonable accommodation to the known physical and/or mental impairments of a qualified individual with a disability, either an applicant or an employee. The accommodation need not be granted if it would impose an undue hardship or direct threat.**

COMMENT: *Reasonable accommodation* refers to modifications or adjustments, which enable qualified applicants with disabilities to access the job application process or which enable qualified employees with disabilities to perform the essential functions of the job and to enjoy the same terms, conditions, and privileges of employment that are available to persons without disabilities. *Terms, conditions, and privileges of employment* include, but are not limited to:

- recruitment, selection, and hiring
- salary and compensation
- benefits, holidays, leave, and work hours
- promotion and advancement
- staff development, including in-service training
- retirement, resignation, and termination

An *undue hardship* means significant difficulty or expense. *Direct threat* means a significant risk of substantial harm to the health or safety of any person, including the applicant or employee with a disability that cannot be eliminated or reduced by reasonable accommodation. A *qualified individual with a disability* means an individual with a disability who satisfies the requisite skill, experience, education, and other job-related requirements for the employment position such individual holds or desires, and who, with or without reasonable accommodation, can perform the essential functions of such position.

3-JDF-1C-13 **Revised August 2007. A criminal record check is conducted on all new employees in accordance with state and federal statutes. This record will include comprehensive identifier information to be collected and run against law enforcement indices. If suspect information on matters with potential terrorism connections is returned on a desirable applicant, it is forwarded to the local Joint Terrorism Task Force (JTTF) or another similar agency.**

COMMENT: The facility's administrators should know of any criminal conviction that could directly affect an employee's job performance in a facility setting.

3-JDF-1C-15 **Revised January 2012. There is a written agency policy, procedure, and practice that specifies support for a drug-free workplace for all employees. This policy includes at a minimum the following:**

- **prohibition of the use of illegal drugs**
- **prohibition of possession of any illegal drug except in the performance of official duties**
- **the opportunities available for treatment and/or counseling for drug abuse**
- **the procedures to be used to ensure compliance**
- **the penalties for violation of the policy**

COMMENT: None.

3-JDF-1C-19 **Revised August 2010. The institution maintains a current, accurate, confidential personnel record on each employee except where state statutes require open public records and the personnel record cannot be maintained confidentially. Information obtained as part of a required medical examination (and/or inquiry) regarding the medical condition or history of applicants and employees is collected and maintained on separate forms and in separate medical files and treated as a confidential medical record.**

COMMENT: The personnel record should contain the following: initial application; reference letters; results of employment investigation; verification of training and experience; wage and salary information; job performance evaluations; incident reports, if any; and commendations and disciplinary actions, if any.

3-JDF-1D-08 **Revised August 2000. Written policy, procedure, and practice provide that all administrative and managerial staff receive 40 hours of training in addition to orientation training during their first year of employment and 40 hours of training each year thereafter, in areas relevant to their position.**

COMMENT: Ongoing training in topics relevant to an employee's position enhances skill and job performance.

3-JDF-1D-09 **Revised August 2005. Written policy, procedure, and practice provide that all new juvenile care workers receive 120 hours of training during their first year of employment. At a minimum, this training covers the following areas:**

- **security and safety procedures**
- **emergency and fire procedures**
- **supervision of offenders**
- **suicide intervention/prevention**
- **use of force**
- **offender rights**
- **key control**

- **interpersonal relations**
- **communication skills**
- **standards of conduct**
- **cultural awareness**
- **sexual abuse/assault intervention**
- **code of ethics**

Additional topics may be added at the discretion of the agency or facility.

COMMENT: Since the duties of juvenile care workers frequently involve most institutional operations, their training should be comprehensive.

3-JDF-1D-09-1

Added August 2005. Written policy, procedure, and practice provide that all juvenile care workers receive at least 40 hours of annual training. This training shall include at a minimum the following areas:

- **standards of conduct/ethics**
- **security/safety/fire/medical/emergency procedures**
- **supervision of offenders including training on sexual abuse and assault**
- **use of force**

Additional topics shall be included based upon a needs assessment of both staff and institution requirements.

COMMENT: This training will enable employees to sharpen skills, maintain certification and keep abreast of changes in policies, procedures, and legislative, judicial, or executive actions.

3-JDF-1D-10

Revised August 2002. Written policy, procedure, and practice provide that all professional specialist employees who have juvenile contact receive an additional 120 hours of training during their first year of employment and an additional 40 hours of training each subsequent year of employment. At a minimum this training covers the following areas:

- **security procedures**
- **supervision of juveniles**
- **signs of suicide risks**
- **suicide precautions**
- **use-of-force regulations and tactics**
- **report writing**
- **juvenile rules and regulations**
- **rights and responsibilities of juveniles**
- **fire and emergency procedures**
- **key control**
- **interpersonal relations**
- **communication skills**
- **first aid**
- **counseling techniques**
- **social/cultural lifestyles of the juvenile population**
- **sexual abuse/assault**

COMMENT: Since the duties of full-time employees frequently involve most institutional operations, their training should be comprehensive. Ongoing training during subsequent years of employment enables employees to sharpen skills and keep abreast of changes in operational procedure.

3-JDF-1E-01 **Revised January 2012. Written agency policy, procedure and practice governing case record management includes, but is not limited to, the establishment, use, content, privacy, security, preservation, and destruction of case records**

COMMENT: None.

3-JDF-1G-01 **Deleted August 2007.**

3-JDF-1G-02 **Revised August 2007. Written policy and procedure specify who is responsible for operating a citizen involvement and volunteer service program, and his or her lines of authority, responsibility, and accountability.**

COMMENT: A citizen involvement and volunteer service program can generate a wide variety of services for juveniles during confinement and after release; for example, information on referrals to release programs and recreational and cultural activities in the community. The staff member responsible for the program may be full-time or part-time, and the position may be filled by volunteer or contract personnel. The responsible person should have or receive appropriate training. Some jurisdictions mandate a citizen advisory board for each facility. Written policy should provide direction for the program, listing the goals and objectives, types of services offered, and so forth. Clear lines of accountability and authority should be established and communicated to staff and volunteers. Any volunteer activity that is shown to threaten the facility's order and security or the safety of a volunteer should be limited or discontinued until the problem is resolved.

3-JDF-2B-02 **Revised August 2006 (Existing only). The detention facility operates with living units of no more than 25 juveniles. The detention facility does not exceed a bed capacity of 150 juveniles.**

COMMENT: A small living and treatment unit is more conducive to enhancing student and staff interaction. The living unit's maximum size should be no more than 25; however, smaller units of 10, 15, or 20 permit services on a more manageable scale. A classification system that is departmentalized allows for the grouping/separation of youth who are in need of special management, such as separation of gang members, classification by age, and/or size, and so on. Through both design and operation, a 150-bed facility permits the cost efficiencies to service delivery advantages of a larger facility while preserving the programmatic advantages of smaller facility size.

3-JDF-2B-02-1

Added August 2006. (Renovations, Additions, New Construction). The detention facility operates with living units of no more than 16 juveniles. The detention facility does not exceed a bed capacity of 150 juveniles.

COMMENT: A small living and treatment unit is more conducive to enhancing student and staff interaction. A classification system that is departmentalized allows for the grouping/separation of youth who are in need of special management, such as separation of gang members, classification by age, and/or size, and so on. Through both design and operation, a 150-bed facility permits the cost efficiencies to service delivery advantages of a larger facility while preserving the programmatic advantages of smaller facility size.

3-JDF-2B-05

Revised August 1992. (New Construction). The facility location is selected with participation from the community in which it is to be located.

COMMENT: The support of citizens from the community should be enlisted. They should be informed of the purpose of detention facilities, the nature of the building, the program, and the extent of supervision and control. Once their support has been gained, they can help to interpret the project to others.

3-JDF-2C-02

Revised January 1996. Single cells/rooms and multiple-occupancy cells/rooms may be used for housing juveniles in medium/minimum custody when the classifications system, cell/room size, and level of supervision meet the following requirements:

1. Number of occupants — Amount of Unencumbered Space*

Number of occupants	**Amount of Unencumbered Space***
1	**35 square feet per occupant**
2-50	**25 square feet**

***Unencumbered space* is usable space that is not encumbered by furnishings or fixtures. At least one dimension of the unencumbered space is no less than seven feet. In determining unencumbered space in the cell or room, the total square footage is obtained and the square footage of fixtures and equipment is subtracted. All fixtures and equipment must be in operational position and must provide the following minimums per person: bed, plumbing fixtures (if inside the cell/room), desk, locker, and chair or stool.**

2. **When confinement exceeds 10 hours per day, there are at least 80 square feet of total floor space per occupant.**
3. **Housing is in compliance with American Correctional Association standards 3-JDF-2C-06, 3-JDF-2C-07, 3-JDF-2C-08, and 3-JDF-2C-09.**
4. **Medium-security juveniles housed in multiple-occupancy cells/rooms require direct supervision.**

A classification system is used to divide the occupants into groups that reduce the probability of assault and disruptive behavior. At a minimum, the classification system evaluates the following:

- **mental and emotional stability**
- **escape history**
- **history of assaultive behavior**
- **medical status**
- **age**
- **enemies of record**
- **male and female juveniles are housed in separate cells/rooms**

COMMENT: None.

3-JDF-2C-02-1

Added August 1991. Written policy, procedure, and practice provide that single-occupancy rooms shall be available when indicated for the following:
- **juveniles with severe medical disabilities**
- **juveniles suffering from serious mental illness**
- **sexual predators**
- **juveniles likely to be exploited or victimized by others**
- **juveniles who have other special needs for single housing**

COMMENT: While standards permit the housing of juveniles in multiple rooms, there is a need for single rooms for the juvenile groups listed above. The caveat, "when indicated," refers to determinations made by the classification system, medical diagnosis, or other professional conclusion.

3-JDF-2C-03

Revised January 1996. Each sleeping room has, at a minimum, the following facilities and conditions:
- **sanitation facilities, including access to toilet facilities that are available for use without staff assistance 24-hours a day**
- **a washbasin with hot and cold running water**
- **a bed, and adequate space for storage**
- **a desk and chair or stool in facilities that do not have scheduled program activities outside youth sleeping rooms for eight hours or more per day**
- **natural light**
- **temperatures that are appropriate to the summer and winter comfort zones**

COMMENT: Sensory awareness is enhanced by providing variety in terms of space, surface textures, and colors. Natural lighting should be available either by room windows to the exterior or from a source within 20 feet of the room. The bed should be elevated from the floor and have a clean, covered mattress with blankets provided, as needed.

3-JDF-2C-04

Revised August 1995. Dayrooms with space for varied juvenile activities are situated immediately adjacent to the juvenile sleeping areas. Dayrooms provide a minimum of 35 square feet of space per juvenile (exclusive of lavatories, showers, and toilets) for the maximum number of juveniles who use the dayroom at one time, and no dayroom encompasses less than 100 square feet of space (exclusive of lavatories, showers, and toilets).

COMMENT: While the standard establishes a minimum square footage for any dayroom, total square footage is calculated for the maximum number of users at one time rather than the total number of juveniles served.

3-JDF-2C-05 **Revised August 1998. Dayrooms provide sufficient seating and writing surfaces. Dayroom furnishings are consistent with the custody level of the juveniles assigned.**

COMMENT: The standard provides managers and designers with flexibility in designing and furnishing dayrooms and takes into consideration the range of activities that may occur (for example, dayroom activities usually include television viewing, reading, recreation, conversation, and games, and sometimes include eating and work). In lower security settings, the use of "normalized" furnishings should be considered.

3-JDF-2C-08 **Revised August 1995. Juveniles have access to operable showers with temperature-controlled hot and cold running water, at a minimum ratio of one shower for every eight juveniles, unless national or state building or health codes specify a different ratio. Water for showers is thermostatically controlled to temperatures ranging from 100 degrees Fahrenheit to 120 degrees Fahrenheit to ensure the safety of juveniles and to promote hygienic practices.**

COMMENT: Juveniles can use scalding showers as a weapon against, or punishment for, other juveniles. Also, accidental injury could occur when cold water is drawn in other areas, thereby unexpectedly elevating the hot water in showers to scalding temperatures. Water temperatures below 100 degrees Fahrenheit are uncomfortable and may deter an individual from pursuing good hygienic practices. The temperature controls should not preclude the use of water at higher temperatures, if needed, in other areas of the institution, such as kitchens.

3-JDF-2C-09 **Revised August 1995. Juveniles with disabilities are housed in a manner that provides for their safety and security. Housing used by juveniles with disabilities is designed for their use and provides for integration with other juveniles. Programs and services are accessible to juveniles with disabilities who reside in the facility.**

COMMENT: If the facility accepts individuals with disabilities, it must provide for their housing and use of facility resources. Housing includes, but is not limited to, sleeping quarters/areas, furnishings, dayrooms, toilets, washbasins, facilities, showers/ bathing, and other common elements. Program and service areas include, but are not limited to, exercise and recreation areas, visiting rooms, laundry facilities, private counseling space, group meeting rooms, dining rooms, telephone facilities, admission and intake areas, and administrative areas, where appropriate.

3-JDF-2C-09-1 **Added January 2002. Written policy, procedure, and practice provide for the assignment of appropriately trained individuals to assist disabled juveniles who cannot otherwise perform basic life functions.**

COMMENT: None.

3-JDF-2C-09-2 **Added August 2002. Written policy, procedure, and practice provide education, equipment and facilities, and the support necessary for juveniles with disabilities to perform self-care and personal hygiene in a reasonably private environment.**

COMMENT: A reasonably private environment will vary, depending on individual and institutional circumstances, but is one which will maintain the dignity of the disabled individual in light of that person's disability.

3-JDF-2D-01 **Revised January 2008. Written policy, procedure, and practice require that all housing areas provide at a minimum the following:**

- **lighting of at least 20 foot-candles at desk level and in the personal grooming area, as documented by a qualified source, at least once per accreditation cycle**
- **natural light available from an opening or window that has a view to the outside, or from a source within 20 feet of the room**
- **other lighting requirements for the facility determined by tasks to be performed**
- **access to drinking fountain**
- **heating, ventilation, and acoustical systems to ensure healthful and comfortable living and working conditions for juveniles and staff**

COMMENT: None.

3-JDF-2D-03 **Revised August 2006. Temperatures in indoor living and work areas are appropriate to the summer and winter comfort zones.**

COMMENT: Temperature should be capable of being mechanically raised or lowered to an acceptable comfort level.

3-JDF-2F-02 **Revised August 1995. Reasonable accommodation is made to ensure that all parts of the facility that are accessible to the public are accessible and usable by staff and visitors with disabilities.**

COMMENT: None.

3-JDF-2G-01 **Deleted January 2007.**

3-JDF-3A-02

Revised January 2007. Space is provided for a 24-hour control center for monitoring and coordinating the facility's security, safety, and communications systems. The control center provides access to a washbasin and toilet. There is a communication system between the control center and juvenile living areas.

COMMENT: The control center should contain sufficient space for monitoring and coordinating all internal and external security systems, communication systems, safety alarms, detection systems, and other mechanical and electrical systems. A mechanical or audio communication system should be used to supplement direct staff supervision activities (for example, to advise staff of emergency needs), not as a substitute for staff supervision.

3-JDF-3A-16-1

Revised January 2011 (Mandatory). Four/five point restraints are used only in extreme instances and only when other types of restraints have proven ineffective or the safety of the inmate is in jeopardy. Advance approval is secured from the facility administrator/designee before a juvenile is placed in a four/five point restraint. Subsequently, the health authority or designee must be notified to assess the juvenile's medical and mental health condition, and to advise whether, on the basis of serious danger to self or others, the juvenile should be in a medical/mental health unit for emergency involuntary treatment with sedation and/or other medical management, as appropriate. If the juvenile is not transferred to a medical/mental health unit and is restrained in a four/five point position, the following minimum procedures are followed:

- **Direct visual observation by staff is continuous prior to obtaining approval from the health authority or designee**
- **Subsequent visual observation is made at least every 15 minutes**
- **Restraint procedures are in accordance with guidelines approved by the designated health authority**
- **All decisions and actions are documented**

COMMENT: Four/five-point restraints should be used only in extreme instances and only when other types of restraints have proven to be ineffective. Restraint guidelines should include consideration of an individual's physical condition, such as body weight.

3-JDF-3A-16-2

Added August 2008 (Mandatory). Written policy, procedure and practice, in general, prohibit the use of restraints on female offenders during active labor and the delivery of a child. Any deviation from the prohibition requires approval by, and guidance on, methodology from the medical authority and is based on documented serious security risks. The medical authority provides guidance on the use of restraints on pregnant offenders prior to active labor and delivery.

COMMENT: Restraints on pregnant offenders during active labor and the delivery of a child should only be used in extreme instances and should not be applied for more time than is absolutely necessary. Restraints used on pregnant offenders prior to active labor and delivery should not put the pregnant offender nor the fetus at risk.

3-JDF-3A-21 **Revised January 1994. Written policy, procedure, and practice provide that, except in emergency situations, visual inspections of juvenile body cavities are conducted by care workers of the same sex and in private and based on reasonable belief that the juvenile is carrying contraband or other prohibited material. Reasonable belief is not required when juveniles return from contact with the general public or from outside the institution. In all cases, this inspection is conducted by trained personnel.**

COMMENT: None.

3-JDF-3A-22 **Revised January 2001 (Mandatory). Written policy, procedure, and practice govern the control and use of keys.**

COMMENT: None.

3-JDF-3A-23 **Revised January 2001 (Mandatory). Written policy, procedure, and practice govern the control and use of tools and culinary and medical equipment.**

COMMENT: None.

3-JDF-3A-27 **Revised August 1991. Written policy, procedure, and practice provide that written reports are submitted to the superintendent or designee no later than the conclusion of the tour of duty when any of the following occur:**

- **use of chemical agents to control juveniles**
- **use of force to control juveniles**
- **juvenile(s) remain in restraints at the end of the shift**

COMMENT: Any incident involving the use of force that has the potential for injury should be recorded to establish the identities of the staff, juveniles, or others involved and to describe the nature of the incident.

3-JDF-3A-30 **Revised August 2000 (Mandatory). Written policy, procedure, and practice restrict the use of physical force to instances of justifiable self-defense, protection of others, protection of property, prevention of escapes, and to maintain or regain control, and then only as a last resort and in accordance with appropriate statutory authority. In no event is physical force justifiable as punishment. A written report is prepared following all uses of force and is submitted to administrative staff for review.**

COMMENT: Correctional personnel should be prepared to justify their use of physical force. The phrase as a last resort may be defined through appropriate statutory authority.

3-JDF-3A-31

Added new subtitle January 1995.

Preservation of Physical Evidence

Written policy, procedure, and practice provide for the preservation, control, and disposition of all physical evidence obtained in connection with a violation of law and/or institutional regulation. At a minimum, the procedures shall address the following:

- **chain of custody**
- **evidence handling**
- **location and storage requirements**

COMMENT: Strict accountability of physical evidence collected in connection with a crime must be established to preserve the integrity of the disciplinary and/or legal process. Minor rule violations should be exempt from the procedural requirements of evidence control, preservation, and disposition.

3-JDF-3B-09

Revised January 1998. Emergency equipment and systems are tested at least quarterly. Power generators are inspected weekly and load tested quarterly at a minimum or in accordance with manufacturer's recommendations and instruction manuals.

COMMENT: Emergency equipment, such as standby lighting, batteries, power generators, fire-fighting apparatus, communications systems, and alarms should be checked frequently to ensure their reliability.

3-JDF-3B-14

Added January 2003. Written policy, procedure, and practice define critical incidents for the facility and provide for a debriefing to be conducted after each such incident. The debriefing process includes coordination and feedback about the incident with designated staff of the facility as soon as possible after the incident. A debriefing includes, but is not limited to:

- **a review of staff and juvenile actions during the incident**
- **a review of the incident's impact on staff and juveniles**
- **a review of corrective actions taken and still needed**
- **plans for improvement to avoid another incident**

COMMENT: A *critical incident* is any event or situation that threatens staff or offenders in their community (criminal justice setting). While debriefings should occur as soon as possible, some information may not be available until later. All staff impacted by a critical incident should be included in the debriefings and referred to appropriate services to mitigate the stress associated with these events. All critical incidents should be reviewed by the administration, security, and health services. A two-week follow-up debriefing should occur to review the validity and appropriateness of all policies, plans, and information used during the critical incident and immediately after.

3-JDF-3C-03 **Revised August 2013. A rulebook that contains all chargeable offenses, ranges of penalties, and disciplinary procedures is given to each juvenile and staff member and is translated into those languages spoken by significant numbers of juveniles. Signed acknowledgment of receipt of the rulebook is maintained in each juvenile's file. When a literacy or language problem prevents a juvenile from understanding the rulebook, a staff member or translator assists the juvenile in understanding the rules. This information is provided to juveniles in a written and/or electronic format. If the inmate handbook is provided electronically, juveniles in segregation are provided the information in a written format so that their access to the information is not impeded by their custody status. The handbook is translated into those languages spoken by significant numbers of juveniles.**

COMMENT: The use of electronic kiosks is allowed as a means of providing the inmate handbook. Agencies using such kiosks should implement strategies to allow access to this information by general population juveniles without interference by facility staff without a valid security-related reason. Juveniles who are unable to read and write should be assisted through case management services provided by the facility.

3-JDF-3C-13 **Revised January 2008. Written policy, procedure, and practice provide that juveniles are scheduled for a hearing as soon as practicable but no later than seven days, excluding weekends and holidays, after being charged with a violation. Juveniles are notified of the time and place of the hearing at least 24 hours in advance of the hearing.**

COMMENT: To ensure fairness and the integrity of the discipline process, juveniles charged with rule violations should receive hearings as soon as possible, unless the hearing is prevented by exceptional circumstances, unavoidable delays, or reasonable postponements. Reasons for all delays should be documented.

3-JDF-3D-04-1 **Added August 1995. Written policy, procedure, and practice prohibit discrimination based on a juvenile's race, religion, national origin, sex, disability, or political views in making administrative decisions and in providing access to programs.**

COMMENT: Juveniles should be assured equal opportunities to participate in all institutional programs.

3-JDF-3D-06-1 **Added January 1992. Written policy, procedure, and practice provide for the reporting of all instances of child abuse and/or neglect consistent with appropriate state law or local laws.**

COMMENT: Whenever a juvenile reports or staff observe indicators of child abuse and/or neglect, there are procedures for juvenile care and investigation of the allegation. Where appropriate, interagency agreements pursuant to child abuse should be implemented.

3-JDF-3D-06-2

Added August 2002. Written policy, procedure, and practice ensure that information is provided to juveniles about sexual abuse/assault including:

- **prevention/intervention**
- **self-protection**
- **reporting sexual abuse/assault**
- **treatment and counseling**

The information is communicated orally and in writing, in a language clearly understood by the juvenile, upon arrival at the facility.

COMMENT: None.

3-JDF-3D-06-3

Added January 2003. Juveniles are screened within 24 hours of arrival at the facility for potential vulnerabilities or tendencies of acting out with sexually aggressive behavior. Housing assignments are made accordingly.

COMMENT: None.

3-JDF-3D-06-4

Added January 2003. Written policy, procedure, and practice require that an investigation is conducted and documented whenever a sexual assault is alleged, threatened, or occurs.

COMMENT: The agency should report occurrences/allegations of sexual assault or threat in accordance with the laws of the jurisdiction. The investigation may be limited by what is allowed by the laws of the jurisdiction.

3-JDF-3D-06-5

Added January 2003. Written policy, procedure, and practice require that juveniles identified as high risk with a history of assaultive behavior are assessed by a mental health or other qualified professional. Such juveniles are identified, monitored, counseled, and provided appropriate treatment.

COMMENT: None.

3-JDF-3D-06-6

Added January 2003. Written policy, procedure, and practice require that juveniles identified as at risk for sexual victimization are assessed by a mental health or other qualified professional. Such juveniles are identified, monitored, and counseled.

COMMENT: None.

3-JDF-3D-06-7

Added January 2003. Written policy, procedure, and practice ensure that sexual conduct between staff and juveniles, volunteers, or contract personnel and juveniles, regardless of consensual status, is prohibited and subject to administrative and criminal disciplinary sanctions.

COMMENT: None.

3-JDF-3D-06-8 **Added January 2003. Victims of sexual assault are referred under appropriate security provisions to a community facility for treatment and gathering of evidence. If these procedures are performed in-house, the following guidelines are used:**

- **A history is taken by health care professionals who conduct an examination to document the extent of physical injury and to determine if referral to another medical facility is indicated. With the victim's consent, the examination includes collection of evidence from the victim, using a kit approved by the appropriate authority.**
- **Provision is made for testing for sexually transmitted diseases (for example, HIV, gonorrhea, hepatitis, and other diseases) and counseling, as appropriate**
- **Prophylactic treatment and follow-up for sexually transmitted diseases are offered to all victims, as appropriate.**
- **Following the physical examination, there is availability of an evaluation by a mental health professional to assess the need for crisis intervention counseling and long-term follow-up.**
- **A report is made to the facility or program administrator or designee to assure separation of the victim from his or her assailant.**

COMMENT: None.

3-JDF-3D-06-9 **Added January 2003. Written policy, procedure, and practice provide that juveniles who are victims of sexual abuse have the option to report the incident to a designated staff member other than an immediate point-of-contact line staff member.**

COMMENT: None.

3-JDF-3D-06-10 **Added January 2003. Written policy, procedure, and practice provide that all case records associated with claims of sexual abuse, including incident reports, investigative reports, offender information, case disposition, medical and counseling evaluation findings, and recommendations for post-release treatment and/or counseling are retained in accordance with an established schedule.**

COMMENT: None.

3-JDF-3E-04 **Revised August 2001. Juveniles placed in confinement are checked visually by staff at least every 15 minutes and are visited at least once each day by personnel from administrative, clinical, social work, religious, or medical units. A log is kept recording who authorized the confinement, persons visiting the juvenile, the person authorizing release from confinement, and the time of release. Suicidal juveniles are under continuous and continuing observation.**

COMMENT: None.

3-JDF-4A-06

Revised August 2001. Therapeutic diets are provided as prescribed by appropriate clinicians. A therapeutic diet manual is available in health services and food services for reference and information. Prescriptions for therapeutic diets should be specific and complete, furnished in writing to the food service manager, and rewritten annually, or more often as clinically indicated.

COMMENT: Therapeutic diets are prepared and served to offenders according to the orders of the treating clinician or as directed by the responsible health authority. Therapeutic diets should be kept as simple as possible and should conform as closely as possible to the foods served other offenders.

3-JDF-4A-09-1

Added August 2011. All staff, contractors, and juveniles who work in the food service department are trained in the use of food service equipment and in the safety procedures to be followed in the food service department.

COMMENT: None.

3-JDF-4A-11

Revised August 1999. Written policy, procedure, and practice provide that stored shelf goods are maintained at 45 degrees to 80 degrees Fahrenheit, refrigerated foods at 35 degrees to 40 degrees Fahrenheit, and frozen foods at 0 degrees Fahrenheit or below, unless national or state health codes specify otherwise.

COMMENT: None.

3-JDF-4B-12

Revised August 2007. Written policy, procedure, and practice provide for the issue of suitable, clean bedding and linen, including two sheets, pillow and pillowcase, one mattress, not to exclude a mattress with integrated pillow, and sufficient blankets to provide comfort under existing temperature controls. There is provision for linen exchange, including towels, at least weekly. Blanket exchange must be available at least quarterly.

COMMENT: Collection, storage, and exchange methods for bedding and linens should be done hygienically; that is, blankets, pillows, and mattresses should be cleaned before reissue, and linen and towels must be laundered before reissue.

3-JDF-4B-14

Revised January 1998. Written policy, procedure, and practice require that articles necessary for maintaining proper personal hygiene are provided to all juveniles.

COMMENT: As part of the admissions process, each juvenile should be given soap, a toothbrush, toothpaste or powder, a comb, and toilet paper. Shaving equipment should be made available upon request, and the special hygiene needs of females should be met. Proper personal hygiene improves juveniles' health and medical conditions.

3-JDF-4C-20

Revised August 1993. Written policy, procedure, and practice provide that the person administering medications has training from the responsible physician and the official responsible for the operation of the facility. The training includes, at a minimum, the following:

- **being accountable for medications**
- **administering medications**
- **record keeping for medications**

COMMENT: Administration of drugs and remedies referred to in this standard does not include medications administered intramuscularly. Such medications may only be administered by medical personnel in accordance with the laws and regulations of the authority having medical jurisdiction.

3-JDF-4C-21-1

Revised January 2003. Written policy, procedure, and practice provide that pregnancy management is specific as it relates to the following:

- **pregnancy testing**
- **routine prenatal care**
- **high-risk prenatal care**
- **management of the chemically addicted pregnant juvenile**
- **postpartum follow up**
- **unless mandated by state law, birth certificate/registry does not list a correctional facility as the place of birth**

COMMENT: None.

3-JDF-4C-21-2

Revised January 2001. Written policy, procedure, and practice provide for the early identification and treatment of juveniles with alcohol and drug abuse problems through a battery assessment. This battery shall be documented and include, at a minimum, the following:

- **screening and sorting**
- **clinical assessment and reassessment**
- **medical assessment for drug and alcohol program assignment appropriate to the needs of the individual juveniles**
- **referrals**

COMMENT: None.

3-JDF-4C-24

Revised August 2001. Written policy, procedure, and practice for the collection and recording of health appraisal data require the following:

- **The process is completed in a uniform manner as determined by the health authority.**
- **Health history and vital signs are collected by health-trained or qualified health personnel.**
- **Review of the results of the medical examination, tests, and identification of problems is performed by a physician or other health care personnel, if such is authorized in the medical practice act.**
- **Collection of all other health appraisal data is performed only by qualified health personnel.**

COMMENT: None.

3-JDF-4C-28

Revised August 2002. Written policy, procedure, and practice require that first aid kit(s) are available. The responsible physician approves the contents, number, location, and procedure for periodic inspection of the kit(s). An automatic external defibrillator is available for use at the facility.

COMMENT: The medical staff develops written procedures outlining the use of first aid kits and an automatic external defibrillator by nonmedical staff.

3-JDF-4C-33-1

Added August 1991. Written policy, procedure, and practice govern the use of restraints for medical and psychiatric purposes. At a minimum, the policy will address the following:

- **conditions under which restraints may be used**
- **types of restraints to be applied for specific conditions**
- **identification of person or persons who may authorize the use of restraints**
- **monitoring procedures for juveniles in restraints**

COMMENT: When restraints are part of a health care treatment regimen, the restraints used should be those that would be appropriate for the general public within the jurisdiction. Written policy should identify the authorization needed and when, where, and how restraints may be used and for how long.

3-JDF-4C-35

Revised August 1994 (Mandatory). There is a written suicide prevention and intervention program that is reviewed and approved by a qualified medical or mental health professional. All staff with responsibility for juvenile supervision are trained in the implementation of the program.

COMMENT: The program should include specific procedures for intake screening, identifying, and supervising of suicide-prone juveniles.

3-JDF-4C-41

Revised January 1992. Written policy, procedure, and practice provide for the clinical management of chemically dependent juveniles and include the following:

- **a standardized diagnostic needs assessment administered to determine the extent of use, abuse, dependency, and/or codependency**
- **a medical examination to determine medical needs and/or observational requirements**
- **an individualized treatment plan developed and implemented by a multidisciplinary team**
- **prerelease relapse-prevention education including risk management**
- **aftercare discharge plans that include the juvenile and the family, when appropriate**

COMMENT: Primary goals with chemical dependency programs are assessment of needs and the development of a treatment plan. A key component to support the educational program, recovery process, and ongoing stability of the juvenile/family includes relapse prevention. Relapse prevention is necessary to support long-term recovery and identify high-risk areas needing management. Referral resources for ongoing services should be updated and used in discharge planning for the juvenile and/or family as available.

3-JDF-5A-06

Revised January 1990. Written policy, procedure, and practice provide that an alleged juvenile held in detention be brought to court for a detention hearing and assignment of counsel within 24 hours.

COMMENT: None.

3-JDF-5B-01-1

Revised August 2002. Written policy, procedure, and practice prohibit discrimination on the basis of disability in the provision of services, programs, and activities administered for program beneficiaries and participants.

COMMENT: Services, programs, and activities include, but are not limited to, the following:

- academic and vocational education (including developmental and rehabilitative programs)
- work programs/work release programs (by providing reasonable accommodations or alternatives for juveniles with disabilities so that the benefits of these programs, including sentence-reduction credits, are available to juveniles with disabilities)
- recreation, exercise, and activities
- mail, telephone, and visiting
- library
- religious programs
- reception and orientation
- transportation services (to provide for safety and security, and to avoid undue discomfort, in light of the offender's disabilities)
- classification

- food service
- sanitation and hygiene
- health care
- social services
- release
- discipline, grievance procedures, and due process proceedings
- safety and emergency procedures
- access to media, courts, counsel, and law library
- commissary/canteen
- volunteer programs
- psychological and psychiatric services

Program beneficiaries and participants include, but are not limited to: juveniles, family members, clergy, attorneys, volunteers, and other authorized visitors.

The institution may be required to take remedial action, when necessary, to afford program beneficiaries and participants with disabilities an opportunity to participate in, and enjoy the benefit of services, programs, or activities. *Remedial action* may include, but is not limited to: 1) making reasonable modifications to policies, practices, or procedures, 2) providing auxiliary aids and services to the hearing and visually impaired, 3) constructing new or altering existing facilities, and 4) delivering services, and so on, at alternative accessible sites.

3-JDF-5B-01-2

Added August 2002. Written policy, procedure, and practice provide for staff and juvenile access to an appropriately trained and qualified individual who is educated in the problems and challenges faced by juveniles with physical and/or mental impairments, programs designed to educate and assist disabled juveniles, and all legal requirements for the protection of juveniles with disabilities.

COMMENT: An appropriately trained and qualified individual, as used in this standard, is one who has been designated by the warden, superintendent, or other authority, to coordinate efforts to comply with and carry out responsibilities defined by the Americans with Disabilities Act. That individual should develop relationships with, and use the expertise of institutional staff, advocacy groups, nonprofit organizations, agencies of government, and others that have relevant knowledge and experience.

3-JDF-5C-01

Revised August 1991. Written policy, procedure, and practice provide that comprehensive education programs are available to all eligible juveniles at a time when the majority can take advantage of the programs.

COMMENT: Educational programs should not have to compete with work assignments, visitation, counseling, other work programs, and so forth. Encouragement to participate should be provided by using a reward system and limiting barriers to attendance.

3-JDF-5C-01-1

Added January 1992. Written policy, procedure, and practice provide for an educational program that is consistent with the needs of the juvenile population.

COMMENT: While many detention facilities house juveniles with sentences of a few days or weeks, there are increasing numbers that are held for longer periods, sometimes up to five years. An educational program for those longer-term juveniles includes an evaluation of educational needs and a method for providing for those needs.

3-JDF-5C-04-1

Added August 1991. Written policy, procedure, and practice govern the maintenance and handling of educational/vocational records. Students' rights to privacy and confidentiality in accordance with state and federal law should be maintained.

COMMENT: Academic/vocational information should become a part of the master file and be transferred when juveniles are moved to other facilities or relocated in the community during prerelease. Accurately maintained student files and records are part of staff accountability and are essential for program needs, assessments, and evaluations.

3-JDF-5C-04-2

Added August 1991. Written policy, procedure, and practice provide incentives for educational participation and formal recognition of specific educational accomplishments.

COMMENT: Recognition of academic and vocational achievements, such as certification or graduation, is helpful to juveniles and provides general support for educational programs. Incentives may include pay, access to preferred jobs and/or educational programs, or other special privileges.

3-JDF-5C-04-3

Added August 1991. Written policy, procedure, and practice provide that the academic and vocational training programs are recognized, certified, or licensed by the state department of education or other recognized agency having jurisdiction. Programs up to the completion of high school and/or the GED are available at no cost to juveniles. Provision is made for formal recognition of specific educational accomplishments.

COMMENT: Correctional education programs must be at least equal in quality and requirements to equivalent programs in the community to ensure that student credits, certificates, and diplomas are accepted by employers and transferable to schools and colleges after release. Recognition, certification, or licensing by the authority having jurisdiction legitimizes the correctional education program and allows opportunity for self-evaluation and outside evaluation; it also facilitates obtaining funding from state, federal, and private sources.

3-JDF-5C-04-4 **Added August 1991. There is a written, standardized, competency-based curriculum supported by appropriate materials and classroom resources.**

COMMENT: Standardization of curriculum assists in monitoring student progress from class to class or between facilities. Emphasis should be on individual student progress as measured by observable or assessable instructional objectives. Programmed instruction, teaching machines, and educational television may be used in addition to traditional teaching methods.

3-JDF-5C-04-5 **Added August 1991. All academic and vocational training personnel are certified by a state department of education or other comparable authority.**

COMMENT: All teachers, supervisors, and administrators should be certified and should receive additional training to meet the special needs of juveniles. Policies should also provide for emergency or temporary certification to facilitate hiring qualified personnel who lack complete or current certification.

3-JDF-5C-04-6 **Added August 1991. Written policy, procedure, and practice provide for a system of academic and vocational counseling as well as initial screening, assessment, and evaluation to determine each juvenile's educational needs.**

COMMENT: There should be a systematic procedure for screening, assessment, and evaluation at intake that includes standardized testing so that each juvenile can be placed in appropriate educational programs. Staff should be qualified to interpret tests and decide when additional testing is needed.

3-JDF-5C-04-7 **Added August 1991. The educational program allows for flexible scheduling that permits juveniles to enter at any time and to learn at their own pace.**

COMMENT: Flexible scheduling is open-entry, open-exit instruction with emphasis on individualized instruction. If a program has no vacancies, juveniles may be placed on a waiting list.

3-JDF-5C-04-8 **Added August 1991. The facility uses business, industry, and community resources in developing academic and vocational education programs for selected juveniles.**

COMMENT: Academic and vocational programs in the community can supplement the facility's programs. Based on predetermined criteria, arrangements should be made for selected juveniles to attend classes at nearby schools. Such community contacts also encourage staff to design institutional instruction that is realistic and relevant to the needs and requirements of the current labor market. A trade and craft advisory committee can assist in updating curricula and facilitating job placement of released juveniles.

3-JDF-5C-04-9

Added August 1991. The educational program coordinates with other institutional services to provide instruction in functional social skills.

COMMENT: Social skills include consumer activities, life skills, and parenting/family life skills. Courses should be coordinated with social services, leisure activities, and religious programs, as well as a comprehensive social skills development program.

3-JDF-5C-07

Added January 1992. Written policy, procedure, and practice provide for a vocational program that is consistent with the needs of the juvenile population.

COMMENT: While many detention facilities house juveniles with sentences of a few days or weeks, there are increasing numbers that are held for longer periods, sometimes up to five years. A vocational program for those longer-term juveniles should include an evaluation of vocational needs and a method for providing for those needs.

3-JDF-5C-08

Added August 1995. The juvenile work plan provides for employment for juveniles with disabilities.

COMMENT: None.

3-JDF-5F-02

Revised January 1990. Written policy, procedure, and practice require that the facility provide space and equipment needed to conduct and administer religious programs. The facility makes available adult clergy to ensure confidentiality.

COMMENT: Sufficient space should be available for congregate worship/religious services, individual counseling, group counseling and/or religious studies, and chaplaincy offices. Equipment, office supplies, and secretarial help should be adequate to meet the needs of the religious program.

3-JDF-5F-04

Added August 1990. The chaplain, in cooperation with the facility administrator or designee, approves donations of equipment or materials for use in religious programs.

COMMENT: Approval of donations helps ensure that equipment and materials are available for approved religious practices and helps avoid the accumulation of duplicate or inappropriate materials.

3-JDF-5F-05

Added August 1990. The chaplain has physical access to all areas of the institution to minister to juveniles and staff.

COMMENT: None.

3-JDF-5F-06

Revised August 2004. The chaplain or staff person develops and maintains close relationships with religious sources in the community.

COMMENT: Community resources can help administer religious services on special holidays or as needed to meet the requirements of the diversity of religious faiths among youth.

3-JDF-5G-04

Revised August 2002. Written policy, procedure, and practice specify that juveniles are permitted to send sealed letters to a specified class of persons and organizations, including but not limited to the following: courts, counsel, officials of the confining authority, administrators of grievance systems, and members of the releasing authority. Staff, in the presence of the juvenile, may be allowed to inspect outgoing privileged mail for contraband before it is sealed. Mail to juveniles from this specified class of persons and organizations may be opened only to inspect for contraband and only in the presence of the juveniles, unless waived in writing, or in circumstances which may indicate contamination.

COMMENT: Suspicious mail may include packages and letters unusual in appearance or which appear different from mail normally received or sent by the individual; packages and letters of a size or shape not customarily received or sent by the individual; packages and letters with a city and/or state postmark that is different from the return address; or packages and letters leaking, stained, or emitting a strange or unusual odor, or that have a powdery residue.

3-JDF-5G-08

Revised August 1994. Written policy, procedure, and practice require that all funds received through the mail are held for the juvenile in accordance with procedures approved by the parent agency. The facility may refuse acceptance of cash or personal checks by returning the items to the sender.

COMMENT: The administration should have discretion to control the flow of cash to juveniles. However, when cash is intercepted and withheld by the facility, it must be in accordance with written procedures that specify who is responsible for the cash, where it is to be deposited, and the method of return or transfer on the juvenile's release or placement.

3-JDF-5G-09

Revised August 2006. Written policy, procedure, and practice require that, excluding weekends and holidays, or emergency situations, incoming and outgoing letters are held for no more than 48 hours and packages (if allowed) are held no more than 72 hours.

Interpretation August 2002. The term *emergency situation* is interpreted as any significant disruption of normal facility or agency procedure, policy, or activity caused by riot, escape, fire, natural disaster, employee action, or other serious incident.

COMMENT: Inspection for contraband letters should take no longer than 48 hours to complete so that incoming letters should be distributed to inmates and outgoing letters sent to the post office within 48 hours of receipt. Similarly, inspection of packages normally should take no longer than 72 hours to complete. The standard does not prohibit the holding of mail for inmates who are temporarily absent from the facility (for example, in a hospital or court).

3-JDF-5G-11

Revised August 2002. Written policy, procedure, and practice provide for juvenile access to public telephones. Juveniles with hearing and/or speech disabilities, and juveniles who wish to communicate with parties who have such disabilities, shall be afforded access to a Telecommunications Device for the Deaf (TDD), or comparable equipment. Public telephones with volume control also shall be made available to hearing-impaired juveniles.

COMMENT: Sufficient telephone facilities should permit reasonable and equitable access to all inmates and permit a reasonable amount of privacy. Procedures should specify the hours during which the telephone is available, the maximum length of calls, and any limitation on calls. All long distance calls should be made collect.

3-JDF-5G-11-1

Added August 2002. Written policy, procedure, and practice ensure that juveniles have access to reasonably priced telephone services. Correctional agencies ensure that:

- **Contracts involving telephone services for juveniles comply with all applicable state and federal regulations.**
- **Contracts are based on rates and surcharges that are commensurate with those charged to the general public for like services. Any deviation from ordinary consumer rates reflects actual costs associated with the provision of services in a correctional setting.**
- **Contracts for juvenile telephone services provide the broadest range of calling options determined by the agency administrator to be consistent with the requirements of sound correctional/juvenile management.**

COMMENT: When procuring and renewing telephone services, correctional officials should inquire into the reasons for proposed deviations from standard charges and seek the best possible rates for the broadest possible range of calling options.

3-JDF-5G-14-1

Added August 2003. Written policy, procedure, and practice require that a juvenile is informed in a timely manner of the verifiable death or critical illness of an immediate family member. In case of the critical illness of an immediate family member, the juvenile is allowed, whenever statutes and circumstances allow, to go to the bedside under escort or alone.

COMMENT: Classification, status, geography, security level, and other specified criteria should determine eligibility. Immediate family is usually defined as parent, spouse, child, sibling, grandparent, or legal guardian.

Appendix B Revised January 2001. Refer to *Standards Supplement* Appendix D.

Juvenile Probation and Aftercare Services (JPAS), 2nd Edition

2-7005 **Revised August 1986. There is a written description and organizational chart that reflect the current structure of authority, responsibility, and accountability within the field agency. These documents are reviewed at least annually and are updated, as needed.**

COMMENT: A current organizational chart is necessary for providing a clear administrative picture. The chart should reflect the grouping of similar functions, the effective span of control, lines of authority, and an orderly channel of communication.

2-7006-1 **Added August 2010. The facility/agency shall demonstrate it has examined, and where appropriate and feasible, implemented strategies that promote recycling, energy and water conservation, pollution reduction, and utilization of renewable energy alternatives.**

COMMENT: Correctional facilities and programs have the responsibility to implement strategies that allow correctional facilities to be managed in ways that are most cost-effective and deliver superior performance, while improving environmental responsibility and sustainability. This includes recycling (including paper, metal, and plastic products), energy conservation (including building insulation, heating and ventilation, temperature controls, vehicle fuel efficiency, water economies, physical plant engineering, and energy measures), pollution reduction (including composting sewer treatment, litter abatement, and carbon emissions), and utilization of renewable energy alternatives (bio-fuels, solar collection, turbine energy production, and methane collection).

2-7020-1 **Added August 1993. Written policy, procedure, and practice establish the agency's commitment to informing the public and the media of events within the agency's areas of responsibility. The procedures address emergency and nonemergency responses to the media and, at a minimum, include the following:**

- **identification of areas in the facility that are accessible to media representatives**
- **the contact person for routine requests for information**
- **identification of data and information protected by federal or state privacy laws, or federal and state freedom of information laws**
- **special events coverage**
- **news release policy**
- **the designation of individuals or positions within the agency authorized to speak with the media on behalf of the agency**

COMMENT: The complexity of the policy statement should be consistent with the size and complexity of the operation.

2-7025 **Revised August 2003. To be considered qualified, an agency administrator, at a minimum, must possess the following: a bachelor's degree in an appropriate discipline, two years of experience working with juveniles and three years in staff supervision and administration; and/or the completion of a career development program that includes work-related experience, training, or college credits providing a level of achievement equivalent to a bachelor's degree.**

COMMENT: The parent agency should be able to demonstrate that the employee is able to handle a variety of tasks relevant to the job, which include an understanding of legislation and relevant case law, the ability to learn and use basic management principles, to understand fiscal processes, to work with public officials, to express oneself logically, and to use relevant information in decision making.

2-7026 **Deleted August 2002.**

2-7030 **Deleted August 1986.**

2-7030-1 **Added August 1995. Written policy, procedure, and practice provide a mechanism to process requests for reasonable accommodation to the known physical and/or mental impairments of a qualified individual with a disability, either an applicant or an employee. The accommodation need not be granted if it would impose an undue hardship or direct threat.**

COMMENT: *Reasonable accommodation* refers to modifications or adjustments, which enable qualified applicants with disabilities to access the job application process or which enable qualified employees with disabilities to perform the essential functions of the job and to enjoy the same terms, conditions, and privileges of employment that are available to persons without disabilities. *Terms, conditions, and privileges of employment* include, but are not limited to:

- recruitment, selection, and hiring
- salary and compensation
- benefits, holidays, leave, and work hours
- promotion and advancement
- staff development, including in-service training
- retirement, resignation, and termination

An *undue hardship* means significant difficulty or expense. *Direct threat* means a significant risk of substantial harm to the health or safety of any person, including the applicant or employee with a disability that cannot be eliminated or reduced by reasonable accommodation. A *qualified individual with a disability* means an individual with a disability who satisfies the requisite skill, experience, education, and other job-related requirements for the employment position such individual holds or desires, and who, with or without reasonable accommodation, can perform the essential functions of such position.

2-7031 **Deleted August 1984.**

2-7032 **Revised August 1995. Written policy specifies that equal employment opportunities exist for all positions. When deficiencies exist regarding the employment of minority groups and women, the agency can document the implementation of an affirmative action program that is approved by the appropriate government agency and can document annual reviews and the changes needed to keep the program current.**

COMMENT: Equal employment opportunity is a public policy goal. All qualified persons should be able to compete equally for entry into and promotion within the agency, and the affirmative action program should actively encourage the participation of members of minority groups, individuals with a disability, and women in the agency's staff development program. The affirmative action program also should include corrective actions, when needed, in policies regarding pay rate, demotion, transfer, layoff, termination, and upgrades.

2-7032-1 **Added January 1992. Written policy, procedure, and practice prohibit sexual harassment.**

COMMENT: Agency administrators should have as their objective the creation of a workplace that is free from all forms of discrimination, including sexual harassment. Agency policy clearly indicates that sexual harassment, either explicit or implicit, is strictly prohibited. Employees and agents of the agency, including volunteers, contractors, and vendors, must be advised that they are subject to disciplinary action, including dismissal and termination of contracts and/or services, if found guilty of sexual harassment charges brought by employees or juveniles.

2-7037 **Revised August 1986. Written policy and procedure require that employees whose jobs involve use of force or law enforcement responsibilities, which may include the power of arrest, receive a physical examination prior to the job assignment. All other employees receive a medical screening prior to the job assignment. Provisions exist for reexamination according to a defined need or schedule.**

COMMENT: Probation and parole assignments can be physically demanding, and all staff members should be physically fit. Staff whose responsibilities include the potential for physically demanding tasks must have physical examinations to protect their health, ensure their ability to perform effectively, and avoid appointments or assignments incompatible with their physical condition. The basic health status of all employees should be evaluated against the specific job requirements of their assignments. Physical examination and screening procedures may be established by the appropriate medical authority for the agency in accordance with applicable laws and regulations. Policy should encourage the hiring of persons with disabilities.

2-7039 **Deleted August 1986.**

2-7041 **Revised August 1995. The agency maintains a current, accurate, confidential personnel record on each employee. Information obtained as part of a required medical examination (and/or inquiry) regarding the medical condition or history of applicants and employees is collected and maintained on separate forms and in separate medical files and treated as a confidential medical record.**

COMMENT: The personnel record should contain the following: initial application; reference letters; results of employment investigation; verification of training and experience; wage and salary information; job performance evaluations; incident reports, if any; and commendations and disciplinary actions, if any.

2-7049-1 **Added August 1985. The training curriculum is developed, evaluated, and updated based on an annual needs assessment that identifies current job-related training needs.**

COMMENT: Training should be responsive to job requirements; professional development needs; new theories, techniques, and technologies; and current correctional issues. A needs assessment may entail observation and analysis of job tasks and components, surveys of staff to identify perceived training needs, reviews of agency/facility operations, reports and documents generated by staff, and use of previously developed resources in this area, with recommendations and specific objectives for training to be made based on findings resulting from these efforts.

2-7058 **Revised August 1986. The field agency encourages employees to attend professional meetings, seminars, and similar work-related activities, and provides administrative leave and/or reimburses employees for expenses connected with these activities.**

COMMENT: Outside training and educational programs may provide new ideas and insights into probation, parole, and related activities. Participation in these activities should be encouraged, and the budget should include adequate funds for staff participation.

2-7059 **Deleted August 1986.**

2-7064 **Deleted August 1986.**

2-7073 **Deleted August 1986.**

2-7093 **Revised August 1992. Written policy, procedure, and practice permit non-judicial voluntary informal probation by the intake unit or its parent agency, in accordance with the statute of the authority having jurisdiction.**

COMMENT: Non-judicial or informal probation can be used to divert a juvenile from the formal juvenile justice system.

2-7100 **Interpretation August 1983. A judicial review is a proceeding to reexamine the course of action or continued confinement of a juvenile in a secure detention facility. Arguments, witnesses, or evidence are not required as a part of the review. Reviews may be conducted by a judge, judicial officer, or other administrative person who has been delegated the authority to detain or release juveniles from secure detention with the approval of the judge.**

2-7104 **Revised August 1983. Written policy and procedure provide that group residential facilities meet applicable building, sanitation, health, and fire safety codes.**

COMMENT: Local and state codes should be strictly enforced to ensure the safety and well-being of the juveniles involved. Reports of periodic inspections and action taken with respect to these reports should be available. In the event local and state codes are not available or applicable, appropriate national codes will be applied to the program.

2-7107 **Revised January 1995. Written policy, procedure, and practice require a minimum of monthly person-to-person contact between field staff and juveniles in placement other than their own homes and with the person(s) responsible for the care of the juveniles in placement, unless under interstate compact supervision. When the private placement facility is at least 500 miles (round trip) from the base station, bimonthly person-to-person contact is required. Telephonic contact between the probation officer and the juvenile in placement, as well as, the placement authority must be made at least twice during the month the juvenile will not be visited.**

COMMENT: The agency's responsibility for supervision of juveniles and for ensuring that their care and program needs are being met requires regular contact with the juveniles and those who are sharing responsibility for their care and supervision.

2-7127 **Revised August 1991. Field staff who have caseloads report to a designated supervisor who is trained in the supervisory function.**

COMMENT: Regular case conferences between field staff and their supervisors can provide training and improve professional development. Such contacts also can help to ensure maximum effectiveness and efficiency in job performance. The span of control for a supervisor should not exceed 10 staff members, and the job of supervising field staff should be full-time.

2-7131 **Revised August 1983. The initial contact between the juvenile newly released from confinement and/or placed on probation and the assigned field staff member occurs no later than 24-hours after release or placement on probation/aftercare.**

COMMENT: The field staff member should immediately explain to the juvenile and his/her parents the purpose of probation/aftercare, special conditions imposed, and the range of services available. It is also important that the field staff member, the juvenile, and his/her parents determine if there are other specific program needs that must be met immediately, such as alternative home placement.

2-7133-1 **Added January 1992. Written policy, procedure, and practice provide for the reporting of all instances of child abuse and/or neglect consistent with appropriate state law or local laws.**

COMMENT: Whenever a juvenile reports or staff observe indicators of child abuse and/or neglect, there are procedures for juvenile care and investigation of the allegation. Where appropriate, interagency agreements pursuant to child abuse should be implemented.

2-7164 **Revised August 2000 (Mandatory). Written policy, procedure, and practice provide that all personnel receive appropriate training before being issued authorization to carry a firearm or other weapon. Training covers the use of, safety, and care of the weapon and the constraints on its use. All personnel issued authorization to use a weapon must demonstrate competency in its use at least annually.**

COMMENT: None.

2-7164-1 **Added August 2000. Written policy, procedure, and practice require all personnel authorized to carry a weapon receive a medical/physical evaluation, a mental health screening, and drug and alcohol screening prior to being issued a weapon.**

COMMENT: None.

2-7166 **Deleted August 1986.**

Small Jail Facilities (SJ), 1st Edition

SJ-002-1

Added August 2010. The facility/agency shall demonstrate it has examined and, where appropriate and feasible, implemented strategies that promote recycling, energy and water conservation, pollution reduction, and utilization of renewable energy alternatives.

COMMENT: Correctional facilities and programs have the responsibility to implement strategies that allow correctional facilities to be managed in ways that are most cost-effective and deliver superior performance, while improving environmental responsibility and sustainability. This includes recycling (including paper, metal, and plastic products), energy conservation (including building insulation, heating and ventilation, temperature controls, vehicle fuel efficiency, water economies, physical plant engineering, and energy measures), pollution reduction (including composting sewer treatment, litter abatement, and carbon emissions), and utilization of renewable energy alternatives (bio-fuels, solar collection, turbine energy production, and methane collection).

SJ-009-1

Added October 1997. Written policy, procedure, and practice establish the facility's commitment to informing the public and the media of events within the facility's areas of responsibility. The procedures address emergency and nonemergency responses to the media and, at a minimum, include the following:

- **the identification of areas in the facility that are accessible to media representatives**
- **the contact person for routine requests for information**
- **identification of data and information protected by federal or state privacy laws, or federal and state freedom of information laws**
- **special events coverage**
- **news release policy**
- **the designation of individuals or positions within the facility authorized to speak with the media on behalf of the facility**

COMMENT: The complexity of the policy statement should be consistent with the size and complexity of the operation.

SJ-018-1

Added October 1997. Written policy specifies that equal employment opportunities exist for all positions. When deficiencies exist regarding the employment of minority groups and women, the facility can document the implementation of an affirmative action program that is approved by the appropriate government agency and can document annual reviews and the changes needed to keep the program current.

COMMENT: Equal employment opportunity is a public policy goal. All qualified persons should be able to compete equally for entry into and promotion within the facility, and the affirmative action program should actively encourage the participation of members of minority groups, individuals with disability, and women in the facility's staff development program. The affirmative action program also should include corrective actions, when needed, in policies regarding pay rate, demotion, transfer, layoff, termination, and upgrades.

SJ-018-2 **Added October 1997. Written policy, procedure, and practice prohibit sexual harassment.**

COMMENT: Facility administrators should have as their objective the creation of a workplace that is free from all forms of discrimination, including sexual harassment. Facility policy clearly indicates that sexual harassment, either explicit or implicit, is strictly prohibited. Employees and agents of the facility, including volunteers, contractors, and vendors, must be advised that they are subject to disciplinary action, including dismissal and termination of contracts and/or services, if found guilty of sexual harassment charges brought by employees or inmates.

SJ-018-3 **Added October 1997. Written policy, procedure, and practice provide a mechanism to process requests for reasonable accommodation to the known physical and/or mental impairments of a qualified individual with a disability, either an applicant or an employee. The accommodation need not be granted if it would impose an undue hardship or direct threat.**

COMMENT: *Reasonable accommodation* refers to modifications or adjustments which enable qualified applicants with disabilities to access the job application process or which enable qualified employees with disabilities to perform the essential functions of the job and to enjoy the same terms, conditions, and privileges of employment that are available to persons without disabilities. *Terms, conditions, and privileges of employment* include, but are not limited to:

- recruitment, selection, and hiring
- salary and compensation
- benefits, holidays, leave, and work hours
- promotion and advancement
- staff development, including in-service training
- retirement, resignation, and termination

An *undue hardship* means significant difficulty or expense. *Direct threat* means a significant risk of substantial harm to the health or safety of any person, including the applicant or employee with a disability that cannot be eliminated or reduced by reasonable accommodation. A *qualified individual with a disability* means an individual with a disability who satisfies the requisite skill, experience, education, and other job-related requirements for the employment position such individual holds or desires, and who, with or without reasonable accommodation, can perform the essential functions of such position.

SJ-019 **Revised January 2007. In accordance with state and federal statutes, a criminal record check is conducted on all new employees prior to entry on duty to ascertain whether there are criminal convictions that have a specific relationship to job performance. This record will include comprehensive identifier information to be collected and run against law enforcement indices. If suspect information on matters with potential terrorism connections is returned on a desirable applicant, it is forwarded to the local Joint Terrorism Task Force (JTTF) or another similar agency.**

COMMENT: The facility administrator should know of any criminal conviction that could directly affect an employee's job performance.

SJ-024

Revised August 2010. The institution maintains a current, accurate, confidential personnel record on each employee except where state statutes require open public records and the personnel record cannot be maintained confidentially. Information obtained as part of a required medical examination (and/or inquiry) regarding the medical condition or history of applicants and employees is collected and maintained on separate forms and in separate medical files and treated as a confidential medical record.

COMMENT: The personnel record should contain the following: initial application; reference letters; results of employment investigation; verification of training and experience; wage and salary information; job performance evaluations; incident reports, if any; commendations; and disciplinary actions, if any.

SJ-024-1

Revised January 2003. A written code of ethics requires employees to conduct themselves and perform their duties in such a way as to set a good example for inmates and thereby command their respect. The code of ethics prohibits employees from using their official position to secure privileges for themselves or others and from engaging in activities that constitute a conflict of interest. This code is available to all employees.

COMMENT: To protect the integrity of the institution, its staff, and the parent agency, all personnel must be thoroughly familiar with the code of ethics and the code must be strictly enforced.

SJ-025

Revised August 2005. Written policy, procedure, and practice provide that the facility's training programs for all employees are specifically planned, coordinated, and supervised by a qualified employee. The training plan is reviewed annually.

COMMENT: Staff development should be an integral part of the management and operation of the facility. Therefore, a staff member should be selected to maintain continuity and ensure cooperation in the training function. The training plan should include pre-service and in-service training curriculum for the various subcategories with specific timelines for completion of each training unit. It should also consider the physical characteristics of the institution, its overall mission, and the type of offenders served.

SJ-028

Revised August 2005. Written policy, procedure, and practice provide that all new correctional officers receive 120 hours of training during their first year of employment. At a minimum, this training covers the following areas:

- **security and safety procedures**
- **emergency and fire procedures**
- **supervision of offenders**

- **suicide intervention/prevention**
- **use of force**
- **offender rights**
- **key control**
- **interpersonal relations**
- **communication skills**
- **standards of conduct**
- **cultural awareness**
- **sexual abuse/assault intervention**
- **code of ethics**

Additional topics may be added at the discretion of the agency or facility.

COMMENT: Since the duties of correctional officers frequently involve most institutional operations, their training should be comprehensive.

SJ-028-1

Added August 2005. Written policy, procedure, and practice provide that all correctional officers receive at least 40 hours of annual training. This training shall include at a minimum the following areas:

- **standards of conduct/ethics**
- **security/safety/fire/medical/emergency procedures**
- **supervision of offenders including training on sexual abuse and assault**
- **use of force**

Additional topics shall be included based upon a needs assessment of both staff and institution requirements.

COMMENT: This training will enable employees to sharpen skills, maintain certification, and keep abreast of changes in policies, procedures, and legislative, judicial, or executive actions.

SJ-030

Revised August 2005. When there is an emergency unit, written policy, procedure, and practice provide that correctional officers assigned to an emergency unit have at least one year of experience as a correctional officer and 40 hours of specialized training before undertaking their assignments. The specialized training may be part of the officer's first year training program. Officers on emergency units receive 40 hours of training annually, at least 16 of which are specifically related to the emergency unit assignment.

COMMENT: Members of these units should receive training that will enable them to implement new knowledge and techniques.

SJ-048-1

Added October 1997. Inmates have access to operable showers with temperature-controlled hot and cold running water, at a minimum ratio of one shower for every eight inmates, unless local building health codes specify a different ratio. Water for showers is thermostatically controlled to temperatures ranging from 100 degrees Fahrenheit to 120 degrees Fahrenheit to ensure the safety of inmates and to promote hygienic practices.

COMMENT: Offenders can use scalding showers as a weapon against, or punishment for, other inmates. Also, accidental injury could occur when cold water is drawn in other areas, thereby unexpectedly elevating the hot water in showers to scalding temperatures. Water temperatures below 100 degrees Fahrenheit are uncomfortable and may deter an individual from pursuing good hygienic practices. The temperature controls should not preclude the use of water at higher temperatures, if needed, in other areas of the facility, such as kitchens.

SJ-049

Revised October 1997. Segregation rooms provide living conditions that approximate those of the general inmate population; all exceptions are clearly documented. Segregation housing units provide:

- **single-occupancy rooms or cells with a floor area of at least 70 square feet, of which 35 square feet is unencumbered**
- **a bed above floor level, a desk or writing space, and a stool**
- **continuous access to above-floor level toilet facilities**
- **hot and cold running water, and natural light**

There is documentation by an independent, qualified source that lighting is at least 20 foot-candles at desk level and in the personal grooming area, circulation is at least 10 cubic feet of outside or recirculated filtered air per minute, and temperatures are appropriate to summer and winter comfort zones.

COMMENT: None.

SJ-051

Revised October 1997. Written policy, procedure, and practice provide that single-occupancy cells/rooms shall be available when indicated for the following:

- **inmates with severe medical disabilities**
- **inmates suffering from serious mental illness**
- **sexual predators**
- **inmates likely to be exploited or victimized by others**
- **inmates who have other special needs for single-occupancy housing**

COMMENT: While the standard permits the housing of medium-security inmates in multiple cells/rooms, there is a need for single cells/rooms for the inmate groups listed above. The caveat *when indicated* refers to determinations made by the classification system, cell/room size, medical diagnosis, or other professional conclusion.

SJ-061 **Revised January 2006. The facility provides space for religious services, educational programs, and visiting.**

COMMENT: None.

SJ-069 **Revised October 1997. Inmates with disabilities are housed in a manner that provides for their safety and security. Housing used by inmates with disabilities is designed for their use and provides for integration with other inmates. Programs and services are accessible to inmates with disabilities who reside in the facility.**

COMMENT: If the facility accepts individuals with disabilities, it must provide for their housing and use of facility resources. Housing includes, but is not limited to, rooms, sleeping areas, furnishings, dayrooms, toilets, washbasins, showers, and other common elements. An offender with disability should not be placed in a special unit (for example, the infirmary, security room, or protective custody) that cannot accommodate the offender's disability. Program and service areas include, but are not limited to, exercise and recreation areas, visiting rooms, classrooms, dining rooms, commissary/canteen, telephone facilities, library, reception and classification areas, chapel, and administrative areas, where appropriate.

SJ-070 **Revised October 1997. Reasonable accommodation is made to ensure that all parts of the facility that are accessible to the public are accessible and usable by staff and visitors with disabilities.**

COMMENT: None.

SJ-070-1 **Added January 2002. Written policy, procedure, and practice provide for the assignment of appropriately trained individuals to assist disabled offenders who cannot otherwise perform basic life functions.**

COMMENT: None.

SJ-070-2 **Added August 2002. Written policy, procedure, and practice provide education, equipment, and facilities, and the support necessary for inmates with disabilities to perform self-care and personal hygiene in a reasonably private environment.**

COMMENT: A *reasonably private environment* will vary, depending on individual and institutional circumstances, but is one which will maintain the dignity of the disabled individual in light of that person's disability.

SJ-071

Revised August 2013. Segregation units have either outdoor uncovered or outdoor covered exercise areas. The minimum space requirements for outdoor exercise areas for segregation units are as follows:

- **Group yard modules: 330-square feet of unencumbered space can accommodate two inmates. For each additional 150-square feet of unencumbered space, an additional inmate may use the exercise area simultaneously. (Formula: for each 150-square feet of unencumbered space exceeding the base requirement of 180-square feet for the first inmate, equals the maximum number of inmates change to who which may use the recreation area space simultaneously). No more than five inmates are to use a group module at one time.**
- **Individual yard modules: 180-square feet of unencumbered space**

In cases where cover is not provided to mitigate the inclement weather, appropriate weather-related equipment and attire should be made available to the inmates who desire to take advantage of their authorized exercise time.

COMMENT: Indoor and outdoor exercise areas should be secure and available to all inmates. Indoor exercise programs may be conducted in a multipurpose room provided the space requirements are met, the space is available, and the location is acceptable.

SJ-076-1

Added January 2003. Written policy, procedure, and practice define critical incidents for the facility and provide for a debriefing to be conducted after each such incident. The debriefing process includes coordination and feedback about the incident with designated staff of the facility as soon as possible after the incident. A debriefing includes, but is not limited to:

- **a review of staff and offender actions during the incident**
- **a review of the incident's impact on staff and offenders**
- **a review of corrective actions taken and still needed**
- **plans for improvement to avoid another incident**

COMMENT: A *critical incident* is any event or situation that threatens staff or offenders in their community (criminal justice setting). While debriefings should occur as soon as possible, some information may not be available until later. All staff impacted by a critical incident should be included in the debriefings and referred to appropriate services to mitigate the stress associated with these events. All critical incidents should be reviewed by the administration, security, and health services. A two-week follow-up debriefing should occur to review the validity and appropriateness of all policies, plans, and information used during the critical incident and immediately after.

SJ-090-1 **Added October 1997.**

Preservation of Physical Evidence

Written policy, procedure, and practice provide for the preservation, control, and disposition of all physical evidence obtained in connection with a violation of law and/or institutional regulation. At a minimum, the procedures shall address the following:

- **chain of custody**
- **evidence handling**
- **location and storage requirements**

COMMENT: Strict accountability of physical evidence collected in connection with a crime must be established to preserve the integrity of the disciplinary and/or legal process. Minor rule violations should be exempt from the procedural requirements of evidence control, preservation, and disposition.

SJ-096 **Revised October 1997. Written policy, procedure, and practice provide that written reports are submitted to the facility administrator or designee no later than the conclusion of the tour of duty when any of the following occur:**

- **discharge of a firearm or other weapon**
- **use of chemical agents to control inmates**
- **use of force to control inmates**
- **inmate(s) remain in restraints at the end of the shift**

COMMENT: All incidents involving use of force that have the potential for injury should be recorded to establish the identities of the staff, inmate(s), or others involved and to describe the nature of the incident.

SJ-098 **Revised January 2001 (Mandatory). Written policy and procedure govern the control and use of keys, tools, and culinary and medical equipment.**

COMMENT: The key control system should provide a current accounting of the location and possessor of each key. Tools and utensils should be locked in control panels and issued in accordance with a prescribed system.

SJ-099 **Revised October 1997. Written policy, procedure, and practice provide that personnel read the appropriate post order each time they assume a new post and sign and date the post order. A review of the post orders by supervisory staff shall be documented at least annually.**

COMMENT: None.

SJ-105-1

Added October 1997 (Mandatory). Written policy, procedure, and practice provide that when an offender is placed in a four/five-point restraint (arms, head, and legs secured), advance approval must be obtained from the facility administrator or designee. Subsequently, the health authority or designee must be notified to assess the inmate's medical and mental health condition, and to advise whether, on the basis of serious danger to self or others, the inmate should be placed in a medical/mental health unit for emergency involuntary treatment with sedation and/or other medical management, as appropriate. If the offender is not transferred to a medical/mental health unit and is restrained in a four/five-point position, the following minimum procedures will be followed:

- **Direct visual observation by staff must be continuous prior to obtaining approval from the health authority or designee.**
- **Subsequent visual observation must be made at least every 15 minutes.**
- **Restraint procedures are in accordance with guidelines endorsed by the designated health authority.**

COMMENT: Four/five-point restraints should be used only in extreme instances and only when other types of restraints have proven to be ineffective. Restraint guidelines should include consideration of an individual's physical condition, such as body weight.

SJ-114-1

Added October 1997. If an inmate uses food or food service equipment in a manner that is hazardous to self, staff, or other inmates, alternative meal service may be provided. Alternative meal service is on an individual basis, is based on health or safety considerations only, meets basic nutritional requirements, and occurs with the written approval of the facility administrator and responsible health authority. The substitution shall not exceed seven days.

COMMENT: None.

SJ-127

Revised August 2004. Therapeutic diets are provided as prescribed by appropriate clinicians. A therapeutic diet manual is available in health services and food services for reference and information. Prescriptions for therapeutic diets should be specific and complete, furnished in writing to the food service manager, and rewritten annually, or more often as clinically indicated.

COMMENT: Therapeutic diets are prepared and served to offenders according to the orders of the treating clinician or as directed by the responsible health authority. Therapeutic diets should be kept as simple as possible and should conform as closely as possible to the foods served other offenders.

SJ-132-1

Added October 1997. Written policy, procedure, and practice provide that stored shelf goods are maintained at 45 degrees to 80 degrees Fahrenheit, refrigerated foods at 35 degrees to 40 degrees Fahrenheit, and frozen foods at 0 degrees Fahrenheit or below.

COMMENT: The American Dietary Association recommends storage temperatures for freezers to be -10 degrees to 0 degrees Fahrenheit and refrigerated storage at 32 degrees to 36 degrees Fahrenheit. However, the requirements may differ under certain conditions. When the requirements vary from the above, laws and regulations of the health authority having jurisdiction shall prevail.

SJ-133-1

Added August 2011. All staff, contractors, and inmate workers who work in the food service department are trained in the use of food service equipment and in the safety procedures to be followed in the food service department.

COMMENT: None.

SJ-150

Revised October 1997. Written policy, procedure, and practice govern the use of restraints for medical and psychiatric purposes. At a minimum, the policy will address the following:

- **conditions under which restraints may be used**
- **types of restraints to be applied for specific purposes**
- **identification of person or persons who may authorize the use of restraints**
- **monitoring procedures for inmates in restraints**

COMMENT: When restraints are part of a health care treatment regimen, the restraints used should be those that would be appropriate for the general public within the jurisdiction. Written policy should identify the authorization needed and when, where, and how restraints may be used and for how long.

SJ-155-1

Added October 1997. Written policy, procedure, and practice govern the administration of involuntary psychotropic drugs in compliance with the applicable laws of the jurisdiction.

COMMENT: None.

SJ-157-1

Revised January 2003. Written policy, procedure, and practice provide that pregnancy management is specific as it relates to the following:

- **pregnancy testing**
- **routine prenatal care**
- **high-risk prenatal care**
- **management of the chemically addicted pregnant inmate**
- **postpartum follow-up**
- **unless mandated by state law, birth certificates/registry does not list a correctional facility as the place of birth**

COMMENT: Management should include family planning services prior to release.

SJ-157-2

Revised January 2001. Written policy, procedure, and practice provide for early identification and treatment of inmates with alcohol and drug abuse problems through a standardized battery assessment. This battery shall be documented and include, at a minimum, the following:

- **screening and sorting**
- **clinical assessment and reassessment**
- **medical assessment for drug and alcohol program assignment appropriate to the needs of the individual offenders**
- **referrals**

COMMENT: None.

SJ-157-3

Added October 1997 (Mandatory). There is a written suicide-prevention and intervention program that is reviewed and approved by a qualified medical or mental health professional. All staff with responsibility for inmate supervision are trained in the implementation of the program.

COMMENT: The program should include specific procedures for intake screening, identifying, and supervising of suicide-prone inmates.

SJ-158-1

Added October 1997. Written policy, procedure, and practice provide that foreign nationals have access to the diplomatic representative of their country of citizenship.

COMMENT: Staff assistance should be provided to enable foreign nationals to contact their diplomatic representative.

SJ-162-1

Added August 2002. Written policy, procedure, and practice ensure that information is provided to offenders about sexual abuse/assault including:

- **prevention/intervention**
- **self-protection**
- **reporting sexual abuse/assault**
- **treatment and counseling**

The information is communicated orally and in writing, in a language clearly understood by the offender, upon arrival at the facility.

COMMENT: None.

SJ-162-2

Added January 2003. Inmates are screened within 24 hours of arrival at the facility for potential vulnerabilities or tendencies of acting out with sexually aggressive behavior. Housing assignments are made accordingly.

COMMENT: None.

SJ-162-3

Added January 2003. Written policy, procedure, and practice require that an investigation is conducted and documented whenever a sexual assault or threat is reported.

COMMENT: The agency should report occurrences/allegations of sexual assault or threat in accordance with the laws of the jurisdiction. The investigation may be limited by what is allowed by the laws of the jurisdiction.

SJ-162-4

Added January 2003. Written policy, procedure, and practice require that inmates identified as high risk with a history of sexually assaultive behavior are assessed by a mental health or other qualified professional. Inmates with a history of sexually assaultive behavior are identified, monitored, and counseled.

COMMENT: None.

SJ-162-5

Added January 2003. Written policy, procedure, and practice provide that inmates identified as at risk for sexual victimization are assessed by a mental health or other qualified professional. Inmates at risk for sexual victimization are identified, monitored, and counseled.

COMMENT: None.

SJ-162-6

Added January 2003. Written policy, procedure, and practice ensure that sexual conduct between staff and inmates, volunteers, or contract personnel and inmates, regardless of consensual status, is prohibited and subject to administrative and criminal disciplinary sanctions.

COMMENT: None.

SJ-162-7

Added January 2003. Victims of sexual assault are referred under appropriate security provisions to a community facility for treatment and gathering of evidence. If these procedures are performed in-house, the following guidelines are used:

- **A history is taken by health care professionals who conduct an examination to document the extent of physical injury and to determine if referral to another medical facility is indicated. With the victim's consent, the examination includes collection of evidence from the victim, using a kit approved by the appropriate authority.**
- **Provision is made for testing for sexually transmitted diseases (for example, HIV, gonorrhea, hepatitis, and other diseases) and counseling, as appropriate.**
- **Prophylactic treatment and follow-up for sexually transmitted diseases are offered to all victims, as appropriate.**

- **Following the physical examination, there is availability of an evaluation by a mental health professional to assess the need for crisis-intervention counseling and long-term follow-up.**
- **A report is made to the facility administrator, designee, or program administrator to assure separation of the victim from his or her assailant.**

COMMENT: None.

SJ-162-8

Added January 2003. Written policy, procedure, and practice provide that inmates who are victims of sexual abuse have the option to report the incident to a designated staff member other than an immediate point-of-contact line officer.

COMMENT: None.

SJ-162-9

Added January 2003. Written policy, procedure, and practice provide that all case records associated with claims of sexual abuse, including incident reports, investigative reports, offender information, case disposition, medical and counseling evaluation findings, and recommendations for post-release treatment and/or counseling are retained in accordance with an established schedule.

COMMENT: None.

SJ-170-1

Added October 1997. Written policy, procedure, and practice provide that inmates charged with rule violations are scheduled for a hearing as soon as practical but no later than seven days, excluding weekends and holidays, after the alleged violation. Inmates are notified of the hearing at least 24 hours in advance of the hearings.

COMMENT: To ensure fairness and the integrity of the disciplinary process, inmates charged with rule violations should receive hearings as soon as possible unless the hearing is prevented by exceptional circumstances, unavoidable delays, or reasonable postponements. Reasons for all delays should be documented.

SJ-177

Revised August 2002. Written policy, procedure, and practice require that, excluding weekends, holidays, or emergency situations, incoming and outgoing letters are held for no more than 24 hours and packages are held for no more than 48 hours.

Interpretation August 2002. The words *emergency situation* are interpreted as any significant disruption of normal facility or agency procedure, policy, or activity caused by riot, escape, fire, natural disaster, employee action, or other serious incident.

COMMENT: Inspection for contraband letters should take no longer than 24 hours to complete so that incoming letters should be distributed to inmates and outgoing letters sent to the post office within 24 hours of receipt. Similarly, inspection of packages normally should take no longer than 48 hours to complete. The standard does not prohibit the holding of mail for inmates who are temporarily absent from the facility (for example, in a hospital or court).

SJ-178

Revised January 2002. Written policy and procedure specify that inmates are permitted to send sealed letters to specified groups and organizations, including, but not limited to: courts, counsel, officials of the confining authority, government officials, administrators of grievance systems, and members of the parole authority. Mail to inmates from this specified class of persons and organizations may be opened only to inspect for contraband and only in the presence of the inmate or in circumstances which may indicate contamination. Staff, in the presence of the inmate, may be allowed to inspect outgoing privileged mail for contraband before it is sealed.

COMMENT: Suspicious mail may include packages and letters unusual in appearance or that appear different from mail normally received or sent by the individual; packages and letters of a size or shape not customarily received or sent by the individual; packages and letters with a city and/or postmark that is different from the return address; or packages and letters leaking, stained, or emitting a strange or unusual odor, or which have a powdery residue.

SJ-179

Revised August 2002. Written policy, procedure, and practice provide for inmate access to public telephones. Inmates with hearing and/or speech disabilities, and inmates who wish to communicate with parties who have such disabilities, shall be afforded access to a Telecommunications Device for the Deaf (TDD), or comparable equipment. Public telephones with volume control also shall be made available to inmates with hearing impairments.

COMMENT: Telephone facilities should permit reasonable and equitable access to all inmates and permit a reasonable amount of privacy. Procedures should specify the hours during which the telephone is available, the maximum length of calls, and any limitation on calls. All long distance calls should be made collect.

SJ-179-1

Added August 2002. Written policy, procedure, and practice ensure that offenders have access to reasonably priced telephone services. Correctional agencies ensure that:

- **Contracts involving telephone services for offenders comply with all applicable state and federal regulations.**
- **Contracts are based on rates and surcharges that are commensurate with those charged to the general public for like services. Any deviation from ordinary consumer rates reflects actual costs associated with the provision of services in a correctional setting.**
- **Contracts for offender telephone services provide the broadest range of calling options determined by the agency administrator to be consistent with the requirements of sound correctional management.**

COMMENT: When procuring and renewing telephone services, correctional officials should inquire into the reasons for proposed deviations from standard charges and seek the best possible rates for the broadest possible range of calling options.

SJ-184-1

Added August 2003. Written policy, procedure, and practice require that an inmate is informed in a timely manner of the verifiable death or critical illness of an immediate family member. In case of the critical illness of an immediate family member, the inmate is allowed, whenever statutes and circumstances allow, to go to the bedside under escort or alone.

COMMENT: Classification, status, geography, security level, and other specified criteria should determine eligibility. *Immediate family* is usually defined as parent, spouse, child, sibling, grandparent, or legal guardian.

SJ-188

Revised August 2013. Written policy, procedure, and practice provide that:

- **All newly admitted inmates receive written or oral orientation information in the language in which they are fluent.**
- **Completion of orientation is documented by a statement that is signed and dated by the inmate.**
- **Newly admitted inmates are permitted to complete at least three local or collect long distance telephone calls during the admission process.**

This information is provided to inmates in a written and/or electronic format. If the inmate handbook is provided electronically, inmates in segregation are provided the information in a written format so that their access to the information is not impeded by their custody status. The handbook is translated into those languages spoken by significant numbers of inmates.

COMMENT: The use of electronic kiosks is allowed as a means of providing the inmate handbook. Agencies using such kiosks should implement strategies to allow access to this information by general population inmates without interference by facility staff without a valid security-related reason. Inmates who are unable to read and write should be assisted through case management services provided by the facility.

SJ-196-1

Revised August 2002. Written policy, procedure, and practice prohibit discrimination on the basis of disability in the provision of services, programs, and activities administered for program beneficiaries and participants.

COMMENT: Services, programs, and activities include, but are not limited to, the following:

- academic and vocational education (including developmental and rehabilitative programs)
- work programs/work release programs (by providing reasonable accommodations or alternatives for offenders with disabilities so that the benefits of these programs, including sentence-reduction credits, are available to offenders with disabilities)
- recreation, exercise, and activities
- mail, telephone, and visiting
- library
- religious programs
- reception and orientation
- transportation services (to provide for safety and security, and to avoid undue discomfort, in light of the offender's disabilities)
- classification
- food service
- sanitation and hygiene
- health care
- social services
- release
- discipline, grievance procedures, and due process proceedings
- safety and emergency procedures
- access to media, courts, counsel, and law library
- commissary/canteen
- volunteer programs
- psychological and psychiatric services

Program beneficiaries and participants include, but are not limited to: inmates, family members, clergy, attorneys, volunteers, and other authorized visitors.

The institution may be required to take remedial action, when necessary, to afford program beneficiaries and participants with disabilities an opportunity to participate in, and enjoy the benefit of services, programs, or activities. Remedial action may include, but is not limited to: 1) making reasonable modifications to policies, practices, or procedures, 2) providing auxiliary aids and services to the hearing and visually impaired, 3) constructing new or altering existing facilities, and 4) delivering services, and so on, at alternative accessible sites.

SJ-196-2 **Added August 2002. Written policy, procedure, and practice provide for staff and offender access to an appropriately trained and qualified individual who is educated in the problems and challenges faced by offenders with physical and/or mental impairments, programs designed to educate and assist disabled offenders, and all legal requirements for the protection of offenders with disabilities.**

COMMENT: An *appropriately trained and qualified individual*, as used in this standard, is one who has been designated by the warden, superintendent, or other authority, to coordinate efforts to comply with and carry out responsibilities defined by the Americans with Disabilities Act. That individual should develop relationships with, and use the expertise of institutional staff, advocacy groups, nonprofit organizations, agencies of government, and others that have relevant knowledge and experience.

SJ-199-1 **Added October 1997. Written policy, procedure, and practice prohibit discrimination based on an inmate's race, religion, national origin, sex, disability, or political views in making administrative decisions and in providing access to programs.**

COMMENT: Inmates should be assured equal opportunities to participate in all institutional programs.

SJ-203-1 **Added October 1997. Written policy, procedure, and practice provide that consistent with the law of the jurisdiction, there is a system for providing notification to the registered victim(s) of a crime prior to any release from confinement of the convicted inmate and/or escape from custody. Follow-up notification to victim(s) occurs when escapees are returned to custody.**

COMMENT: An increasing number of jurisdictions are requiring notification of the victims of criminal act(s) prior to release of the person(s) convicted of the crime. When such legislation exists, the facility should provide the staff with a clear set of instructions to implement the legislation.

Appendix B Revised January 2001. Refer to *Standards Supplement* Appendix D.

Small Juvenile Detention Facilities (SJD), 1st Edition

1-SJD-1A-03-1 **Added January 1990. Written policy, procedure, and practice provide that the facility is used solely for pretrial holding and not as a post-trial treatment center. Juveniles may be held post-trial awaiting placement.**

COMMENT: None.

1-SJD-1A-03-2 **Added August 2010. The facility/agency shall demonstrate it has examined, and where appropriate and feasible, implemented strategies that promote recycling, energy and water conservation, pollution reduction, and utilization of renewable energy alternatives.**

COMMENT: Correctional facilities and programs have the responsibility to implement strategies that allow correctional facilities to be managed in ways that are most cost-effective and deliver superior performance, while improving environmental responsibility and sustainability. This includes recycling (including paper, metal, and plastic products), energy conservation (including building insulation, heating and ventilation, temperature controls, vehicle fuel efficiency, water economies, physical plant engineering, and energy measures), pollution reduction (including composting sewer treatment, litter abatement, and carbon emissions), and utilization of renewable energy alternatives (bio-fuels, solar collection, turbine energy production, and methane collection).

1-SJD-1A-12 **Deleted August 2002.**

1-SJD-1A-23-1 **Added August 1993. Written policy, procedure, and practice establish the facility's commitment to informing the public and the media of events within the facility's areas of responsibility. The procedures address emergency and nonemergency responses to the media and, at a minimum, include the following:**

- **the identification of areas in the facility that are accessible to media representatives**
- **the contact person for routine requests for information**
- **identification of data and information protected by federal or state privacy laws, or federal and state freedom of information laws**
- **special events coverage**
- **news release policy**
- **the designation of individuals or positions within the facility authorized to speak with the media on behalf of the facility**

COMMENT: The complexity of the policy statement should be consistent with the size and complexity of the operation.

1-SJD-1B-10

Revised January 2001. Written policy, procedure, and practice provide for an independent financial audit of the facility. This audit is conducted annually or as stipulated by statute or regulation, but at least every three years. If the facility is a part of a state system, an internal audits section or department of the agency's central administration and/or statutory agency shall be considered independent of the facility to be audited.

COMMENT: None.

1-SJD-1B-16

Deleted August 1993.

1-SJD-1C-04

Revised August 1995. Written policy specifies that equal employment opportunities exist for all positions. When deficiencies exist regarding the employment of minority groups and women, the facility can document the implementation of an affirmative action program that is approved by the appropriate government agency and can document annual reviews and the changes needed to keep the program current.

COMMENT: Equal employment opportunity is a public policy goal. All qualified persons should be able to compete equally for entry into and promotion within the facility, and the affirmative action program should actively encourage the participation of members of minority groups, individuals with a disability, and women in the facility's staff development program. The affirmative action program also should include corrective actions, when needed, in policies regarding pay rate, demotion, transfer, layoff, termination, and upgrades.

1-SJD-1C-04-1

Added January 1993. Written policy, procedure, and practice prohibit sexual harassment.

COMMENT: Facility administrators should have as their objective the creation of a workplace that is free from all forms of discrimination, including sexual harassment. Facility policy clearly indicates that sexual harassment, either explicit or implicit, is strictly prohibited. Employees and agents of the facility, including volunteers, contractors, and vendors, must be advised that they are subject to disciplinary action, including dismissal and termination of contracts and/or services, if found guilty of sexual harassment charges brought by employees or juveniles.

1-SJD-1C-04-2

Added August 1995. Written policy, procedure, and practice provide a mechanism to process requests for reasonable accommodation to the known physical and/or mental impairments of a qualified individual with a disability, either an applicant or an employee. The accommodation need not be granted if it would impose an undue hardship or direct threat.

COMMENT: *Reasonable accommodation* refers to modifications or adjustments, which enable qualified applicants with disabilities to access the job application process or which enable qualified employees with disabilities to perform the essential functions of the job and to enjoy the same terms, conditions, and privileges of employment that are available to persons without disabilities. *Terms, conditions, and privileges of employment* include, but are not limited to:

- recruitment, selection, and hiring
- salary and compensation
- benefits, holidays, leave, and work hours
- promotion and advancement
- staff development, including in-service training
- retirement, resignation, and termination

An *undue hardship* means significant difficulty or expense. *Direct threat* means a significant risk of substantial harm to the health or safety of any person, including the applicant or employee with a disability that cannot be eliminated or reduced by reasonable accommodation. A *qualified individual with a disability* means an individual with a disability who satisfies the requisite skill, experience, education, and other job-related requirements for the employment position such individual holds or desires, and who, with or without reasonable accommodation, can perform the essential functions of such position.

1-SJD-1C-11

Revised August 2007. A criminal record check is conducted on all new employees in accordance with state and federal statutes. This record will include comprehensive identifier information to be collected and run against law enforcement indices. If suspect information on matters with potential terrorism connections is returned on a desirable applicant, it is forwarded to the local Joint Terrorism Task Force (JTTF) or another similar agency.

COMMENT: The facility's administrators should know of any criminal convictions or charges (particularly abuse or sexual misconduct) that could directly affect an employee's job performance in a facility setting.

1-SJD-1C-13

Revised January 2012. There is a written agency policy, procedure, and practice that specifies support for a drug-free workplace for all employees. This policy includes at a minimum the following:

- **prohibition of the use of illegal drugs**
- **prohibition of possession of any illegal drug except in the performance of official duties**
- **the opportunities available for treatment and/or counseling for drug abuse**
- **the procedures to be used to ensure compliance**
- **the penalties for violation of the policy**

COMMENT: None.

1-SJD-1C-16

Revised August 2010. The institution maintains a current, accurate, confidential personnel record on each employee except where state statutes require open public records and the personnel record cannot be maintained confidentially. Information obtained as part of a required medical examination (and/or inquiry) regarding the medical condition or history of applicants and employees is collected and maintained on separate forms and in separate medical files and is treated as a confidential medical record.

COMMENT: The personnel record should contain the following: initial application; reference letters; results of employment investigation; verification of training and experience; wage and salary information; job performance evaluations; incident reports, if any; and commendations and disciplinary actions, if any.

1-SJD-1D-04

Revised August 2000. Written policy, procedure, and practice provide that all administrative and managerial staff receive 40 hours of training in addition to orientation training during their first year of employment and 40 hours of training each year thereafter, in areas relevant to their position.

COMMENT: Ongoing training in topics relevant to an employee's position enhances skill and job performance.

1-SJD-1D-05

Revised August 2005. Written policy, procedure, and practice provide that all new juvenile care workers receive 120 hours of training during their first year of employment. At a minimum, this training covers the following areas:

- **security and safety procedures**
- **emergency and fire procedures**
- **supervision of offenders**
- **suicide intervention/prevention**
- **use of force**
- **offender rights**
- **key control**
- **interpersonal relations**
- **communication skills**
- **standards of conduct**
- **cultural awareness**
- **sexual abuse/assault intervention**
- **code of ethics**

Additional topics may be added at the discretion of the agency or facility.

COMMENT: Since the duties of juvenile care workers frequently involve most institutional operations, their training should be comprehensive.

1-SJD-1D-05-1 **Added August 2005. Written policy, procedure, and practice provide that all staff receive at least 40 hours of annual training. This training shall include at a minimum the following areas:**

- **standards of conduct/ethics**
- **security/safety/fire/medical/emergency procedures**
- **supervision of offenders including training on sexual abuse and assault**
- **use of force**

Additional topics shall be included based upon a needs assessment of both staff and institution requirements.

COMMENT: This training will enable employees to sharpen skills, maintain certification, and keep abreast of changes in policies, procedures, and legislative, judicial, or executive actions.

1-SJD-1E-03 **Revised August 1997. Written policy, procedure, and practice provide for a daily population report on every juvenile in detention, including full name, date of birth, race, sex, date of arrival, accumulated days of stay, court date, charge (violation of probation is not acceptable, the charge causing the violation of probation must be given), probation officer assigned, county, and any other pertinent information. The report is provided to the court, the chief probation officer of each jurisdiction using the facility, the parent agency, and the licensing agency.**

COMMENT: Strong administrative control over intake and release procedures must be maintained through the availability of current population statistics to those who use, operate, and monitor the detention facility. This practice will ensure that juveniles who are court committed to a program are removed from the facility in a timely manner. It also will make certain that juveniles are not being placed in detention for excessive lengths of time prior to a court hearing.

1-SJD-1G-01 **Deleted August 2007.**

1-SJD-1G-02 **Revised August 2007. Written policy and procedure specify who is responsible for operating a citizen involvement and volunteer service program, and his or her lines of authority, responsibility, and accountability.**

COMMENT: A citizen involvement and volunteer service program can generate a wide variety of services for juveniles during confinement and after release; for example, information on, and referrals to, release programs and recreational and cultural activities in the community. The staff member responsible for the program may be full-time or part-time, and the position may be filled by volunteer or contract personnel. The responsible person should have or receive appropriate training. Some jurisdictions mandate a citizen advisory board for each facility. Written policy should provide direction for the program, listing the goals and objectives, types of services offered, and so forth. Clear lines of accountability and authority should be established and communicated to staff and volunteers. Any volunteer activity that is shown to threaten the facility's order and security or the safety of a volunteer should be limited or discontinued until the problem is resolved.

1-SJD-2B-05 **Revised August 1992. (New plant). The facility location is selected with participation from the community in which it is to be located.**

COMMENT: The support of citizens from the community should be enlisted. They should be informed of the purpose of detention facilities, the nature of the building, the program, and the extent of supervision and control. Once their support has been gained, they can help to interpret the project to others.

1-SJD-2C-03 **Revised January 1996. Each sleeping room has, at a minimum, the following facilities and conditions:**

- **sanitation facilities, including access to toilet facilities that are available for use without staff assistance 24 hours a day**
- **a washbasin with hot and cold running water**
- **a bed and adequate space for storage**
- **a desk and chair or stool in facilities that do not have scheduled program activities outside youth sleeping rooms for eight hours or more per day**
- **natural light**
- **temperatures that are appropriate to the summer and winter comfort zones**

COMMENT: Sensory awareness is enhanced by providing variety in terms of space, surface textures, and colors. Natural lighting should be available either by room windows to the exterior or from a source within 20 feet of the room. The bed should be elevated from the floor and have a clean, covered mattress with blankets provided, as needed.

1-SJD-2C-04 **Revised August 1995. Dayrooms with space for varied juvenile activities are situated immediately adjacent to the juvenile sleeping areas. Dayrooms provide a minimum of 35 square feet of space per juvenile (exclusive of lavatories, showers, and toilets) for the maximum number of juveniles who use the dayroom at one time, and no dayroom encompasses less than 100 square feet of space (exclusive of lavatories, showers, and toilets).**

COMMENT: While the standard establishes a minimum square footage for any dayroom, total square footage is calculated for the maximum number of users at one time rather than the total number of juveniles served.

1-SJD-2C-05 **Revised August 1998. Dayrooms provide sufficient seating and writing surfaces. Dayroom furnishings are consistent with the custody level of the juveniles assigned.**

COMMENT: The standard provides managers and designers with flexibility in designing and furnishing dayrooms and takes into consideration the range of activities that may occur (for example, dayroom activities usually include television viewing, reading, recreation, conversation, and games, and sometimes include eating and work). In lower security settings, the use of "normalized" furnishings should be considered.

1-SJD-2C-08

Revised August 1995. Juveniles have access to operable showers with temperature-controlled hot and cold running water, at a minimum ratio of one shower for every eight juveniles, unless national or state building or health codes specify a different ratio. Water for showers is thermostatically controlled to temperatures ranging from 100 degrees Fahrenheit to 120 degrees Fahrenheit to ensure the safety of juveniles and to promote hygienic practices.

COMMENT: Juveniles can use scalding showers as a weapon against, or punishment for, other juveniles. Also, accidental injury could occur when cold water is drawn in other areas, thereby unexpectedly elevating the hot water in showers to scalding temperatures. Water temperatures below 100 degrees Fahrenheit are uncomfortable and may deter an individual from pursuing good hygienic practices. The temperature controls should not preclude the use of water at higher temperatures, if needed, in other areas of the facility, such as kitchens.

1-SJD-2C-09

Revised August 1995. Juveniles with disabilities are housed in a manner that provides for their safety and security. Housing used by juveniles with disabilities is designed for their use and provides for integration with other juveniles. Programs and services are accessible to juveniles with disabilities who reside in the facility.

COMMENT: If the facility accepts individuals with disabilities, it must provide for their housing and use of facility resources. Housing includes, but is not limited to, rooms, sleeping areas, furnishings, dayrooms, toilets, washbasins, showers, and other common elements. A juvenile with disability should not be placed in a special unit (for example, the infirmary, security room, or protective custody) that cannot accommodate the juvenile's disability. Program and service areas include, but are not limited to, exercise and recreation areas, visiting rooms, classrooms, dining rooms, commissary/canteen, telephone facilities, library, reception and classification areas, chapel, and administrative areas, where appropriate.

1-SJD-2C-09-1

Added January 2002. Written policy, procedure, and practice provide for the assignment of appropriately trained individuals to assist disabled juveniles who cannot otherwise perform basic life functions.

COMMENT: None.

1-SJD-2C-09-2

Added August 2002. Written policy, procedure, and practice provide education, equipment and facilities, and the support necessary for juveniles with disabilities to perform self-care and personal hygiene in a reasonably private environment.

COMMENT: A *reasonably private environment* will vary, depending on individual and institutional circumstances, but is one which will maintain the dignity of the disabled individual in light of that person's disability.

1-SJD-2D-01

Revised January 2008. Written policy, procedure, and practice require that all housing areas provide at a minimum the following:

- **lighting of at least 20 foot-candles at desk level and in the personal grooming area, as documented by a qualified source, at least once per accreditation cycle**
- **natural light available from an opening or window that has a view to the outside or from a source within 20 feet of the room**
- **other lighting requirements for the facility determined by tasks to be performed**
- **access to a drinking fountain**
- **heating, ventilation, and acoustical systems to ensure healthful and comfortable living and working conditions for juveniles and staff**

COMMENT: None.

1-SJD-2D-03

Revised August 2006. Temperatures in indoor living and work areas are appropriate to the summer and winter comfort zones.

COMMENT: Temperature should be capable of being mechanically raised or lowered to an acceptable comfort level.

1-SJD-2D-04

Added August 2010. The facility/agency shall demonstrate it has examined, and where appropriate and feasible, implemented strategies that promote recycling, energy and water conservation, pollution reduction, and utilization of renewable energy alternatives.

COMMENT: Correctional facilities and programs have the responsibility to implement strategies that allow correctional facilities to be managed in ways that are most cost-effective and deliver superior performance, while improving environmental responsibility and sustainability. This includes recycling (including paper, metal, and plastic products), energy conservation (including building insulation, heating and ventilation, temperature controls, vehicle fuel efficiency, water economies, physical plant engineering, and energy measures), pollution reduction (including composting sewer treatment, litter abatement, and carbon emissions), and utilization of renewable energy alternatives (bio-fuels, solar collection, turbine energy production, and methane collection).

1-SJD-2F-02

Revised August 1995. Reasonable accommodation is made to ensure that all parts of the facility that are accessible to the public are accessible and usable by staff and visitors with disabilities.

COMMENT: None.

1-SJD-2G-01

Deleted January 2007.

1-SJD-3A-02

Revised January 2007. Space is provided for a 24-hour control center for monitoring and coordinating the facility's security, safety, and communications systems. There is a communication system between the control center and juvenile living areas.

COMMENT: The control center should contain sufficient space for monitoring and coordinating all internal and external security systems, communication systems, safety alarms, detection systems, and other mechanical and electrical systems. A mechanical or audio communication system should be used to supplement direct staff supervision activities (for example, to advise staff of emergency needs), not as a substitute for staff supervision.

1-SJD-3A-14-1

Added January 1995 (Mandatory). Written policy, procedure, and practice provide that when a juvenile is placed in a four/five-point restraint (arms, head, and legs secured), advance approval must be obtained from the warden/superintendent or designee. Approval also must be subsequently obtained from the designated health authority or designee. Subsequently, the health authority or designee must be notified to assess the juvenile's medical and mental health condition, and to advise whether, on the basis of serious danger to self or others, the juvenile should be placed in a medical/mental health unit for emergency involuntary treatment with sedation and/or other medical management, as appropriate. If the juvenile is not transferred to a medical/mental health unit and is restrained in a four/five-point position, the following minimum procedures will be followed:

- **direct visual observation by staff must be continuous prior to obtaining approval from the health authority or designee**
- **subsequent visual observation must be made at least every 15 minutes**
- **restraint procedures are in accordance with guidelines endorsed by the designated health authority**

COMMENT: Four/five-point restraints should be used only in extreme instances and only when other types of restraints have proven to be ineffective. Restraint guidelines should include consideration of an individual's physical condition, such as body weight.

1-SJD-3A-14-2

Added August 2008. Written policy, procedure and practice, in general, prohibit the use of restraints on female juveniles during active labor and the delivery of a child. Any deviation from the prohibition requires approval by and guidance on methodology from the medical authority and is based on documented serious security risks. The medical authority provides guidance on the use of restraints on pregnant juveniles prior to active labor and delivery.

COMMENT: Restraints on pregnant juveniles during active labor and the delivery of a child should only be used in extreme instances and should not be applied for more time than is absolutely necessary. Restraints used on pregnant juveniles prior to active labor and delivery should not put the pregnant juveniles nor the fetus at risk.

1-SJD-3A-18 **Revised January 1994. Written policy, procedure, and practice provide that, except in emergency situations, visual inspections of juvenile body cavities are conducted by officers of the same sex and in private and based on reasonable belief that the juvenile is carrying contraband or other prohibited material. Reasonable belief is not required when juveniles return from contact with the general public or from outside the facility. In all cases, this inspection is conducted by trained personnel.**

COMMENT: None.

1-SJD-3A-19 **Revised January 2001 (Mandatory). Written policy, procedure, and practice govern the control and use of keys.**

COMMENT: None.

1-SJD-3A-20 **Revised January 2001 (Mandatory). Written policy, procedure, and practice govern the control and use of tools and culinary and medical equipment.**

COMMENT: None.

1-SJD-3A-27 **Revised August 2000. Written policy, procedure, and practice restrict the use of physical force to instances of justifiable self-defense, protection of others, protection of property, prevention of escapes, and to maintain or regain control, and then only "as a last resort" and in accordance with appropriate statutory authority. In no event is physical force justifiable as punishment. A written report is prepared following all uses of force and is submitted to administrative staff for review.**

COMMENT: Correctional personnel should be prepared to justify their use of physical force. The phrase "as a last resort" may be defined through appropriate statutory authority.

1-SJD-3A-28 **Added/new subtitle January 1995.**

Preservation of Physical Evidence

Written policy, procedure, and practice provide for the preservation, control, and disposition of all physical evidence obtained in connection with a violation of law and/or facility regulation. At a minimum, the procedures shall address the following:

- **chain of custody**
- **evidence handling**
- **location and storage requirements**

COMMENT: Strict accountability of physical evidence collected in connection with a crime must be established to preserve the integrity of the disciplinary and/or legal process. Minor rule violations should be exempt from the procedural requirements of evidence control, preservation, and disposition.

1-SJD-3B-12

Added January 2003. Written policy, procedure, and practice define critical incidents for the facility and provide for a debriefing to be conducted after each such incident. The debriefing process includes coordination and feedback about the incident with designated staff of the facility as soon as possible after the incident. A debriefing includes, but is not limited to:

- **a review of staff and juvenile actions during the incident**
- **a review of the incident's impact on staff and juveniles**
- **a review of corrective actions taken and still needed**
- **plans for improvement to avoid another incident**

COMMENT: A *critical incident* is any event or situation that threatens staff or juveniles in their community (criminal justice setting). While debriefings should occur as soon as possible, some information may not be available until later. All staff impacted by a critical incident should be included in the debriefings and referred to appropriate services to mitigate the stress associated with these events. All critical incidents should be reviewed by the administration, security, and health services. A two-week follow-up debriefing should occur to review the validity and appropriateness of all policies, plans, and information used during the critical incident and immediately after.

1-SJD-3C-13

Revised January 2008. Written policy, procedure, and practice provide that juveniles are scheduled for a hearing as soon as practicable but no later than seven days, excluding weekends and holidays, after being charged with a violation. Juveniles are notified of the time and place of the hearing at least 24 hours in advance of the hearing.

COMMENT: To ensure fairness and the integrity of the disciplinary process, juveniles charged with rule violations should receive hearings as soon as possible unless a hearing is prevented by exceptional circumstances, unavoidable delays, or reasonable postponements. Reasons for all delays should be documented.

1-SJD-3D-03

Revised August 1995. Written policy, procedure, and practice prohibit discrimination based on a juvenile's race, religion, national origin, sex, disability, or political views in making administrative decisions and in providing access to programs.

COMMENT: Juveniles should be assured equal opportunities to participate in all facility programs.

1-SJD-3D-06-1

Added January 1992. Written policy, procedure, and practice provide for the reporting of all instances of child abuse and/or neglect consistent with appropriate state law or local laws.

COMMENT: Whenever a juvenile reports or staff observe indicators of child abuse and/or neglect, there are procedures for juvenile care and investigation of the allegation. When appropriate, interagency agreements pursuant to child abuse should be implemented.

1-SJD-3D-06-2 **Added August 2002. Written policy, procedure, and practice ensure that information is provided to juveniles about sexual abuse/assault including:**

- **prevention/intervention**
- **self-protection**
- **reporting sexual abuse/assault**
- **treatment and counseling**

The information is communicated orally and in writing, in a language clearly understood by the juvenile, upon arrival at the facility.

COMMENT: None.

1-SJD-3D-06-3 **Added January 2003. Juveniles are screened within 24 hours of arrival at the facility for potential vulnerabilities or tendencies of acting out with sexually aggressive behavior. Housing assignments are made accordingly.**

COMMENT: None.

1-SJD-3D-06-4 **Added January 2003. Written policy, procedure, and practice require that an investigation is conducted and documented whenever a sexual assault is alleged, threatened, or occurs.**

COMMENT: The agency should report occurrences/allegations of sexual assault or threat in accordance with the laws of the jurisdiction. The investigation may be limited by what is allowed by the laws of the jurisdiction.

1-SJD-3D-06-5 **Added January 2003. Written policy, procedure, and practice require that juveniles identified as high risk with a history of assaultive behavior are assessed by a mental health or other qualified professional. Such juveniles are identified, monitored, counseled, and provided appropriate treatment.**

COMMENT: None.

1-SJD-3D-06-6 **Added January 2003. Written policy, procedure, and practice require that juveniles identified as at risk for sexual victimization are assessed by a mental health or other qualified professional. Such juveniles are identified, monitored, and counseled.**

COMMENT: None.

1-SJD-3D-06-7 **Added January 2003. Written policy, procedure, and practice ensure that sexual conduct between staff and juveniles, volunteers, or contract personnel and juveniles, regardless of consensual status, is prohibited and subject to administrative and criminal disciplinary sanctions.**

COMMENT: None.

1-SJD-3D-06-8 **Added January 2003. Victims of sexual assault are referred under appropriate security provisions to a community facility for treatment and gathering of evidence. If these procedures are performed in-house, the following guidelines are used:**

- **A history is taken by health care professionals who conduct an examination to document the extent of physical injury and to determine if referral to another medical facility is indicated. With the victim's consent, the examination includes collection of evidence from the victim, using a kit approved by the appropriate authority.**
- **Provision is made for testing for sexually transmitted diseases (for example, HIV, gonorrhea, hepatitis, and other diseases) and counseling, as appropriate**
- **Prophylactic treatment and follow-up for sexually transmitted diseases are offered to all victims, as appropriate**
- **Following the physical examination, there is availability of an evaluation by a mental health professional to assess the need for crisis intervention counseling and long-term follow-up**
- **A report is made to the facility or program administrator or designee to assure separation of the victim from his or her assailant**

COMMENT: None.

1-SJD-3D-06-9 **Added January 2003. Written policy, procedure, and practice provide that juveniles who are victims of sexual abuse have the option to report the incident to a designated staff member other than an immediate point-of-contact line staff member.**

COMMENT: None.

1-SJD-3D-06-10 **Added January 2003. Written policy, procedure, and practice provide that all case records associated with claims of sexual abuse, including incident reports, investigative reports, juvenile information, case disposition, medical and counseling evaluation findings, and recommendations for post-release treatment and/or counseling are retained in accordance with an established schedule.**

COMMENT: None.

1-SJD-4A-06 **Revised August 2004. Therapeutic diets are provided as prescribed by appropriate clinicians. A therapeutic diet manual is available in health services and food services for reference and information. Prescriptions for therapeutic diets should be specific and complete, furnished in writing to the food service manager, and rewritten annually, or more often as clinically indicated.**

COMMENT: Therapeutic diets are prepared and served to offenders according to the orders of the treating clinician or as directed by the responsible health authority. Therapeutic diets should be kept as simple as possible and should conform as closely as possible to the foods served other offenders.

1-SJD-4A-09-1 **Added August 2011. All staff, contractors, and inmate workers who work in the food service department are trained in the use of food service equipment and in the safety procedures to be followed in the food service department.**

COMMENT: None.

1-SJD-4A-11 **Revised August 1999. Written policy, procedure, and practice provide that stored shelf goods are maintained at 45 degrees to 80 degrees Fahrenheit, refrigerated foods at 35 degrees to 40 degrees Fahrenheit, and frozen foods at 0 degrees Fahrenheit or below, unless national or state health codes specify otherwise.**

COMMENT: None.

1-SJD-4B-11 **Revised August 2007. Written policy, procedure, and practice provide for the issue of suitable, clean bedding and linen, including two sheets, pillow and pillowcase, one mattress, not to exclude a mattress with integrated pillow, and sufficient blankets to provide comfort under existing temperature controls. There is provision for linen exchange, including towels, at least weekly. Blanket exchange must be available at least quarterly.**

COMMENT: None.

1-SJD-4B-13 **Revised January 1998. Written policy, procedure, and practice require that articles necessary for maintaining proper personal hygiene are provided to all juveniles.**

COMMENT: As part of the admissions process, each juvenile should be given soap, a toothbrush, toothpaste or powder, a comb, and toilet paper. Shaving equipment should be made available upon request, and the special hygiene needs of females should be met. Proper personal hygiene improves juveniles' health and medical conditions.

1-SJD-4C-18-1 **Added January 1990. Written policy, procedure, and practice provide that pregnancy management is specific as it relates to the following:**

- **pregnancy testing**
- **routine prenatal care**
- **high-risk prenatal care**
- **management of the chemically addicted pregnant juvenile**
- **postpartum follow up**

COMMENT: None.

1-SJD-4C-18-2 **Added August 1994. Written policy, procedure, and practice provide for early identification and treatment of juveniles with alcohol and drug abuse problems through a standardized battery assessment. This battery shall be documented and include, at a minimum, the following:**

- **screening and sorting**
- **clinical assessment and reassessment**
- **medical assessment for drug and alcohol program assignment appropriate to the needs of the individual juveniles**
- **referrals**
- **monitoring and drug testing**

COMMENT: None.

1-SJD-4C-20 **Revised August 2001. Written policy, procedure, and practice for the collection and recording of health appraisal data require the following:**

- **The process is completed in a uniform manner as determined by the health authority.**
- **Health history and vital signs are collected by health-trained or qualified health personnel.**
- **Review of the results of the medical examination, tests, and identification of problems is performed by a physician or other health care personnel, if such is authorized in the medical practice act.**
- **Only qualified health personnel perform collection of all other health appraisal data.**

COMMENT: None.

1-SJD-4C-24 **Revised August 2002. Written policy, procedure, and practice require that first aid kit(s) are available. The responsible physician approves the contents, number, location, and procedure for periodic inspection of the kit(s). An automatic external defibrillator is available for use at the facility.**

COMMENT: The medical staff develops written procedures outlining the use of first aid kits by nonmedical staff.

1-SJD-4C-28 **Revised August 1994 (Mandatory). There is a written suicide prevention and intervention program that is reviewed and approved by a qualified medical or mental health professional. All staff with responsibility for juvenile supervision are trained in the implementation of the program.**

COMMENT: The program should include specific procedures for intake screening, identifying, and supervising of suicide-prone juveniles.

1-SJD-4C-34

Revised January 1992. Written policy, procedure, and practice provide for the clinical management of chemically dependent juveniles and include the following:

- **a standardized diagnostic needs assessment administered to determine the extent of use, abuse, dependency, and/or codependency**
- **a medical examination to determine medical needs and/or observational requirements**
- **an individualized treatment plan developed and implemented by a multidisciplinary team**
- **prerelease relapse prevention education including risk management**
- **aftercare discharge plans shall include the juvenile and the family, when appropriate**

COMMENT: Primary goals with chemical dependency programs are assessment of needs and the development of a treatment plan. A key component to support the educational program, recovery process, and ongoing stability of the juvenile/family includes relapse prevention. Relapse prevention is necessary to support long-term recovery and identify high-risk areas needing management. Referral resources for ongoing services should be updated and used in discharge planning for the juvenile and/or family as available.

1-SJD-4C-42

Added August 2008. Written policy, procedure, and practice govern the use of restraints for medical and psychiatric purposes. At a minimum, the policy will address the following:

- **conditions under which restraints may be used**
- **types of restraints to be applied for specific conditions**
- **identification of person or persons who may authorize the use of restraints**
- **monitoring procedures for juveniles in restraints**

COMMENT: When restraints are part of a health care treatment regimen, the restraints used should be those that would be appropriate for the general public within the jurisdiction. Written policy should identify the authorization needed and when, where, and how restraints may be used and for how long.

1-SJD-5A-05

Revised January 1990. Written policy, procedure, and practice provide that an alleged juvenile held in detention be brought to court for a detention hearing and assignment of counsel within 24 hours.

COMMENT: None.

1-SJD-5B-01-1

Revised August 2002. Written policy, procedure, and practice prohibit discrimination on the basis of disability in the provision of services, programs, and activities administered for program beneficiaries and participants.

COMMENT: Services, programs, and activities include, but are not limited to, the following:

- academic and vocational education (including developmental and rehabilitative programs)
- work programs/work release programs (by providing reasonable accommodations or alternatives for juveniles with disabilities so that the benefits of these programs, including sentence-reduction credits, are available to juveniles with disabilities)
- recreation, exercise, and activities
- mail, telephone, and visiting
- library
- religious programs
- reception and orientation
- transportation services (to provide for safety and security, and to avoid undue discomfort, in light of the juvenile's disabilities)
- classification
- food service
- sanitation and hygiene
- health care
- social services
- release
- discipline, grievance procedures, and due process proceedings
- safety and emergency procedures
- access to media, courts, counsel, and law library
- commissary/canteen
- volunteer programs
- psychological and psychiatric services

Program beneficiaries and participants include, but are not limited to: juveniles, family members, clergy, attorneys, volunteers, and other authorized visitors.

The institution may be required to take remedial action, when necessary, to afford program beneficiaries and participants with disabilities an opportunity to participate in, and enjoy the benefit of services, programs, or activities. Remedial action may include, but is not limited to: 1) making reasonable modifications to policies, practices, or procedures, 2) providing auxiliary aids and services to the hearing and visually impaired, 3) constructing new or altering existing facilities, and 4) delivering services, and so on, at alternate accessible sites.

1-SJD-5B-01-2 **Added August 2002. Written policy, procedure, and practice provide for staff and juvenile access to an appropriately trained and qualified individual who is educated in the problems and challenges faced by juveniles with physical and/or mental impairments, programs designed to educate and assist disabled juveniles, and all legal requirements for the protection of juveniles with disabilities.**

COMMENT: An *appropriately trained and qualified individual*, as used in this standard, is one who has been designated by the warden, superintendent, or other authority, to coordinate efforts to comply with and carry out responsibilities defined by the Americans with Disabilities Act. That individual should develop relationships with, and use the expertise of institutional staff, advocacy groups, nonprofit organizations, agencies of government, and others that have relevant knowledge and experience.

1-SJD-5C-01-1

Added January 1992. Written policy, procedure, and practice provide for an educational program that is consistent with the needs of the juvenile population.

COMMENT: While many detention facilities house juveniles with sentences of a few days or weeks, there are increasing numbers that are held for longer periods, sometimes up to five years. An educational program for those longer-term juveniles should include an evaluation of educational needs and a method for providing for those needs.

1-SJD-5C-01-2

Added January 1992. Written policy, procedure, and practice provide for a vocational program that is consistent with the needs of the juvenile population.

COMMENT: While many detention facilities house juveniles with sentences of a few days or weeks, there are increasing numbers that are held for longer periods, sometimes up to five years. A vocational program for those longer-term juveniles should include an evaluation of vocational needs and a method for providing for those needs.

1-SJD-5C-06

Added August 1995. The juvenile work plan provides for employment for juveniles with disabilities.

COMMENT: None.

1-SJD-5F-02

Revised January 1990. Written policy, procedure, and practice require that the facility provide space and equipment needed to conduct and administer religious programs. The facility makes available adult clergy to ensure confidentiality.

COMMENT: Sufficient space should be available for congregate worship/religious services, individual counseling, group counseling, religious studies, and chaplaincy offices. Equipment, office supplies, and secretarial help should be adequate to meet the needs of the religious program.

1 SJD 5F-04

Added August 1990. The chaplain, in cooperation with the facility administrator or designee, approves donations of equipment or materials for use in religious programs.

COMMENT: Approval of donations helps ensure that equipment and materials are available for approved religious practices and helps avoid the accumulation of duplicate or inappropriate materials.

1-SJD-5F-05

Added August 1990. The chaplain has physical access to all areas of the facility, to minister to juveniles and staff.

COMMENT: None.

1-SJD-5F-06

Revised August 2004. The chaplain or staff person develops and maintains close relationships with religious sources in the community.

COMMENT: Community resources can help administer religious services on special holidays or as needed to meet the requirements of the diversity of religious faiths among youth.

1-SJD-5G-04

Revised August 2002. Written policy, procedure, and practice specify that juveniles are permitted to send sealed letters to a specified class of persons and organizations, including but not limited to, the following: courts, counsel, officials of the confining authority, administrators of grievance systems, and members of the releasing authority. Staff, in the presence of the juvenile, may be allowed to inspect outgoing privileged mail for contraband before it is sealed. Mail to juveniles from this specified class of persons and organizations may be opened only to inspect for contraband and only in the presence of the juveniles, unless waived in writing, or in circumstances which may indicate contamination.

COMMENT: Suspicious mail may include packages and letters unusual in appearance or which appear different from mail normally received or sent by the individual; packages and letters of a size or shape not customarily received or sent by the individual; packages and letters with a city and/or state postmark that is different from the return address; or packages and letters leaking, stained, or emitting a strange or unusual odor, or which have a powdery residue.

1-SJD-5G-08

Revised August 1994. Written policy, procedure, and practice require that all funds received through the mail are held for the juvenile in accordance with procedures approved by the parent agency. The facility may refuse acceptance of cash or personal checks by returning the items to the sender.

COMMENT: The administration should have discretion to control the flow of cash to juveniles. However, when cash is intercepted and withheld by the facility, it must be in accordance with written procedures that specify who is responsible for the cash, where it is to be deposited, and the method of return or transfer upon the juvenile's release or placement.

1-SJD-5G-09

Revised August 2006. Written policy, procedure, and practice require that, excluding weekends and holidays, or emergency situations, incoming and outgoing letters are held for no more than 48 hours and packages (if allowed) are held no more than 72 hours.

Interpretation August 2002. The term *emergency situation* is interpreted as any significant disruption of normal facility or agency procedure, policy, or activity caused by riot, escape, fire, natural disaster, employee action, or other serious incident.

COMMENT: Inspection for contraband letters should take no longer than 48 hours to complete so that incoming letters should be distributed to inmates and outgoing letters sent to the post office within 48 hours of receipt. Similarly, inspection of packages normally should take no longer than 72 hours to complete. The standard does not prohibit the holding of mail for inmates who are temporarily absent from the facility (for example, in a hospital or court).

1-SJD-5G-11

Revised August 2002. Written policy, procedure, and practice provide for juvenile access to public telephones. Juveniles with hearing and/or speech disabilities, and juveniles who wish to communicate with parties who have such disabilities, shall be afforded access to a Telecommunications Device for the Deaf (TDD), or comparable equipment. Public telephones with volume control also shall be made available to juveniles with hearing impairments.

COMMENT: Sufficient telephone facilities should permit reasonable and equitable access to all juveniles and permit a reasonable amount of privacy. Procedures should specify the hours during which the telephone is available, the maximum length of calls, and any limitation on calls. All long distance calls should be made collect.

1-SJD-5G-11-1

Added August 2002. Written policy, procedure, and practice ensure that juveniles have access to reasonably priced telephone services. Correctional agencies ensure that:

- **Contracts involving telephone services for juveniles comply with all applicable state and federal regulations.**
- **Contracts are based on rates and surcharges that are commensurate with those charged to the general public for like services. Any deviation from ordinary consumer rates reflects actual costs associated with the provision of services in a correctional setting.**
- **Contracts for juvenile telephone services provide the broadest range of calling options determined by the agency administrator to be consistent with the requirements of sound correctional management.**

COMMENT: When procuring and renewing telephone services, correctional officials should inquire into the reasons for proposed deviations from standard charges and seek the best possible rates for the broadest possible range of calling options.

1-SJD-5G-14-1 **Added August 2003. Written policy, procedure, and practice require that a juvenile is informed in a timely manner of the verifiable death or critical illness of an immediate family member. In case of the critical illness of an immediate family member, the juvenile is allowed, whenever statutes and circumstances allow, to go to the bedside under escort or alone.**

COMMENT: Classification, status, geography, security level, and other specified criteria should determine eligibility. *Immediate family* is usually defined as parent, spouse, child, sibling, grandparent, or legal guardian.

Appendix B Revised January 2001. Refer to *Standards Supplement* Appendix D.

Performance-Based Standards for Therapeutic Communities (TC), 1st Edition

1-TC-1B-2

Revised January 2010. There is an evacuation plan to be used in the event of fire or other major emergency. Evacuation drills are conducted at least quarterly in all locations, including housing and administrative areas and are conducted when the majority of program members are present. All program members participate in evacuation drills except when clear and convincing evidence demonstrates that facility security will be jeopardized. The plan is reviewed annually, updated if necessary, and reissued to the local fire jurisdiction. The plan includes the following: (a) location of building and room floor plans, (b) use of exit signs and directional arrows for traffic flow, (c) location and identification of hazardous material storage, and (d) location of publicly posted plan.

COMMENT: The evacuation plan should specify evacuation routes, subsequent disposition and housing of inmates, and provision for medical care or hospital transportation for injured inmates and/or staff. Fire drills should include evacuation of all inmates except when there is clear and convincing evidence that institutional security is jeopardized; upon such showing, actual evacuation during drills is not required, although staff supervising such inmates should be required to perform their roles/activity in quarterly drills.

1-TC-6D-01

Revised January 2012. There is a written agency policy, procedure, and practice that specifies support for a drug-free workplace for all employees. This policy includes at a minimum the following:

- **prohibition of the use of illegal drugs**
- **prohibition of possession of any illegal drug except in the performance of official duties**
- **the opportunities available for treatment and/or counseling for drug abuse**
- **the procedures to be used to ensure compliance**
- **the penalties for violation of the policy**

COMMENT: None.

Appendix A
Guidelines for Institution Security Levels

The following descriptions illustrate the numbers and types of barriers that separate inmates from the community. These guidelines are designed for illustrative purposes. Segments may be interchanged to compensate for strengths or weaknesses in other segments. Some agencies and systems use more or less than three levels of security. For those systems, these guidelines can be adjusted.

SECURITY ELEMENTS	SECURITY LEVELS		
	I (Minimum)	**II (Medium)**	**III (Maximum)**
Housing	Dormitories, cubicles, or rooms	Rooms and/or multiple occupancy cells and/or dormitories	Single cells, very secure, with heavy-duty hardware
Perimeter Security	None, or single fence; occasional patrol	Double fence; electric alarm system; patrol of perimeter or towers	A combination of double fence, wall, towers, and/or constant armed perimeter surveillance; and/or an electronic alarm system
Internal Security Measures	Inmate census taken at least three times daily	Inmate movement is controlled by pass system. Formal census is taken at least four times daily, plus frequent informal censuses.	Formal census is taken at least five times daily. Capability to quickly separate the inmates into smaller groups. Inmates are directly supervised and/or escorted when outside cell house or living area.

Appendix B
Classification Guidelines

The following descriptions illustrate behavioral characteristics typical of inmate custody levels.

Typical Behavior Patterns* for Various Levels of Custody for Inmates in a Correctional Facility

*These characteristics are used only as guidelines; decisions should also be based on evaluations by classification committee (including mental health and security staff) to determine the proper custody level assignment. Inmates also may be assigned increased or decreased levels of custody based on behavior during incarceration or extenuating circumstances relating to the behavior pattern.

TYPICAL BEHAVIOR PATTERNS	CUSTODY LEVELS		
	I (Minimum)	II (Medium)	III (Maximum)
Risk of Escape	No history of escape or escape attempts from secure or nonsecure settings (within past five years). Length of sentence is three years or less to projected release date.	No escape history (including flight from custody) during past seven years. No history of escape attempts from a secure setting (within past five years). Length of sentence is five years or less to projected release date.	Conduct that indicates high probability of escape attempts. History of escape or escape attempts from secure setting during the past 10 years. Length of sentence is 10 years or more to projected release date.
Behavior	No history of violent behavior (within past five years). No pattern of threats or violence.	No history of institution violence involving weapons or serious injury (within past five years). No history of assault on staff (within past five years). No pattern of serious institutional misconduct. No active participation in prison gangs.	Recent history of violent crimes and/or violent institutional conduct within past five years. Active membership in gangs/groups advocating violence. Serious assault on staff.

Definition of Direct Supervision

- A method of inmate management that ensures continuing direct contact between inmates and staff by posting an officer(s) inside each housing unit.
- Officers in general housing units are not separated from inmates by a physical barrier.
- Officers provide frequent, nonscheduled observation of and personal interaction with inmates.

Appendix C
Definition of "Qualified Individual" for Safety and Sanitation Inspections

Several standards refer to documentation and inspections by qualified individuals. (For example, Building and Safety Codes (2A), Fire Safety (3B), Food Service (4C), Sanitation and Hygiene (4D), and Work and Correctional Industries (5A) standards.) Such persons also may be referred to as an independent, qualified source, qualified departmental staff member, qualified designee, or qualified fire and safety officer.

A qualified individual is a person whose training, education, and/or experience specifically qualifies him or her to do the job indicated in the standard.

I. General Requirements

When a standard calls for inspections, the individual conducting them needs to be trained in the application of appropriate codes and regulations. Standards do not specify the number of hours of training required, as this is determined in part by the tasks assigned. At a minimum, though, the qualified individual must (1) be familiar with the applicable codes and regulations and their requirements; (2) be able to use the appropriate instruments for measuring and documenting code compliance; (3) be able to complete checklists and prepare the necessary reports; and (4) have the authority to make corrections when deficiencies are found.

Training is often obtained from code officials or inspectors (fire marshals, building officials); government agencies that have statutory authority for inspections in a particular area (health department, labor department); or private organizations, such as the National Fire Protection Association. Often, the individual obtains written certification or approval from these authorities to conduct in-house inspections. When trained and certified by the above sources to do so, a central office specialist may train and assist facility staff to conduct inspections.

II. Specific Requirements

A. Authority Having Jurisdiction

The term *authority having jurisdiction* is defined as follows:

The authority having jurisdiction must be knowledgeable about the requirements of the National Fire Protection Life Safety Code. The authority having jurisdiction may be a federal, state, local, or other regional department or individual, such as the fire chief, fire marshal, chief of a fire prevention bureau, labor department, health department, building official, electrical inspector, or others with statutory authority. The authority having jurisdiction may be employed by the department/agency, provided that he or she is not under the authority of the facility administrator and that the report generated is referred to higher authorities within the department/agency independent of influence by the facility administrator or staff. This rule applies no matter who generates the report.

The definition also applies to the terms independent, qualified source and independent, outside source.

B. Inspections

Qualified individuals conducting the monthly and weekly inspections required in the standards may be institutional staff members.

The qualified individual responsible for conducting monthly inspections (for example, fire and safety officer, safety/sanitation specialist) may be an institutional staff member trained in the application of jurisdictional codes and regulations. Periodically, and as needed, this individual receives assistance from the independent authority or central office specialist(s) on requirements and inspections. This assistance may include participation in quarterly or biannual inspections. Training for the individual conducting the monthly inspections may be provided by the applicable agencies or through the agency's central office specialist(s).

The qualified departmental staff member who conducts weekly inspections of the facility may be an institutional staff member who has received training in and is familiar with the safety and sanitation requirements of the jurisdiction. At a minimum, on-the-job training from the facility's safety/sanitation specialist or the fire and safety officer regarding applicable regulations is expected, including use of checklists and methods of documentation.

The periodic weekly and monthly inspections may be conducted by either a combination of qualified individuals or one specialist, as long as the schedules and minimum qualifications described above are met. Safety and sanitation inspections may be conducted by the same person, provided this individual is familiar with the regulations for both types of inspections. When safety and sanitation requirements differ substantially, it may sometimes be necessary to call on several qualified individuals to conduct the inspections required by the standards. Using more than one person is strongly recommended.

III. Compliance Audits

In conducting standards compliance audits, the commission visiting committees will review documentation submitted by the facilities to assist them in judging the qualifications of these individuals. In making compliance decisions, the audit teams will look closely at the facility's entire program—both practices and results—for ensuring safety and sanitation.

Appendix D
Guidelines for the Control and Use of Flammable, Toxic, and Caustic Substances

(Revised January 2001)

This appendix provides definitions and recommendations to assist agencies in the application of standards that address the control of materials that present a hazard to staff and inmates.

Substances that do not contain any of the properties discussed in the guidelines, but are labeled "Keep out of reach of children" or "May be harmful if swallowed," are not necessarily subject to the controls specified in the guidelines. Their use and control, however, including the quantities available, should be evaluated and addressed in agency policy. Questions concerning the use and control of any substance should be resolved by examining the manufacturer's material safety data sheet.

I. Definitions

Caustic material—A substance capable of destroying or eating away by chemical reaction.

Combustible liquid—A substance with a flash point at or above 100 degrees Fahrenheit. Classified by flash point as Class II or Class III liquid.

Flammable liquid—A substance with a flash point below 100 degrees Fahrenheit (37.8 degrees Centigrade).

Flash Point—The minimum temperature at which a liquid will give off sufficient vapors to form an ignitable mixture with the air near the surface of the liquid (or in the vessel used).

Label—A written, printed, or graphic material, displayed on or affixed to containers of hazardous chemicals.

Material Safety Data Sheet (MSDS)—A document required by government regulation for all hazardous chemical substances produced and/or sold in the United States. Each MSDS shall be in English and shall contain the following information: the identity used on the label, physical and chemical characteristic (vapor pressure, flash point, and so forth), physical and health hazards, primary routes of entry, exposure limits, precautions for safe handling and use, control measures, emergency and first aid procedures, and the chemical manufacturer's name, address, and telephone number.

NFPA Flammability Hazard (Red)—This degree of hazard is measured by using the flash point assigned to the product as specified on the material safety data sheet. (0, will not burn; 1, above 200 F; 2, above 100 and below 200 F; 3, below 100 F; 4, below 73 F).

NFPA Health Hazard (Blue)—The likelihood of a material to cause, either directly or indirectly, temporary or permanent injury or incapacitation due to an acute exposure by contact, inhalation, or ingestion. (0, normal material; 1, slightly hazardous; 2, moderately hazardous; 3, extremely dangerous; 4, deadly).

NFPA Reactivity Hazard (Yellow)—The violent chemical reaction associated with the introduction of water, chemicals also could polymerize, decompose or condense, become self-reactive, or otherwise undergo a violent chemical change under conditions of shock, pressure, or temperature. (0, stable; 1, unstable if heated; 2, violent chemical change; 3, shock and heat detonate; 4, may detonate).

NFPA Specific Hazard (White)—Other properties of the material that cause special problems or require special fire-fighting techniques (ACID=acid, ALK=alkali, COR=corrosive, OXY=oxidizer, P=polymerization, Y-radioactive).

Personal Protective Equipment (PPE)—Equipment intended to be worn by an individual to create a barrier against workplace hazards.

Secondary Container—A portable container into which chemicals are transferred for use.

Toxic Material—A substance that through which chemical reaction or mixture can produce possible injury or harm to the body by entry through the skin, digestive tract, or respiratory tract. The toxicity is dependent on the quantity absorbed and the rate, method, and the site of absorption, and the concentration of the chemical.

II. Procedural Guidelines

Facility staff should control the use of flammable, toxic, and caustic substances through the use of a comprehensive program that begins with a review of what chemicals are in use in a particular facility. Controlling what is purchased is the critical first step in limiting the use of dangerous materials in increasing the safety and security of both staff and inmates. A thorough review process by the safety officer or other appropriate person or group can help to insure that the least dangerous product is used for a particular task. The information contained in the MSDS is critical in choosing products.

Limiting the use of extremely dangerous materials whenever possible is the best method of insuring the highest degree of safety for staff and inmates alike.

Diluted products with a hazardous rating (0) or (1) for health, flammability, and reactivity, using the guidelines from the MSDS, do not meet the definition of toxic material. Issue logs for these substances are not required but all containers must be labeled. MSDS sheets must be maintained on these substances and be readily available. An inventory of these products should be maintained in the primary storage area for general control purposes but is not required at the usable area.

When more dangerous materials (2, 3, or 4) must be used, a system of inventories, issue logs, and controlled storage must be instituted. At a minimum, the following areas must be addressed:

1. Stored materials must be dispensed and inventoried in accordance with written operating procedures.

2. Storage areas or cabinets and/or storage areas must be kept inventoried and locked along with the MSDS information pertaining to the items, which are contained in that area. Flammable materials must be stored in accordance with all appropriate codes and approved by the authority having jurisdiction.

3. When possible, all chemicals should be stored in their original container with the manufacturer's label intact. When chemicals are removed from the original to a secondary container, it will be labeled to identify the contents.

4. The facility safety officer or other designated person must maintain a master index of all flammable, caustic, and toxic substances used by a facility. Included with this will be all MSDS material on each substance.

5. Spills and disposal must be addressed in accordance with the guidelines indicated on the MSDS sheet.

6. A hazard communication program should be incorporated in the general staff training curriculum and a specific training program instituted for all offenders using a particular substance in either work or training activities.

7. At least annually, the control of toxic flammable and caustic chemicals should be reviewed to insure continued compliance with all aspects of the program. Any deficiencies will be addressed with remedial action.

Appendix E
ACA Health Care Outcome Measures Technical Guidance

MRSA

1A (1) (NEW) The number of offenders diagnosed with a MRSA infection within the past 12 months divided by the average daily population.

Purpose: Methicillin-resistant staphylococcus aureus (MRSA) infections are readily transmitted from person to person within congregate settings such as jails and prisons. Outbreaks of MRSA infections among offender populations have occurred throughout the United States. Although most MRSA infections can be effectively treated with incision and drainage or antibiotics, serious life-threatening infections requiring hospitalization may develop particularly if the cases are not diagnosed. Furthermore, MRSA infections occur in correctional staff and their families. This measure estimates the incidence of MRSA infections in a given facility over time. This calculation is important to chief executive officers because MRSA infections can disrupt correctional operations, can be costly to treat if not effectively managed, and can affect the morale and health of correctional workers and offender populations. This may be a useful indicator to determine if appropriate hygiene practices are used.

Methodology: A continuous manual or automated method should be established for tracking all offenders diagnosed with MRSA infections within the institution or during infirmary or community hospitalization that ensures ongoing reporting to the chief executive officer. The tracking of MRSA and other skin infections can be facilitated by referring all bacterial culture results to a single infection control officer and notifying the officer of all clinically evaluated skin infections. Skin and soft tissue infections empirically treated as MRSA should also be tracked as a component of this outcome measure. Periodic bacterial cultures should be obtained in correctional settings where MRSA infections are chronically suspected and empirically treated to both confirm that MRSA infections are an ongoing problem and to assess the resistant patterns of the isolates. A designated health care authority should notify the chief executive officer of any increases in MRSA cases or suspected outbreaks within the facility and ensure that multidisciplinary infection control meetings identify potential interventions to reduce the incidence of MRSA in the facility.

Outcome Measure Calculation:

MRSA bacteria are a type of "staph" bacterium that are resistant to beta-lactam antibiotics, including: Penicillin, Ampicillin, Amoxicillin, Augmentin, Methicillin, Oxacillin, Dicloxacillin, Cephalosporins, Carbapenems (for example, Imipenem), and the Monobactams (for example, Aztreonam).

Numerator
Assess offenders in the facility during a set 12-month reporting period (Recommend ending the reporting period at the end of the calendar year.)

1. Include offenders with new positive MRSA cultures from blood, sterile body fluids, and abscesses.

2. Include offenders with new positive MRSA cultures from purulent drainage of skin or soft tissue infection (avoid contacting external skin when culturing drainage).

3. Include new empiric (clinically diagnosed) MRSA infections within a facility with ongoing, previously confirmed MRSA infections.

4. Include recurrent infections that occur in a single offender as separate MRSA cases.

5. Consider concurrent infections at multiple sites in one offender as one infection.

6. Include both community-associated and nosocomial (hospital-acquired) cases.

7. Exclude inmates with MRSA colonization without evidence of infection.

8. Exclude inmates diagnosed with MRSA but housed in another correctional system, community-based facility, or home detention.

9. Exclude inmates who may have been initially diagnosed while housed at another correctional facility, but still may be on active treatment or observation.

Denominator
Average daily population during the 12-month reporting period.

Limitations: The measure is a detection rate that provides an approximated incidence of MRSA infections within a given facility. It does not take into account the total number of offenders who move through the facility during a given year since the average daily population is used as the denominator. Therefore, a facility with a large turnover of the offender population may have a skewed increase in the incidence of reported MRSA infections compared to a facility with a similar average daily population but which has a much lower offender turnover. Because not all skin and soft tissue infections are cultured and some cases resolve without being clinically detected or reported, the number of MRSA infections reported in this measure is only an estimate. Empirically diagnosed skin and soft tissue infections, however, serve as a proxy for MRSA infections because of the widespread prevalence of this pathogen nationwide. Distinguishing between MRSA infections acquired within the correctional setting versus the hospital or elsewhere in the community is difficult; therefore, MRSA cases detected within a specific facility may or may not represent transmission within the correctional setting.

Resource: http://www.cdc.gov/ncidod/dhqp/ar_mrsa_ca.html

Tuberculosis

1A (2) Number of offenders diagnosed with active tuberculosis in the past 12 months divided by the average daily population.

Purpose: The measure approximates the incidence of active tuberculosis disease (TBD) among offenders in a facility during an established reporting period and assumes real time reporting of active TB cases to the chief executive officer. Pulmonary TB is a contagious airborne disease that can easily spread in congregate settings, such as jails and prisons, and threaten correctional workers and offenders alike. Readily identifying TB cases and determining the incidence of TBD among the offender population helps the chief executive officer assess the risk of TB transmission within the facility and allocate resources for containing this public health threat.

Methodology: A continuous manual or automated method should be established for tracking all offenders diagnosed with active TBD within the institution or during infirmary or community hospitalizations that permit real time reporting to the chief executive officer by a designated health care authority. A log of active TBD cases should be maintained. Additionally, all TB cases must be reported to local and state authorities in accordance with applicable laws and regulations. The designated health care authority should ensure that each TB case is effectively treated, contained, and monitored in accordance with Centers for Disease Control (CDC) guidelines. Contact investigations shall be conducted within the institutions for potentially contagious TB cases in order to prevent or contain TB outbreaks.

Outcome Measure Calculation:

Numerator
Include offenders in the facility diagnosed with TBD during the 12-month reporting period. (Recommend ending reporting period at the end of the calendar year.)

1. Include all offenders diagnosed by a qualified health care practitioner with newly diagnosed TBD by a positive culture for M. tuberculosis, whether pulmonary or extra-pulmonary.
2. Include all offenders with pathologic evidence of TBD, for example, caseating granulomas, even if cultures are unobtainable or negative.
3. Include all offenders who have clinical and radiographic evidence of TBD who are empirically treated for TBD and clinically and radiographically improve even though TB cultures are negative.
4. Exclude offenders on continuing treatment for previously diagnosed TBD during other reporting periods or diagnosed prior to arrival at the facility.
5. Exclude inmates diagnosed and/or treated for latent tuberculosis infection (LTBI).
6. Exclude inmates diagnosed with TBD but housed in another correctional system, community-based facility, or home detention.

Denominator
Average daily population during the 12-month reporting period.

Limitations: This measure is an approximated incidence of TBD within a given facility/system. It does not take into account the total number of offenders who move through the facility/system during a given year since average daily population is used as the denominator. Therefore, a facility with a large turnover of the offender population may have a skewed increase in TB incidence compared to a facility with a similar average daily population but which has a much lower offender turnover.

Resource: http://www.cdc.gov/nchhstp/Default.htm

TB Converters

1A (3) Number of offenders who are new converters on a TB test that indicates newly acquired TB infection in the past 12 months divided by the number of offenders administered tests for TB infection in the past 12 months as part of periodic or clinically based testing, but not intake screening.

Purpose: The measure estimates the incidence of newly acquired TB infections among offenders within a given facility. The detection of airborne TB transmission within the facility is critically important for chief executive officers since TB is a serious, but treatable, disease that can affect correctional staff and inmates and can spread unabated if not detected and controlled.

Methodology: A continuous manual or automated method should be established for tracking all offenders who newly acquire LTBI within the facility that permits ongoing reporting to the chief executive officer. Policies and procedures must be established to ensure that periodic (for example, annual) and clinically indicated screening for TB infection (for example, contact investigations) are conducted in accordance with CDC guidance. Newly acquired TB infections within a facility should be rare, carefully documented, and thoroughly investigated by the designated health care authority and infection control committee. Offenders who are new converters (in other words, are recently infected) must be high priority candidates for treatment of LTBI.

Outcome Measure Calculation:

Numerator
Include all offenders with newly acquired TB infections diagnosed in the facility during the 12-month reporting period. (Recommend ending reporting period at the end of the calendar year.)

1. Include offenders with a newly positive blood test for TB infection (for example, Quanti-FERON) while incarcerated in the facility, in other words, not an intake screening test.

2. Include offenders with a newly positive tuberculosis skin test (TST) while incarcerated in the facility, in other words, not an intake screening test. These offenders will have had previously documented negative TSTs but now have a TST that has increased by 10 millimeters. They are considered new converters.

3. Exclude offenders who have a new TST that is greater than or equal to 10 millimeters, but the increase from the previous test was less than 10 millimeters (for example, TST increases from 7 mm to 12 mm). Consider these offenders as previously infected; therefore, they are not new convertors; yet, they should still be considered candidates for LTBI treatment.

4. Exclude all offenders with a past positive screening test for TB infection.

5. Exclude all offenders with accepted negative documentation for LTBI on intake, but were not retested and confirmed as negative within the last 12 months and now have a positive screening test for tuberculosis infection.

Denominator
Number of offenders administered annual or clinically indicated screening tests for TB infection. Exclude offenders with positive tuberculosis screening tests conducted at intake during the reporting period.

Limitations: This may produce a higher estimate of new conversions as differentiating between boosted test and new conversions is difficult if two-step TSTs are not done. These boosted reactions may otherwise be included. Furthermore, this measure does not assess the number of offenders who were not screened for newly acquired TB infection but should have been based on facility policy or clinical indications.

Resource: http://www.cdc.gov/nchhstp/Default.htm

Completed Treatment for Latent Tuberculosis

1A (4) Number of offenders who completed treatment for latent tuberculosis infection in the past 12 months divided by the number of offenders treated for latent tuberculosis infection in the past 12 months.

Purpose: The measure estimates the proportion of offenders who complete treatment for LTBI. Effectively treating LTBI should reduce the incidence of TBD and associated outbreaks within the facility. Measuring LTBI treatment success helps the chief executive officer assess the effectiveness of this important TB control strategy.

Methodology: Within the first month of the 12-month reporting period, establish a cohort of inmates who are either on or are starting treatment for LTBI. All data collected for the reporting period will be based on the outcomes of this cohort.

Accurately assessing LTBI treatment requires a careful clinical evaluation of treatment candidates and prescribed regimens as recommended by the Centers for Disease Control (CDC). Administration by directly observed therapy is recommended.

— Isoniazid (INH)/6-9 months: 180 - 270 doses of a daily regimen, or 52 - 76 doses of twice weekly dosing, has been completed (NOTE: 6 months of therapy is suboptimal, but still has significant treatment efficacy so is considered a successful treatment regimen for the purpose of this outcome measure); or

— Rifampin (RIF)/4 months: 120 doses of a daily regimen, has been completed. The designated health care authority should report to the chief executive officer the proportion of offenders who successfully complete treatment for LTBI on an annual basis and pursue strategies to improve adherence and LTBI completion rates, as appropriate.

Outcome Measure Calculation:

Numerator
Identify within the first month of the reporting period a cohort of all offenders on LTBI treatment to be tracked within the 12-month reporting period (Recommend ending the reporting period at the end of the calendar year.)

1. Include offenders who started treatment for LTBI during the cohort identification period and completed an adequate treatment course in the facility during the 12-month reporting period.

2. Include offenders who arrived on treatment for LTBI, whether new admissions or transfers, during the cohort identification period and then completed adequate therapy during the 12-month reporting period.

3. Exclude inmates that have either started or arrived to the facility on treatment, but are outside of the first month cohort identification period.

4. Exclude offenders who have discontinued treatment for any reason.

5. Exclude offenders who were started on treatment but transferred to another facility, inmates that might have died, or were released prior to completion.

6. Exclude offenders completing LTBI treatment but housed in another correctional system, community-based facility, or home detention.

Denominator
The denominator is the total number of offenders in the facility who were appropriately prescribed treatment for LTBI or were on a treatment regimen during the cohort identification period (the first month of the reporting period) that remain within the facility. These inmates would have the opportunity to complete therapy within the following 11 months of the reporting period and, therefore, have the 9-month window to complete therapy.

Limitations: This measure does not take into account the number of offenders in the facility who are candidates for LTBI treatment, but are not identified or offered therapy. This measure does not specify the reasons for why treatment was discontinued.

Resource: http://www.cdc.gov/tb/

Hepatitis C

1A (5) Number of offenders diagnosed with hepatitis C viral infection at a given point in time divided by the total offender population at that time.

Purpose: The measure estimates a point prevalence of chronic hepatitis C viral infection diagnosed in the offender population within a given facility. Chief executive officers can better manage their health care budgets and better assess health care delivery needs by an annual measurement of offenders with hepatitis C. These cases often require significant resources and can be a risk management concern for a correctional system if not effectively and consistently managed.

Methodology: Hepatitis C viral infection is diagnosed with the detection of anti-HCV by immunoassay (EIA) or chemiluminescence immunoassay (CIA). A secondary test documenting viremia is not required for the purposes of this outcome measure. Tracking of chronic hepatitis C cases can be operationalized by requiring reporting of positive laboratory tests via electronic or manual methods through a single point of contact. The designated health care authority should report the annual point prevalence of hepatitis C viral infection to the chief executive officer. It will be important to report the facility's routine testing protocols or criteria for determining testing the need for HCV testing.

Outcome Measure Calculation:

Numerator
Include all offenders who are diagnosed with chronic hepatitis C infection a given point of time. (Recommend selecting the midpoint of a calendar year to be the data reporting point. It is highly suggested that all facilities within a correctional system use the same reporting date for systemwide data aggregation capability.)

1. Include all offenders within the facility with a current laboratory test indicative of hepatitis C viral infection whether or not they have received antiviral treatment.

2. Exclude inmates diagnosed with chronic hepatitis C infection but housed in another correctional system, community-based facility, or home detention.

3. Exclude inmates with suspected acute hepatitis C viral infection who are currently under evaluation for clearance of their infection (in other words, viremia).

Denominator
The total offender population in the facility at the time the number of offenders with hepatitis C infection was counted.

Limitations: Diagnosed hepatitis C cases may not represent the true number of offenders infected with HCV, since not all offenders may have been tested.

Resource: http://www.cdc.gov/hepatitis/HCV/index.htm

HIV

1A (6) Number of offenders diagnosed with HIV infection at a given point in time divided by the total offender population at that time.

Purpose: The measure estimates a point prevalence of diagnosed HIV infection among an offender population within a given facility. Chief executive officers can better manage their health care budgets and better assess health care delivery needs by an annual measurement of offenders with HIV infection. These cases often require significant resources and can be a risk-management concern for a correctional system if not effectively managed.
Methodology: HIV infection is diagnosed with a positive anti-HIV enzyme immunoassay (EIA), with a confirmatory test, for example, Western blot (WB) or an immunofluorescence antibody test (IFA), or positive result or report of a detectable quantity on any of the following HIV virologic (nonantibody) tests:

— HIV detected through a FDA-approved nucleic acid test

— HIV p24 antigen test, including neutralization assay

— HIV isolation (viral culture)

Tracking offenders diagnosed with HIV infection requires a manual or automated method for collecting these data. If automated methods are unavailable, establishing a single point of contact to receive/review laboratory diagnostic information and chronic care enrollee information can facilitate data collection. The designated health care authority should report the annual point prevalence of HIV infection to the chief executive officer.

Outcome Measure Calculation:

Numerator
(Recommend selecting the midpoint of a calendar year to be the data reporting point. It is highly suggested that all facilities within a correctional system use the same reporting date for systemwide data aggregation capability.)

1. Include all offenders in the facility who are diagnosed with HIV infection at a given point of time.

2. Exclude inmates diagnosed with HIV infection but housed in another correctional system, community-based facility, or home detention.

Denominator
Total offender population in the facility at the point in time the offenders with HIV infection were counted.

Limitations: The number of offenders diagnosed with HIV infection may not represent the total number of offenders infected, since not all offenders may have been tested.

Resource: http://www.cdc.gov/hiv/default.html

Offenders with HIV Receiving Treatment (HAART)

1A (7) Number of offenders with HIV infection who are being treated with highly active antiretroviral treatment (HAART) at a given point in time divided by the total number of offenders diagnosed with HIV infection at that time.

Purpose: The measure estimates the proportion of offenders with HIV infection who are receiving treatment with antiviral therapy at a given point in time. Antiretroviral therapy is indicated for a subset of persons diagnosed with HIV infection and is proven to reduce hospitalization and deaths from AIDS when appropriately prescribed and administered. Chief executive officers can better manage their HIV programs, including budgetary needs, by an annual assessment of affected offenders who are receiving treatment.

Methodology: Tracking offenders with HIV infection who are receiving effective antiviral therapy requires monitoring pharmacy or medical records through automated or manual methods. The indications for antiretroviral therapy and recommended drug regimens are determined by community standards that constantly evolve and are frequently updated by the U.S. Public Health Service (USPHS). Therefore, this outcome measure is not constructed to determine the percentage of offenders with HIV infection who are appropriately prescribed therapy. The designated health care authority, however, should establish a method for reviewing antiretroviral prescribing practices, and improving patient care, as appropriate. The designated health care authority should report the annual point prevalence of HIV-treated offenders to the chief executive officer and establish a method for assessing whether treatment is being provided in accordance with USPHS guidelines and other relevant evidence-based guidelines.

Outcome Measure Calculation:

Numerator
(Recommend selecting the midpoint of a calendar year to be the data reporting point. It is highly suggested that all facilities within a correctional system use the same reporting date for systemwide data aggregation capability.)

1. Include all offenders who are being treated with antiretroviral therapy at a given point of time.

2. Exclude offenders with HIV infection on antiretroviral therapy who are housed in another correctional facility, community-based facility, or home detention.

Denominator
The total number of offenders diagnosed with HIV infection housed in the facility at the time that the treated offenders were counted.

Limitations: This measure does not assess whether or not the specific antiretroviral therapies are medically appropriate or warranted. The measure also does not take into account offenders who may be candidates for treatment who are currently being evaluated or awaiting release.

Resource: http://www.aidsinfo.nih.gov

Medically Managed Offenders with HIV

1A (8) Number of selected offenders with HIV infection at a given point in time who have been on antiretroviral therapy for at least six months with a viral load of less than 50 cps/ml divided by the total number of treated offenders with HIV infection that were reviewed.

Purpose: This measure assesses how well offenders with HIV infection are medically managed. Poorly treated HIV infection may progress to the Acquired Immunodeficiency Syndrome (AIDS) and its associated complications. The measure is important to chief executive officers from a risk management, security, and fiscal perspective, since well managed offenders with HIV infection are less likely to transmit infection, require outside medical trips for related complications, or suffer a sentinel event such as a preventable injury or death.

Methodology: This measure requires tracking viral loads for offenders with HIV infection under treatment with medications. Testing is done by an ultra-sensitive nucleic acid test that is capable of detecting HIV in the blood at < 50 cps/ml. Monitoring HIV viral loads can most efficiently be achieved by automated methods or separately documenting readings at each chronic care evaluation as a reportable outcome measure. Otherwise, assessing treatment response among offenders with HIV infection requires retrospective chart reviews, which is very time consuming.

If not all evaluations of treated offenders with HIV infection can be reviewed, then a random subset of offenders under treatment for at least 6 months should be selected for analysis. If the total population is less than 10 offenders, then report data on all inmates. If the study population is greater than 10, report either 25 percent of affected offenders or 10 offenders, whichever number is greater. If a subset of the population is used, a random sample is vital. In selecting this random sample, ensure there are offender cases among all providers to monitor treatment variations.

Outcome Measure Calculation:

Numerator
(Recommend selecting the midpoint of a calendar year to be the data reporting point. It is highly suggested that all facilities within a correctional system use the same reporting date for systemwide data aggregation capability.)

1. Include, on a given date, the number of offenders from the selected sample with HIV infection who have been under treatment for at least 6 months and have a viral load less than 50 cps/ml on their most recent evaluation. If not all offenders with HIV infection are selected for review, then a random subset should be evaluated (*see above*).

2. Exclude offenders who have been under treatment for HIV infection for less than 6 months within the facility.

3. Exclude offenders with HIV infection who are housed in other correctional systems, community-based facilities, or home detention.

Denominator
Include all offenders in the review sample with HIV infection on antiretroviral therapy for at least 6 months who were reviewed on the given date. (The denominator should be at least 10 unless there were fewer than 10 offenders with HIV infection in the facility who warranted evaluation.)

Limitations: The reported outcome measurements do not account for offenders with HIV infection who were prescribed effective treatment, but who were not adherent to their regimen and did not meet therapeutic targets. Furthermore, successful treatment for HIV infection, for example, maximal viral suppression, is in large part related to the degree of viral resistance present at the time treatment is initiated. This outcome measurement does not take into consideration whether or not individual offenders were not successfully treated because of inherent viral resistance present at the time of incarceration.

If a subset is used to report this measure, then some margin of error will be included.

Resource: http://aidsinfo.nih.gov/ (adult and adolescent guidelines)

Axis I Disorder

1A (9) Number of offenders diagnosed with an Axis I disorder (excluding sole diagnosis of substance abuse) at a given point in time divided by the total offender population at that time.

Purpose: The measure estimates a point prevalence of serious mental illness diagnosed in the offender population within a given facility. Chief executive officers can better manage their health care budgets and better assess health care delivery needs by an annual assessment of mentally ill offenders who often require significant resources and can be a risk-management concern for a correctional system if not effectively and consistently managed.

Methodology: Axis I disorders, excluding substance abuse as a sole diagnosis, are defined by the most current *Diagnostic and Statistical Manual* (DSM) published by the American Psychiatric Association. Axis I disorders do not include personality disorders. Tracking offenders with serious mental illness requires a manual or automated method for collecting this information. If automated methods are unavailable, establishing a single point of contact for whenever offenders with mental illness are assigned to chronic care clinics can facilitate data collection. A process for assessing and improving the validity of the diagnostic information should also be established.

Outcome Measure Calculation:

Numerator
(Recommend selecting the midpoint of a calendar year to be the data reporting point. It is highly suggested that all facilities within a correctional system use the same reporting date for systemwide data aggregation capability.)

1. Include all offenders who are diagnosed with an Axis I mental health disorder at a given point of time.

2. Exclude offenders with Axis I mental health disorders but housed in another correctional system, community-based facility, or home detention.

Denominator
The total number of offenders in the facility at the time the offenders with Axis I mental health disorders were counted.

Limitations: The number of diagnosed offenders with Axis I mental health disorders may not represent the true number of offenders with serious mental illness since affected offenders may be undetected. Further, calculation of this measure at one point in time each year underrepresents the complexity of mental health issues for high-turnover facilities.

Resource: http://www.nimh.nih.gov

Offender Admission to Off-Site Hospitals

1A (10) Number of offender admissions to off-site hospitals in the past 12 months divided by the average daily population.

Purpose: This measure estimates the annual rate at which offenders are admitted to off-site hospitals. Chief executive officers should monitor offender hospitalization rates since this is a relevant measure for monitoring current and future security risks, medical costs, and the adequacy of preventive and ambulatory care within the correctional setting.

Methodology: The designated health care authority should ensure that all offender off-site hospitalizations are monitored on a daily basis to ensure the adequacy of health care delivery and minimize the length of stay as medically feasible. An automated or manual method should be established to track the number of offsite hospitalizations, including length of stay whenever possible. The designated health care authority should annually report the offender hospitalization rate to the chief executive officer. Unnecessary or preventable hospitalizations should be identified by the health care authority and related health care delivery concerns addressed.

Outcome Measure Calculation:

Numerator

1. Include all offenders admitted to an outside hospital for any reason within the 12-month reporting period, including those offenders still hospitalized at the end of the reporting period. (Recommend ending reporting period at the end of the calendar year.)

2. Count multiple admissions separately, for any individual offender if these admissions occurred in the reporting period.

3. Exclude offenders who are admitted to hospitals for same day procedures, including ambulatory surgery and observation for less than 24 hours.

4. Exclude inmates admitted to department of correction-operated hospitals as a result of an intra-system transfer.

5. Exclude inmates admitted to outside hospitals directly from other correctional systems, community-based facilities, or home detention.

Denominator
Average daily population for the 12-month reporting period.

Limitations: The measure does not account for the significant variations in on-site correctional health care services, or the variations in community hospital capabilities and discharge criteria. The measure is only an approximated calculation of the facility's hospitalization rate. It does not take into account the total number of offenders who move through the facility during a given year since average daily population is used as the denominator. Therefore, a facility with a large population turnover may have a skewed increase in their rate of hospitalizations compared to a facility with a similar average daily population but which has a much lower offender turnover.

Off-Site Emergency Treatment

1A (11) Number of offenders transported off-site for treatment of emergency health conditions in the past 12 months divided by the average daily population in the past 12 months.

Purpose: The measure estimates the annual rate of off-site emergency visits within a given facility. Chief executive officers and the health care authority should regularly assess the extent of emergency transfers of offenders outside the facility to monitor potential security risks, medical costs, and the adequacy of preventive and ambulatory care within the correctional setting.

Methodology: The designated health care authority should ensure that all off-site offender emergency visits are evaluated to assess the quality of emergency care provided to the offender prior to transfer, identify any potential lapses in providing ambulatory care, and ensure that adequate follow-up is provided upon return to the facility. The designated health care authority should annually report the rate of off-site emergency services to the chief executive officer.

Outcome Measure Calculation:

Numerator

1. Include all offenders sent to an off-site emergency care facility for any unscheduled reason within the 12-month reporting period. (Recommend ending reporting period at the end of the calendar year.)

2. Count multiple emergency care visits separately, for any individual inmate if these visits occurred within the 12-month reporting period; except as referred from one emergency department to another.

4. Exclude inmates treated on-site or at other department of correction-operated facilities as a result of an intra-system transfer.

5. Exclude inmates sent to emergency care facilities directly from other correctional systems, community-based facilities, or home detention.

Denominator
Average daily population for the 12-month reporting period.

Limitations: The measure does not account for inherent variances in the morbidities of offender populations in different facilities or variations in onsite correctional health care services. This outcome measure could also be influenced by the practitioner's skills and capabilities. The measure is only an approximated calculation of the facility's rate of offsite emergency visits. It does not take into account the total number of offenders who move through the facility during a given year since average daily population is used as the denominator. Therefore, a facility with a large population turnover may have a skewed increase in their rate of off-site emergency visits compared to a facility with a similar average daily population that has much lower offender turnover.

Offender Specialty Consults

1A (12) Number of offender specialty consults completed during the past 12 months divided by the number of specialty consults (on-site or off-site) ordered by primary health care practitioners in the past 12 months.

Purpose: Measures the access that offenders have to specialty consults ordered by primary care practitioners. Measures the rate at which institution resources are utilized to obtain specialty consultations. These data may be an indicator for the chief executive officer and the health authority of whether it is feasible and cost effective to provide specialty service in-house.

Methodology: A consult is a patient evaluation as requested by a primary care practitioner and approved by a utilization review process and/or by the health care authority. This must be approved within the reporting period.

Outcome Measure Calculation:

Numerator

1. A specialty consult included an approved referral and completed evaluation by a medical specialist (for example, surgeon, dermatologist, nephrologists, pulmonary specialist, orthopedic specialist, cardiologist, obstetrician, or gynecologist) within the reporting period. (Recommend ending the reporting period at the end of the calendar year.)

2. Count all approved on-site, off-site, or electronic telemedicine specialty consults for medical conditions ordered by a primary care practitioner. Do not include subsequent pre- or post- procedure follow ups ordered by the specialists.

3. The consult may occur off-site or on-site or via a telemedicine process as the medical specialist may make periodic rounds to the facility so the consult may occur in the facility.

Denominator
Count all requested evaluations ordered for the offender and while the offender remained in the facility, which were approved by the utilization review process and/or reviewed by the health care authority within the reporting period.

Limitations: The number of consults completed will not address the appropriateness of the need for specialty services in the event of a suboptimal utilization process. Further, it does not refer to the skill set of in-house physicians or the availability of community services.

Hypertensive Offenders

1A (13) Number of selected hypertensive offenders at a given point in time with a B/P reading > 140 mm Hg/ > 90 mm Hg divided by the total number of offenders with hypertension who were reviewed.

Purpose: This measure assesses hypertensive offenders whose hypertension is poorly controlled. Inadequately controlled hypertension can lead to end-stage disease such as heart failure, stroke, and kidney failure. The measure is important to chief executive officers from a risk management, security, and fiscal perspective, since poorly controlled offenders with hypertension are more likely to require outside medical trips for related complications, costly inpatient care, and are more likely to suffer a sentinel event such as a preventable injury or death.

Methodology: This measure requires tracking blood pressure readings of offenders who are treated with medication for hypertension. Monitoring blood pressure readings can most efficiently be achieved by automated methods or separately documenting blood pressure readings at each chronic care evaluation as a reportable outcome measure. Otherwise, assessing the control of hypertension among affected offender populations requires retrospective chart reviews, which is very time-consuming.

If not all evaluations of treated hypertensive offenders can be reviewed, then a random subset of offenders under treatment for at least 6 months should be selected for analysis. If the total population is less than 30 offenders, then report data on all inmates. If the study population is greater than 30, report either 25 percent of affected offenders or 30 offenders, whichever number is greater. If a subset of the population is used, a random sample is vital. In selecting this random sample, ensure there are offender cases among all providers to monitor treatment variations.

Outcome Measure Calculation:

Numerator
(Recommend selecting the midpoint of a calendar year to be the data reporting point. It is highly suggested that all facilities within a correctional system use the same reporting date for systemwide data aggregation capability.)

1. Include, at a given date, the number of offenders with hypertension who have been under treatment for at least 6 months and have a blood pressure reading of > 140/90 mm Hg on the most recent evaluation. If not all hypertensive offenders are selected for review, then a random subset should be evaluated (see above).

2. Exclude offenders who have been treated for hypertension for less than 6 months within the facility.

4. Exclude offenders with hypertension who are housed in other correctional systems, community-based facilities, or home detention.

Denominator
Include all offenders in the review sample with hypertension under treatment for at least 6 months who were reviewed on the given date. (The denominator should be at least 30 unless there were fewer than 30 offenders with hypertension who warranted evaluation.)

Limitations: This measure does not reflect optimal hypertension control. The outcome measurement also does not account for offenders prescribed effective treatments who are not adherent to therapy and, therefore, do not meet therapeutic goals. If a subset is used to report this measure, then some margin of error will be included.

Resource: http://www.nhlbi.nih.gov/guidelines/hypertension

Diabetics

1A (14) Number of selected diabetic offenders at a given point in time who are under treatment for at least 6 months with a hemoglobin A1C level measuring greater than 9 percent divided by the total number of diabetic offenders who were reviewed.

Purpose: This measure assesses diabetic offenders whose diabetes is poorly controlled. Inadequately controlled diabetes can lead to end-stage diseases such as blindness, neuropathy, and kidney failure. The measure is important to chief executive officers from a risk management, security, and fiscal perspective, since poorly controlled offenders with diabetes are more likely to require outside medical trips for related complications and are more likely to suffer a sentinel event such as a preventable injury or death.

Methodology: This measure requires tracking hemoglobin A1C readings of diabetic offenders who are treated with medication for their diabetes. Monitoring hemoglobin A1C readings can most efficiently be achieved by automated methods or separately documenting readings at each chronic care evaluation as a reportable outcome measure. Otherwise, assessing the control of diabetes among affected offender populations requires retrospective chart reviews, which is very time-consuming.

If not all evaluations of treated diabetic offenders can be reviewed, then a random subset of offenders under treatment for at least 6 months should be selected for analysis. If the total population is less than 30 offenders, then report data on all inmates. If the study population is greater than 30, report either 25 percent of affected offenders or 30 offenders, whichever number is greater. If a subset of the population is used, a random sample is vital. In selecting this random sample, ensure there are offender cases among all providers to monitor treatment variations.

Outcome Measure Calculation:

Numerator
(Recommend selecting the midpoint of a calendar year to be the data reporting point. It is highly suggested that all facilities within a correctional system use the same reporting date for systemwide data aggregation capability.)

1. Include, at a given date, the number of offenders from the selected sample with diabetes who have been under treatment for at least 6 months and have a hemoglobin A1C reading of > 9 percent on the most recent A1C. If not all diabetic offenders are selected for review, then a random subset should be evaluated (*see above*).

2. Exclude offenders with diabetes who have been under treatment for less than 6 months within the given facility.

4. Exclude offenders with diabetes who are housed in other correctional systems, community-based facilities, or home detention.

Denominator
Include all offenders in the review sample with diabetes under treatment for at least 6 months who were reviewed on the given date. (The denominator should be at least 30 unless there were fewer than 30 offenders with diabetes in the facility who warranted evaluation.)

Limitations: This measure does not reflect optimal diabetic control. The reported outcomes also do not account for offenders prescribed effective treatments who are not adherent to therapy and therefore do not meet therapeutic goals. If a subset is used to report this measure, then some margin of error will be included.

Resource: http://professional.diabetes.org/

Comprehensive Dental Care

1A (15) The number of completed dental treatment plans within the past 12 months divided by the average daily population during the reporting period.

Purpose: Inmates present with an array of oral health needs ranging from periodontal disease, caries, and edentulism. If not addressed, incipient conditions can progress into acute disease, which is often non-restorable, and inmates can be left in a state of poor masticatory function. Costly litigation has focused on the inability to manage and address identified dental conditions.

This calculation measures an inmate's access to continuous routine care resulting in the completion of planned treatment. By tracking completed treatment plans, the chief executive officer and health care authority can assess the availability of dental resources and improve the inmate's access to routine dental care at the facility. This measures a program's ability to provide comprehensive dental care.

Methodology: A continuous manual or automated method should be established for tracking all offenders that ensures ongoing reporting to the chief executive officer. Data should be maintained by the provider showing that planned care has been completed. Emphasis is placed on the completion of planned care as opposed to the development of a treatment plan. Daily and monthly statistical reports should provide the number of inmates whose care has been completed for the reporting period.

Outcome Measure Calculation:

Numerator
(Recommend ending reporting period at the end of the calendar year.)

1. Include inmates who have a completed treatment plan during the reporting period as determined by the facility's dentist. A completed treatment plan requires that a documented individual treatment plan (ITP) with radiographs has been developed for the inmate and according to the ITP all oral hygiene appointments, tooth restorations, extractions of non-restorable teeth, and tooth replacements (as determined by the department of corrections' guidelines) have been performed in their entirety.

2. Exclude inmates for which routine or emergency care was rendered but require continued dental appointments to restore dental health.

Denominator
Average daily population during the 12-month reporting period.

Limitations: The measure is a rate of completed dental treatment plans within a given facility. It does not take into account the total number of offenders who move through the facility during a given year since average daily population is used as the denominator. Therefore, a facility with a large turnover of the offender population may have a skewed increase in the dental completion rate (depending on the amount of care required for completion) compared to a facility with a similar average daily population but which has much lower offender turnover. Further, since the ability to complete dental treatment plans would typically require many appointments (and are therefore time consuming), the reported completion rate does not imply that all treatment was rendered at the reporting facility.

Conversely, processing centers with high turnover populations may have comparatively lower rates if that facility has an emergency-only dental mission.

Low rates of completed dental treatment plans will not distinguish between causes such as the length of time required to complete a dental case, the number or complexity of procedures required for completion, or even the lack of dental resources available to provide routine care.

Staff Licensure and Certification

2A (1)(NEW) Number of health care staff with lapsed licensure or certification during a 12-month period divided by the number of licensed or certified staff during a 12-month period.

Purpose: The measure assesses the degree to which the facility ensures that all licensed or certified staff maintain their ability to practice their profession in accordance with state regulations. The chief executive officer should ensure that health care staff are qualified to deliver medical services to minimize the delivery of substandard medical care to the offender population and prevent associated medical-legal risks.

Methodology: The health care authority must ensure that systems are in place to regularly monitor all personnel files of health care staff that require licensure or certification to practice their profession. This system must validate that all providers who must possess current, valid, and unrestricted licenses do so. Any provider who cannot produce a current, valid, and unrestricted license for verification is considered to have a lapsed license. Lapsed licensure includes change to inactive status, non-renewal, expiration, suspension, or revocation and also includes anyone whose license lapsed in the reporting period even if it was subsequently reinstated. Lapsed certifications apply only to those professions where certification is required by the governing state. Health care staff should be prohibited from delivering patient care if they are no longer licensed or certified when such qualification is required.

Outcome Measure Calculation:

Numerator

1. Include any health care staff for whom licensure or certification is required, who worked during the reporting period and whose licensure or certification has lapsed within the reporting period. This would include in-house contractors as well as facility employees. (Recommend ending the reporting period at the end of the calendar year.)

2. Include all staff with lapses during their term of employment even if they are no longer working at the institution at the end of the reporting period.

3. Exclude health care staff who can achieve certifications for their profession, but work in a profession where certification is not required to practice within the given state.

4. Exclude staff who do not have current licensure due to state administrative errors during the renewal process. (Staff must be able to demonstrate they fulfilled their obligation to the requirements for licensure.)

Denominator
Include any health care staff, in-house contractors as well as facility employees, requiring licensure or certification who were working in the facility during the reporting period.

Limitations: This would not address the cause of lapsed licensure, the length of time the practitioner was without a valid license, or the impact of this on the provision of health care in the facility.

Resource: State licensing boards.

Orientation Training

2A (2) Number of new health care staff during a 12-month period who completed orientation training prior to undertaking their job divided by the number of new health care staff during the 12-month period.

Purpose: The measure assesses the degree to which the facility ensures that new health care staff receive orientation training prior to performing their job duties. Chief executive officers should ensure that orientation to duty assignments are routinely provided since properly trained staff are safer and more productive workers.

Methodology: The orientation of health care staff should be both correctional and clinically focused. The orientation program should include definitive learning objectives, a delineated course content, and sufficient hours to provide adequate training. Optimally, the training should include an assessment of acquired knowledge and skills prior to duty assignment.

Outcome Measure Calculation

Numerator
All new health care staff in the reporting period who completed the required orientation training prior to performing any routine job-specific duties. (Recommend ending the reporting period at the end of the calendar year.)

Denominator
All new health care staff in the reporting period.

Limitations: This is not an indicator of the adequacy of orientation training, participant learning, or the relevancy of its content.

Occupational Exposure

2A (3) Number of occupational exposures to blood or other potentially infectious materials in the past 12 months divided by the number of employees.

Purpose: The purpose of this measure is to estimate the annual incidence of occupational exposures to blood or other potentially infectious material within the facility. Surveillance of work-related injuries is important for the chief executive officer to maintain a safe work environment for correctional workers and is required by federal regulations.

Methodology: Each chief executive officer must ensure that a system is in place to document all occupational exposures to blood or other potentially infectious material, including injuries from sharp devices, in accordance with OSHA standards. Sharps include, but are not limited to needles, scalpels, dental instruments, utensils, knifes, homemade weapons, and tattoo devices. Health care, safety, and security authorities should assess occupational exposures to blood or other potentially infectious material, as applicable to their disciplines, and amend policies and operational procedures as warranted reducing future exposures within the facility.

Outcome Measure Calculation

Numerator
(Recommend ending the reporting period at the end of the calendar year.)

1. Include the number of incidents where occupational exposures to blood or other potentially infectious material among correctional employees and contract staff have occurred during the reporting period. Exposures include any percutaneous (injuries that occur when the skin is penetrated by a contaminated sharp object) or mucous membrane (inside the eyes, nose, or mouth), exposures to potentially infectious body fluids that can spread blood-borne pathogens, for example, blood; fluids that contain visible blood, semen, vaginal secretions; and cerebrospinal, synovial, pleural, peritoneal, pericardial, and amniotic fluids.

2. Include exposures of potentially infectious body fluids to compromised skin.

3. Count recurrent exposures during separate incidents to a single employee separately.

4. Exclude contacts to human body substances that are not considered exposures to blood-borne pathogens, for example, contact with saliva, urine, feces, sputum, sweat, tears, or vomitus, not visibly contaminated with blood.

5. Exclude contacts of potentially infectious body to intact skin.

6. Exclude percutaneous contacts from a sterile sharp object.

7. Exclude volunteer and inmate exposures, even though these exposures also warrant emergency evaluation.

Denominator
The number of correctional employees and contract staff (those employed for greater than 20 hours weekly) in the facility at the end of the reporting period.

Limitations: The measure is limited by discrepancies in defining occupational exposures to blood or other potentially infectious material and the potential for underreporting of occupational exposures by correctional staff. This number may be skewed by the turnover rate of employees and contract staff within the reporting period.

Resources:
http://www.cdc.gov/mmwr/preview/mmwrhtml/rr5409a1.htm
http://www.osha.gov/SLTC/healthcarefacilities/standards.html
http://professional.diabetes.org/

TB Infection of Staff

2A (4) (NEW) The number of direct care staff (employees and contractors) with a conversion of a TB test that indicates newly acquired TB infection in the past 12 months divided by the number of direct care staff tested for TB infection in the past 12 months during periodic or clinically indicated evaluations.

Purpose: The measure estimates the incidence of newly acquired TB infections among direct care staff within a given facility. The detection of airborne TB transmission within the facility is critically important for chief executive officers since TB is a serious, but treatable, disease that can affect correctional staff and inmates and can spread unabated if not detected and controlled.

Methodology: Newly acquired TB infections among direct care staff (employees and contract staff that work more than 20 hours per week) should be assessed through periodic (for example, annual) and clinically indicated tuberculosis screening tests. Suspected new TB infections among direct care correctional staff should be rare, carefully documented, and thoroughly investigated by the clinical authority and infection control committee. Since correctional staff may be exposed to TBD in the community, evidence of new TB infections among direct care staff may not reflect transmission within the prison setting.

Outcome Measure Calculation

Numerator

1. Include direct care staff, including contract staff, with a newly positive blood test for TB infection obtained via periodic or clinically indicated testing, in other words, not upon initial hire. (Recommend ending the reporting period at the end of the calendar year.)
2. Include direct care staff with a newly positive TST in the reporting period obtained via periodic or clinically indicated testing, in other words, not upon initial hire. Staff who had previously documented negative TSTs but now have a TST that has increased by at least 10 millimeters are considered to be new converters.

3. Exclude all direct care staff with a past positive screening test for TB infection.

Denominator
The number of direct care employees and contract staff who work more than 20 hours per week screened for tuberculosis infection during the past 12 months through periodic (for example, annual testing) and clinically indicated testing (for example, contact investigations).

Limitations: This may produce a higher estimate of new conversions as differentiating between boosted test and new conversions is difficult if two-step TSTs are not done. These boosted reactions may otherwise be included. Periodic testing for TBI may not be mandatory nor conducted in all jurisdictions.

Resource: http://www.cdc.gov/tb/

Offender Health Care Grievances

3A (1) Number of offender grievances related to health care services found in favor of the offender in the past 12 months divided by the number of evaluated offender grievances related to health care services in the past 12 months.

Purpose: The measure assesses offender grievances that have been sustained concerning the delivery of health care services within a facility during a given year. The chief executive officer should monitor the grievance process and assess whether or not offender complaints related to the delivery of health care services are warranted in order to improve offender health care, reduce unnecessary health costs, and reduce future medical-legal risks.

Methodology: All facilities should have an offender grievance procedure that is tracked through manual or automated systems. The designated health care authority should investigate all sustained offender grievances related to medical care to ensure that justified complaints are adequately addressed.

Outcome Measure Calculation:

Numerator

1. Include all offender grievances sustained during the 12-month reporting period related to the delivery of health care services. (Recommend ending the reporting period at the end of the calendar year.)

2. Exclude all offender grievances/complaints related to health care delivery in other correctional systems, community-based facilities, or home detention.

Denominator
The number of offender grievances related to health care delivery that were formally submitted in writing at the local facility level and completely reviewed during the 12-month reporting period. Count repeated grievances on the same issue by the same offender as only one grievance.

Limitations: The measure is greatly limited by the differences in thresholds for "sustaining" offender grievances between facilities and systems.

Offender Grievances on Safety or Sanitation

3A (2) The number of offender grievances related to safety or sanitation sustained during a 12-month period divided by the number of evaluated offender grievances related to safety or sanitation during a 12-month period.

Purpose: The measure assesses offender grievances that are granted within a given facility regarding safety and sanitation concerns. By regularly evaluating safety and sanitation concerns, the chief executive officer can ensure a healthier and safer correctional environment.

Methodology: All facilities should have an offender grievance procedure that is monitored through manual or automated systems. Safety and sanitation issues include, but are not limited to occupational health, hand hygiene programs, environmental protection, pest management, fire safety, and chemical abatement. Chief executive officers should regularly assess offender grievances that are sustained regarding safety or sanitation, since these matters not only directly affect offenders, but just as much affect the health and safety of correctional workers and the immediate community.

Outcome Measure Calculation:

Numerator

1. Include all offender grievances granted during the 12-month reporting period related to safety and sanitation. (Recommend ending the reporting period at the end of the calendar year.)

2. Exclude all offender grievances/complaints related to safety or sanitation for offenders housed in other correctional facilities/systems, community-based facilities, or home detention.

Denominator
The number of offender grievances regarding issues of safety or sanitation that were formally submitted in writing at the local facility level and completely reviewed during the 12-month reporting period. Count repeated grievances on the same sanitation issue by the same offender as only one grievance.

Limitations: The measure is greatly limited by the differences in thresholds for "granting" offender grievances between facilities and systems.

Offender Lawsuits on Health Care Delivery

3A (3) Number of adjudicated offender lawsuits related to the delivery of health care found in favor of the offender in the past 12 months divided by the number of offender adjudicated lawsuits related to health care delivery in the past 12 months.

Purpose: This outcome measure defines the rate of favorable legal outcomes for offenders on health care issues within a facility. This indicator cannot be used without reviewing other data concerning the provision of health care within a facility, but when used in concert with other indicators, may indicate possible systemic problems.

Methodology: The numerator will include all lawsuits that were filed by or on behalf of offenders that relate to health care delivery at the facility. Health care delivery will encompass those services provided by the facility or on behalf of the facility while the inmate was under this correctional authority. It shall include cases for any medical or mental health claim.

Outcome Measure Calculation:

Numerator

1. Include all health care lawsuits that were complete in being adjudicated within the reporting period and were found in favor of the offender. (Recommend ending the reporting period at the end of the calendar year.)

2. Include lawsuits settled in favor of the plaintiff in lieu of trial.

3. Include cases won by the offender on appeal.

Denominator
All health care lawsuits filed by inmates or on behalf of inmates that had been adjudicated or settled in the reporting period.

Limitations: This will not differentiate between the varying degrees of severity of the underlying failures in health care delivery (for example, inappropriate surgery versus failure to allow soft shoes without adverse clinical consequences). This does not differentiate between cases settled for merit versus administrative reasons. However, it is important to capture all these instances in as much as they represent actual instances of adverse actions against the organization.

Problems Identified by Quality Assurance

4A (1) Number of problems identified by the quality assurance program that were corrected during a 12-month period divided by the number of problems identified by quality assurance program during a 12-month period.

Purpose: This indicator establishes a rate of resolved health care problems as identified by a quality assurance program and as certified by the facility leadership. The number of issues corrected during a 12-month period reveals how vigilant institution and health care leadership is in correcting found deficiencies. Upon examination, if a number of issues identified were not resolved, it would indicate a lack of leadership, resources, or both.

Methodology: The quality assurance department or function conducts a periodic assessment of the number of process outcome or systemic health care deficiencies identified as important for the delivery of health care services. This assessment is to be conducted at least once a year and indicates the beginning of the reporting year. Findings from these reviews are further assessed and prioritized through a deliberative process by facility leadership. Problems certified through this process will be monitored for completion during the reporting period. The quality assurance department shall compare the number of issues found against those corrected.

Outcome Measure Calculation:

Numerator

1. Include the number of problems determined to be resolved by the quality assurance department and certified by facility leadership.

2. Include only those problems which could be completed within the reporting period. (Recommend ending the reporting period at the end of the calendar year.)

Denominator

1. Include the number of problems found through a formal assessment process and certified by facility leadership within the reporting period.

2. Include only those problems that could be completed within the reporting period.

Adverse Outcomes Identified by Quality Assurance

4A (2) (NEW) Number of high-risk events or adverse outcomes identified by the quality assurance program during a 12-month period.

Purpose: This measure requires the assessment and reporting of certain adverse outcomes to the chief executive officer. By identifying and evaluating health care risk management issues, the chief executive officer can implement policies and procedures to reduce the incidence of adverse outcomes in the future, improve offender care, reduce unnecessary health care costs, and avoid litigation. The health care authority, designated by the chief executive officer, is responsible for the surveillance for high-risk processes and outcomes, analysis of these events, and recommending corrective actions to the chief executive officer.

Methodology: The measure requires identifying high-risk events and adverse health outcomes, analyzing the occurrences for root cause, and implementing corrective actions to prevent recurrences. These events are defined as the omission or commission of diagnostics, procedures, or treatments that result in the risk of or actual serious physical or psychological injury, especially injury resulting in permanent loss of function or limb or offender death. Examples include treatment administered to the wrong patient, failure to diagnose a serious medical condition despite available objective evidence, or delay in delivering health care that results in preventable complications.

Outcome Measure Calculation:

Numerator
(Recommend ending the reporting period at the end of the calendar year.)

1. Include the number of omissions or commissions of diagnostic tests, procedures, or treatments that result in serious physical or psychological injury producing permanent loss of function.

2. Include the number of omissions or commissions of diagnostic tests, procedures, or treatments that result in serious physical injury producing permanent loss of limb or organ.

3. Include omissions or commissions in health care delivery related to offender suicides or suicide attempts, which are examined in psychological reconstructions or mortality review processes that result in the death or serious physical or psychological injury of the offender.

4. Include omissions or commissions in health care delivery related to offender deaths, which are examined in mortality review processes.

5. Include all serious medication errors as defined and counted in a separate outcome measure.

This measure is the total number of healthcare risk management omissions and commissions for the given year, not a rate. Therefore, there is no denominator.

Limitations: The measure does not determine whether or not all high risk events and adverse outcomes are identified within the facility and that staff have the skills to analyze the events and synthesize the necessary preventive actions. The measure also does not account for the tremendous variance in the number of health care encounters in a given facility dependent upon the offender general population and turnover.

Offender Suicide Attempts

4A (3) The number of offender suicide attempts in the past 12 months divided by the average daily population.

Purpose: The measure estimates the annual rate of offender suicide attempts in a facility. Chief executive officers should monitor the rate of offender suicide attempts in their facilities since offender suicides are a major risk management concern and are, at times, preventable. By tracking and evaluating serious offender suicide attempts, the chief executive officer and health care authority can improve the facility's suicide prevention program.

Methodology: A continuous manual or automated method should be established for tracking all offenders in the facility who attempt suicide that permits ongoing reporting to the chief executive officer. Incident report forms documenting suicide attempts should be reviewed by health care staff. A qualified mental health professional should determine whether or not a single event is classified as a suicidal attempt versus a "gesture" or "accident." Each facility should develop a mechanism for a formal review of the suicide prevention program to address risk management concerns and reduce future suicide attempts.

Outcome Measure Calculation:

Numerator
(Recommend ending the reporting period at the end of the calendar year.)

1. Include all offenders who attempt suicide and are placed on suicide precautions during a 12-month reporting period. (Attempts are offender actions intended to cause their own death as determined on a case-by-case basis by a mental health professional).

2. Include all offenders who seriously harm themselves even if the self-inflicted incident was potentially a "gesture" and not an attempt in the mind of the offender (for example, swallowing a razor blade with intestinal trauma requiring abdominal surgery).

3. Exclude offenders who commit self-injuries that are deemed suicidal gestures (in other words, not true attempts) by the designated mental health professional (for example, superficial self-inflicted scratches and cuts not requiring suturing).

4. Exclude offenders who attempt suicide but are housed in other correctional systems, community-based facilities, or home detention.

Denominator
Average daily offender population during the 12-month reporting period.

Limitations: The measure is only an approximated rate of suicide attempts within a given facility. It does not take into account the total number of offenders who move through the facility during a given year since average daily population is used as the denominator. Therefore, a facility with a large turnover of the offender population may have a skewed increase in their suicide attempt rate compared to a facility with a similar average daily population but which has much lower offender turnover. Furthermore, the accuracy of this measure is limited by the difficulty in differentiating suicidal attempts from suicidal gestures, even by qualified mental health professionals.

Suicides

4A (4) The number of offender suicides in the past 12 months divided by the average daily population.

Purpose: The measure estimates the proportion of offenders who annually commit suicide in the facility and assumes the immediate reporting of all apparent suicides to the chief executive officer. Chief executive officers should review each offender suicide to identify interventions that may reduce the risk of future suicides among the offender population. Annual suicide measurements give the chief executive officer a barometer to assess the effectiveness of the facility's suicide prevention program.

Methodology: A reporting method should be established to ensure that all apparent suicides are immediately reported to the chief executive officer or designated official. The chief executive officer should establish a method for making a final determination if an offender's death is classified as a suicide, using autopsy findings (if available), the clinical assessments provided by the designated health care authority, and any relevant investigations. An automated or manual tracking system should be maintained to document all offender suicides over time. A designated health care authority should ensure that all offender suicides undergo a careful evaluation. Potential concerns (when identified) and recommended interventions for preventing future offender suicides should be forwarded to the chief executive officer for review.

Outcome Measure Calculation:

Numerator
(Recommend ending the reporting period at the end of the calendar year.)

1. The numerator is the number of offender suicides within the past 12 months.
2. Exclude offenders who commit suicide while housed in other correctional systems, community-based facilities, or home detention.

Denominator
The denominator is the average daily population of the facility during the 12-month reporting period.

Limitations: The measure is only an approximated rate of offender suicides within the facility. It does not take into account the total number of offenders who move through the facility during a given year since average daily population is used as the denominator. Therefore, a facility with a large population turnover may have a skewed increase in their annual suicide rate compared to a facility with a similar average daily population but which has much lower offender turnover. Furthermore, certain offender deaths may be difficult to accurately classify as suicides versus accidents, for example, certain drug overdoses.

Unexpected Natural Deaths

4A (5) The number of unexpected natural deaths in the past 12 months divided by the total number of deaths in the same reporting period.

Purpose: The measure estimates the proportion of unexpected natural deaths among the offender population within a given facility. Chief executive officers should monitor the rate of unexpected offender deaths in the facility since a subset of these deaths may be preventable. Furthermore, a multidisciplinary review of these deaths may detect risk management or health care delivery concerns that if addressed, could further reduce offender morbidity and decrease future health care costs, for example, community hospitalizations.

Methodology: The chief executive officer should establish a method for making a final determination if an offender's death is classified as unexpected using autopsy findings (if available), the clinical assessments provided by the designated health care authority, and any relevant investigations. An automated or manual tracking system should be maintained to document all unexpected natural deaths over time. A designated health care authority should ensure that all unexpected natural deaths undergo a thorough evaluation. Potential concerns (when identified) and recommended interventions for preventing future unexpected natural deaths should be forwarded to the chief executive officer for review.

Outcome Measure Calculation:

Numerator
(Recommend ending the reporting period at the end of the calendar year.)

1. Include all medically unexpected deaths during the 12-month reporting period. Medically unexpected deaths are those that occur suddenly without any clinical warning (in other words, sudden death) and are not a result of a previously diagnosed medical condition(s) that is life threatening, for example, certain cancers, AIDs, congestive heart failure, kidney or liver failure, and geriatric co-morbidities. Offenders with terminal medical conditions, however, can die "unexpectedly" from other causes and should be included in the numerator. Additionally, "medically unexpected deaths" include offenders who succumb despite well managed chronic conditions, for example, an offender with an acute myocardial infarction with a history of well-controlled hypertension.

2. Include offender deaths from injuries.

3. Exclude offender deaths from suicide, homicide, or executions.

4. Exclude any offender deaths occurring in other correctional systems, community-based facilities, or home detention at the time of their death.

Denominator
Number of offender deaths in the 12-month reporting period.

Limitations: The measure is a calculation of the rate of unexpected offender deaths within the facility. The total number of deaths might be skewed from correctional facility to facility, since it does not take into account the total number of offenders who move through a facility within a given year.

Serious Medication Errors

4A (6) The number of serious medication errors in the past 12 months.

Purpose: This measure requires the cumulative reporting of the most serious medication errors to the chief executive officer. Medication dispensing, prescribing, distribution, and administration errors are a serious risk management issue in any health care system and can be the source of preventable hospitalizations and litigation. All chief executive officers should require medication error reporting for their health care delivery system. A "no fault" approach to medication error reporting should be adopted with the exception of gross negligence by the health care provider. A "no fault" approach has been proven to increase the reporting of medication errors and secondarily improve the medication delivery system. By tracking serious medication errors, the chief executive officer can determine how health care policies and operations can be improved to reduce the incidence of future medication errors.

Methodology: Each chief executive officer should establish a policy that requires the reporting of serious medication errors to the health care authority. In turn, the health care authority should provide a summary of medication errors to the chief executive officer during the past year. The report should assess risk management issues that require attention to improve the medication delivery system within the facility.

Outcome Measure Calculation:

1. Count the number of medication errors that caused temporary offender harm (in other words, complication, which is completely reversible) and required the need for treatment or intervention. An example might be prescribing something despite a known drug allergy to that class of agents.

2. Count the number of medication errors that caused the offender harm and resulted in initial or prolonged hospitalization.

3. Count the number of medication errors that resulted in permanent offender harm (in other words, lifelong treatment or irreversible sequelae as a direct result of the error).

4. Count the number of medication errors that resulted in a near-death event.

5. Count the number of medication errors that resulted in an offender's death. This measure is the total number of serious medication errors for the year, not a rate.

Limitations: This measure does not determine whether or not all serious medication errors are identified within the facility and that staff have the skills to analyze these errors and synthesize the necessary corrective actions. The measure also does not account for the tremendous variance in the number of medications prescribed, dispensed, and administered within a given facility dependent on the offender census, morbidity, clinician prescribing practices, and population turnover.

Name of Facility ______________________ Date______________

Number of Months Data Collected ______________

Health Care Outcome Measures

Standard	Outcome Measure	Numerator/Denominator	Value	Calculated O.M.
1A	(1)	Number of offenders diagnosed with a MRSA infection within the past 12 months		
	divided by	Average daily population.		
	(2)	Number of offenders diagnosed with active tuberculosis in the past 12 months		
	divided by	Average daily population.		
	(3)	Number of offenders who are new converters on a TB test that indicates newly acquired TB infection in the past 12 months		
	divided by	Number of offenders administered tests for TB infection in the past 12 months as part of periodic or clinically based testing, but not intake screening.		
	(4)	Number of offenders who completed treatment for latent tuberculosis infection in the past 12 months		
	divided by	Number of offenders treated for latent tuberculosis infection in the past 12 months.		
	(5)	Number of offenders diagnosed with Hepatitis C viral infection at a given point in time		
	divided by	Total offender population at that time.		
	(6)	Number of offenders diagnosed with HIV infection at a given point in time		
	divided by	Total offender population at that time.		
	(7)	Number of offenders with HIV infection who are being treated with highly active antiretroviral treatment (HAART) at a given point in time		
	divided by	Total number of offenders diagnosed with HIV infection at that time.		
	(8)	Number of selected offenders with HIV infection at a given point in time who have been on antiretroviral therapy for at least six months with a viral load of less than 50 cps/ml		
	divided by	Total number of treated offenders with HIV infection that were reviewed.		
	(9)	Number of offenders diagnosed with an Axis I disorder (excluding sole diagnosis of substance abuse) at a given point in time		

	divided by	Total offender population at that time.		
	(10)	Number of offender admissions to offsite hospitals in the past 12 months		
	divided by	Average daily population.		
	(11)	Number of offenders transported offsite for treatment of emergency health conditions in the past 12 months		
	divided by	Average daily population.		
	(13)	Number of selected hypertensive offenders at a given point in time with a B/P reading > 140 mm Hg/ >90 mm Hg		
	divided by	Total number of offenders with hypertension who were reviewed.		
	(14)	Number of selected diabetic offenders at a given point in time who are under treatment for at least six months with a hemoglobin A1C level measuring greater than 9 percent		
	divided by	Total number of diabetic offenders who were reviewed.		
	(15)	The number of completed dental treatment plans within the past 12 months		
	divided by	Average daily population during the reporting period.		
2A	(1)	Number of health care staff with lapsed licensure or certification during a 12-month period		
	divided by	Number of licensed or certified staff during a 12-month period.		
	(2)	Number of new health care staff during a 12-month period that completed orientation training prior to undertaking their job		
	divided by	Number of new health care staff during the 12-month period.		
	(3)	Number of occupational exposures to blood or other potentially infectious materials in the past 12 months		
	divided by	Number of employees.		
	(4)	Number of direct care staff (employees and contractors) with a conversion of a TB test that indicates newly acquired TB infection in the past 12 months		
	divided by	Number of direct care staff tested for TB infection in the past 12 months during periodic or clinically indicated evaluations.		

3A	(1)	Number of offender grievances related to health care services found in favor of the offender in the past 12 months		
	divided by	Number of evaluated offender grievances related to health care services in the past 12 months.		
	(2)	Number of offender grievances related to safety or sanitation sustained during a 12-month period		
	divided by	Number of evaluated offender grievances related to safety or sanitation during a 12-month period.		
	(3)	Number of adjudicated offender lawsuits related to the delivery of health care found in favor of the offender in the past 12 months		
	divided by	Number of offender adjudicated lawsuits related to healthcare delivery in the past 12 months.		
4A	(1)	Number of problems identified by quality assurance program that were corrected during a 12-month period		
	divided by	Number of problems identified by quality assurance program during a 12-month period.		
	(2)	Number of high-risk events or adverse outcomes identified by the quality assurance program during a 12-month period		
	(3)	Number of offender suicide attempts in the past 12 months		
	divided by	Average daily population.		
	(4)	Number of offender suicides in the past 12 months		
	divided by	Average daily population.		
	(5)	Number of unexpected natural deaths in the past 12 months		
	divided by	Total number of deaths in the same reporting period.		
	(6)	Number of serious medication errors in the past 12 months		
5A	None			
6A	None			
7A	None			
7B	None			
7C	None			

Appendix F
Revised Definitions of Learning and Training

The following definitions related to formal and informal learning, classroom training, online training, and blended learning are derived from the American Society of Training and Development (ASTD) (http://www.astd.org), and are accepted by ACA as industry standard definitions.

Formal learning is structured learning, where the instructor/facilitator is responsible for all aspects of the learning process, including what, how, and when the learners learn. Formal learning includes both classroom and online training.

Classroom training is defined as training that occurs within the confines of a formal classroom at a training academy, hotel/meeting space, or in some other type of educational setting. All training participants are gathered in the same room at the same time for the learning experience. Classroom training is sometimes referred to informally as "face-to-face" training.

A subset of formal learning, which takes place outside of the classroom, is on-the-job training (OJT). On-the-job training takes place in a normal working situation, using the actual tools, equipment, documents, or materials students will use when fully trained.

Online training is defined as, essentially, the computer and network-enabled transfer of skills and knowledge. Content is delivered via the Internet, intranet/extranet, audio or videotape, satellite TV, CD-ROM, and other technologically leveraged formats, which mirror the processes of a face-to-face session. It can be self-paced, instructor-led, or virtual instructor-led and includes media in the form of text, image, animation, streaming video, and audio. Effective online training offers links to other learning resources such as references, e-mail, bulletin boards, discussion groups, readings, and more to enrich the learning.

Online can be synchronous or asynchronous in nature. Synchronous online learning includes virtual-instructor-led training, such as training where the group convenes using an online virtual learning platform, which mirrors the processes of a face-to-face session. Asynchronous online learning uses formats outside the constraints of time and place and is usually delivered in the form of a course. Effective online training courses that meet the requirements of defensible training are interactive, and include a final exam to assess the learner's knowledge.

As technology continues to advance, online training can and will be delivered to the learner through multiple devices (computers, laptops, smartphones, etc.).

Blended learning refers to a mixing of different learning environments (classroom and online learning) and multiple instructional strategies. Blended learning can be both synchronous and asynchronous in design and delivery. It combines traditional face-to-face classroom methods with more modern technology-mediated activities. By "blending" the learning, an integrated training approach results.

Informal learning refers to anything that is not easily recognizable as formal training and performance support (such as organized classes, workshops, individualized instruction, job aids, and just-in-time, on-the-job learning). It may be individualized to meet specific needs, is personal and limited in scope, and usually occurs in small timeframes or "chunks."

Defendable Formal Training

Defendable formal training is an organized, planned, documented and evaluated learning activity designed to enhance job performance or professional development. This type of training is based on enhancing specific job-related competencies, skills, and objectives, which are based upon a needs assessment or job evaluation and prepared by a credible source. Defendable formal training can be delivered in the classroom, online, or in a blended format.

Defendable formal training occurs when the seven elements, as detailed, are achieved.

Elements of Defendable Formal Training:

1. **Based on specific competencies**
   — Applied skills and knowledge necessary to perform the assigned tasks successfully.
   — Tasks identified through a formal job evaluation process.

2. **Based on specific performance objectives targeted to outcomes**
   — Goals of the training are identifiable and measurable.
   — The training is designed based upon information and research that is credible and applicable to the audience group to which it will be delivered.

3. **Documented for Records**
   — A formal lesson plan or equivalent is used to reflect performance objectives, instructional content, instructional delivery strategies and evaluation methods at a minimum.
   — The format or requirements of the required documentation may be more rigorous at the agency level, and are dependent upon prevailing agency/organizational standards or requirements.

4. **Delivered by a qualified source**
   — Credentialed: Instructors/facilitators possess a documented credential, qualification or certification for the content area for which they are training, such as instructors in firearms, self-defense or specific counseling techniques.
   — Knowledgeable and skilled in the field of study and the content to be taught.
   — Possess solid instructional delivery skills appropriate for the delivery format (classroom, online facilitation skills, or blended delivery skills).

5. **Conducted in a sufficient amount of time**
   — Time required to gain the knowledge or acquire the skills being taught includes appropriate time for skills and knowledge practice, feedback, and evaluation of student learning through practical activities, as appropriate to the format (classroom, technology-based, or a blend of both).

6. Relevant to the student and organization

Relevancy is determined through:

— Job requirements and competencies
— Staff feedback on the training
— Evaluation of the student during the training (including required proficiency testing)
— Evaluation of the student's performance on the job
— Agency annual training review and assessments
— Supervisor's input
— Agency performance assessments

7. Delivered to the correct population

— Topics related to job tasks and/or performance problems.
— Attendance documented with name roster and title/positions of staff that perform tasks or share problems, or certificate of completion of valid training through a qualified source.

Glossary

Absconder—an individual who fails to report for probation, parole, or aftercare supervision or leaves supervision of correctional or assigned staff.

Accreditation cycle—the three-year cycle between audits.

Accreditation manager—an agency employee designated by the agency administrator to supervise the planning and implementation of accreditation activities in the agency. He/she has comprehensive knowledge of the agency and sufficient authority within the agency to design and administer a successful accreditation strategy.

Accreditation panel—the subunit of the Commission on Accreditation for Corrections empowered to review applications and make final decisions on agency accreditation.

Accredited status—the three-year period during which the agency maintains and improves upon its standards compliance levels that were achieved at the time of the accreditation award.

Adjudicatory hearing—a hearing to determine whether the allegations of a petition are supported by the evidence beyond a reasonable doubt or by the preponderance of the evidence.

Administrative segregation—a form of separation from the general population administered by the classification committee or other authorized group when the continued presence of the inmate in the general population would pose a serious threat to life, property, self, staff, or other inmates or to the security or orderly running of the institution. Inmates pending investigation for trial on a criminal act or pending transfer also can be included. (*See* Protective custody, Segregation.)

Administrator—*See* Program director.

Administrator of field services—the individual directly responsible for directing and controlling the operations of the adult probation and/or parole field services program. This person may be a division head in a large correctional agency, a chief probation officer answering to a judge, or the administrative officer of a court or parole authority with responsibility for the field services program.

Admission—the process of entry into a program. During admission processing, the juvenile or adult offender receives an orientation to program goals, rules, and regulations. Assignment to living quarters and to appropriate staff also is completed at this time.

Adult community residential service—also referred to as halfway house, a community-based program providing group residence (such as a house, work release center, prerelease center) for probationers, parolees, residents in incarcerated status, and referrals through the courts or other agencies. Clients also may receive these services from the agency on a nonresidential basis. (*See* Out-client.)

Adult correctional institution—a confinement facility, usually under state or federal auspices, that has custodial authority over adults sentenced to confinement for more than one year.

Adult detention facility or jail—a local confinement facility with temporary custodial authority. Adults can be confined pending adjudication for forty-eight hours or more and usually for sentences of up to two years.

Affirmative action—a concept designed to ensure equal opportunity for all persons regardless of race, religion, age, sex, or ethnic origin. These equal opportunities include all personnel programming, such as selection, promotion, retention, rate of pay, demotion, transfer, layoff, and termination.

Aftercare—control, supervision, and care exercised over juveniles and in some case adults released from facilities through a stated release program. (*See* Releasing authority.)

Agency—the unit of a governing authority that has direct responsibility for the operations of a corrections program, including the implementation of policy as set by the governing authority. For a community residential center, this would be the administrative headquarters of the facilities. A single community facility that is not a part of a formal consolidation of community facilities is considered to be an agency. In a public agency, this could be a probation department, welfare department, or similar agency. For a juvenile correctional organization, this would be the central office responsible for governing the juvenile correctional system for the jurisdiction.

Agency administrator—the administrative officer appointed by the governing authority or designee who is responsible for all operations of the agency, such as the department of corrections or parole, and all related programs under his or her control.

Agency industries administrator—the individual who has functional responsibility for industries operations throughout the correctional system. Titles, such as head of industries, superintendent, chief, director, or general manager, may be used to denote this position.

Alternative meal service—special foods provided to comply with the medical, religious, or security requirements. Alternative meals always must be designed to ensure that basic health needs are met and are provided in strict compliance with the policies signed by the chief executive officer, the chief medical officer, and for the religious diets, by the appropriate religious leader.

Annual certification statement—the document an accredited agency submits to ACA to verify continued compliance with the standards, report on its progress of implementing plans of action, and advise the Association of any significant events that may have occurred. It is due on the anniversary of the accreditation award.

Appeal—the agency's attempt to change the visiting committee's decision on a standard. The result of a successful appeal is a change in the status of the standard, either compliance or applicability, and a recalculation of the compliance tally.

Applicant agency—an agency involved in the exchange of materials, information, and correspondence with ACA while preparing to participate in the accreditation process.

Appropriately trained and qualified individual for working with offenders with disabilities—one who has been designated by the warden, superintendent, or other authority to coordinate efforts to comply with and carry out responsibilities defined by the Americans with Disabilities Act. This individual should develop relationships with, and use the expertise of institutional staff, advocacy groups, nonprofit organizations, agencies of government, and others who have relevant knowledge and experience.

Audit—an examination of agency or facility records or accounts to check their accuracy. It is conducted by a person or persons not directly involved in the creation and maintenance of these records or accounts. An independent audit results in an opinion that either affirms or disaffirms the accuracy of records or accounts. An operational or internal audit usually results in a report to management that is not shared with those outside the agency.

Auditor—the term frequently used to refer to ACA consultants who conduct the pre-accreditation assessments, technical assistance visits, standards compliance audits, and monitoring visits.

Authority having jurisdiction—may be a federal, state, local, or other regional department or individual, such as the fire chief, fire marshal, chief of a fire prevention bureau, labor department, health department, building official, electrical inspector, or other with standing authority who are knowledgeable about the requirements of the National Fire Protection Life Safety Code. This person may be employed by the department/agency, provided that he or she is not under the authority of the facility administrator and that the report generated is referred to higher authorities within the department/agency independent of influence by the facility administrator or staff, no matter who generates the report.

Booking—both a law enforcement process and a detention-facility procedure. As a police administrative action, it is an official recording of an arrest and the identification of the person, place, time, arresting authority, and reason for the arrest. In a detention facility, it is a procedure for the admission of a person charged with or convicted of an offense, which includes searching, fingerprinting, photographing, medical screening, and collecting personal history data. Booking also includes the inventory and storage of the individual's personal property.

Boot camp—a short-term correctional unit designed to combine elements of basic military training programs and appropriate correctional components.

Camp—a nonsecure residential program located in a relatively remote area. The residents participate in a structured program that emphasizes outdoor work, including conservation and related activities. There are often twenty to sixty residents in these facilities.

Candidate status—the period after an agency has completed its self-evaluation report. Candidate status continues until standards compliance is verified during the audit and the accreditation decision is made.

Career development plan—the planned sequence of promotions within an agency that contains provision for (1) vertical movement throughout the entire range of a particular discipline, (2) horizontal movement encouraging lateral and promotional movement among disciplines, and (3) opportunity for all to compete for the position of head of the agency. Progression along these three dimensions can occur as long as the candidate has the ambition, ability, and required qualifications.

Case conference—a conference between individuals working with the juvenile or adult offender to see that court-ordered services are being provided.

Case record—information concerning an offender's or juvenile's criminal, personal, and medical history, behavior, and activities while in custody. The record typically includes commitment papers, court orders, detainers, personal property receipts, visitor's list, photographs, fingerprints, type of custody, disciplinary infractions and action taken, grievance reports, work assignments, program participation, and miscellaneous correspondence.

Cases of exceptional merit—outstanding prison adjustment beyond that normally expected, performance of a meritorious deed by the inmate or juvenile, or existence of an unusual employment opportunity for which the inmate or juvenile is especially qualified and which would not be available at the time of the normal parole or release date.

Casework—the function of the caseworker, social worker, or other professional in providing social services, such as counseling, to individuals in custody.

Caustic material—a substance capable of destroying or eating away by chemical reaction.

Cellblock—a group or cluster of single and/or multiple occupancy cells or detention rooms immediately adjacent and directly accessible to a day or activity room. In some facilities, the cellblock consists of a row of cells fronted by a day-room of corridor-like proportions.

Chemical agent—an active substance, such as tear gas, used to defer activities that might cause personal injury or property damage.

Chemical dependency—a compulsive use of alcohol or other drugs to the point that stopping is difficult and causes physical and mental reactions.

Chief—*See* Agency industries administrator.

Chief of police—a local law enforcement official who is the appointed or elected chief executive of a police department and is responsible for the operation of the city jail or lockup.

Chronic care—health care provided to patients over a long period of time; health care services provided to patients with long-term health conditions or illnesses. Care usually includes initial assessment, treatment, and periodic monitoring to evaluate the patient's condition.

Chronic illness—a disease process or condition that persists over an extended period of time. Chronic illnesses include diabetes, hypertension, asthma, HIV, seizures, and mental health diagnosis.

Classification—a process for determining the needs and requirements of those for whom confinement has been ordered and for assigning them to housing units and programs according to their needs and existing resources.

Clinical services—health care services administered to offenders in a clinic setting by persons qualified to practice in one of the health care disciplines.

Clinicians—persons qualified to assess, evaluate and treat patients according to the dictates of their professional practice act. These may include physicians, nurses, physician assistants, nurse practitioners, dentists, psychologists, psychiatrists, and social workers.

Co-correctional facility—an institution designed to house both male and female juvenile or adult offenders.

Code—any set of standards set forth and enforced by a local government agency for the protection of public safety, health, and so forth, as in the structural safety of buildings (building code), health requirements for plumbing, ventilation, and so forth (sanitary or health code), and the specifications for fire escapes or exits (fire code).

Code of ethics—a set of rules describing acceptable standards of conduct for all employees.

Combustible liquid—a substance with a flash point at or above 100 degrees Fahrenheit, a Class II or Class III liquid.

Commissary—an area or system where approved items are available for purchase by juveniles or inmates.

Commission on Accreditation for Corrections (CAC)—the term used collectively to refer to the elected and appointed members empowered to render accreditation decisions.

Committing authority—the agency or court responsible for placing a juvenile in a program.

Communicable disease—a disease that can be transmitted from person to person.

Community-based program—*See* Adult community residential service.

Community resources—human services agencies, service clubs, citizen interest groups, self-help groups, and individual citizen volunteers that offer services, facilities, or other functions that can meet the needs of the facility or have the potential to assist residents. These various resources, which may be public or private and national or local, may assist with material and financial support, guidance, counseling, and supportive services.

Consult—a patient evaluation as requested by a primary care practitioner and approved by a utilization review process or by the health care authority.

Contact visiting—a program inside or outside the facility that permits offenders or juveniles to visit with designated person(s). The area is free of obstacles or barriers that prohibit physical contact.

Continuity of care—health care provided on a continual basis beginning with the offender's initial contact with health care personnel and all subsequent health care encounters including referrals to community providers/facilities for offsite care during incarceration and when discharged from the institution.

Contraband—any item possessed by confined juvenile or adult offenders or found within the facility that is illegal by law or expressly prohibited by those legally charged with the administration and operation of the facility or program.

Contract—the written, signed agreement between the ACA and the agency specifying responsibilities, activities, and financial obligations.

Contractor—a person or organization that agrees to furnish materials or to perform services for the facility or jurisdiction at a specified price. Contractors operating in correctional facilities are subject to all applicable rules and regulations of the facility.

Contractual arrangement—an agreement with a private party (such as an incorporated agency or married couple) to provide services to juveniles or adult offenders for compensation. (*See* Independent operator.)

Control center—a very secure, self-contained unit designed to maintain the security of the facility. Policies governing the design, staffing, and accessibility of the control center ensure that it cannot be commandeered by unauthorized persons.

Controlled substance—any drug regulated by the Drug Enforcement Act.

Copayment—a fee charged an offender by the correctional institution for health care or other services.

Corporal punishment—any act of inflicting punishment directly on the body, causing pain or injury.

Correctional facility—a place used for the incarceration of individuals accused of or convicted of criminal activity. A correctional facility is managed by a single chief executive officer with broad authority for the operation of the facility. This authorization typically includes the final authority for decisions concerning the employment or termination of staff members, and the facility operation and programming within guidelines established by the parent agency or governing body. A correctional facility also must have (1) a separate perimeter that precludes the regular commingling of the inmates with inmates from other facilities, (2) a separate facility budget managed by a chief executive officer within guidelines established by the parent agency or governing authority, and (3) staff that are permanently assigned to the facility.

Correspondent status—the initial period after an agency applies for accreditation. At this time, the agency evaluates its compliance with the standards and prepares a self-evaluation report.

Counseling—planned use of interpersonal relationships to promote social adjustment. Counseling programs provide opportunities to express feelings verbally with the goal of resolving the individual's problems. At least three types of counseling may be provided: individual (a one-to-one relationship), small-group counseling, and large-group counseling in a living unit.

County parole—the status of a county jail inmate who, convicted of a misdemeanor and conditionally released from a confinement facility prior to the expiration of his or her sentence, has been placed under supervision in the community for a period of time.

Credentials—documentation that demonstrates health care professionals are qualified and currently licensed, certified, and/or registered as applicable to provide health services within their scope of practice.

Criminal record check—process of investigating whether the background of an individual has any criminal convictions. It is conducted in accordance with state and federal statutes.

Custody—level of restriction of inmate movement within a detention/correctional facility, usually divided into maximum, medium, and minimum risk levels.

Dayroom—space for activities that is situated immediately adjacent to the offender/juvenile sleeping areas and separated from them by a wall.

Delinquent act—an act that, if committed by an adult, would be considered a crime.

Delinquent youth—also referred to as a juvenile delinquent or a criminal-type offender, a juvenile who has been charged with or adjudicated for conduct that would, under the law of the jurisdiction in which the offense was committed, be a crime if committed by an adult. (*See also* Status offender; Juvenile.)

Dental exam—an examination by a licensed dentist that includes a dental history, exploration and charting of teeth, examination of the oral cavity, and x-rays.

Detainee—any person confined in a local detention facility not serving a sentence for a criminal offense.

Detainer—a warrant placed against a person in a federal, state, or local correctional facility that notifies the holding authority of the intention of another jurisdiction to take custody of that individual when he or she is released.

Detention warrant—a warrant that authorizes the arrest and temporary detention of a parolee pending preliminary revocation proceedings. A detention warrant should be distinguished from a warrant for the return of a parolee to prison, although return warrants are sometimes used as detainers. For the purpose of these standards, return warrants used as detainers also are deemed to be detention warrants.

Detoxification—the treatment of a person who is demonstrating symptoms of intoxication or withdrawal and/or the process of gradually withdrawing alcohol or drugs from a person who is chemically dependent.

Developmental disabilities—a disorder in which there is a delay in the expected age-specific development stages. These disabilities originate prior to age twenty-one, can be expected to continue indefinitely, and may constitute a substantial impairment in behavior and coping skills.

Direct care staff—any staff member who routinely has contact with the inmate or juvenile population.

Direct supervision—a method of inmate management that ensures continuing direct contact between inmates and staff by posting an officer(s) inside each housing unit. Officers in general housing units are not separated from inmates by a physical barrier. Officers provide frequent, nonscheduled observation of and personal interaction with inmates.

Direct threat—significant risk of substantial harm to the health or safety of any person including the applicant or employee with a disability that cannot be eliminated or reduced by reasonable accommodation.

Director—*See* Agency industries administrator.

Disability—a physical or mental impairment that substantially limits one or more of the major life activities of an individual; a record of such an impairment; or being regarded as having such an impairment.

Disciplinary detention—a form of separation from the general population in which inmates committing serious violations of conduct regulations are confined by the disciplinary committee or other authorized group for short periods of time to individual cells separated from the general population. Placement in detention only may occur after a finding of a rule violation at an impartial hearing and when there is not an adequate alternative disposition to regulate the inmate's behavior. (*See* Protective custody; Segregation.)

Disciplinary hearing—a nonjudicial administrative procedure to determine if substantial evidence exists to find an inmate guilty of a rule violation.

Dispositional hearing—a hearing held subsequent to the adjudicatory hearing to determine what order of disposition (for example, probation, training school, or foster home) should be made concerning a juvenile adjudicated as delinquent.

Diversion—the official halting or suspension, at any legally prescribed point after a recorded justice system entry, of formal criminal or juvenile justice proceedings against an alleged offender. The suspension of proceedings may be in conjunction with a referral of that person to a treatment or care program administered by a nonjudicial agency or a private agency, or there may be no referral.

Due process safeguards—procedures that ensure just, equal, and lawful treatment of an individual involved in all stages of the juvenile or criminal justice system, such as a notice of allegations, impartial and objective fact finding, the right to counsel, a written record of proceedings, a statement of any disposition ordered with the reasons for it, and the right to confront accusers, call witnesses, and present evidence.

Ectoparasites—parasites that live on the outside of the host, such as fleas or lice.

Education program—a program of formal academic education or a vocational training activity designed to improve employment capability.

Educational release—the designated time when residents or inmates leave the program or institution to attend school in the community and return to custody after school hours.

Elective surgery—surgery that is not essential and is not required for survival; especially surgery to correct a condition that is not life-threatening.

Emergency—any significant disruption of normal facility or agency procedure, policy, or activity caused by riot, escape, fire, natural disaster, employee action, or other serious incident.

Emergency care—care of an acute illness or unexpected health care need that cannot be deferred until the next scheduled sick call. Emergency care shall be provided to the resident population by the medical director, physician, or other staff, local ambulance services, and/or outside hospital emergency rooms. This care shall be expedited by following specific written procedures for medical emergencies described in the standards.

Emergency plans—written documents that address specific actions to be taken in an institutional emergency or catastrophe such as a fire, flood, riot, or other major disruption.

Emergency power—an alternate power system that is activated when the primary source of electricity is interrupted. The system may be an emergency generator, battery-operated power pack or an alternate supply source.

Environmental health—all conditions, circumstances, and surrounding influences that affect the health of individuals or groups in the area.

Escape—the act of breaking free of confinement or control while inside, or in the custody of, a correctional facility.

Expected practices—actions and activities that if implemented properly (according to protocols) will produce the desired outcome. They are what we think is necessary to achieve and maintain compliance with the standard—but not necessarily the only way to do so. They are activities that represent the current experience of the field, but that are not necessarily supported by research. As the field learns and evolves, so will the practices.

Facility—a place, institution, building (or part thereof), set of buildings, or area (whether or not enclosing a building or set of buildings) that is used for the lawful custody and/or treatment of individuals. It may be owned and/or operated by public or private agencies and includes the staff and services as well as the buildings and grounds.

Facility administrator—any official, regardless of local title (for example sheriff, chief of police, administrator, warden/superintendent), who has the ultimate responsibility for managing and operating the facility.

Field agency—the unit of a governing authority that has direct responsibility for the provision of field supervision services and for the carrying out of policy as set by the governing authority.

Field services—services provided to delinquent juveniles, status offenders, or adult offenders in the community by probation, parole, or other agencies.

Field staff/field workers—the professionals assigned case responsibility for control, supervision, and provision of program services to delinquent juveniles or adult offenders.

Firearm—a small arms weapon, such as a rifle or pistol, from which a projectile is fired by gunpowder.

First aid—care for a condition that requires immediate assistance from an individual trained in first aid care and the use of the facility's first aid kits.

Fiscal position control—the process that ensures that individuals on the payroll are legally employed, positions are authorized in the budget, and funds are available.

Flammable liquid—a substance with a flashpoint below 100 degrees Fahrenheit, classified as a Class I liquid.

Flash point—the minimum temperature at which a liquid will give off sufficient vapors to form an ignitable mixture with the air near the surface of the liquid (or in the vessel used).

Foot-candle—a unit for measuring the intensity of illumination, defined as the amount of light thrown on a surface one-foot away from the light source.

Formulary—a list of prescription and nonprescription medications that have been approved by the health authority and are stocked or routinely procured for use in an institution.

Furlough/temporary leave—a period of time during which a resident is allowed to leave the facility and go into the community unsupervised.

Goal statement—a general statement of what is sought within the functional area of the performance- based standard.

Good time—a system established by law whereby a convicted offender is credited a set amount of time, which is subtracted from his or her sentence, for specified periods of time served in an acceptable manner.

Governing authority—in public/governmental agencies, the administrative department or division to which the agency reports; the policy-setting body. In private agencies, this may be an administrative headquarters, central unit, or the board of directors or trustees.

Grievance/grievance process—a circumstance or action considered to be unjust and grounds for complaint or resentment and/or a response to that circumstance in the form of a written complaint filed with the appropriate body.

Halfway house—*See* Adult community residential service.

Handicapped—having a mental or physical impediment or disadvantage that substantially limits an individual's ability to use programs or services.

Hardship cases—serious mental or terminal medical illness, imminent death or death of a member of the inmate's immediate family.

Head of industries—*See* Agency industries administrator.

Health agency—an organization that provides health care services to an institution or a system of institutions.

Health authority—the health administrator, or agency responsible for the provision of health care services at an institution or system of institutions; the responsible physician may be the health authority.

Health care—the sum of all action taken, preventative and therapeutic, to provide for the physical and mental well-being of a population. It includes medical and dental services, mental health services, nursing, personal hygiene, dietary services, and environmental conditions.

Health care personnel—individuals whose primary duty is to provide health services to juveniles or inmates in keeping with their respective levels of health care training or experience.

Health care practitioner—clinicians trained to diagnose and treat patients, such as physicians, dentists, psychologists, podiatrists, optometrists, nurse practitioners, and physician assistants.

Health care professional—staff who perform clinical duties, such as health care practitioners, nurses, social workers, and emergency medical technicians in accordance with each health care professional's scope of training and applicable licensing, certification, and regulatory requirements.

Health care provider—an individual licensed in the delivery of health care.

Health care services—a system of preventative and therapeutic services that provide for the physical and mental well-being of a population. Includes medical and dental services, mental health services, nursing, pharmaceutical services, personal hygiene, dietary services, and environmental conditions.

Health/medical screen—a structured inquiry and observation to prevent newly arrived offenders who pose a health or safety threat to themselves or others from being admitted to the general population and to identify offenders who require immediate medical attention. The screen can be initiated at the time of admission by health care personnel or by a health-trained correctional officer.

Health-trained personnel/Medically trained personnel—correctional officers or other correctional personnel who may be trained and appropriately supervised to carry out specific duties with regard to the administration of health care.

Hearing—a proceeding to determine a course of action, such as the placement of a juvenile or adult offender, or to determine guilt or innocence in a disciplinary matter. Argument, witnesses, or evidence are heard by a judicial officer or administrative body in making the determination.

Hearing examiner—an individual appointed by the parole authority who conducts hearings for the authority. His or her power of decision making may include, but not be limited to, making parole recommendations to granting, denying, or revoking parole.

Holding facility/Lockup—a temporary confinement facility, for which the custodial authority is usually less than forty-eight hours, where arrested persons are held pending release, adjudication, or transfer to another facility.

Holidays—all days legally designated as non-workdays by statute or by the chief governing authority of a jurisdiction.

House parent—*See* Program director.

Improvement—*See* Quality assurance.

Incident report—a written document reporting a special event such as use of force, use of chemical agents, discharge of firearms, and so forth. The term is often used interchangeably with the term "disciplinary report."

Independent audit—an audit that is completed independent of influence by the agency or organization being audited.

Independent operator—a person or persons who contract with a correctional agency or other governmental agency to operate and manage a correctional program or facility.

Independent outside source—*See* Authority having jurisdiction.

Independent source—a person, organization or group that acts independently from the correctional unit being evaluated. An independent source may not be a staff member who reports to the chief executive officer of the unit being audited.

Indigent—an individual with no funds or source of income.

Industries—an activity existing in a correctional system that uses inmate labor to produce goods and/or services for sale. These goods and/or services are sold at prices calculated to recover all or a substantial portion of costs associated with their production and may include a margin of profit. Sale of the products and/or services is not limited to the institution where the industries activity is located.

Infection control program—a program designed to investigate, prevent, and control the spread of infections and communicable disease.

Infirmary—a specific area within an institution, separate from other housing areas, where offenders are admitted for health observation and care under the supervision and direction of health care personnel.

Information system/Management information system—the concepts, personnel, and supporting technology for the collection, organization, and delivery of information for administrative use. There are two such types of information: (1) standard information, consisting of the data required for operations control such as the daily count, payroll data in a personnel office, probation/parole success rates, referral sources, and caseload levels; (2) demand information, consisting of information that can be generated when a report is required, such as information on the number of residents in educational and training programs, duration of residence, or the number of residents eligible for discharge during a twelve-month period by offense, sentence, and month of release.

Informed consent—the agreement by a patient to a treatment, examination, or procedure after the patient receives the material facts regarding the nature, consequences, risks, and alternatives concerning the proposed treatment, examination, or procedure.

Inmate—any individual, whether in pretrial, unsentenced, or sentenced status, who is confined in a correctional facility.

Inmate compensation—incentives that are given for services provided. Incentives may be monetary compensation, special housing, extra privileges, good time credits, and other items of value.

Institution industries manager—the individual designated as responsible for industries operations at a specific institution in the correctional system.

Interstate Compact on Juveniles—This program established in 1955 regulates the interstate movement of juveniles under court supervision, specifically, juveniles who have run away from home without consent of a parent or legal guardian; been placed on probation/parole and want to reside in another state; those absconded or escaped from an institution in another state; or those who require institutional care/specialized services in another state; or those who have a pending hearing and have run away to another state.

Interstate Compact for the Supervision of Probationers and Parolees—an agreement entered into by eligible jurisdictions in the United States and its territories that provides the criteria for these jurisdictions to cooperate in working with probation and release.

Intersystem transfers—transfers from one distinct correctional system to another.

Intra-system transfers—transfers from facility to facility within a correctional system. This only applies to contractual relationships if the contracting agency is ACA accredited.

Jail—*See* Adult detention facility.

Judicial review—a proceeding to reexamine the course of action or continued confinement of a juvenile in a secure detention facility. Arguments, witnesses, or evidence are not required as part of the review. Reviews may be conducted by a judge, judicial officer, or an administrator who has been delegated the authority to release juveniles from secure detention with the approval of the judge.

Juvenile—a person under the age of 21, or as defined in the local jurisdiction as under the age of majority.

Juvenile community residential program—a program housed in a structure without security fences and security hardware or other major restraining construction typically associated with correctional facilities, such as a converted apartment building or private home. They are not constructed as or intended to be detention facilities. Except for daycare programs, they provide twenty-four-hour care, programs, and supervision to juveniles in residence. Their focus is on providing the juvenile with positive adult models and program activities that assist in resolving problems specific to this age group in an environment conducive to positive behavior in the community.

Juvenile correctional facility—an institution that may provide supervision, programs, and residential services for more than 100 residents. These facilities are designed and operated to be secure institutions. Juvenile development centers, juvenile treatment centers, secure training schools, and other facilities in the category may serve relatively smaller populations ranging from 40 to 100 juveniles. The age range served is generally from 13 to 18 years of age, although in many jurisdictions, residents may be as young as 10 or as old as 25 years of age. Older residents are usually juveniles who have been returned to the facility as parole violators.

Juvenile day treatment program—a program that provides services to juveniles who live at home and report to the program on a daily basis. Juveniles in these programs require more attention than that provided by probation and aftercare services. Often the program operates its own education program through the local school district. The population usually is drawn from court commitments but may include juveniles enrolled as a preventive or diversionary measure. The program may operate as part of a residential program, and it may provide space for occasional overnight stays by program participants where circumstances warrant additional assistance.

Juvenile delinquent—*See* Delinquent youth.

Juvenile detention—temporary care of juvenile offenders and juveniles alleged to be delinquent who require secure custody in a physically restricting facility.

Juvenile development center—*See* Juvenile correctional facility.

Juvenile group home—nonsecure residential program emphasizing family-style living in a homelike atmosphere. Program goals are similar to those for large community residential programs. Although group homes usually house juveniles who are court-committed, they also house abused or neglected juveniles who are placed by social agencies. Small group homes serve from four to eight juveniles; large group homes serve eight to twelve. Participating juveniles range in age from 10 to 17, with the concentration from 13 to 16.

Juvenile intake—process of determining whether the interests of the public or the juvenile require the filing of a petition with the juvenile court. Generally, an intake officer receives, reviews, and processes complaints, recommends detention or release, and provides services for juveniles and their families, including diversion and referral to other community agencies.

Juvenile nonresidential program—a program that provides services to juveniles who live at home and report to the program on a daily basis. Juveniles in these programs require more attention than that provided by probation and aftercare services. Often the program operates its own education program through the local school district. The population of non-residential programs may be as many as 50 boys and girls ranging in age from 10 to 18. The population is usually drawn from court commitments but may include juveniles enrolled as a preventive or diversionary measure. The program may operate as part of a residential program, and it may provide space for occasional overnight stays by program participants where circumstances warrant additional assistance.

Juvenile ranch—nonsecure residential program providing services to juveniles in a rural setting. Typically, the residents participate in a structured program of education, recreation, and facility maintenance, including responsibility for the physical plant, its equipment, and livestock. Often there are 20-to-60 juveniles in the ranch setting, ranging in age from 13-to-18.

Juvenile service center—*See* Juvenile correctional facility.

Juvenile village—*See* Juvenile correctional facility.

Library service—a service that provides reading materials for convenient use; circulation of reading materials; service to help provide users with library materials, educational and recreational audio/visual materials, or a combination of these services.

Life Safety Code—a manual published and updated by the National Fire Protection Association specifying minimum standards for fire safety necessary in the public interest. Two chapters are devoted to correctional facilities.

Lockup—*See* Holding facility.

Mail inspection—examination of incoming and outgoing mail for contraband, cash, checks, and money orders.

Major equipment—equipment that is securely and permanently fastened to the building or any equipment with a current book value of $1,000 or more.

Major infraction—rule violation involving a grievous loss and requiring imposition of due process procedures. Major infractions include (1) violations that may result in disciplinary detention or administrative segregation; (2) violations for which punishment may tend to increase an inmate's sentence; (3) violations that may result in a forfeiture, such as loss of good-time or work time; and (4) violations that may be referred for criminal prosecution.

Mandatory standard—a standard that has been determined by the American Correctional Association to directly affect the life, health, and safety of offenders and correctional personnel.

Management information system—*See* Information system.

Master index file—used in an institution to keep track of the inmates who are housed in particular housing units.

Medical records—separate records of medical examinations and diagnoses maintained by the responsible physician. The date and time of all medical examinations and copies of standing or direct medical orders from the physician to the facility staff should be transferred to the resident's or staff 's record.

Medical restraints—chemical restraints, such as sedatives, or physical restraints, such as straitjackets, applied only for medical or psychiatric purposes. Metal handcuffs and leg shackles are not considered medical restraints.

Medical screen—*See* Health screen.

Medically trained personnel—*See* Health trained personnel.

Medically unexpected deaths—those that occur suddenly without any clinical warning (in other words, sudden death) and are not a result of a previously diagnosed medical condition(s) that is life-threatening, for example, certain cancers, AIDS, congestive heart failure, kidney or liver failure, and geriatric co-morbidities. This may also include offenders who succumb despite well managed chronic conditions.

Medication administration—process of giving a dose of a prescribed or over-the-counter medication to a patient.

Medication dispensing—the process of placing one or more doses of a medication into a container that is labeled to indicate the name of the patient, the contents of the container, and other necessary information by health care staff member as authorized by the jurisdiction.

Medication disposal—destruction or removal of medication from a facility after discontinuation of its use per local, state, and federal regulation.

Mental health care practitioner—staff who perform clinical duties for mentally ill patients, for example, physicians, psychologists, nurses, and social workers in accordance with each health care professional's scope of training and applicable licensing, certification, and regulatory requirements.

Mental health screening—review by a qualified, mental health professional of any history of psychological problems and examination of any current psychological problems to determine, with reasonable assurances, that the individuals pose no significant risk to themselves or others.

Mental health staff—individuals whose primary duty is to provide mental health services to inmates commensurate with their respective levels of education, experience, training, and credentials.

Mental illness—psychiatric illness or disease expressed primarily through abnormalities of thought, feeling, and behavior producing either distress and/or impaired function.

Mental retardation—developmental disability marked by lower-than-normal intelligence and impaired daily living skills.

Mid-level practitioner—nurse practitioner or physician's assistant licensed or credentialed to assume an expanded role in providing medical care under the supervision of a physician.

Minor infraction—a violation of the facility's rules of conduct that does not require due process and can be resolved without the imposition of serious penalties. Minor infractions do not violate any state or federal statutes and may be resolved informally by the reporting staff.

Natural light—the illumination from the sun; daylight.

New construction—standards regulating "new construction" will be deemed applicable to a facility if the final plans were approved or legal permit was issued later than six months after the release of the *Standards Supplement*, which includes no official change to the standard. For example, a standard regulating new construction passed in 2010 will be applicable to all facilities whose final plans were approved or legal permits were issued in or after June 2012 (following the January release of the *2012 Standards Supplement*).

NFPA—National Fire Protection Association publishes the Life Safety Code.

National uniform parole report system—cooperative effort sponsored by the National Parole Institute that calls for the voluntary cooperation of all federal and state authorities having responsibility for felony offenders in developing some common terms to describe parolee (age, sex, and prior record) and some common definitions to describe parole performance. These types of data allow comparisons across states and other jurisdictions.

Not applicable—term used in the accreditation process to describe a standard that does not apply to the correctional unit being audited. While the initial determination of applicability is made by American Correctional Association staff and/or the audit team, the final decision rests with the Commission on Accreditation.

Noncontact visiting—a program that restricts inmates from having physical contact with visitors. Physical barriers usually separate the offender from the visitors with screens and/or glass. Voice communications between the parties are typically accomplished with phones or speakers. Offenders who present a serious escape threat, are a threat to others, or require protection are often designated for noncontact visits.

Non-formulary medication—medications not listed in the approved institution or agency formulary.

Occupational exposure—exposure to potentially harmful chemical, physical, or biological agents that occur as a result of one's occupation.

Offender—individual convicted or adjudicated of a criminal offense.

Official personnel file—current and accurate record of the employee's job history, including all pertinent information relating to that history.

Operating unit—one distinct operation of the industry's activity, which may be operated as a cost center or separate accounting entity. It may take the form of a manufacturing operation (for example, furniture making or clothing production), an agricultural operation (for example, dairy or poultry farming, crop or orchard farming, cow or pig farming), or a service activity (for example, a warehouse, keypunch operation, microfilming process, laundering, auto repair, and so forth).

Orientation and reception—the reception period includes interviews, testing, and other admissions-related activities, including distribution of information about programs, services, rules, and regulations.

Out-client—individual who does not live at the facility but who may use facility services and programs.

Outcome measure—measurable events, occurrences, conditions, behaviors, or attitudes that demonstrate the extent to which a condition described has been achieved.

Parent—individual with whom a juvenile regularly lives and who is the biological, adoptive, or surrogate parent.

Parent agency—administrative department or division to whom the agency seeking accreditation reports; the policy-setting body.

Parole authority/Parole board/Parole commission—decision-making body that has responsibility to grant, deny, and/or revoke parole. The term "parole authority" includes all of these bodies.

Parole hearing—procedure conducted by a parole authority member and/or hearing examiner in which all pertinent aspects of an eligible inmate's case are reviewed to make a decision or recommendation that would change the inmate's legal status and/or degree of freedom.

Peer review—process of having patient care provided by a clinician reviewed and evaluated by a peer with similar credentials. An external peer review is completed by a medical professional not employed by the facility being reviewed.

Perimeter security—a system that controls ingress and egress to the interior of a facility or institution. The system may include electronic devices, walls, fences, patrols, and/or towers.

Permanent status—personnel status that provides due process protection prior to dismissal.

Personal property—property that legally belongs to the offender.

Personnel policies manual—a manual that is available to each employee and contains the following: an affirmative action program, an equal opportunity program, a policy for selection, retention, and promotion of all personnel on the basis of merit and specified qualifications, a code of ethics, rules for probationary employment, a compensation and benefit plan, provisions of the Americans with Disabilities Act (ADA), sexual harassment and sexual misconduct policy, grievance and appeal procedures, infection control procedures, and employees disciplinary procedures.

Personnel record—contains the following: initial application; reference letters; results of employment investigation; verification of training and experience; wage and salary information; job performance evaluations; incident reports, if any; and commendations and disciplinary actions, if any.

Petition—application for a court order or other judicial action. For example, a delinquency petition is an application for the court to act in the matter of a juvenile apprehended for a delinquent act.

Physical examination—evaluation of a patient's current physical condition and medical history conducted by or under the supervision of a licensed professional.

Placing authority—agency or body with the authority to order a juvenile into a specific dispositional placement. This may be the juvenile court, the probation department, or another duly constituted and authorized placement agency.

Policy—course or line of action adopted and pursued by an agency that guides and determines present and future decisions and actions. Policies indicate the general course or direction of an organization within which the activities of the personnel must operate. They are statements of guiding principles that should be followed in directing activities toward the attainment of objectives. Attainment may lead to compliance with standards and compliance with the overall goals of the agency or system.

Population center—geographical area containing at least 10,000 people, along with public safety services, professional services, employment and educational opportunities, and cultural/recreational opportunities.

Preliminary hearing—hearing to determine whether probable cause exists to support an allegation of parole violation pending a revocation hearing by the parole authority.

Pretrial release—procedure whereby an accused individual who had been taken into custody is allowed to be released before and during his or her trial.

Preventive maintenance—a system designed to enhance the longevity and or usefulness of buildings or equipment in accordance with a planned schedule.

Private agency—the contracting agency of the governing authority that has direct responsibility for the operation of a corrections program.

Probation—court-ordered disposition alternative through which a convicted adult offender or an adjudicated delinquent is placed under the control, supervision, and care of a probation field staff member.

Probationary period—a period of time designated to evaluate and test an employee to ascertain fitness for the job.

Procedure—detailed and sequential actions that must be executed to ensure that a policy is fully implemented. It is the method of performing an operation or a manner of proceeding on a course of action. It differs from a policy in that it directs action in a particular situation to perform a specific task within the guidelines of policy.

Process indicators—documentation and other evidence that can be examined periodically and continuously to determine that practices are being properly implemented.

Professional association—collective body of individuals engaged in a particular profession or vocation.

Professional staff—social workers, probation officers, and other staff assigned to juvenile and adult offender cases. These individuals generally possess bachelor's degrees and advanced training in the social or behavioral sciences.

Program—plan or system through which a correctional agency works to meet its goals. This program may require a distinct physical setting, such as a correctional institution, community residential facility, group home, or foster home.

Program director—individual directly in charge of the program.

Prosthesis—functional or cosmetic artificial device that substitutes for a missing body part such as an arm, leg, eye, or tooth.

Protective custody—form of separation from the general population for inmates requesting or requiring protection from other inmates for reasons of health or safety. The inmate's status is reviewed periodically by the classification committee or other designated group. (*See* Administrative segregation; Disciplinary detention.)

Protocols—written instructions that guide implementation of expected practices, such as policies and procedures, training curriculum, offender handbooks, diagrams, and internal forms and logs.

Psychotropic medication—medication that exerts an effect on thought, mood, and/or behavior. Psychotropic medications are used to treat mental illness and a variety of disorders.

Public agency—the governing authority that has direct responsibility for the operation of a corrections program.

Qualified medical person—*See* Health care professional.

Qualified mental health person—*See* Mental health care practitioner.

Quality assurance—formal, internal monitoring program that uses standardized criteria to insure quality and consistency. The program identifies opportunities for improvement, develops improvement strategies, and monitors effectiveness.

Rated capacity—the original architectural design plus, or minus, capacity changes resulting from building additions, reductions, or revisions.

Reasonable accommodation—modifications or adjustments, which enable qualified applicants with disabilities to access the job application process or which enable qualified employees with disabilities to perform the essential functions of the job and to enjoy the same terms, conditions, and privileges of employment that are available to persons without disabilities.

Reasonably private environment—this may vary, depending on individual and institutional circumstances, but it is one which will maintain the dignity of the disabled individual in light of that person's disability.

Records (juvenile and adult offenders)—information concerning the individual's delinquent or criminal, personal and medical history and behavior, and activities while in custody, including but not limited to commitment papers, court orders, detainers, personal property receipts, visitors' lists, photographs, fingerprints, type of custody, disciplinary infractions and actions taken, grievance reports, work assignments, program participation, and miscellaneous correspondence.

Referral—process by which a juvenile or adult offender is introduced to an agency or service that can provide the needed assistance.

Release on bail—release by a judicial officer of an accused individual who has been taken into custody on the accused's promise to appear in court as required for criminal proceedings.

Releasing authority—decision-making body and/or individual who has the authority to grant, deny, and revoke release from a juvenile institution or program of supervision. In some jurisdictions, it is called the parole board or the parole commission. *See* Aftercare.

Renovation—significant structural or design change in the physical plant of a facility.

Responsible physician—individual licensed to practice medicine and provide health services to the inmate population of the facility and/or the physician at an institution with final responsibility for decisions related to medical judgments.

Restraints—devices used to restrict physical activity; for example, handcuffs, leg irons, straight- jackets, belly chain.

Revocation hearing—hearing before the parole authority to determine whether revocation of parole should be made final.

Rule book, offender—a collection of the facility's rules of conduct and sanctions for violations defined in writing.

Safety equipment—primarily fire-fighting equipment, such as chemical extinguishers, hoses, nozzles, water supplies, alarm systems, sprinkler systems, portable breathing devices, gas masks, fans, first aid kits, stretchers, and emergency alarms.

Safety vestibule—grille cage that divides the inmate areas from the remainder of the institution. It must have two doors or gates, only one of which opens at a time, to permit entry to or exit from inmate areas in a safe and controlled manner.

Sallyport—enclosure situated in the perimeter wall or fence of a correctional facility containing gates or doors at both ends, only one of which opens at a time, ensuring there will be no breach in the perimeter security of the institution. The sallyport may handle either pedestrian or vehicular traffic.

School or home for boys and girls—*See* Juvenile correctional facility.

Secure institution—facility that is designed and operated to ensure that all entrances and exits are under the exclusive control of the facility's staff preventing a juvenile or inmate/resident from leaving the facility unsupervised or without permission.

Security devices—locks, gates, doors, bars, fences, screens, ceilings, floors, walls, and barriers used to confine and control detained individuals. Also included are electronic monitoring equipment, security alarm systems, security lights, auxiliary power supplies, and other equipment used to maintain facility security.

Security perimeter—outer portions of a facility that provide for secure confinement of facility inmates/residents. The design of the perimeter may vary dependent on the security classification of the facility.

Segregation—confinement of an inmate to an individual cell separated from the general population. There are three forms of segregation: administrative segregation, disciplinary detention, and protective custody.

Segregation unit—a housing section that separates offenders who threaten the security or orderly management of the institution from the general population.

Self-insurance coverage—system designed to insure the payment of all legal claims for injury or damage incurred as a result of the actions of state officials, employees, or agents. In public agencies, the self-insurance program is usually authorized by the legislature. A "memorandum of insurance" or similar document is required that acts as a policy, setting the limits of liability for various categories of risk, including deductible limits. Approval of the policy by a cabinet-level official is also required.

Serious incident—situation in which injury serious enough to warrant medical attention occurs involving a resident, employee, or visitor on the grounds of the institution. A situation creating an imminent threat to the security of the institution and/or to the safety of residents, employees, or visitors on the grounds of the institution.

Severe mental disturbance—condition in which an individual is a danger to self or others or is incapable of attending to basic physiological needs.

Shelter facility—non-secure public or private facility designated to provide either temporary placement for alleged or adjudicated status offenders prior to the issuance of a disposition order or longer-term care under a juvenile court disposition order.

Special management inmates—individuals whose behavior presents a serious threat to the safety and security of the facility, staff, general inmate population, or themselves. Special handling and/or housing are required to regulate their behavior.

Special needs—mental and/or physical condition that requires accommodations or arrangements differing from those a general population offender or juvenile normally would receive. Offenders or juveniles with special needs may include, but are not limited to, the emotionally disturbed, developmentally disabled, mentally ill, physically handicapped, chronically ill, the disabled or infirm, and the drug or alcohol addicted.

Standard—statement that defines a required or essential condition to be achieved and/or maintained.

Status offender—juvenile who has been charged with or adjudicated for conduct that under the law of the jurisdiction in which the offense was committed would not be a crime if committed by an adult. (*See also* Delinquent youth.)

Strip search—examination of an inmate's/resident's naked body for weapons, contraband, and physical abnormalities. This also includes a thorough search of all of the individual's clothing while it is not being worn.

Superintendent—*See* Warden.

Suspicious mail—This may include packages and letters unusual in appearance or that appear different from mail normally received or sent by the individual; packages and letters of a size or shape not customarily received or sent by the individual; packages and letters with a city and/or state postmark that is different from the return address; or packages and letters leaking, stained, or emitting a strange or unusual odor, or that have a powdery residue.

Syringe—A syringe consists of a barrel, plunger, and/or a needle. Any of the parts of a syringe are to be counted, controlled, and inventoried. Medical and dental instruments and supplies (which include syringes, needles, and blades) that are stocked for daily use are inventoried, controlled, and counted at a minimum daily. A perpetual inventory of bulk stock needles, syringes, blades, and other sharps is maintained in a locked storage area. Needles, syringes, blades, and other sharps are considered contraband in the correctional setting. When items are identified as having the potential for causing harm to offenders or staff, such items must be inventoried, controlled, and counted.

Temporary disability—a condition that can be treated with an expectation of full recovery. It is not the result of a chronic condition, but short-term in nature and resolved over time.

Temporary leave—*See* Furlough.

Temporary release—period of time during which an inmate is allowed to leave the program or institution and go into the community unsupervised for various purposes consistent with the public interest.

Terms, conditions, privileges of employment—include, but are not limited to: recruitment, selection, and hiring; salary and compensation; benefits, holidays, leave, and work hours; promotion and advancement; staff development, including in-service training; and retirement, resignation, and termination

Therapeutic community—a designed social environment with programs for substance-use-disordered patients within a residential or day unit in which the social and group process is used with therapeutic intent.

Therapeutic diet—diet prescribed by a health care practitioner as part of the patient's medical treatment. Therapeutic diets can be ordered by physicians, physician's assistants, or nurse practitioners.

Toxic materials—substances that through chemical reaction or mixture can produce possible injury or harm to the body by entering through the skin, digestive tract, or respiratory tract (for example, zinc chromate paint, ammonia, chlorine, antifreeze, herbicides, pesticides).

Training—an organized, planned, documented, and evaluated or assessed activity designed to impart knowledge and skills to enhance job performance. Training is based on specific objectives, is job related, from an appropriate source, of sufficient duration, relevant to organizational need, and delivered to appropriate staff. *See* Appendix F.

Training plan—a set of long- or short-range training activities that equip staff with the knowledge, skills, and attitudes that they need to accomplish the goals of the agency.

Training school—*See* Juvenile correctional facility.

Treatment plan—series of written statements that specify the particular course of therapy and the roles of medical and nonmedical personnel in carrying it out. A treatment plan is individualized, based on assessment of the individual patient's needs, and includes a statement of the short- and long-term goals and the methods by which the goals will be pursued. When clinically indicated, the treatment plan provides inmates with access to a range of supportive and rehabilitative services, such as individual or group counseling and/or self-help groups that the physician deems appropriate.

Triage—screening and classification of offender health care concerns by qualified medical staff to determine the priority of need and the appropriate level of intervention.

Undue hardship—an accommodation that would be unduly costly, extensive, or substantial.

Unencumbered space—Usable space that is not encumbered by furnishings or fixtures. At least one dimension of the unencumbered space is no less than seven feet. In determining unencumbered space in the area, the total square footage is obtained and the square footage of fixtures and equipment is subtracted. All fixtures and equipment must be in operational position.

Unit management—Management system that subdivides an institution into units. The unit management system has several basic requirements:

1. Each unit holds a relatively small number of inmates. Ideally, there should be fewer than 150 but not more than 500 inmates.
2. Inmates are housed in the same unit for a major portion of their confinement.
3. Inmates assigned to a unit work in a close relationship with a multidisciplinary staff team who are regularly assigned to the unit and whose officers are located within the unit.
4. Staff members have decision-making authority for the institutional programming and living conditions for the inmates assigned to the unit within broad rules, policies, and guidelines established by the agency and/or the facility administrator.
5. Inmate assignments to a unit are based on the inmate's need for control, security, and programs offered.

Unit management increases contact between staff and inmates, fosters increased interpersonal relationships, and leads to more knowledgeable decision making as a direct result of staff dealing with a smaller, more permanent group. At the same time, the facility benefits from the economies inherent in centralized service facilities, such as utilities, food service, health care, educational systems, vocational programs, and recreational facilities.

Urine surveillance program—program whereby urine samples are collected on an irregular basis from offenders suspected of having a history of drug use to determine current or recent use.

Use of force—refers to the right of an individual or authority to settle conflicts or prevent certain actions by applying measures to either dissuade another party from a particular course of action, or physically intervene to stop them. The use of force is governed by statute and is usually authorized in a progressive series of actions, referred to as a "use-of-force continuum."

Volunteer—individual who donates his or her time and effort to enhance the activities and programs of the agency. They are selected on the basis of their skills or personal qualities to provide services in recreation, counseling, education, religion, and so forth.

Warden—individual in charge of the institution; the chief executive or administrative officer. This position is sometimes referred to by other titles, but "warden" and "superintendent" are the most commonly used terms.

Work release—formal arrangement sanctioned by law whereby an inmate/resident is released into the community to maintain approved and regular employment.

Workers' compensation—statewide system of benefits for employees who are disabled by job-related injury.

Work stoppage—a planned or spontaneous discontinuation of work. The stoppage may involve employees or inmates, acting separately or in concert by refusing to participate in institutional activities.

Youthful offender—person under the age of criminal majority in the jurisdiction in which he or she is confined who has been charged and/or sentenced as an adult.

Members of the Standards Committee 1976–2016

A

Adams, Betty (TN) 1996-1999
Alarcon, Francisco (FL) 1997-2001
Albrecht, Thomas (DC) 1988-1990
Allen, Frederick R. (NY) 1982-1986, 1988-1990
Angelone, Ron (NV) 1986-1988, 1999-2004
Ammons, Lori (KS) 2011-2013
Antoine, Janitta (LA) 1996-2000
Atchison, Jim (KY) 1976-1978
Aud, Kenneth J. (MI) 1994-1998

B

Bachmeier, Kathleen (ND) 2009-2013
Bailey, Paul E. (NV) 1980-1982
Beard, Jeffrey (PA) 2005-2011
Belleque, Lester E. (OR) 1982-1986
Bertrand, Roma (Canada) 1984-1986
Bittick, John Cary (GA) 2004-2008
Black, James (CO) 1988-1990
Blake, Gary R. (GA) 1986-1988
Bogard, David (NY) 2002-2004
Borjeson, Terry (CT) 2000-2004
Bradley, Michael (FL) 2011-2016
Braithwaite, John W. (Canada) 1976-1980
Branham, Lynn S. (IL) 1990-1992, 1994-1998
Breaux, Donald J. (LA) 1992-1994
Breed, Allen F. (DC) 1976-1982
Brown, Melvin, Jr. (TX) 1992-1998
Brown, Robert, Jr. (MI) 1988-1990
Brutsche, Robert L. (CA) 1988-1998
Budzinski, Ron (IL) 2006-2010
Burrell, Joyce L. (DC) 2010-2013

C

Campbell, Nancy M. (WA) 1986-1988
Carlson, Norman A. (DC) 1976-1978
Caruso, Patricia (MI) 2006-2008
Chamberlain, Norman F. (WA) 1980-1982
Clute, Penelope D. (NY) 1988-1990
Cocoros, John A. (TX) 1990-1992
Coleman, Ray (WA) 1986-1988
Collins, William C. (WA) 1984-1986
Corsentino, Dan L. (CO) 1996-1998
Coughlin, Thomas A. (NY) 1988-1994
Craig, Daniel (IA) 2006-2010
Crist, Roger W. (CO) 1982-1984
Crawford, Jacqueline (AZ) 1976-1992
Crosby, James V., Jr., (FL) 2001-2005
Cunningham, Su (TX) 1994-1996

D

Davis, Pamela Jo (FL) 1986-1990
Decell, Grady A. (SC) 1979-1982
Dennehy, Kathleen (MA) 2006-2008
Diggins, Elias (CO) 2013-2015
Dismukes, Hugh C. (TX) 1980-1982
Dixon, Leonard (MI) 2002-2004
Dorsey, Helen Brown (WA) 1982-1984
Dorsey, Neil (NM) 1982-1984
Dunning, James (VA) 1994-1996

E

Enomoto, J. J. (CA) 1979-1980
Estelle, W. J., Jr. (TX) 1976-1980
Evans, David C. (GA) 1988-1990

F

Farkas, Gerald M. (DC) 1978-1986
Farrier, Harold A. (IA) 1986-1992
Fitzgibbons, Mark (SC) 2001-2004
Fischer, Brian (NY) 2008-2012
Frawley, Michael F. (MO) 1996-2002, 2006-2008

G

Gagnon, John R. (WI) 1976-1980
Gamby, Jacqueline Jones (CO) 1980-1986
Garvey, Robert (MA) 2000-2004, 2006-2008
Gaudio, Anthony C. (VA) 1976-1978
Ghee, Margarette (OH) 1996-1998
Gibson, Steve (MT) 2006-2010
Giesen, Linda (IL) 1982-1984
Gispert, Ana (FL) 1982-1984
Glanz, Stanley (OK) 2008-2012
Goodall, Paula (OK) 1982-1984
Goord, Glenn S. (NY) 1996-1999, 2002-2006
Guillen, Rudy F. (VA) 1976-1982

H

Haasenritter, David K. (VA) 2008-2012
Hahn, Paul H. (OH) 1984-1986
Hamden, Michael S. (NC) 1998-2002, 2004-2006
Hawk, Kathleen M. (DC) 1992-1998
Hegmann, Michael, M.D. (LA) 1998-2000
Hershberger, Gregory L. (KS) 1998-2002
Hill, Gary (NE) 1976-1980
Hill-Christian, Sheila (VA) 1996-1998
Hofacre, Rob (OH) 2006-2008
Holden, Tamara (OR) 1986-1988
Housewright, Vernon G. (IL) 1976-1982, 1984-1986
Humphrey-Barnett, Susan (AK) 1988-1992

I

Irving, James R. (IL) 1988-1994

J

Jackson, Ronald G. (TX) 1978-1980
Johnson, Perry M. (NH) 1984-1992
Jones, Justin W. (OK) 2008-2010, 2013-2015
Jordan, James M. (IL) 1986-1988

K

Kehoe, Charles J. (VA) 1978-1982
Kelly, Marton (OH) 1976-1978
Kelly, Ralph (KY) 2000-2004
Kennedy, Robert (NY) 2006-2008
Keohane, Patrick (MO) 1998-2000

L

Lappin, Harley (DC) 2002-2015
Larivee, John (MA) 1997-2005
LeBlanc, James M. (LA) 2008-2015
Lehman, Joseph D. (ME) 1994-1996
Lejins, Peter P. (MD) 1976-1978
Lindamood, Cherry (TN) 2013-2015
Linthicum, Lannette, M.D., CCHP-A (TX) 2002-2006, 2008-2013
Livers, Mary L. (OK) 1996-1997, 2008-2011
Livingston, Brad (TX) 2006-2014
Livingston, Shirley H. (FL) 1976-1979
Lucero, Penny (NM) 1997-2001

M

Manley, Harry A. (MD) 1990-1996
Martin, Bill (MI) 2000-2004
Maynard, Gary D. (OK) 1989-1992
McCartt, John M. (OH) 1976-1978
McCotter, O. L. (TX) 1984-1986
McGehee, R. Daniel (SC) 1998-2002
McMahon, John F. (NY) 1976-1978
Michael, Venetia T. (LA) 1998-2002
Milliken, William V. (UT) 1982-1984
Minor, John (MI) 1992-1994
Mitchell, Anabel P. (FL) 1984-1986
Mohr, Gary C. (OH) 2011-2015
Moore, Margaret A. (PA) 1990-1996
Moore, Michael (FL) 2001-2005
Morton, Joann B. (SC) 1976-1980
Murray, Albert (GA) 2006
Myers, Kevin Bradley (TN) 2010-2013
Myers, Victoria C. (MO) 1980-1994, 2005-2009

N

Natalucci-Persichetti, Geno (OH) 1994-2004
Nelson, Ray (CO) 1984-1986

O

Owens, George (OH) 2002-2004

P

Pappert, Ruth M. (IL) 1980-1982
Parrish, David (FL) 1992-1998
Patrick, Allen L. (OH) 1992-1994
Perry, Gloria (MS) 2013-2015
Peters, Howard A. III (IL) 1992-1998
Petrovsky, Joseph (MO) 1982-1984
Phyfer, George M. (AL) 1976-1978
Pointer, Donald W. (MD) 1978-1980
Pugh, Julian U. (VA) 1978-1980

Q

Quinlan, Michael J. (DC) 1986-1990

R

Rapp, Marcella (CO) 1984-1986
Rees, John D. (LA) 1988-1992
Ridley-Turner, Evelyn (IN) 1999-2003
Riggin, Viola (KS) 2013-2017
Rion, Sharon Johnson (TN) 1996-1997
Robinette, Michelle (OK) 2013-2017
Robinson, Carl (CT) 1982-1984
Robinson, Denise (OH) 2008-2017
Robinson, William B. (PA) 1980-1984
Robuck, Lucille (KY) 1976-1978
Rogan, Marilyn (NV) 2008-2010
Ross, Howard (TN) 2001-2005
Rosser, Paul (GA) 1984-1986
Rossi, Linda D'Amario (RI) 1980-1982
Rustin, Ramon C. (NM) 2011-2016
Ryan, Timothy (SC) 2004-2006

S

Samuels, Charles (VA) 2012-2014
Scott, Wayne (TX) 1998-2002
Sexton, Ted (AL) 1998-2002
Sheridan, Francis (NY) 2002-2004
Shirley, Sue (TX) 1980-1982
Shope, John T. (NC) 1976-1978
Schmidt, Robert (DC) 1986-1988
Shumate, Denis (KS) 1990-1996
Simonet, John (CO) 1990-1996
Singh, Raman (LA), 2010-2015
Singletary, Harry (FL) 1988-1994
Sipos, Chiquita (CA) 1984-1986, 1992-1998
Smith, Paula (NC) 2009-2013
Spencer, Luis (MA) 2013-2015
Stalder, Richard (MA) 1994-1996
Stickrath, Thomas J. (OH) 1997-2000
Sublett, Samuel J. (IL) 1976-1986, 1996-1997
Swanson, Virginia (WA) 1988-1990, 1992-1994, 1996-1998

T

Thomas, David (FL) 2002-2004
Thomas, Penny (TX) 1997-2001
Townsend, Cheryln (AZ) 2002-2004, 2006-2008

V

Vassar, B. Norris (VA) 1986-1988
Vigil, Celedonio (NM) 1990-1996

W

Wade, Michael (VA) 2010-2012
Ward, Frederick J. (NJ) 1976-1978
Washington, Odie (DC) 1998-2002
Weber, J. Robert (NC) 1982-1984
Webster, Marge (NH) 2008-2015
Weldon, Paul I. (SC) 1978-1980
Wetzel, John (PA) 2011-2014
White, William S. (IL) 1986-1988
Wilber, Harold (FL) 1998-2000, 2001-2004
Williams, Jr., Clarence (KY) 2013-2015
Williams, Joe (NM) 2002-2004
Wilson, George W. (OH) 1988-1990
Wirkler, Norman E. (CO) 1988-1990, 1992-1998
Wrenshall, Allen F. (Canada) 1982-1984
Wright, Lester (NY) 2000-2002

Y

Young, Marjorie H. (GA) 1986-1988, 1990-1992
Youngken, Michael (KS) 1994-1998, 2000-2002

Members of the Commission on Accreditation for Corrections 1976–2016

A

Ammons, Lori (KS) 2011-2017
Ackermann, John (NY) 1976-1977
Anderson, Elizabeth (DC) 2002-2004, 2008-2010
Andrashko, Steve (VA) 2013-2017

B

Black, James (CO) 1986-1988*
Blake, Gary (MD) 1979-1984
Bogard, David A. (NY) 2000-2004
Borjeson, Terry (CT) 1999-2000
Boswell, Anita (AL) 2002-2004
Braithwaite, John (Canada) 1980-1986
Branham, Lynn S. (IL) 1990-1998, 2000-2002, 2008-2010, 2013-2015
Breaux, Donald J. (LA) 1990-1996
Brown, Mel (TX) 2000-2004
Brutsche, Robert L. (VA) 1986-1998
Budzinksi, Ron (IL) 2006-2010
Burrell, Joyce L. (DC) 2010-2015
Buss, Edwin G. (IN) 2008-2013

C

Campbell, Donal (TN) 1999-2000
Caruso, Patricia (MI) 2003-2004
Casselbury, Parkes (FL) 2002-2004
Catley, Dan (VA) 2000-2004
Charters, Paul (FL) 1979-1984
Chin, Arleen (NH) 2000-2002
Clarke, Harold (NE) 2000-2004
Clute, Penelope D. (NY) 1984-1990
Coate, Alfred B. (MT) 1975-1980
Cocoros, John (TX) 1988-1994
Coleman, Raymond J. (WA) 1984-1990
Corsentino, Dan L. (CO) 1996-1998
Crawford, Jacqueline (AZ) 1986-1992, 2002-2004
Crosby, James V. (FL) 2001-2005
Cunningham, Su (TX) 1992-1998
Curran, Patrick J., III (TN) 2008-2017
Cushwa, Patricia (MD) 2002-2004

D

David, Monica (FL) 2004-2008
Davis, Hasan (KY) 2013-2015
Dennehy, Kathleen M. (MA) 2004-2006
DePrato, Debra, M.D., (LA) 2004-2008
Dietz, Christopher D. (NJ) 1980-1986
Diggins, Elias (CO) 2013-2017
Dooley, Barbara (TN) 2000-2004
Donahue, J. David (KY) 2008-2010
Downey, Kevin (TX) 2013-2017
Dunbar, Walter (NY) 1974-1975
Dunning, James (VA) 1990-1996
Dupree, James (AL) 1996-2002

E

Elias, Al (NJ) 1979-1980
Elrod, Richard J. (IL) 1984-1986
Enomoto, J. J. (CA) 1980-1986
Epps, Christopher (MS) 2004-2008
Evans, David C. (CA) 1988-1990

F

Fant, Fred D. (NJ) 1974-1978
Farkas, Gerald M. (PA) 1974-1978
Fitzgibbons, Mark (SC) 1996-2004
Frawley, Michael H. (MO) 1996-2002
Fryer, Gordon L. (IL) 1974-1978

G

Galey, Mary S. (AZ) 2010-2015
Garvey, Robert (MA) 2000-2004
George, B. James, Jr. (NY) 1979-1984
Ghee, Margarette (OH) 1996-2004
Gladstone, William E. (FL) 1981-1986
Goehring, Angela (FL) 2010-2015
Goodrich, Edna L. (WA) 1978-1982
Goord, Glenn (NY) 2002-2006
Green, Leslie R. (MN) 1979-1984

H

Haas, Scott (KY) 2008-2012
Hamden, Michael (NC) 1999-2004
Hamilton, William (OH) 2000-2004
Hammergren, Donald R. (MN) 1975-1979

*Based on an extension of the original term to correspond with ACA election year.

Hattaway, George (TN) 1995-1996
Hays, Bonnie L. (OR) 1987-1992
Heard, John (TX) 1974-1978
Hearn, Pamela (LA) 2006-2015
Hegmann, M.D., Michael (LA) 1999-2000
Heyne, Robert P. (IN) 1974-1977
Hill, Janice (FL) 2006-2010
Hill-Christian, Sheila (VA) 1996-2004
Hofacre, Robert (OH) 2000-2004
Holcomb, Beth (VA) 2002-2006
Hopkins, Wayne (DC) 1974-1977
Horn, Martin F. (NY) 2010-2014
Houston, Bob P. (NE) 2011-2017
Huggins, M. Wayne (VA) 1983-1988*

I

Irving, James R. (IL) 1981-1986

J

Jackson, Ron (TX) 1990-1996
Jackson, Ronald W. (GA) 1992-1998
Jefferson, Ralph A. (WI) 1978-1983
Johnson, Perry M. (MI) 1986-1992
Jones, Justin W. (OK) 2008-2012
Jordan, James M. (IL) 1984-1996

K

Kehoe, Charles J. (VA) 1983-1988*
Kennedy, Robert (NY) 2006-2010
Keohane, Patrick (MO) 1999-2000
Kinker, Jeannette (NM) 2000-2002, 2004-2008

L

Lamberti, Al (FL) 2008-2010
Lappin, Harley (DC) 2002-2006
Larivee, John (MA) 2001-2005
LeBlanc, James M. (LA) 2010-2015
Lewis, Lester (TN) 2010-2015
Lick, Alton (ND) 2003-2007
Liddell, Wayne (MI) 1996-2002
Lindamood, Cherry (TN) 2013-2017
Linthicum, Lannette, M.D., CCHP-A (TX) 2002-2012
Lucas, William (MI) 1978-1983
Luttrell, Mark H. (TN) 2010-2015

M

Maciekowich, Z. C. (AZ) 1974-1975
Mangogna, Thomas J. (MO) 1974-1979
Martinez, Orlando L. (CO) 1986-1992
Maue, Frederick (PA) 2000-2004
Mausser, Cynthia (OH) 2008-2012
Maynard, Gary D. (OK) 1990-1994, 2002-2004
McGehee, R. Daniel (SC) 1999-2002
McGough, John (WA) 1979-1984
McGowan, Patrick D. (MN) 1996-2000
McKune, David R (KS) 2010-2015
McVey, Catherine (PA) 2006-2008
Miller, Jeaneene E. (CO) 2010-2015
Minor, John (MI) 1988-1994
Moeller, H. G. (NC) 1974-1980
Moore, Edgar C. (Ted) (SC) 1982-1988*
Morrissey, Thomas H. (NC) 1979-1980
Murray, Albert (GA) 2004-2010
Myers, Kevin Bradley (TN) 2004-2012
Myers, Victoria C. (MO) 1982-1994

N

Natalucci-Persichetti, Geno (OH) 1996-2004
Nelsen, Anne M. (UT) 1999-2000
Newberger, Jay M. (SD) 1984-1990
Nichols, R. Raymond (NM) 1974-1976
Northrup, Madeline K. (OH) 2006-2010
Nuernberger, W. W. (NE) 1974-1979

O

Omodt, Don (MN) 1979-1980
Orlando, Frank A. (FL) 1986-1992
Owens, George III, CCO (OH) 2003-2007

P

Parsons, Michael (OK) 1994-1998
Patrick, Allen L. (OH) 1990-1996
Patterson, Wayne K. (CO) 1978-1983
Perry, Gloria (MS) 2013-2017
Phyfer, George M. (AL) 1986-1998
Pinson, Michael D. (VA) 2006-2010
Pointer, W. Donald (MD) 1974-1977

*Based on an extension of the original term to correspond with ACA election year.

Q

Quinn, Luke (MI) 1988-2000

R

Ramirez, Teresa V. (TX) 1994-2000
Rapp, Marcella C. (CO) 1977-1982
Reed, Amos E. (NC) 1976-1981
Riedman, Irvin M. (ND) 1975-1980
Rion, Sharon Johnson (TN) 2000-2004
Robinson, Denise M. (OH) 2008-2012
Rodriguez, Felix (NM) 1979-1980
Rogan, Marilyn (NV) 2008-2012
Ross, Howard R. (TN) 2001-2005
Rossi, Linda D'Amario (RI) 1981-1986
Rowan, Joseph R. (IL) 1974-1980
Rowland, Claudia (IL) 1999-2000
Ryan, Timothy (FL) 2004-2008

S

Scott, Thomas (FL) 1999-2002
Seidelman, Charles (KY) 2004-2008
Sexton, Ted (AL) 1999-2004
Sheridan, Francis (NY) 2002-2004
Shirley, Sue (TX) 1981-1986
Shoemaker, Joan (CO) 2010-2015
Shumate, Denis (KS) 1999-2000, 2002-2004
Simonet, John (CO) 1990-1996
Singletary, Harry (FL) 1992-1998
Slater, Brad (UT) 2008-2012
Skeen, Barbara (SC) 2002-2004
Skoler, Daniel (DC) 1974-1979
Spencer, Luis (MA) 2013-2017
Stalder, Richard (LA) 1994-2000
Stickrath, Thomas J. (OH) 1997-2000, 2008-2015
Swanson, Virginia (WA) 1984-1998

T

Thomas, David (FL) 2000-2004, 2013-2015
Thompson, William (TX) 2008-2010
Townsend, Cheryln (AZ) 2000-2004
Tremont, J. Steven (LA) 1977-1982

V

Van DeKamp, John (CA) 1974-1976

W

Wade, Michael (VA) 2010-2014
Washington, Odie (DC) 1999-2002
Watson, Robert J. (OR) 1977-1982
Weber, J. Robert (KY) 1974-1981
Webster, Marge (NH) 1992-1998, 2002-2006, 2008-2015
Wheeler, Martha E. (MI) 1974-1977
White, William S. (IL) 1983-1988
Wilber, Harold B. (FL) 2001-2004
Williams, Clarence (KY) 2009-2017
Williams, Joe R. (NM) 2003-2010
Wilson, George W. (KY) 1982-1988*
Wirkler, Norman E. (CO) 1984-1990
Wright, Lester, M.D., MPH (NY) 2000-2006

Y

Young, Marjorie H. (GA) 1986-1998
Youngken, Michael (KS) 1994-2002

*Based on an extension of the original term to correspond with ACA election year.